Human Rights Protection in the Field

International Studies in Human Rights

VOLUME 87

Human Rights Protection in the Field

edited by

Bertrand G. Ramcharan

MARTINUS NIJHOFF PUBLISHERS
LEIDEN / BOSTON

A C.I.P. record for this book is available from the Library of Congress.

Printed on acid-free paper.

ISBN 90-04-14847-7

Koninklijke Brill NV incorporates the imprints Brill Academic Publishers, Martinus Nijhoff Publishers and VSP.

Printed in the Netherlands

CONTENTS

Introduction 1
Bertrand G. Ramcharan

Chapter One
Human Rights Protection Strategies in a Time of Crises 13
Bertrand G. Ramcharan

Chapter Two
We are Failing the Victims of War 41
Michael O'Flaherty

Chapter Three
The Protection of Civilians 59
Mark Bowden

Chapter Four
Operationalising the Protection of Civilians 71
Elissa Golberg

Chapter Five
The Protection of Refugees and Displaced Persons 79
Kamel Morjane

Chapter Six
Implementing International Humanitarian Law: Old and New Ways 87
Michel Veuthey

Chapter Seven
Protection in the Field: Human Rights Perspectives 119
OHCHR Staff

Chapter Eight
Human Rights Field Operations: A New Protection Tool 127
William G. O'Neill

Chapter Nine
The Protection Methods of Human Rights Field Offices 141
Bertrand G. Ramcharan

Chapter Ten
The Human Rights Components of UN Peacekeeping and Peacebuilding Operations, and the Field Offices of UNDP and the Office of High Commissioner for Human Rights 153
OHCHR Staff

Chapter Eleven
Enhancing Protection of Women and Girls in Conflict and Post-Conflict Environments 211
Comfort Lamptey

Chapter Twelve
The OHCHR Kosovo Emergency Operation: Lessons Learned 225
OHCHR Staff

Chapter Thirteen
Protecting Human Rights in a Situation of Humanitarian Crisis: The Case of Colombia 231
OHCHR Staff

Chapter Fourteen
The UN Centre for Human Rights and Democracy in Central Africa 235
Teffera Shiawal-Kidanekal

Conclusion 247

Bibliography 249

About the Authors 250

Annexes
I. The UN Aide Memoire 253
II. Memorandum of Understanding Between the Office of the High Commissioner for Human Rights and the Department of Peacekeeping Operations 269
III. The Guiding Principles on Internal Displacement 277

IV. Annual Report of the OHCHR Field Office in Cambodia (2004) 289
V. Annual Report of the OHCHR Field Office in Colombia (2004) 311
VI. Annual Report on Human Rights Field Operations in Sierra Leone (2004) 387
VII. Consolidating the Profession: The Human Rights Field Officer 407

Index 419

INTRODUCTION

Human Rights are violated on a massive scale the world over. International Humanitarian Law is flouted without compunction in conflict after conflict. Some twenty-five million people have been internally displaced. Some fourteen million refugees have taken refuge in foreign lands. Civilians are deliberately targeted in war. Women are raped. Children are abused. The protection of human rights can no longer take place only from offices in capitals or the headquarters of international organizations. Protection is needed on the ground, where people are at risk. It is far from an easy task.

United Nations peacekeeping operations regularly have, these days, human rights components with a variety of functions. Humanitarian agencies are called upon to respond to protection challenges more and more. Human rights and humanitarian NGOs deploy staff on the ground in the hope of helping people in need and bringing their plight to the outside world. The Office of UN High Commissioner for Human Rights has field offices that try to protect people to the extent they can. Sometimes, specifically human rights field operations are established as in Haiti.

How are human rights field offices faring? What can we learn from the experiments so far for future operations? How can we discharge the responsibility to protect in today's conflict and crisis-riddled world? That is the objective of this volume: to look at what has been tried so far and to try to come to a better understanding of how protection can be developed in the future. The difficulties are many, but try we must. For a start, there is the question, what is protection?

The Meaning of Protection

'Strengthening Protection in War' is the title of a publication of the International Committee of the Red Cross that summarises the reflections of four workshops of humanitarian and human rights organizations. The participants in the workshops considered that the concept of protection encompasses "... all activities aimed at ensuring full respect for the rights of the individual in accordance with the letter and the spirit of the relevant bodies of law, i.e. human rights law, international humanitarian law and refugee law. Human rights and humanitarian organizations must conduct these

Bertrand G. Ramcharan (Ed.), Human Rights Protection in the Field, 1–11.

activities in an impartial manner (not on the basis of race, national or ethnic origin, language or gender."[1]

The participants in the workshops considered a protection activity to be any activity which:

- prevents or puts a stop to a specific pattern of abuse and/or alleviates its immediate effects;
- restores people's dignity and ensures adequate living conditions through reparation, restitution, and rehabilitation;
- fosters an environment conducive to respect for the rights of individuals in accordance with the relevant bodies of law.

They recognized that "No single organization is able to meet the sheer diversity of protection needs as this requires a wide array of skills and means". It is therefore natural that various organizations operate in the same arena and often cater to the same beneficiaries, regardless of the situation.[2]

To develop better protection approaches we must understand the roots of the problems of violations.

The Roots of the Problem of Violations of International Humanitarian Law

An ICRC study of The Roots of Behaviour in War reached the conclusion that "supervision of weapons-bearers, strict orders relating to proper conduct and effective penalties for failure to obey those orders are essential conditions which must all be met if there is to be any hope of securing better respect for International Humanitarian Law. The ICRC will have to engage in a whole range of representations and activities, combined in a coherent effort of diplomacy, if it hopes to make progress in this regard."[3]

Another conclusion reached by the ICRC in the same study was the following: "(W)e have to make international humanitarian law a judicial and political rather than a moral issue."[4] A related ICRC publication, The Roots of Behaviour in War: Understanding and Preventing IHL Violations spelled this out further as follows: "The study's main lessons may be summarized by the following three points: (1) Efforts to disseminate IHL must be made a legal and political matter rather than a moral one, and focus more on norms than on their underlying values, because the idea that the

[1] ICRC, Strengthening Protection in War (2001), pp. 20–21.
[2] Ibid., p. 28.
[3] ICRC, The Roots of Behaviour in War. A Survey of the Literature (2004), p. 110.
[4] Ibid., p. 111.

combatant is morally autonomous is mistaken. (2) Greater respect for IHL is possible only if bearers of weapons are properly trained, if they are under strict orders as to the conduct to adopt and if effective sanctions are applied in the event they fail to obey such orders. (3) It is crucial that the ICRC be perfectly clear about its aims when it seeks to promote IHL and prevent violations: does it want to impart knowledge, modify attitudes or influence behaviour? *The ICRC must develop strategies genuinely aimed at preventing violations of IHL.*"[5]

We know that that there is a bedrock of rules and principles.

A Bedrock of Principles and Rules

In its Advisory Opinion of 8 July, 1996 on the *Legality of the Threat or Use of Nuclear Weapons* the International Court of Justice held that "the protection of the International Covenant on Civil and Political Rights does not cease in times of war, except by operation of Article 4 of the Covenant whereby certain provisions may be derogated from in time of national emergency. Respect for the right to life is not, however, such a provision. In principle, the right not arbitrarily to be deprived of one's life applies also in hostilities. The test of what is an arbitrary deprivation of life, however, falls to be determined by the applicable *lex specialis*, namely the law applicable in armed conflict which is designed to regulate the conduct of hostilities."[6]

In a later Advisory Opinion, on the *Legal Consequences of the Construction of A Wall in the Occupied Palestinian Territory*, the Court reaffirmed that the protection offered by human rights conventions does not cease in case of armed conflict, save through the effect of provisions for derogation of the kind found in Article 4 of the International Covenant on Civil and Political Rights. As regards the relationship between international humanitarian law and human rights law, "there are thus three possible situations: some rights may be exclusively humanitarian matters of international humanitarian law; others may be exclusively matters of human rights law; yet others may be matters of both these branches of international law."[7]

An ICRC Report, "International Humanitarian Law and the Challenges of Contemporary Armed Conflicts", submitted to the 28th International Conference of the Red Cross and Red Crescent in December 2003 reached

[5] Pp. 2–3. Emphasis added.
[6] I.C.J. Reports 1996 (1), para. 25.
[7] I.C.J. Reports 2000, para. 106.

the following conclusions: "First, the ICRC believes . . . that the four Geneva conventions and their Additional Protocols, as well as the range of other IHL treaties and the norms of customary law provide a bedrock of principles and rules that must continue to guide the conduct of hostilities and the treatment of persons who have fallen into the hands of a party to an armed conflict. Second, some of the dilemmas that the international community grappled with decades ago were, in general, satisfactorily resolved by means of IHL development. Today, the primary challenge in these areas is to either ensure clarification or further elaboration of the rules. Thirdly, international opinion—both governmental and expert, as well as public opinion—remains largely divided on how to deal with new forms of violence, primarily acts of transnational terrorism."[8]

The highest protection organ of the United Nations, the Security Council, has been endeavouring to generate greater protection for civilians in armed conflicts. The UN Aide Memoire is evidence of this.

Protection of Civilians in Armed Conflict: UN Aide Memoire

The UN Aide Memoire on the Protection of Civilians in Armed Conflict[9] set out an agenda for protection of civilians including the following:

1. Prioritize and support the immediate protection needs of displaced persons and civilians in host communities through measures to enhance security for displaced persons, measures to enhance security for civilians who remain in their communities and for host communities living in or around areas where refugees or internally displaced persons take shelter.
2. Facilitate safe and unimpeded access to vulnerable populations as the fundamental prerequisite for humanitarian assistance and protection through appropriate security arrangements, engagement in sustained dialogue with all parties to the armed conflict, facilitation of the delivery of humanitarian assistance, compliance with obligations under relevant international humanitarian, human rights and refugee law, and counter-terrorism measures in full compliance with all obligations under international law, in particular international human rights, refugee and humanitarian law.
3. Strengthen the capacity of local police and judicial systems to physically protect civilians and enforce law and order through deployment of qualified and well-trained international civilian police, technical

[8] Pp. 5–6.
[9] S/PRST/2003/27.

assistance for local police, judiciary and penitentiaries, reconstruction and rehabilitation of institutional infrastructure, and mechanisms for monitoring and reporting of alleged violations of humanitarian, human rights and criminal law.

4. Address the specific needs of women for assistance and protection through special measure to protect women and girls from gender based discrimination and violence, rape and other forms of sexual violence; implementation of measures for reporting on and prevention of sexual abuse and exploitation of civilians by humanitarian workers and peacekeepers; mainstreaming of gender perspective, including the integration of gender advisers in peace operations.
5. Address the specific needs of children for assistance and protection through prevention of and putting an end to the recruitment of child soldiers in violation of international law, initiatives to secure access to war-affected children, negotiated release of children abducted in situations of armed conflict, effective measures to disarm, demobilize, reintegrate and rehabilitate children recruited or used in hostilities, specific provisions for the protection of children, including where appropriate, the integration of child protection advisers in peace operations, implementation of measures for reporting on and prevention of sexual abuse and exploitation of civilians by humanitarian workers and peacekeepers, family reunification of separated children, and monitoring and reporting on the situation of children.
6. Put an end to impunity for those responsible for serious violations of international humanitarian, human rights and criminal law through establishment and use of effective arrangements for investigating and prosecuting serious violations of humanitarian and criminal law; exclusion of genocide, crimes against humanity and war crimes from amnesty provisions; referral of situations, where possible and appropriate, to international courts and tribunals.

Specific attention has been given to the issue of protecting children in armed conflicts.

Protection of Children in Armed Conflicts

A Report of the Secretary-General submitted to the fifty-ninth session of the General Assembly in 2004 provided a Comprehensive Assessment of the United Nations System response to children affected by armed conflict.[10]

---

[10] A/59/331.

The report grouped recommendations for improving and sustaining efforts on CAAC into four categories, which constitute the medium-term strategic priorities for the United Nations system to improve its response to children affected by armed conflict:

A. Continued vigorous advocacy for children and armed conflict.
B. An effective and credible monitoring and reporting system on child rights violations.
C. Enhanced mainstreaming of CAAC issues across the United Nations system.
D. Improved coordination of CAAC issues across the United Nations system.[11]

On advocacy, the report concluded that there was continuing need for a SRSG-CAAC as an independent advocate reporting directly to the Secretary-General and recommended the introduction of appropriate mechanisms for measurement of progress against benchmarks established each year. The mandated functions of the SRSG-CAAC should focus on the following:

- Integrating children's rights and concerns into the United Nations' peace and security, humanitarian and development agendas throughout all phases of conflict prevention, peace-building, peacemaking and peacekeeping activities.
- Unblocking political impasses to secure commitments from political actors on child protection on the national and regional levels and ensuring adequate follow-up to these commitments.
- Ensuring the inclusion of children and armed conflict concerns in all relevant reports submitted to the Security Council by the Secretary-General.
- Reporting child rights violations to relevant bodies, e.g. the Secretary-General, the Security Council, governments and regional mechanisms, and advocating the inclusion of appropriate measures in resolutions, e.g. sanctions, for actors who are violating CAAC norms and standards.
- Leading a collaborative process to produce the annual Secretary-General's report to the Security Council on CAAC. The report should focus on progress in the application of CAAC norms and standards including reporting on child rights violations in situations of conflict; suggestions for measures to ensure compliance to norms and standards; and high-level analysis of CAAC trends with recommendations on

[11] Ibid., para. 46.

improvements to the United Nations system response, particularly with suggestions on how United Nations peace and security mechanisms can respond better to CAAC and progress on the development of a monitoring and reporting system for child rights violations.

- Producing an annual report to the General Assembly and the Commission on Human Rights, using inputs from key United Nations actors. The report should include a high-level analytical assessment of the state of CAAC in all conflict situations (i.e. not just countries on the Security Council's agenda); progress in the United Nations system's advocacy, mainstreaming and coordination efforts on CAAC issues; and prioritized next steps for the United Nations system in improving its response to CAAC.
- Providing proactive advocacy support to the Secretary-General, Heads of Agencies, Special Representatives, RCs/HCs and other high-level United Nations officials, primarily through inter-agency committees such as ECHA, the Executive Committee on Peace and Security (ECPS), the Senior Management Group, and annual meetings of RCs and HCs.
- Co-chairing a coordination mechanism at United Nations Headquarters on children affected by armed conflict.
- Maintaining a high-profile public awareness on CAAC issues as required to achieve political advocacy objectives including cooperation with the Department of Public Information (DPI).[12]

The report urged that the advocacy role of the ERC and the High Commissioner for Human Rights should also be systematically resorted to in support of CAAC concerns and issues.[13]

The report urged that a robust monitoring and reporting system for child rights violations in conflict situations should be developed in three distinct stages:

(i) Developing an accepted, standardized and practical methodology to identify, document and verify child rights violations.
(ii) Setting up and coordinating of networks of actors on the ground to document child rights concerns.
(iii) Establishing responsibilities and procedures for disseminating and leveraging the information.[14]

The protection of women has also engaged the attention of the Security Council.

[12] Ibid., para. 49.
[13] Ibid., para. 51.
[14] Ibid., para. 52.

Protection of Women

In its resolution 1325 (2000), the Security Council called upon all parties to armed conflict to respect fully international law applicable to the rights and protection of women and girls, especially as civilians, in particular the obligations applicable to them under the Geneva Conventions of 1949 and the Additional Protocols thereto of 1977, the Refugee Convention of 1951 and the Protocol thereto of 1967, the Convention on Elimination of All Forms of Discrimination against Women of 1979 and the Optional Protocol thereto of 1999 and the United Nations Convention on the Rights of the Child of 1989 and the two Optional Protocols thereto of 25 May 2000, and to bear in mind the relevant provisions of the Rome Statute of the International Criminal Court. (Paragraph 9). The Council further called on all parties to armed conflict to take special measures to protect women and girls from gender-based violence, particularly rape and other forms of sexual abuse, and all other forms of violence in situations of armed conflict. (Paragraph 10).

Enhancing Protection of Refugees has particularly engaged the attention of the UN High Commissioner for Human Rights.

Protection of Refugees

The United Nations High Commissioner for Refugees published in 2002 an "Agenda for Protection" whose programme of action has six goals:

1. Strengthening implementation of the 1951 Convention and 1967 Protocol;
2. Protecting refugees within broader migration movements;
3. Sharing burdens and responsibilities more equitably and building capacities to receive and protect refugees;
4. Addressing security-related concerns more effectively;
5. Redoubling the search for durable solutions; and
6. Meeting the protection needs of refugee women and children.[15]

The protection of internally displaced persons has also been highlighted.

[15] UNHCR, Agenda for Protection (2002), p. 29.

Protection of Internally-Displaced Persons

The Guiding Principles on Internal Displacement provide that National authorities have the primary duty and responsibility to provide protection and humanitarian assistance to internally displaced persons within their jurisdiction. Certain internally displaced persons, such as children, especially unaccompanied minors, expectant mothers, mothers with young children, female heads of household, persons with disabilities and elderly persons shall be entitled to protection and assistance required by their condition and to treatment which takes into account their special needs.

All authorities and international actors shall respect and ensure respect for their obligations under international law, including human rights and humanitarian law, in all circumstances, so as to prevent and avoid conditions that might lead to displacement of persons. The Principles contain, in addition to general principles, guidance on protection from displacement (prevention), protection during displacement, humanitarian assistance, and principles relating to return, resettlement and reintegration.

A Special Representative of the Secretary-General on Internally Displaced persons has sought to generate protection for IDPs and there is a special inter-agency unit on displaced persons within the UN system.

The protection role of United Nations peacekeeping operations has received high-level attention.

UN Field Operations and Human Rights: The 'Brahimi Report'

The 'Brahimi report' advocated:

- The essential importance of the United Nations system adhering to and promoting international human rights instruments and standards and international humanitarian law in all aspects of its peace and security activities.
- Improving respect for human rights through the monitoring, education and investigation of past and existing abuses, providing technical assistance for democratic development; and promoting conflict resolution and reconciliation techniques.
- Addressing variables that affect peace implementation such as issues of ethnicity or religion or gross violations of human rights.
- Addressing past violations of human rights.
- Working for respect of minority rights: "Long-term preventive strategies . . . must . . . work to promote human rights, to protect minority rights and to institute political arrangements in which all groups are represented".

- Building a culture of respect for human rights.
- Observing international standards for democratic policing and human rights.
- Integrating human rights specialists in peace-building missions.
- Upholding the rule of law and respect for human rights through team work on the part of judicial, penal, human rights and policing experts.
- Human rights components of peace operation are critical to effective peace-building.
- Training military, police and other civilian personnel on human rights issues and on the relevant provisions of international humanitarian law.
- A doctrinal shift in the use of civilian police, other rule of law elements and human rights experts in complex peace operations to reflect an increased focus on strengthening rule of law institutions and improving respect for human rights in a post-conflict environment.
- Human rights monitoring.
- Meeting threshold conditions in the implementation of ceasefire or peace agreements, such as consistency with international human rights standards.
- Rebuilding civil society and promoting respect for human rights in places where grievance is widespread, keeping in mind international conventions and declarations relating to human rights.

A special Memorandum of Understanding has been concluded between the Office of High Commissioner for Human Rights and the Department of Peacekeeping Operations with a view to developing better protection of human rights by peacekeeping operations.

The MOU between OHCHR and DPKO

Paragraph 2 of the MOU urges that "The activities of human rights components of peacekeeping operations shall be based on international human rights standards, as defined in the relevant international treaties, declarations, guidelines and other instruments. In the implementation of their activities, whether of a monitoring or of a technical cooperation nature, and within the framework of their mandate, human rights components of peacekeeping operations will seek to promote an integrated approach to human rights promotion and protection, paying due attention to civil, cultural, economic, political and social rights, including the right to development, and to the special needs of women, children, minorities, internally displaced persons and other groups requiring special protection."

In an effort to strengthen protection, principles of universal criminal jurisdiction are being developed.

Universal Criminal Jurisdiction

The Princeton Principles of Universal Jurisdiction (2001) offered a recapitulation of international law that is relevant to the issue of impunity that has been identified as a key issue to be tackled if successful prevention of violations of international human rights and humanitarian law is to be achieved. According to the Principles:

(a) Universal jurisdiction may be exercised by a competent and ordinary judicial body of any state in order to try a person accused of committing serious crimes under international law, provided the person is present before such judicial body.[16]

(b) Serious crimes under international law include: (1) piracy; (2) slavery; (3) war crimes; (4) crimes against peace; (5) crimes against humanity; (6) genocide; and (7) torture.[17]

Violations of human rights and humanitarian law persist: The Search for Protection must go on

Notwithstanding all of this, violations of human rights and humanitarian law are rampant the world over. The search for protection must go on. Protection in the field.

[16] Principle 1 (2).
[17] Principle 2 (1).

CHAPTER ONE

HUMAN RIGHTS PROTECTION STRATEGIES IN A TIME OF CRISES

Bertrand G. Ramcharan[1]

Introduction

Human rights are under attack across the globe and different governments are advancing all sorts of troubling justifications for their violations. At the same time there is also perplexity among defenders of human rights about how to move forward in a time of crises. Yet, the human rights movement can never allow itself to be thrown off course by those who flout international human rights brazenly. It is imperative to uphold international human rights guarantees. How are we to do this in a time of crises? This chapter will review the crises facing the international human rights movement and then seek to explore courses of action that might help take international protection forward.

I. *A Time of Crises for the Human Rights Movement*

In the preparation of this chapter the author interviewed a number of human rights defenders and felt their sense of anguish about what was happening in the world of human rights. Motions in the Third Committee of the General Assembly to take no action on draft resolutions expressing concern about situations of gross violations of human rights[2] led a seasoned human rights professional from Amnesty International, who had spent many years in the cause, to exclaim about developments at the General Assembly, "Many things I have believed in are crumbling around me. If we have no-action motions in the Commission on Human Rights and now in the General Assembly what are we left with at the United Nations."[3]

---

[1] Former UN High Commissioner for Human Rights a.i. (2003–2004).

[2] See, 'Danforth Faults U.N. Assembly on Sudan Ruling', New York Times, 24 November, 2004, p. A.6.

[3] Interview on 15 December, 2004.

Bertrand G. Ramcharan (Ed.), Human Rights Protection in the Field, 13–39.

Human Rights Watch, in its 2005 World Report just released, is anguished about the failure of the international community to come to the protection of the victims in Darfur, Western Sudan, as well about the situation in the Abu Ghraib prison in Iraq.[4] Violations of human rights in the struggle against terrorism were also lamented in the report. In a Foreword to the Report of the High-Level Panel on Threats, Challenges and Change, Secretary-General Kofi Annan cautions, in respect of the Commission on Human Rights in particular, ". . . we cannot move forward without restoring the credibility and effectiveness of our human rights mechanisms and refocusing ourselves on the protection of individual rights."[5] Yes, we are living in a time of crises for the human rights movement. In order to help us to assess how to move forward let us look more closely at key aspects of the problems we are dealing with.

A. *Threats and Challenges*

The Secretary-General's High-Level Panel on Threats Challenges and Change recalled that the United Nations was created in 1945 to save succeeding generations from the scourge of war. Sixty years later, it cautioned,

> ". . . the biggest security threats we face now, and in the decades ahead go far beyond States waging aggressive war. They extend to poverty, infectious disease and environmental degradation; war and violence within States; the spread and possible use of nuclear, radiological, chemical and biological weapons, terrorism, and transnational organized crime. The threats are from non-State actors as well as States, and to human security as well as State security."[6]

A former United Nations High Commissioner for Human Rights, in his Human Rights Day Message, 2003, recapitulated that the human rights movement had to come to terms with poverty, conflicts, terrorism, State violence against its own people, prejudice, and bad governance.[7] Another former High Commissioner for Human Rights, speaking at the Seventh Meeting of the International Council on Human Rights Policy looked ahead to emerging challenges such as the following:

> ". . . movements of people, changes in the notion of citizenship, the evolution of the state in relation to human rights and on the ground, global

[4] Human Rights Watch, World Report, 2005, Introduction.

[5] A More Secure World: Our Shared Responsibility. Report of the High-level Panel on Threats, Challenges and Change. United Nations, 2004, p. ix.

[6] Ibid., p. 9.

[7] Bertrand Ramcharan, Human Rights Day Message as High Commissioner, 10 December, 2003.

> inequity, scientific innovation, challenges to civil liberties, reform of the UN and the need for more adequate international governance, the possibility that human rights might be marginalized in favour of a new paradigm."[8]

The OECD, in a study of future risks has drawn attention to a host of issues that would have to be kept in mind if we are to achieve human security and uphold human rights. We shall look briefly at these next.

The Chief of the Research and Right to Development Branch of the Office of High Commissioner for Human Rights sees seven issues that should engage the attention of the international community in the coming period:

- The relationship between differences in cultures and the universalism of human rights
- Inequalities, discrimination, poverty
- The deficit of democracy and weaknesses in the rule of law
- Globalization
- Terrorism and the strain between security requirements and human rights
- Armed conflicts
- Progress in science and technology
- Internal divisions in human rights
- Politicization of human rights.

He sees many paradoxes in the contemporary human rights situation: "The international community must cope with a situation marked both by positive and negative trends. Over the recent half-century a significant distance has been covered, but we still have a long way to go. The foundations of human rights in law, practice, politics and consciousness have grown stronger. Human Rights are said to have become the common language of humanity."[9]

B. *Emerging Risks*

A recent study by the OECD on Emerging Risks in the 21st century, which discusses changes likely to affect the world in the coming years, identified four contexts: demography, the environment, technology and socio-economic structure. On the demographic front, world population is

---

[8] Mary Robinson, recounted in Quarterly Newsletter of the International Council on Human Rights Policy, Vol. 7, No. 2, p. 1.

[9] Zdzislaw Kedzia, "Present-Day Challenges to Human Rights", Polish Review of International Affairs, 2003.

projected to increase to 9 billion by 2050, in comparison with today's figure of 6 billion. In this scenario, migration is expected to intensify and, by 2050, South-North migration might become the norm.

On the environmental front, the earth's climate is changing and will continue to do so. Water will be increasingly scarce. Over half of the 12,500 km^3 of freshwater available for human use is already used and 90% will be used in 2030 if current trends continue. Worldwide, polluted water is already estimated to affect the health of about 1.2 billion people and to contribute to the death of about 15 million children aged under-five every year. Reduction in biodiversity could have dramatic consequences.[10]

According to the study three aspects of emerging technologies will influence risk: connectedness; the speed and pervasiveness of technological change; and the fundamental changes in the landscape they might induce. Some emerging technologies change living matter and represent an unprecedented potential to change the environment. They are even starting to challenge the definition of 'living' and could ultimately change the whole notion of 'human'. While the hope is that biotechnology, for instance, will improve living conditions and the quality of life, the long term consequences of interfering at such a basic level are impossible to evaluate and irreversible damage could be done before the danger is understood or when it is too late to stop it.

As to socio-economic structures, governments' role in directly managing the economy has been shrinking over several decades, and especially in the past 20 years through privatization, deregulation and regulatory reform. Poverty has persisted and in some cases increased in recent years. The living conditions of the poor render them exposed to risks, but poverty and income gaps also have direct impacts on risk in that they fuel social tensions and weaken the social cohesion needed to assess and respond to potential dangers.

It is in relation to this emerging world and these risks that we must contemplate future strategies for the protection and promotion of human rights. For the present, however, we already have serious problems of gross violations on our hands, as we shall see next.

C. *Flouting of International Norms*

Massive violations of human rights are all around us. The evidence is overwhelming.

---

[10] Emerging Systemic Risks in the 21st Century. ISBN 92-64-19947-0. OECD, 2003.

(1) *The UN High Commissioner for Human Rights*
UN High Commissioner for Human Rights Louise Arbour, on the occasion of Human Rights Day, 2004, lamented that the vision and promise of the Universal Declaration of Human Rights are under considerable strain: "Few of us are free from fear; many of us are still not free from want. The sinister shadow of terrorism is generating a confused response, unanchored in the principles that have guided us in the search for a proper balance between our desire for collective security and our need for liberty and individual freedom."[11]

(2) *The President of the International Committee of the Red Cross*
In an address to the UN Commission on Human Rights on 18 March, 2003, the President of the International Committee of the Red Cross, Jakob Kellenberger, noted that human rights law, refugee law, and international law shared the common objective of protecting human life, safety and dignity. These bodies of law and their supervisory mechanisms formed an interlocking web of guarantees for individuals in particular in times of emergency. Sadly, breaches of all three bodies of law were widespread in the contemporary world. President Kellenberger urged:

> "Improving respect for international humanitarian law remains a huge challenge. Without greater respect for existing rules the credibility and protective value of existing and also of any new rules is very limited.
>
> "How can respect be improved? First, and quite simply, by spreading knowledge of the rules to authorities, to combatants, including of course, organized armed groups, and to civil society.
>
> "Secondly, by the adoption of preventive steps in times of peace, such as the implementation of relevant treaties and national laws, military manuals and other instruments.
>
> "Thirdly, in the heat of conflict, by the mobilization of all those who can contribute to the better respect of the law. The representations made on a daily basis by ICRC delegates in the field to those participating in hostilities are often a life-saving contribution."[12]

(3) *The UN High Commissioner for Refugees*
The Office of the UN High Commissioner for Refugees has repeatedly expressed concern over disregard for the 1951 Convention Relating to the Status of Refugees, which defines the rights of refugees, including asylum

---

[11] UN Press Release, Human Rights Vision and Promise under Considerable Strain, says High Commissioner for Human Rights, 9 December, 2004.
[12] Extracted from the original text.

and sets out legal obligations of States. The Convention is the cornerstone of international protection. Faced with widespread breaches of the Convention, UNHCR launched, in 2003, 'Convention Plus', an initiative aimed at strengthening the original convention. The objective is to improve refugee protection worldwide and to facilitate the resolution of refugee problems through special multilateral agreements that are expected to focus on three priority areas: the strategic use of resettlement as a tool of protection, a durable solution and a tangible form of burden-sharing; more effective targeting of development assistance to support durable solutions for refugees, whether in countries of asylum or upon return home; and clarification of the responsibilities of States in the event of secondary movements of refugees and asylum seekers from an initial country of refugee to another country. These measures are intended to secure for refugees a higher standard of protection as close to home as possible and also to increase the level of State involvement as an effective system of international burden-sharing. It remains to be seen whether these strategies will contribute to strengthened protection for refugees. As to the plight of millions of internally displaced persons protection remains a mirage.

(4) *Special Procedures of the Commission on Human Rights*

At a recent meeting of the International Council on Human Rights Policy, the Special Representative on Human Rights Defenders recounted serious problems on the ground:

> "A host of questions emerged—new challenges to democracy, new forms of authoritarianism, the privatization of prisons and security, the impact on civil liberties of anti-terrorism policies, the evolution of the UN and human rights institutions within it, corruption as a human rights issue, and access to information."[13]

In a joint statement issued on the occasion of Human Rights Day, 2004, 28 Independent Experts of the Commission on Human Rights pleaded:

> "Over the years, we have witnessed the immense obstacles certain persons and groups face in enjoying their human rights fully. Among the groups most at risk and in need of protection are indigenous peoples, who have suffered perennial prejudice and discrimination . . .
>
> "In many countries indigenous peoples are the victims of extrajudicial executions, arbitrary detention, torture, forced evictions and many forms of discrimination, in particular in the administration of justice. In too many places, they also lack access to basic social rights, such as the rights to health, food, culturally appropriate education and adequate housing.

[13] Quarterly Newsletter of the International Council on Human Rights Policy, Vol. 7, No. 2, November, 2004, p. 1.

> "Within the indigenous community, the plight of women and human rights defenders is often exacerbated. Indigenous women face multiple forms of discrimination, both as women and as members of the indigenous community. There must be effective implementation of international human rights laws to eradicate gender-based violence and tackle its causes effectively."[14]

(5) *Human Rights NGOs*

In Amnesty International's 2004 Report its Secretary-General cautioned:

> "The challenges facing the global movement for human rights today are stark. As activists we must confront the threat posed by callous, cruel and criminal acts of armed groups and individuals. We must resist the backlash against human rights created by the single-minded pursuit of a global security doctrine that has deeply divided the world. We must campaign to redress the failure of governments and the international community to deliver on social and economic justice."[15]

The Legal Adviser of Human Rights Watch advised:

> ". . . The question . . . is what to do? We need to figure out how we position ourselves when serious abuses are committed by democratic nations who are simultaneously engaged in armed conflict abroad and under serious threat of terrorism at home. We need to strike a new balance between our ability to engage these mostly Western governments in highly sophisticated debates, and the bluntness required by campaigning techniques that blame and shame those responsible for torture. In brief, we need to achieve a modus operandi that allows for complementarity between strategic thinking and principled action."[16]

The challenges facing the global human rights movement today are indeed stark. How did the Secretary-General's High Level Panel on Threats, Challenges and Change see the situation? It excoriated gross violations of human rights in the world today and was particularly critical of the Commission on Human Rights. It saw the problems of the Commission as reflecting adversely on the reputation of the United Nations. Its recommendations were targeted mainly at this problem. When it referred to the relevant law it repeatedly used the term 'international humanitarian law', giving the impression that there was the well-known sensitivity on this issue. In referring to international conventions it hardly ever mentioned the key international human rights conventions. Its recommendations will have to stand the test of time. It is to those recommendations that we turn next.

---

[14] Human Rights Protection a Must, UN Independent Experts Affirm on Human Rights Day. United Nations Press Release, 8 December, 2004.

[15] Amnesty International, Report 2004, p. 3.

[16] Wilder Taylor, "Towards an Advocacy Strategy for Human Rights in the Fight Against Terrorist Acts".

II. *The Report of the High-Level Panel on New Threats, Challenges and Change*

The High Level Panel on New Threats, Challenges and Change designated by the United Nations Secretary-General in its report submitted to him[17] formulated significant recommendations to the Secretary-General on human rights issues.

Recommendation No. 91 suggests that all members of the Commission on Human Rights should designate prominent and experienced human rights figures at the heads of their delegations. This is surely worthy of broad support in the human rights movement. When the current commission was established the ground rules were that Members States on the Commission would submit the names of their nominees to the Secretary-General, that there would be a process of consultation with the Secretary-General, and that the nominee would be subject to confirmation by the Economic and Social Council. The consultations have never taken place. Should the Commission remain as it is, it would be urgent to devise a consultation process and to set down some criteria for being a Head of Delegation on the Commission. Should the Commission become universal, it would be even more important to devise criteria for serving as a Head of Delegation. The Secretary-General may wish to have prepared such a set of criteria and submit it to the Membership for endorsement. That would help develop a consensus on the kind of person who should be a Head of Delegation on the Commission.

Recommendation No. 93 suggests that the High Commissioner for Human Rights should be called upon to prepare an annual report on the situation of human rights worldwide. The High Commissioner has the competence to do so. The basis for such a report could be a recapitulation of the principal findings of the special rapporteurs, representatives, and working groups established by the Commission and reporting to it. The High Commissioner could preface these findings with an Introduction of her own highlighting issues or situations of particular concern to her. Such a report would be an important step forward in the protection of human rights globally. It would not entail much additional outlay of resources.

Recommendation No. 94 suggests that the Security Council and the proposed Peace building Commission should request the High Commissioner for Human Rights to report to them regularly on the implementation of all human rights-related provisions of Security Council resolutions, thus

[17] Recommendations 91–96.

enabling focused, effective monitoring of those provisions. This is surely a sensible recommendation to Members of the Security Council.

There are two aspects to this recommendation. In the first place, the High Commissioner could have prepared and publish such a report in any event, say, on a quarterly basis. Such a written report would be at the disposal of the Security Council and, indeed, all other United Nations bodies. The second aspect of this recommendation is that the High Commissioner could present her report personally to the Security Council, as needed. There are many ways of achieving this. In the first place, the Office of the High Commissioner already briefs the President of the Security Council monthly. In the second place, the High Commissioner or her representative could brief the Security Council regularly in informal consultations. In the third place, the High Commissioner, as needed, could be invited by the Security Council to brief it in formal sessions. There is thus much room for the constructive implementation of this recommendation.

Recommendation No. 92 suggests that the Commission on Human Rights should be supported in its work by an advisory council or panel. If one takes the Commission as it is, it would seem wise for this advisory council or panel to consist of the rapporteurs, representatives, and chairpersons of working groups, cumulatively called the special procedures. There is a sound rationale for this: they have been mandated by the Commission to monitor the protection of human rights and are therefore in the best position to advise on protection issues. The advisory council or panel could also include the heads of the principal human rights treaty bodies. These two groups already meet annually for a week and then hold a joint meeting. This would be an ideal advisory forum. Making them the advisory panel would give them the opportunity to make protection-related recommendations to the Commission, whether in its current composition or enlarged.

This brings us to the last of the five recommendations, Recommendation No. 90 that Membership of the Commission should be made universal. There are two groups of views on this recommendation. The first is based on the premise that a Commission on Human Rights presupposes special commitment and responsibility on the part of the members, that protection of human rights should be the primary goal, and that Members of the Commission must be able to take principled positions on issues and situations. On top of this, human rights non-governmental organizations participate in large numbers in the Commission and, by their presence, make it a special body attuned to conditions on the ground in countries. The participation of special rapporteurs and other special procedures, the national human rights commission, and regional human rights organizations give the Commission, in the eyes of those loyal to the historic commission a special place in the United Nations that would lost were it enlarged to universal membership. Furthermore, it is argued, the Commission has a lead role in the drafting of standards, in supervising the work of the Sub-Commission, particularly its research reports and studies, and the Commission also occasionally requests studies of its own. Could these all be done, it is asked, in a universal commission?

On the other side, there are those who argue that the election of Members with questionable human rights records presents a problem of credibility for the United Nations as a whole and the High-level panel was obviously moved by this concern in making its recommendation for universal membership. It is further argued that a universal commission would place on each Member State of the United Nations the responsibility to respond to protection challenges. Even further, it is argued, the majority of Member States of the United Nations—at least those with diplomatic representation in Geneva—participate *en masse* in the Commission, contributing to debates, moving procedural motions, and sponsoring resolutions. The only thing non-members cannot do, it is argued, is vote on resolutions.

It needs to be pointed out that should a decision be taken to move to a universal commission it would probably have to meet in New York where all Member States are represented, otherwise it would be necessary to envisage United Nations financial assistance for Member States who would find the costs of sustaining a delegation in Geneva for several weeks taxing. Even should the Commission meet in New York, it might still be necessary to envisage financial assistance to needy Member States if one would like to have real experts from home participate in the Commission. Without such financial assistance one might well end up in a situation in which the Heads and other members of delegations are mostly coming from diplomatic missions to the United Nations—which be at cross purpose with the recommendation that heads of delegations should be prominent and experienced human rights figures. There is need for some hard thinking on this issue.

Be that as it may, were the decision taken to move to a universal human rights commission, how could this be made to work in favour of human rights protection? That would seem to be the crux of the matter. One could envisage a scenario in which the suggested advisory council or panel, consisting of special procedures mandate holders and chairpersons of human rights treaty bodies meets twice annually under the chairpersonship of the High Commissioner. They offer recommendations for the human rights commission, which meets biannually for the purpose of responding to protection challenges. Studies, drafting of norms, and advice and technical assistance issues would be considered principally in the Sub-Commission, which would continue to meet annually. Such an arrangement would give a sharper protection focus to the Commission and would bring it, the special procedures, the treaty bodies, and the High Commissioner into better synergy for the more effective protection of human rights.

The Advisory Council or Panel would continue to meet in Geneva. Where the Commission meets would depend on the issues of policy and financing adduced earlier. Realistically it would probably end up meeting in New York. The Commission currently has a session of six weeks. One could envisage this being split into two sessions of three weeks each. The Third Committee of the General Assembly meets usually in October and November. One could envisage the Commission meeting in the spring and in late summer, on the eve of the General Assembly.

On the line of reasoning being presented here it is envisaged that the Third Committee of the General Assembly would continue to exist. This would seem to be right for reasons of policy and principle. The General Assembly has an important role under the Charter in the advancement of universal realization of human rights. It would therefore be essential for the General Assembly itself to be organized in such a manner as to discharge its human rights role. Besides, the Third Committee also deals with social and humanitarian issues and these must remain the focus of considered discussion in the General Assembly. Having said this, it is quite conceivable for the Third Committee to have shorter sessions during which, as far as human rights issues are concerned, it would be acting mainly on recommendations of the High Commissioner and the Commission on Human Rights.

These observations are offered from the perspective of how, should it be decided to go forward with a universal commission, it might possibly be organized. We have sought to rationalize the recommendations of the High-level panel for a universal commission and an advisory council or panel. The line of organization advanced here leaves unanswered a key question: how would the participation of NGOs, one of the key features of the Commission at the present time, be satisfactorily achieved. A six-week session of the Commission, is predictable from the point of view of planning and enables NGOs to optimize their participation. Likewise, the participation of national human rights commissions is growing to be an important feature of the Commission and it would be essential to think this through so that their participation is optimized.

Having regard to these considerations it would be highly advisable, before taking a decision on this issue of universal membership, to request the Secretariat to canvass the views of NGOs and national human rights commissions so that the most careful consideration is given to them. It would also be important for the Secretariat to present to the decision-making body a detailed 'implementation paper' on what it would entail in delegation costs, meeting costs, and documentation costs, to have a universal commission whether it meets once a year or it meets in biannual session, as would seem to be called for to make optimal use of the proposal.

The recommendation for a universal commission was undoubtedly offered out of a desire to overcome a serious credibility problem for the United Nations. It therefore deserves to be carefully examined from all points of view. At the end of the day, there is a key underlying consideration: change must lead to stronger, not weaker protection and gains achieved slowly over the years must not be given up in the quest for reform. Reform must contribute to stronger, not weaker protection of human rights. Effective protection is, after all, the mission of the Commission on Human Rights.

III. *Views of the Human Rights Movement about the way Forward*

In its 2004 Report Amnesty International summarized the results of its reflections on its future human rights agenda. It set for itself the following challenges: Resisting abuses in the context of the 'war on terror'; defending human rights in armed conflict; protecting the rights of human rights defenders; reforming and strengthening the justice sector; promoting abolition of the death penalty; promoting economic, social and cultural rights; ending violence against women; and upholding the rights of refugees and migrants.[18]

A Committee of Sages (Comité des Sages), in a report they drew up in 1998, recommended a Human Rights Agenda for the European Union for the Year 2000 based on the following foundations:

a. Recognition of legal obligations
b. Universality
c. Indivisibility
d. Consistency between internal and external policy
e. A sound information base to support a sound EU policy
f. Mainstreaming[19]

A collaborative NGO initiative currently underway, Human Rights 2020 seeks to identify key human rights challenges that lie ahead; assess the strengths and weaknesses of human rights activism today, asking difficult

[18] Amnesty International, Report 2004, Chapter: Building an International Human Rights Agenda.

[19] Leading by Example: A Human Rights Agenda for the European Union for the Year 2000. Agenda of the Comite des Sages and Final Project Report. European University Institute, Florence, 1998.

questions; and to propose an agenda for the next generation. Issues intended to be addressed include conceptual questions; the human rights movement and relations with civil society; State, non-state aspects; technology and science; conflicts; social and economic trends; religion and culture.[20] The International Council on Human Rights Policy has commissioned two experts to spend three months taking advice from human rights organizations in different regions about the value of organizing wide consultation on longer-term human rights trends that affect human rights work in a rapidly changing world.[21]

IV. *Strategies of Protection and Promotion*

Against the background of the preceding discussion, we sketch below some thoughts on protection and promotion strategies that might be kept in mind in the future.

A. *Protection*

1. Enhance protection in armed conflict and in situations of exodus and displacement.

It is widely recognized that widespread and massive violations of human rights are taking place in our world in intra-state as well as inter-state conflicts. There is also growing awareness that both international human rights law and international humanitarian law must be called in aid in defence of the victims of conflict. A recent article in the American Journal of International Law noted that "Increasingly, the use of force during armed conflict is being assessed through the perspective of human rights law, as well as under international humanitarian law."[22] A particular strength of the human rights process, the article continued, "has been the development of a strict accountability framework."[23] The confidential modus operandi of the ICRC has many advantages. At the same time, it can lead to situations in which massive violations are taking place, monitored by the ICRC, which submits its reports to the

[20] Concept Paper, Human Rights 2020.

[21] Quarterly Newsletter of the International Council on Human Rights Policy, Vol. 7, No. 2, p. 3: Human Rights 2020.

[22] K. Watkin, "Controlling the Use of Force. A Role for Human Rights Norms in Contemporary Armed Conflict", 98 American Journal of International Law (2004), pp. 1–34, at p. 1.

[23] Ibid., p. 30.

State Party(ies) concerned but the situation persists. The rest of the world may not be aware of the violations taking place. The atrocities in the Abu Ghraib prison are a case in point. The policy issue that is thus joined is: how can the monitoring bodies of international human rights law and those of international humanitarian law work to greater advantage for the defence of human rights?

This gives rise to challenging issues. As the author of the article just cited noted,

> "... (I)ncorporation of human rights principles of accountability can have a positive impact on the regulation of the use of force during armed conflict. Given the close interface between these two normative frameworks in some types of armed conflict, their mechanisms of accountability will inevitably need to be reconciled; but systems of accountability developed to regulate the use of force domestically cannot simply be transferred to the international humanitarian law context. Consequently, both states and human rights supervisory bodies may have to readjust their understanding of the role human rights law can play in enhancing the accountability framework regarding the use of deadly force in armed conflict. No gaps in the effort to apply appropriate norms of humanity can be allowed."[24]

The question that arises for consideration is what more could be done to protect human rights during armed conflicts. The plight of women and children is particularly acute. Women Ministers of Foreign Affairs and other Women Ministers and Representatives of Governments, in a Declaration of 16 March, 2004, during the high-level segment of the Commission on Human Rights, lamented that

> "Armed conflicts continue to stalk the world, becoming ever more vicious. Women and children suffer disproportionately during and after wars. They form the majority of refugees and internally displaced persons. They endure rape and sexual abuse, atrocities that have been used throughout history as weapons of war. It is our firm conviction that much more attention must be given to the consequences of conflicts on women and children, and in particular to their protection from gender-based violence. We strongly support the full implementation of United Nations Security Council resolution 1325 on women, peace and security and underline the important role of women in the prevention and resolution of conflicts."[25]

The protection of refugees and displaced persons is also a topic of special concern. In a Note to the fifty fourth session of the Executive Committee

---

[24] Ibid., p. 34.

[25] Declaration, Women Ministers of Foreign Affairs, their Women Minister Colleagues and Representatives of Governments decry Violence against Women on the margins of the 69th session of the Commission on Human Rights. 16 March 2004.

of the High Commissioner's Programme, the UN High Commissioner for Refugees, advanced a number of measures to strengthen the capacity of his office for protection, including the following:

- I will pursue, vigorously and systematically, the implementation of the Agenda for Protection, including through accessions by States to the 1951 Convention and/or its 1967 Protocol, recognizing that international protection and the search for permanent solutions are the core of UNHCR's mandate.
- My Office will continue to promote new accessions to the 1954 and 1961 conventions on stateless persons and statelessness. I also intend to extend UNHCR's activities in relation to statelessness to achieve global coverage.
- Within the system-wide United Nations approach, I will reinvigorate measures for my Office tobe fully engaged with other partners in pursuing activities for IDPs.
- In partnership with other relevant actors, I will strengthen my Office's activities for the protection of and assistance to returnees.
- I will seek to bring greater attention and a higher profile to refugee issues. I intend to convene, in consultation with the Executive committee, ministerial meetings of States Parties to the 1951 Convention relating to the Status of Refugees and/or the 1967 Protocol as well as other members and observers of the Executive Committee. The meetings will take place normally every five years, in conjunction with the meetings of the Executive Committee.
- I intend to expand and strengthen the linkages between my Office and the Office of the Secretary-General, the United Nations Secretariat, and the bodies and organizations in the areas of peace and security, development, humanitarian affairs and human rights.
- My Office will continue to enhance its partnerships with NGOs in their important roles as advocates, humanitarian actors and international partners.[26]

2. Monitor respect for human rights in the struggle against terrorism.

The Independent Expert on the Protection of Human Rights and Fundamental Freedoms while Countering Terrorism "concludes that given the gaps in coverage of the monitoring systems of the special procedures and treaty bodies and the pressing need to strengthen human

[26] Report by the High Commissioner for Refugees to the General Assembly on Strengthening the Capacity of the Office of the High Commissioner for Refugees to Carry Out its Mandate, A/AC.96/980.

rights protection while countering terrorism, the Commission on Human Rights should seriously consider the creation of a special procedure with a multidimensional mandate to monitor States' counter-terrorism measures and their compatibility with international human rights law."[27] Such a special procedure should have the following attributes: its mandate should encompass all internationally recognized human rights and extend to all States; it should be authorized to provide technical assistance to governments in the design of counter-terrorism measures; it should be authorized to receive credible information from governmental, inter-governmental and non-governmental sources and to dialogue with governments; it should report directly to the Commission on Human Rights; it should be operational and authorized to undertake several *in situ* visits per year; it should be authorized and encouraged to consult with and exchange information with the Security Council's Counter-Terrorism Committee; it should exchange information and engage in cooperative activities with the Office of the High Commissioner for Human Rights, other relevant mandate holders and treaty bodies; and it should consult with regional and sub-regional inter-governmental and human rights bodies.

3. Strengthen the protection role of the High Commissioner.

It has always been the expectation of the human rights movement that the High Commissioner for Human Rights would be the lead international protection actor. A good foundation has been laid for protection,[28] but it must be further strengthened. The recommendation of the High Level Panel on Threats, Challenges and Change that the High Commissioner should prepare an annual report drawing attention to situations of international concern[29] is an important one that would merit careful examination from the point of view of method and political receptivity.

4. Strengthen the protection role of the human rights treaty bodies and international petitions procedures.

The burden of acting for the protection of human rights is one that should be shared by different actors in the human rights movement. The human rights treaty bodies have an important role to play in the quest for better protection. Three issues would deserve particular atten-

[27] E/CN.4/2005/103, p. 2.

[28] See, B.G. Ramcharan, The UN High Commissioner for Human Rights. The Challenges of International Protection (2002); Kluwer; B.G. Ramcharan, A UN High Commissioner in Defence of Human Rights. 2004; Martinus Nijhoff Publishers.

[29] See supra, Section II.

tion here: the role of treaty bodies in reacting urgently to emergency situations; visits on the sport, of the kind that the Committee Against Torture makes; and speeding up the consideration of petitions submitted under petitions procedures established by international treaties.

5. Strengthen the protection role of the special procedures.

There is clearly room to enhance the protection role of special procedures of the Commission on Human Rights: Special Rapporteurs and similar appointees; working groups; and representatives of the Secretary-General. It would be important, in the future, to ask questions such as the following regarding the protection roles of these special procedures: To what extent do they contribute to the prevention of gross violations of human rights? How effective are emergency responses and appeals? Are special procedures able to contain and mitigate situations of gross violations of human rights? How does fact-finding and visits to the spot contribute to protection? Do special procedures contribute to justice and reconciliation? To what extent do they contribute to remedies and compensation.[30]

6. Strengthen the protection role of human rights field offices.

The questions suggested above regarding special procedures should also be asked in respect of human rights field offices. There must be increasing emphasis on their protection role.[31] Since this is the focus of the present book, we shall not expound further on this issue here.

7. Support the role of national courts in human rights protection.

Protection strategies of the future must place increasing emphasis on the role of national courts. A conference organized in Vienna on the occasion of the fifty-fifth anniversary of the Universal Declaration of Human Rights recommended that more be done to support the role of judges in their implementation of international human rights and humanitarian law. It is fundamental that materials on international human rights law and jurisprudence, in local languages, be provided to all national judges on an ongoing basis. There is a great gap here that must be filled urgently. The entire human rights movement has a responsibility to make this happen.

---

[30] See on this, B.G. Ramcharan (Ed.), The Protection Role of UN Human Rights Investigators. Forthcoming. Martinus Nijhoff Publishers.

[31] As of the time of writing the Asian Group at the U.N. is seeking to reduce this role.

8. Build up the role of the International Criminal Court.

Whatever the political controversies still obtaining regarding the role of the International Criminal Court, it is crucial that national leaders and upstarts be aware that they can be taken before the International Criminal Court to answer for criminal violations for which they are responsible. At some point in time it would be vital to launch initiatives with a view to examining how an international consensus can be established on the role of the International Criminal Court.

9. Strengthen the protection role of regional institutions.

An enhanced protection role of regional human rights bodies such as the African, American, and European Court of Human Rights would merit in-depth study in the quest to strengthen human rights protection world-wide. Regional bodies complement national and international ones and have the advantage of local recognition and acceptance. The regional bodies deserve more support.

10. Increase support for rule of law initiatives.

The process engaged in by the Security Council in advancing the rule of law in post-conflict situations is one of the important breakthroughs of recent times. This process should be continued and deepened. Rule of law initiatives are needed not only in the context of post-conflict peace-building but also of development. Without the rule of law in each country the universal realization of human rights will remain illusory.

11. Protect the rights of women more actively.

In a Declaration they adopted on 16 March, 2004, on the margins of the High-Level segment of the sixtieth session of the Commission on Human Rights, Women Ministers of Foreign Affairs, their Women Colleagues and Representatives of Governments decried violence against women:

> "Violence against women nullifies the enjoyment of human rights by women. Around the world, women and girls are victims of countless acts of violence—because they are female. We have come together today to raise our voice against this most pervasive human rights abuse which affects women of all ages, ethnic origins and religions. While recognition of the problem of gender-based violence has changed significantly over the past 20 years, the scope and frequency of assaults against women persist in all layers of world society."

They pleaded:

> "Safeguarding women's dignity and liberty, protecting their health and subsistence and promoting their education and empowerment must be at the core of our political engagement for a democratic, just and equitable society. The strengthening of women will also actively and forcefully contribute to

the fight against HIV/AIDS."[32] The protection of women must remain a priority item on the international human rights agenda.

On the occasion of the tenth anniversary of the Beijing world conference, the UN Commission on the Status of Women adopted a declaration reiterating the continuing validity and relevance of the Beijing recommendations. They must continue to guide the human rights movement. The Commission on the Status of Women called upon the United Nations system, international and regional organizations, all sectors of civil society, including non-governmental organizations, as well as all women and men, to fully commit themselves and to intensify their contributions to the implementation of the Beijing Declaration and Platform for Action and the outcome of the twenty-third special session of the General Assembly on the rights of women.

12. Strengthen protection for groups at risk.

Indigenous peoples, minorities, people with HIV/AIDS, and the victims of trafficking in human beings all require strengthened international protection. The Commission on Human Rights should do its utmost to break the logjam in the adoption of Declaration on the rights of Indigenous Peoples, Indigenous peoples continue to suffer from breaches of their basic economic, social and cultural as well as civil and political rights.

B. *Promotion*

Among promotional strategies that can usefully accompany efforts for strengthened protection, emphasis should be placed on the following:

1. Push harder for Democracy and the Rule of Law.

Human rights function best under democracy and the rule of law. It therefore follows that these two subjects must be given high priority in promotional strategies. This issue has relevance for each country and for the United Nations as a whole. Without moral legitimacy the United Nations cannot prescribe for anyone. A major issue affecting the legitimacy of the United Nations is the undemocratic and oppressive nature of many of the Governments represented in the world body. How can anyone be expected to submit to United Nations authority when this situation prevails? And what role should the law play in helping to give moral legitimacy to the United Nations.

[32] Declaration. Women Ministers of Foreign Affairs, their Women Minister Colleagues and Representatives of Governments decry Violence against Women on the margins of the 60th session of the Commission on Human Rights, 16 December 2004.

We believe that it is urgent to develop principles of democratic legitimacy at the United Nations. We know that it will not be easy, because the very undemocratic and oppressive governments at the United Nations are the ones that will be called upon to ratify them! But this is a challenge not beyond legal ingenuity. The International Law Commission might be able to develop such principles. Or the Secretary-General of the United Nations might be able to establish a group of highly qualified persons to prepare such a set of principles for him that he might publish and disseminate. This is a fundamental problem for the law. If one expects the United Nations to stand in judgment in situations of war and peace it must have the moral legitimacy to do so. Unless it does then it is doomed in its mission.

2. Accentuate the emphasis on preventive strategies.

There is, to date, only incipient work on preventive strategies in the field of human rights. There is need for considerable more work on this front.[33] The more recent jurisprudence of the European Court of Human Rights has emphasized the responsibility of Governments to put preventive strategies in place when rights are at risk. This is an area that is largely undeveloped in international human rights law and practice.

3. Develop human rights education world-wide, particularly in primary and secondary schools.

The General Assembly, at its annual session in 2004, had a debate on how to take forward human rights education world-wide. The work done on this front is still patchy. It is important to put more efforts into human rights education. We have called elsewhere for a Convention on Human Rights Education which would have a simple objective: every country should provide materials, in local languages, for use by teachers in primary, secondary, and higher level institutions of learning. A great deal depends on this simple but powerful idea.

4. Work for the enhancement of national protection systems in each country.

United Nations Secretary-General Kofi Annan has called, as part of his reform package, for intensified efforts to be put into developing the national protection system of each country. An Action Plan was launched by the Office of High Commissioner for Human Rights and other part-

[33] See on this, B.G. Ramcharan (Ed.), Conflict Prevention in Practice. 2005. Martinus Nijhoff Publishers.

ners in 2004. We think that the human rights movement should have a data-base on the national protection system of each country, showing areas of strengths and areas where further work needs to be done. This would be a sort of strategic mapping of the protection system of each country and would allow intelligent decisions to be made as regards projects of technical assistance for particular countries.

5. Disseminate international human rights law and jurisprudence to national courts.

At the present time there is little work done to disseminate international human rights law and jurisprudence to national courts. This work must be of first order importance. We referred to this earlier in this chapter.

6. Develop further cooperation with regional human rights bodies.

One has the feeling that there is a disconnect between United Nations human rights bodies and those of regional organizations. Ways must be found of building synergies among these human rights institutions.

7. Promote cooperation among national human rights institutions.

The Office of High Commissioner for Human Rights has been doing important ground-work to promote cooperation among national human rights bodies, including meeting during the annual sessions of the Commission on Human Rights. The more one puts into cross-fertilization among national human rights institutions the more likely the prospects will be of reaping dividends for human rights promotion and protection.[34]

8. Disseminate international human rights norms more actively.

The dissemination of international human rights norms is a basic activity that remains much neglected. The simple act of distributing materials on human rights to teachers world-wide could make an important difference.

9. Activate further the role of women in the promotion and protection of human rights.

We have discussed the protection challenges affecting women. Here we have in mind drawing more upon the creative energies of women in the promotion and protection of human rights. There is much untapped

---

[34] See, on this, B.G. Ramcharan (Ed.), The Protection Role of National Human Rights Institutions. (2005); Martinus Nijhoff Publishers.

energy here. Women have an important role of play as educators, promoters, and protectors.

We discuss next, some fundamental principles of international human rights law that we feel should be emphasized in the future.

V. *Principles of International Human Rights Law*

Pervading international human rights law, which is *par excellence* the domain of the High Commissioner are fundamental principles of international human rights law that must be ever present in the mind of a High Commissioner—and indeed of the ICRC. A United Nations conference on "Bringing International Human Rights Law Home" held in Vienna in 2000, adopted a Communiqué recommending, "that all judicial officers be guided by international human rights instruments . . ." They specifically urged, "that all citizens, especially judges and lawyers, must be aware of and responsive to international human rights law. Judges and lawyers have a responsibility to familiarize themselves with the growing international jurisprudence of human rights . . ." Surely, this precept would need to be ever present in the minds of all those called upon to uphold international human rights and humanitarian law in the world.

It bears mentioning that Section 39(1) of the South African Constitution provides:

> "When interpreting the Bill of Rights, a court, tribunal or forum:
>
> A. must promote the values that underlie an open and democratic society based on human dignity, equality and freedom;
> B. must consider international law; and
> C. may consider foreign law".

There is guidance to be found from the international human rights treaty bodies on fundamental principles of human rights law such as universality, democratic legitimacy, justice, protection, legality, respect, ensure, equality and non-discrimination and remedy. We deal briefly with each of these in turn.

(a) *Universality*

The World Conference on Human Rights, held in 1993, succinctly expressed the legal consensus of the international community on the universality of human rights as follows: "The universality of these rights and freedoms is beyond question." It went on to say: "While the significance of national and regional particularities and various historical, cultural and religious backgrounds must be borne in mind, it is the duty of States, regardless of their political, economic and cultural systems, to promote and protect all human rights."

(b) *Democratic Legitimacy*

The World Conference on Human Rights also declared that democracy, development and respect for human rights and fundamental freedoms are interdependent and mutually reinforcing. It emphasized that "The international community should support the strengthening and promoting of democracy, development and respect for human rights and fundamental freedoms in the entire world."

Professor Louis Henkin has argued that:

> "The human rights ideology and the law of human rights represented in the International Covenant include, I believe, a right to democracy in the sense of constitutional democracy and its elements—authentic popular sovereignty, respect for individual rights, the rule of law, due process of law and commitment to the principles of justice. I think that these principles of justice were what those who drafted the Covenant contemplated and what states that became parties to the Covenant committed themselves to abide by."[35]

Article 21, paragraph 3 of the Universal Declaration of Human Rights provides that the will of the people shall be the basis of the authority of government: this will shall be expressed in periodic and genuine elections which shall be by universal and equal suffrage and shall be held by secret vote or by equivalent free voting procedures. Article 25 of the International Covenant on Civil and Political Rights states that Everyone shall have the rights and the opportunity, without any of the distinctions mentioned in article 2 and without unreasonable restrictions (a) to take part in the conduct of public affairs, directly or through freely chosen representatives; (b) to vote and to be elected at genuine periodic elections which shall be by universal and equal suffrage and shall be held by secret ballot, guaranteeing the free expression of the will of the electors; (c) to have access, on general terms of equality, to public service in his or her country.

In the case of Peter Chiiko Bwalya v. Zambia, a violation of Article 25 of the Covenant was established when the author had been prevented from participating in a general election campaign as well as from preparing his candidacy for his party.[36]

---

[35] Raoul Wallenberg Institute, Commemorative volume on the occasion of the 25th anniversary of the Human Rights Committee, p. 176.

[36] R. Hanski and M. Scheinin, Leading Cases of the Human Rights Committee, Turku/Åbo, 2003, p. 400.

(c) *Justice*

The Human Rights Committee has invoked the justice principle on occasions. In A *v* Australia, for example, the Committee recalled that the notion of 'arbitrariness' must not be equated with 'against the law' but be interpreted more broadly to include such elements as inappropriateness and injustice.[37]

Section 7 of the Canadian Charter of Rights and Freedoms states that Everyone has the right to life, liberty and security of person and the right not to be deprived thereof except in accordance with the principles of fundamental justice. The Canadian Supreme Court has held that the phrase "principles of fundamental justice" allows the courts to review, from the perspective of substantive as well as procedural justice, laws infringing on life, liberty or security of the person. This means that the courts have the right to strike down laws that do not conform to the judicial view of what is fundamentally just. The principles of fundamental justice are considered the basic tenets of the Canadian legal system and relates to the domain of the judiciary as guardian of the justice system.

(d) *Protection*

The International Commission on Intervention and State Sovereignty, in a widely acclaimed report issued in 2001, elaborated on the core principles of the responsibility to protect. This responsibility embraces three specific duties:

A. The responsibility to prevent: to address both the root causes and direct causes of internal conflict and other man-made crises putting populations at risk.
B. The responsibility to react: to respond to situations of compelling human need with appropriate measures which may include coercive measures like sanctions and international prosecution, and in extreme cases military intervention.
C. The responsibility to rebuild: to provide, particularly after a military intervention, full assistance with recovery, reconstruction and reconciliation, addressing the causes of the harm the intervention was designed to halt or avert.

---

[37] R. Hanski and M. Scheinin, *op. cit.*, p. 121.

(e) *Legality*

In General Comment No. 27, the Human Rights Committee provides general principles applicable in the interpretation of restrictions or limitation clauses. Where, for example, one finds the expression 'as provided by law', the law itself has to establish the conditions under which the rights may be limited. Further, the restriction must not impair the essence of the right, should use precise criteria and may not confer unfettered discretion on those charged with their execution.

In the same vein, a restriction must be legitimate and necessary. 'Restrictive measures must conform to the principle of proportionality; they must be appropriate to achieve their protective function; they must be the least intrusive instrument amongst those which might achieve the desired result; and they must be proportionate to the interest to be protected.' The Committee puts particular emphasis on the fundamental principles of equality and non-discrimination whenever restrictions are made.

(f) *Equality and Non-Discrimination*

In it's General Comment No. 18, the Human Rights Committee took the following approach to the term discrimination:

> "(T)he Committee believes that the term 'discrimination' as used in the Covenant should be understood to imply any distinction, exclusion, restriction or preference which is based on any ground such as race, colour, sex, language, religion, political or other opinion, national or social origin, property, birth or other status, and which the purpose or effect of nullifying or impairing the recognition, enjoyment or exercise by all persons, on an equal footing, of all rights and freedoms."

(g) *Respect and Ensure*

In today's world of pervasive terrorist threats, the Human Rights Committee has provided invaluable guidance on the balance to be struck between security and human rights. Referring to Article 4 of the International Covenant on Civil and Political Rights, the Committee declared in General Comment No. 29:

> "Not every disturbance or catastrophe qualifies as a public emergency which threatens the life of the nation, as required by article 4, paragraph 1. During armed conflict, whether international or non-international, rules of international humanitarian law become applicable and help, in addition to the provisions in article 4 and article 5, paragraph l, of the Covenant, to prevent the abuse of a State's emergency powers. The Covenant requires that even during an armed conflict measures derogating from the Covenant are allowed only if

and to the extent that the situation constitutes a threat to the life of the nation. If States parties consider invoking article 4 in other situations than an armed conflict, they should carefully consider the justification and why such a measure is necessary and legitimate in the circumstances."

(h) *Remedy*

Article 8 of the Universal Declaration of Human Rights states the fundamental principle that "Everyone has the right to an effective remedy by the competent national tribunal . . ." The World Conference on Human Rights emphasized that

> "Every State should provide an effective framework of remedies to redress human rights grievances or violations. The administration of justice, including law enforcement and prosecutorial agencies and, especially, an independent judiciary and legal profession in full conformity with applicable standards contained in international human rights instruments, are essential to the full and non-discriminatory realization of human rights and indispensable to the processes of democracy and sustainable development. In this context, institutions concerned with the administration of justice should be properly funded, and an increased level of both technical and financial assistance should be provided by the international community."

In its views under the Optional Protocol the Human Rights Committee has consistently retained its position that in a case where a violation of the Covenant has been established through the Optional Protocol procedure, the State Party in Question has a legal obligation to provide an effective remedy.[38]

(i) *Principles of Interpretation*

The Human Rights Committee, operating under the International Covenant on Civil and Political Rights, has given extensive guidance on principles of interpretation of human rights provisions. In Views rendered on 5 August, 2003, in a case submitted by one Roger Judge, the Human Rights Committee considered "that the application of human rights evolves and that the meaning of Covenant rights should in principle be interpreted by reference to the time of examination and not, as the State party has submitted, by reference to the time the alleged violation took place."[39]

Mindful of the fundamental principles of international humanitarian law and the fundamental principles of international human rights law are what

[38] M. Scheinin, p. 113.
[39] (Case No. 829/1998).

we would deem operational principles of coexistence that we shall address next.

Conclusion

To conclude this essay, we would recall that a state is obligated to respect the human rights of persons subject to its jurisdiction that it has undertaken to respect by international agreement; that states generally are bound to respect as a matter of customary international law; and that it is required to respect under general principles of law common to the major legal systems of the world. We would urge that the strategies of protection and promotion advanced in the preceding section be built on this foundation and on the following Principles of International Human Rights Law:

1. The principle of universality.
2. The principle of democratic legitimacy.
3. The principle of justice.
4. The principle of protection.
5. The principle of legality.
6. The principles of equality and non-discrimination.
7. The principle of respect, ensuring and guaranteeing international human rights norms.
8. The principle of remedies for wrongs.
9. The principle of faithful compliance with international human rights obligations.
10. The principle of international cooperation for the universal protection of human rights.

These are the fundamental principles of international human rights law on which we must never compromise.

CHAPTER TWO

WE ARE FAILING THE VICTIMS OF WAR[1]

Michael O'Flaherty[2]

The Reality of War

Day in and day out we see and hear stories from Sudan of the massacre of entire villages, sexual abuse, looting and pillaging—as well as of the vast scale of the displacement of people both across Darfur and into Chad.[3] The dimensions of the humanitarian disaster: of starvation, appalling child mortality rates, of death from preventable diseases, challenge us every evening in the TV advertisements of the aid agencies. We hear complex, and sometimes contradictory accounts of the racial, ethnic, economic and other frictions which have fed the violence.[4] Words such as "ethnic cleansing" and "genocide" are used to describe what is happening.[5]

Descriptions of the situation in Sudan could have applied to many other places in the recent past. It could be Bosnia of the early 1990s, Rwanda of a decade ago, Sierra Leone in the late 90s, Afghanistan throughout that time and even, in a way, the Iraq of today. In fact, it could be any one of the 56 major armed conflicts involving more than one thousand conflict deaths per year which occurred between 1990 to 2000.[6]

---

[1] Lecture delivered in Dublin on 10 December 2004 to a public meeting of the Irish Council for Civil Liberties—revised for publication. I express my appreciation to Daniel Moeckli for his research assistance and to Ekkehard Strauss for comments on an earlier draft.

[2] Reader in Human Rights and Co-director of the Human Rights Law Centre at the University of Nottingham; Member of the United Nations Human Rights Committee.

[3] See UN High Commissioner for Human Rights, *Report on the situation of human rights in the Darfur region of the Sudan*, 7 May 2004, UN Doc. E/CN.4/2005/3; Human Rights Watch, *"If We Return, We Will Be Killed": Consolidation of Ethnic Cleansing in Darfur, Sudan*, 15 November 2004 and *Darfur Destroyed: Ethnic Cleansing by Government and Militia Forces in Western Sudan*, May 2004; Amnesty International, *Darfur: What Hope for the Future?*, 16 December 2004. See also the bi-weekly UN Situation Reports available at http://www.unsudanig.org/emergencies/darfur/sitreps/index.jsp.

[4] Ibid.

[5] Ibid. However, at the time of writing, the International Commission of Inquiry on Darfur, established by the UN Secretary General in October 2004 pursuant to Security Council Resolution 1564, had not yet published its findings.

[6] M. Sollenberg and P. Wallensteen, 'Patterns of Major Armed Conflicts, 1990–2000' in *Stockholm International Peace Research Institute Yearbook 2001* (Oxford University Press: Oxford, 2001), available at http://www.sipri.org/contents/conflict/publications.html.

Bertrand G. Ramcharan (Ed.), Human Rights Protection in the Field, 41–57.

It is a story of very particular forms of war, far from the stereotypical images portrayed by literature and the movies. These are not great confrontations of the opposing armies of nation states, engaging in classic battles. Instead, contemporary conflicts typically involve confrontation between a State and one or more rebel groups—often with the involvement in one way or the other of neighbouring States.[7] It may not even be clear who are the opposing forces—in Sierra Leone we used speak of "sobels"—soldiers by day and rebels by night. The fighting is often with light/hand held weapons, or with no modern weapons at all—the machete and axe remain in common use worldwide. Fighters themselves will typically have been conscripted or otherwise forced to serve. Many of them—in some cases, such as Liberia—a majority, will be under the age of 18, often a lot younger than that.[8]

The Impact on Civilians

The single most obvious defining characteristic of these conflicts is their impact on civilians. Typically, civilians are the target. Often, their terrorisation and victimisation is one of the very objectives of the conflict itself.[9]

How does the victimisation of civilians present itself? It is at its gravest in the form of deliberate targeting and killing. We have all heard of the statistic suggesting that, since the time of the First World War, we have moved from a situation where nine soldiers died for every one civilian, to today, when the figures are exactly reversed. I do not know if that is true—I suspect it is one of those statements which takes on its own truth with the retelling—but, be that as it may, recent research does demonstrate the extent to which wars kill civilians. Take Iraq: in October 2004, the medical journal The Lancet, suggested that 100,000 Iraqis—most of them civilians—had been killed since the invasion.[10] Another exercise in counting, that of Iraq Body Count, reported that, in the April 2004 failed assault on Falluja, some 600 of the 800 reported deaths were of civilians, at least 300 of whom were women and children.[11]

---

[7] T. Seybolt, 'Major Armed Conflicts', in ibid.

[8] Amnesty International, *Liberia: The promises of peace for 21,000 child soldiers*, 17 May 2004.

[9] See e.g. *Report of the Secretary-General to the Security Council on the protection of civilians in armed conflict*, 28 May 2004, UN Doc. S/2004/431; report of Graça Machel, *Impact of Armed Conflict on Children*, 26 August 1996, UN Doc. A/51/306.

[10] L. Roberts, R. Lafta, R. Garfield, J. Khudhairi and G. Burnham, 'Mortality before and after the 2003 invasion of Iraq: cluster sample survey' (2004) 364 *The Lancet* 1857.

[11] Iraq Body Count, 'No Longer Unknowable: Falluja's April Civilian Toll is 600', 26 October 2004.

Body counts, in themselves, address only a small part of the actual physical assaults associated with conflict. Just recall the mutilations and the amputations perpetrated during the Sierra Leone war.[12] I spent from 1998 to 2000 in that country and never, before or since, have I witnessed more grotesque infliction of injury. The media focussed on the amputation of arms and legs—less well known were the incidents of cutting off of ears, lips and noses; the carving into the forehead or chest of political slogans and messages; the forced ingestion of fish hooks. The youngest victim whom I saw was a six month old child, the oldest, a bed bound octogenarian woman.[13]

Victimisation takes many other forms, including the uprooting of lives, destruction of communities, displacement and massive humanitarian disaster.[14] Rather than look more deeply at these it is useful to reflect on some of the less well known or, at least until recently, the less well-acknowledged forms of assault on civilians. The most significant of these has got to be sexual violence as a weapon of war.[15] We only ever began to pay proper attention to this phenomenon at the time of the Balkan conflicts—we owe it to people such as Karen Kenny for undertaking the first proper investigations in the early 1990s.[16] And it is thanks to the writings of scholars such as Fionnula Ni Aolain, especially her research on Holocaust-related sexual abuse[17] that we came to understand that common ideas of human rights and human rights law fail to address the extent and the impact of war-time sexual assaults on women.

Another category of victimisation, which is only now receiving proper attention, is that experienced specifically by children. It took the 1996 publication of a seminal study by Graca Machel to wake us up to the global crisis of the deployment of child soldiers and to the multiple other ways in which conflict scars the child.[18] We have yet to come to grips with the

---

[12] See the various reports of the Secretary-General to the Security Council during the years 1998/99, e.g. *Fifth Report of the Secretary-General on the Situation in Sierra Leone*, 9 June 1998, UN Doc. S/1998/486.

[13] M. O'Flaherty, 'Sierra Leone's Peace Process: The Role of the Human Rights Community' (2004) 26 *Human Rights Quarterly* 29.

[14] See supra note 9.

[15] See S. Swiss and J. Giller, 'Rape as a Crime of War—A Medical Perspective' (1993) 270 *Journal of the American Medical Association* 612; Physicians for Human Rights, *War-Related Sexual Violence in Sierra Leone*, 2002.

[16] Final Report of the United Nations Commission of Experts Established Pursuant to Security Council Resolution 780 (1992), Annex IX (Rape and Sexual Assault), 27 May 1994, UN Doc. S/1994/674.

[17] F. Ni Aolain, 'Sex-Based Violence and the Holocaust—A Reevaluation of Harms and Rights in International Law' (2000) 12 *Yale Journal of Law and Feminism* 43.

[18] Supra note 9.

protection needs of unaccompanied children who have been displaced by war. Other issues are still only barely on the table for discussion—such as, for instance, the impact on children of the war-related collapse of birth registration systems.[19]

There are many forms of assault on human rights which have yet to even begin to be acknowledged. One that preoccupies me at the moment has to do with the links between conflict and victimisation for reasons of sexual orientation. On September 29, 2004, Fanny Ann Eddy, the founder of the Sierra Leone Lesbian and Gay Association, was raped and murdered in her office.[20] It is commonly acknowledged in Freetown that the killing was because of she was lesbian and refused to stay in the closet. I think that her killing was facilitated by the general decline in law and order in Sierra Leone since the armed conflict—she was one of the last victims of the war. Her death troubles me personally because I clearly recall, when we were developing the UN's human rights programme for the country, I became aware that homophobia was rife and that that infamous colonial export—the 1861 Offences Against the Person Act—was still on the statute book. At the time I chose not to address the issue on the basis that it was not a priority in the context of the ongoing conflict. Today, perhaps, I would decide differently.

Another range of human rights abuses, crying out for even the most minimal of attention are those affecting the aged. Very little work has been done to identify and address the specific ways in which conflict impacts on their lives. We are left to rely on the anecdotal tales of frail women and men left behind when the able bodied flee from attack or from the bulldozers.[21] I recall myself once visiting a village where, for the preceding four days, there had been a pitched battle between rebel and government forces. All that remained were the smoking ruins of houses, bodies littered across the ground—and a handful of elderly men and women who had somehow survived through it all, but who were profoundly traumatised and near to starvation.

The experience of being a victim does not end with the conflict. In some cases as many people are killed by land mines after as during a war.[22] Only a proportion of physical injuries ever heal. Limbs cannot grow back. Psychological trauma, such as after torture or sexual abuse is little

---

[19] UNICEF Innocenti Research Centre, 'Birth Registration: Right from the Start', 2002.

[20] Human Rights Watch, 'Sierra Leone: Lesbian Rights Activist Brutally Murdered', 5 October 2004.

[21] Half the Iraqis killed in the Fallujah offensive were women, children and elderly people: see Iraq Body Count, 'Fallujah News April 13'.

[22] See e.g. International Campaign to Ban Landmines, *Annual Report 2003*.

understood, never mind treated.[23] And the very notion of treatment can seem very distant indeed when it is entire communities or populations which have been assaulted.

The suffering caused by war very often arrives at our own doorstep, at which point experiences of degradation very likely occur again. Populist and ill-informed asylum and refugee policies of the rich North grow ever more restrictive and disrespectful.[24] It is in this context that we can locate the falling figures for asylum applications in developed States. Last August, UNHCR reported that the second quarter of this year saw a 7% drop in applications in the EU. For Ireland the drop was of 12%.[25]

Everyone can tell a different tale of the disregard for the victims of war in the asylum procedures. I was struck by a story I read on 5 December 2004 in the New York Times,[26] of a Togolese, Kossi Abalo, a conscripted child soldier, imprisoned for refusing to fight against his own tribe, who escaped ten years ago and has been in constant motion ever since, gaining access to and being rejected by what I counted to be at least 12 countries. Last month I got an immediate sense of the ever narrowing welcome for victims, when just three of 50 participants at an international conference which I organised were initially refused either entry or transit visas: the three were prominent human rights activists from Timor Leste, Afghanistan and Sierra Leone.

War—Testimony to Failure

The fact that war happens is a testimony to failure—that civilians are so exposed and violated is a failure. Responsibility for that failure lies at many doors, including those of local, national and regional elites. It is also our responsibility—we the international community.

I suggest that our failure is threefold—a failure to predict, a failure to intervene and a failure to support.

---

[23] But see e.g. the work of the British Medical Foundation for the Care of Victims of Torture, http://www.torturecare.org.uk/

[24] See e.g. European Council on Refugees and Exiles, *Broken Promises—Forgotten Principles: An Evaluation of the Development of EU Minimum Standards for Refugee Protection*, June 2004.

[25] UNHCR, 'Asylum Levels and Trends in Industrialised Countries: January to June 2004', 27 August 2004.

[26] R. Bernstein, 'One African's 10-Year Odyssey Reflects a Growing European Concern', *New York Times*, 5 December 2004.

Failure to Predict

In the first place, the international community has been notoriously unreliable and ineffective in providing early warning of conflict and crisis. Patterns of human rights abuse, most of them longstanding and widespread, preceded all of the conflicts which I have mentioned and made them eminently predictable—yet the signs were not read by the United Nations and other relevant bodies. What is worse, they were sometimes read by parts of the system but ignored by others. This was the case in 1993 when the then UN Commission on Human Rights Special Rapporteur on Summary Executions, Bacre Ndiaye, reported that the genocide in Rwanda was imminent.[27] No one listened. That same year, my then boss, Taduesz Mazowiecki, the Commission's Special Rapporteur for the Former Yugoslavia, predicted that the Bosnian "safe areas", such as Gorazde and Srebrenica, would become killing fields.[28] He was ignored.[29]

These failures were all the more egregious since it is clear that there are some elements of an obligation to "predict" and to "intervene" in the state obligations to protect, promote and ensure human rights.[30] In particular, the Convention on the Prevention and Punishment of the Crime of Genocide,[31] which was considered by the International Court of Justice to reflect international customary law, established an obligation to prevent genocide and other acts.[32]

Cases such as Rwanda and the former Yugoslavia have been widely noted and commented upon.[33] Receiving much less attention, however, are the patterns of violation of economic, social and cultural rights which typically chart the route to war.[34] Despite the repeated evidence that poverty,

---

[27] *Report of the UN Special Rapporteur on extrajudicial, summary or arbitrary executions on mission to Rwanda*, 11 August 1993, UN. Doc. E/CN.4/1994/7/Add.1.

[28] Special Rapporteur on the Former Yugoslavia, *Report on the situation of human rights in the territory of the Former Yugoslavia: Seventh Periodic Reports*, 10 June 1994, UN Doc. E/CN.4/1995/4

[29] F.D. Gaer, 'UN-Anonymous: Reflections on Human Rights in Peace Negotiations' (1997) 19(1) *Human Rights Quarterly* 1.

[30] The recent report of the High-Level Panel on Threats, Challenges and Change expressly endorsed the "emerging norm that there is a collective international responsibility to protect [. . .] in the event of genocide and other large-scale killing, ethnic cleansing or serious violations of international humanitarian law." See *Report of the High-Level Panel on Threats, Challenges and Change*, 2 December 2004, UN Doc. A59/565, para. 203.

[31] 78 U.N.T.S. 277, entered into force 12 January 1951.

[32] Confirming customary nature: *Case Concerning Application of the Convention on the Prevention and Punishment of the Crime of Genocide (Bosnia and Herzegovina v. Yugoslavia), Preliminary Objections*, 11 July 1996, 1996 I.C.J. 595, 616.

[33] K. Kenny, 'UN Accountability for its Human Rights Impact: Implementation through Participation' in N.D. White and D. Klaasen (eds.), *The UN, Human Rights and Post-conflict Situations* (Manchester University Press: Manchester, 2005) 438, p. 452.

[34] See e.g. Mary Robinson's Sidney Peace Prize Lecture, 'Human Rights at the Heart

corruption and discriminatory distribution of wealth destabilise States, we often avert our eyes from the consequences. It is the context of this myopia that we can appreciate the urgent need to develop and implement human rights-based approaches to poverty reduction and to development.[35]

The actual mechanics of early warning also need reform. For instance, the UN systems, to the extent they exist, have shown themselves to be cumbersome and bureaucratic, weighed down not just by complex political game-playing, but also by a chronic inability of the UN to genuinely embrace what the British call "joined-up government".[36]

Failure to Intervene

Even when the crisis is acknowledged, there is a shameful record of inconsistent responses. The UN Security Council, for some years now, has purported to sometimes deploy military/civilian peacekeeping operations on the basis of humanitarian intervention.[37] However, it has failed to clarify a firm doctrine of what might trigger such an intervention and it has been wholly inconsistent in its actions.[38] There is no appetite to seek to deploy a humanitarian intervention force in Sudan, as was again demonstrated the November 2004 meeting of the Security Council in Nairobi.[39] No efforts were made to do so in Sri Lanka or Nepal, notwithstanding the scale of their crises, never mind in humanitarian and human rights disaster zones such as Zimbabwe.

I fully accept of course that many issues of global politics impede the ability of the UN to respond forcefully wherever it is needed—why it is, for instance, pointless to envisage the mounting of sturdy intervention forces in Chechnya or Kashmir. However, in reality, most UN peace missions do not need to invoke a principle of humanitarian intervention in order to engage—the vast majority of them are voluntarily accepted, even sometimes invited in, by the government of the affected state, as was the case in Bosnia, Democratic Republic of Congo, the then East Timor and Afghanistan. But, even regarding situations such as these, practise has

---

of Peace', 6 November 2002, available at http://www.realizingrights.org/index.php?option=content&task=view&id=101.

[35] See e.g. OHCHR, *Draft Guidelines: A Human Rights Approach to Poverty Reduction Strategies*, 2002.

[36] See the *Report of the High-Level Panel on Threats, Challenges and Change*, supra note 32.

[37] See e.g. N.J. Wheeler, *Saving Strangers: Humanitarian Intervention in International Society* (Oxford University Press: Oxford, 2002).

[38] Ibid.

[39] See Security Council resolution 1574 of 19 November 2004, UN Doc. S/RES/1574 (2004).

been highly inconsistent and typically disappointing. These types of UN military/civilian peace missions are only present today in a minority of conflict-affected locations—in just 17 locations.[40]

The figures are even more discouraging when we look at the extent to which the UN has deployed civilian human rights components in its peace missions. As of mid 2004, the UN's Department of Peacekeeping Operations and Department of Political Affairs were either managing or coordinating the planning of only fourteen such "Human rights field presences."[41] The Office of the High Commissioner for Human Rights was, at the same date, operating its own civilian peace-related missions in an additional six countries.[42]

The inconsistent manner in which the UN deploys civilian human rights teams is balanced, albeit to only the most partial of extents, by the occasional mounting of human rights missions by regional organisations. The OSCE operations are the best known,[43] but the African Union is also likely to become active in this area—already a handful of its civilian staff are present in Sudan.[44] The EU is also likely soon to become a player. The deployment of civilian missions is not confined to intergovernmental organisations, for instance small groups of interested states have sent missions to Hebron and Sri Lanka. Even NGOs are somewhat active in this field: the World Council of Churches and Peace Brigades International have deployed volunteers to locations such as Palestine, Mexico and Acceh.[45]

Failure to Support

Let me turn now to the third failure—the failure to support—in other words, once some form of intervention occurs, the failure to identify and respond to the actual needs and requirements of the war-affected civilians. For this purpose I would like to address just one of many aspects by examining the role and activities of the UN human rights field operations.

---

[40] See the website of the UN Department of Peacekeeping Operations (DPKO), http://www.un.org/Depts/dpko/dpko/index.asp.

[41] See OHCHR, *Annual Appeal 2005*, p. 33.

[42] The six countries are: Bosnia and Herzegovina, Burundi, Cambodia, Colombia, The Democratic Republic of the Congo, Serbia and Montenegro. See ibid.

[43] The OSCE has deployed field operations to, *inter alia*, Kosovo, Bosnia and Herzegovina, Moldova and Georgia. For an overview see the OSCE website at http://www.osce.org/about/13510.html.

[44] See African Union press release No. 098/2004, 'The African Union Deploys More Troops in Darfur as Part of its Efforts to Strengthen AMIS', 28 October 2004.

[45] See e.g. L. Mahoney, 'Unarmed Monitoring and Human Rights Field Presences: Civilian Protection and Conflict Prevention' *The Journal of Humanitarian Assistance*, August 2003.

These programmes arrived on the scene just thirteen years ago.[46] They had their origins in a post-Cold War surge of optimism regarding the UN's capacity as a peace-builder. The first specifically human rights mandated mission, established in 1991, was tasked with monitoring the implementation of the San Jose peace agreement in El Salvador. Missions were rapidly established from then in Haiti, the Balkans, Cambodia and elsewhere. Today, these types of mission tend to have wide-ranging mandates to monitor the human rights situation, make sure it is accurately addressed in UN reporting, advocate against human rights violations, undertake human rights capacity building with local institutions, and generally to provide human rights advice to the local UN political leadership.[47]

That the missions should have started off in an ad-hoc way, without much guidance on how to carry out their tasks, is understandable. I vividly recall my own initiation into the UN—when, in 1993, I was sent to Zagreb, told to find a vehicle, fill it with office equipment and get myself to Sarajevo to open the UN's human rights field office. That is what I did. But I look back on the experience with a mixture of horror and amazement—me blithely wandering across the Bosnian battle fields in a battered Cherokee jeep without even the knowledge of how to change a tire, never mind avoid an ambush—it is an utter wonder that I survived.

No less disturbing was the naïve way my colleagues and I sought to do our jobs—or at least, in our defence, how odd were some of the instructions which were sent from headquarters—for instance the instruction, issued at the height of the siege of Sarajevo, to develop a human rights programme at the university—an institution which hadn't functioned in months and whose buildings were on the confrontation line. That was just silly; some other work practices were downright dangerous. I recall, for instance, how a visit made by human rights officers to a concentration camp in western Bosnia may have led to the death of at least one detainee because he was seen speaking with the team.[48]

As I say, it is unremarkable that the first human rights missions should have made many mistakes.[49] What is surprising, and unacceptable is that

[46] See M. O'Flaherty, 'Human Rights Monitoring and Armed Conflict: Challenges for the UN', (2004) (3) *Disarmament Forum* 47.

[47] Ibid.

[48] M. O'Flaherty, 'Report on the Conference on Human Rights in Bosnia and Herzegovina: From Theory to Practice' in Wolfgang Benedek (ed.), *Human Rights in Bosnia and Herzegovina after Dayton: From Theory to Practice* (Martinus Nijhoff, The Hague, 1999), p. 7.

[49] A. Henkin (ed.), *Honoring human rights: from peace to justice: recommendations to the international community* (Aspen Institute: Washington, 1998); D. Garcia-Sayan, 'Human Rights and Peacekeeping Operations', 29 *University of Richmond Law Review* 45; D. Little, 'Protecting Human Rights During and After Conflicts: The Role of the United Nations' (1996) 4 *Tulsa*

many of the mistakes continue to be made—or at least that there remains vast gaps of what might be called "doctrine" or established human rights—law based principles and method for the conduct of field work—entire work areas where no guidance is available and the practitioner is obliged to proceed in a trial and error process of experimentation.

The extent of the problem was highlighted by the results of a questionnaire which I distributed last September to 80 current and former senior staff of field missions.[50] I asked them about what they saw as their role and the extent to which their headquarters supported them in carrying out that role. The results were disturbing. Time and time again, respondents complained that they had no guidance on how to carry out their main responsibilities. For instance, while advocacy and intervention on behalf of victims are among their most important activities, most all respondents said that no guidance whatsoever is available as to how to carry out these functions. Others complained that there are no methods developed to help them engage with rebel groups—notwithstanding the extent to which such groups are the cause of human rights abuses. There was a high level of complaints about a lack of guidance on how to do capacity building work with local civil society. And many respondents wrote that they needed help urgently in order to try to insert human rights considerations into national development programmes and poverty reduction strategies.

The results regarding training in human rights field skills were no less discouraging. Some 50% reported that they had received no pre-deployment training whatsoever, while other complained that what training they did receive was inadequate or irrelevant to the actual situations in which they found themselves. And, as a corollary to the lack of guidance and training, there appear to be a dearth of performance indicators whereby fieldwork can be properly evaluated and staff and management may be held accountable.

Findings such as these[51] go side by side by anecdotal evidence of deep dissatisfaction on the part of national civil societies regarding the activities

---

Journal of Comparative and International Law 87; W. Clarence, 'Field Strategy for the Protection of Human Rights' (1997) 9(2) *International Journal of Refugee Law*; I. Martin, *Human Rights Monitoring and Institution-Building in Post-Conflict Societies: The Role of Human Rights Field Operations*, paper delivered to USAID Conference, Promoting Democracy, Human Rights and Reintegration, 30–31 October 1997, on file with the author, and I. Martin, 'A New Frontier: The Early Experience and Future of International Human Rights Field Operations' (1998) 16(2) *Netherlands Quarterly of Human Rights* 121. See also W.G. O'Neill, 'Gaining Compliance Without Force: Human Rights Field Operations' in S. Chesterman (ed.), *Civilians in War* (Lynne Rienner: Boulder, 2001).

[50] On file with author; for a summary of the findings, see the project report in the annex of this book.

[51] Ibid.

in their countries of some international missions.[52] One hears, for instance, of how the international operation actually undermines the local NGOs by completing ignoring or bypassing them or by damaging their relations with the local government. It seems to be commonplace for an international mission to disregard past achievements and to then to set about with messianic glee on its own programme. Admittedly, the temptation is a strong one. The international mission will often seek to demonstrate swift and impressive achievements—and the infamous acronym, QIPs (Quick Impact Programmes) reflects all that is bad about the approach.[53]

Secondly, the mission will sometimes labour under the illusion that no local civil society could have possible survived whatever period of conflict had gone before—and hence no local consultation is required. This view is almost invariably wrong—I have yet to experience a conflict affected country without some elements of human rights civil society.[54] And those elements always have the capacity to surprise. I recall visiting Peshawar in North West Pakistan during the last days of the Taliban—where I met with an entire law faculty in exile, including human rights scholars, just waiting to get back to Kabul. I visited Solomon Islands following that country's conflict and, given the country's almost total failure to ratify human rights treaties and the lack of available information on human rights organisations, I had next to no expectations. True enough, there was little activity in the country itself, but I learned of an impressive Pacific-regional human rights training project—the Regional Rights Resources Team—doing great work across the island states though with very limited acknowledgement or resources.

Human rights field missions do not exist in vacuums or alone—regardless of the country where they are deployed they form part of complex configurations of international military, police and civilian operations. We can legitimately ask, then, to what extent the other actors compensate for the weakness of the human rights programmes? Among the most important of the other civilian operations from the point of view of human rights are those engaged in humanitarian assistance and development. Large parts of these communities have embraced human rights-based understandings of their work.[55] Major players, like UNICEF and UNHCR, and some of

---

[52] See e.g. K. Kenny, *supra* note 35 and M. O'Flaherty, 'Future Protection of Human Rights in Post-conflict Societies: The Role of the UN' in N.D. White and D. Klaasen (eds.), *The UN, Human Rights and Post-conflict Situations* (Manchester University Press: Manchester, 2005) 379.

[53] See e.g. T. Howland, 'UN Human Rights Field Presence as Proactive Instrument of Peace and Social Change: Lessons from Angola' (2004) 26 *Human Rights Quarterly* 1.

[54] See M. O'Flaherty, *supra* note 13.

[55] See e.g. U. Jonsson, 'A Human Rights Approach to Development Programming',

the largest of the NGOs, are committed to human rights protection and capacity building.[56]

This should be very encouraging—not least because the humanitarian agencies are active in just about every conflict-affected country on the globe. Tragically, though, it seems that, even here, we have to identify a level of failure. A shared commitment to human rights does not seem to always translate into coordinated and effective strategies at the country level.

The deficiencies were highlighted in late 2004 by a damming critique on the record of the UN humanitarian and human rights programme in Sudan issued by the US State Department. Its Assistant Administrator, Roger Winter, on 4 November, in a letter to the UN Humanitarian Coordinator, said, "the current approach to protection within the UN system is fragmented and disjointed. The division of labor in Darfur is unclear even to the personnel involved in protection work on the ground. No central system for reporting and analysis exists. The Protection Working Group in Khartoum lacks leadership, has failed to agree on priorities, and has acted without the sense of urgency called for given the serious problems in Darfur . . . to this day, it remains unclear where a relief agency is supposed to report a protection incident and what the UN system does with information submitted to it."[57]

Reasons for Hope

The picture that I have painted, albeit an incomplete one, is a depressing one, a tale of missed opportunities, inconsistency, disorganisation and, sometimes, of deliberate obstructionism. It is not, however, a hopeless situation. System-wide change is as possible as it is necessary, even if the changes will come slowly and incrementally. We can be particularly encouraged by a number of recent developments.

The first, and by far the most significant, of these is the report issued in November 2004 by the UN Secretary-General's High Level Panel On Threats, Challenges and Change.[58] The Panel, comprising high level former public officials from across the world, achieved consensus on 101 rec-

UNICEF, 2004; J. Darcy, 'Human Rights and Humanitarian Action: A Review of the Issues', paper delivered to a workshop on human rights and humanitarian action convened by OHCHR, UNICEF and ICVA, Geneva, April 2004; Inter-agency Standing Committee (IASC), 'Growing the Sheltering Tree' UNICEF, 2002.

[56] Ibid.

[57] On file with author.

[58] Supra note 32.

ommendations. These have been enthusiastically endorsed by Kofi Annan, who has submitted them for the consideration of the General Assembly.[59]

The panel's report emphasises the importance of the UN's work in preventing conflict and described development as the indispensable foundation for all such efforts. On the subject of humanitarian intervention, the panel proposes five criteria: seriousness of threat, proper purpose, last resort, proportional means and balance of consequences. These criteria, which, at first glance, seem to draw significantly from Scholastic just-war theory, largely reflect a similar set which had been suggested in 2002 by the International Commission on Intervention and State Sovereignty (ICSS).[60] It is noteworthy that the concept, as developed by the ICSS, contains the responsibilities to prevent, react and rebuild.

A second sign of encouragement is the very climate in which the High Level Panel did its work—a climate which seems to accept, at least at the level of principle, that human rights is integral to the pursuit of peace. Foremost, I would refer to the establishment in July 2004 of the office of the United Nations Special Advisor to the Secretary-General on the Prevention of Genocide, which has been presented as a clear, albeit greatly delayed, lesson-learned from the failure of the UN in the case of Rwanda.[61]

This new acceptance is also reflected in the evolving practice of the Security Council—most obviously in its thematic debates and resolutions—such as on women, war and peace; on the protection of civilians and on the impact of armed conflict on children. It can also be seen in the increasing willingness of the Council to be briefed by the High Commissioner for Human Rights (which the High Level panel also encourages) as well as to enter into dialogue with human rights NGOs.[62] For instance, a couple of months ago, the Council, discussing transitional justice, received briefings from Human Rights Watch, Amnesty International and the International Center for Transitional Justice. Unremarkable as this may sound, it would have been unthinkable just a few short years ago.

---

[59] See note by the Secretary-General of 2 December 2004, UN Doc. A/59/565.

[60] See International Commission on Intervention and State Sovereignty, *The Responsibility to Protect*, December 2001, available at http://www.iciss.ca/report-en.asp.

[61] See letter from the Secretary-General addressed to the President of the Security Council, 12 July 2004, UN Doc S/2004/567. The Secretary-General appointed Juan Mendez to this post.

[62] Under the so-called 'Arria Formula', first implemented in 1992, informal meetings can be called for the purpose of a briefing given by one or more persons, considered as expert, in a matter of concern to the Council. It has been used frequently to facilitate briefings by UN officials, UN-appointed independent experts, NGO representatives and others. See J. Paul, 'The Arria Formula', Global Policy Forum paper, October 2003, available at http://www.globalpolicy.org/security/mtgsetc/arria.htm.

It is in the area of transitional justice that it is possible to detect some of the best examples of where solid practice and methodologies are being developing which are based on the link between human rights and peace. Until recently, this was an area of professional hit and miss. I remember, for instance, when the discussions on justice, truth and reconciliation first arose in Sierra Leone, most all we had to go on was the South Africa experience—a very narrow base on which to construct a process for another country.[63] And, a year or so later, at that country's peace talks in Lome, Togo, I had a near impossible job trying to persuade negotiators that amnesties for major human rights-related crimes would be unacceptable.[64] Even as recently as 2002, in East Timor, my colleagues and I faced similar difficulties.

Our job would be at least somewhat easier today, thanks to the availability of guidance on issues such as: the avoidance of impunity in peace processes; the balancing of judicial and non-judicial forms of post-conflict accountability; and even on human rights-based vetting of public employees following regime change.[65] In November 2004, I again saw the value of being able to invoke new forms of guidance and lessons-learned—I was in Jordan meeting with Iraqi government officials to reflect with them on how they can develop human rights approaches for their work. We spent a day discussing transitional justice. At the outset, at least for some of them, transitional justice meant just one thing—the execution of Saddam. It was only after we looked at recent international practice and the guidance by specialist NGOs and the UN, that there was general agreement that Saddam's victims deserved much more—that the future of the country depended on their being a just and comprehensive dealing with the past. To take just one of the issues we discussed—the de-Baathification of the public service—they agreed that some minimum levels of due process of law needed to be guaranteed to the affected officials.[66]

Among the other areas to which we can turn for signs of encouragement, let me return to the work of the UN civilian human rights field operations. Earlier, I criticised them sharply; but I must also acknowledge important shifts and openings. The new High Commissioner for Human

[63] On the Sierra Leone Truth and Reconciliation Commission, see e.g. International Center for Transitional Justice, 'Sierra Leone's Truth and Reconciliation Commission and Special Court: A Citizen's Handbook', 2003, and 'The Sierra Leone Truth and Reconciliation Commission: Reviewing the First Year', January 2004.

[64] M. O'Flaherty, supra note 13.

[65] See International Center for Transitional Justice, 'Vetting and Transitional Justice' (forthcoming 2005), http://www.ictj.org/approaches.asp#vet.

[66] See also International Center for Transitional Justice, 'Iraqi Voices: Attitudes Toward Transitional Justice and Social Reconstruction', May 2004.

Rights, Louise Arbour, has acknowledged the scale of the challenge.[67] She has also made possible the launch of a research project on the role of the human rights field officer. This project is being coordinated at the University of Nottingham. It is trying to identify what is the core content of the professional role of the field officer and to identify methodologies and principles which should guide the work. Based on these findings, sets of training materials will be developed and tested.

This Nottingham project is just one effort, and modest enough in scope at that. Other research and policy work is underway in organisations such as the Geneva-based Centre for Humanitarian Dialogue, in the High Commissioner's office and elsewhere in the UN. In general I think that initiatives such as these, reflecting a new attention to the sector, will at least move it from its infancy to its adolescence.

Turning to Ourselves

Until now I have referred to a "we" or "us" in a very loose way—focussing primarily on the international political bodies such as the UN. By way of a conclusion let me come closer to home and reflect on what we as individuals might do. I have some suggestions:

In the first place, the human rights related findings of the Secretary-General's High Level Panel, if they are to be implemented, will require the firm support of States—all the more so when we consider the rocky soil of anti-UN (and anti Kofi Annan) sentiment into which they fall. It is important for us to call on our governments to show leadership. We have to be dogged in urging them to uphold core principles and to take the necessary action in UN and other fora. We must also persist in demanding that international aid commitments and targets be met, and that those resources are used in ways which best promote and protect human rights. And a consistent concern for the rights of the victims of war also requires us to demand that those who flee conflict are given a welcome—that our countries country stand apart from the mean-spirited tendencies of "Fortress Europe" or of Fortress-anywhere else.

Secondly, we need to examine to what extent we are overly passive observers. It may be the case that we closely follow and speak out on the issues of global crisis and the need for intervention—but do we sufficiently

[67] See High Commissioner for Human Rights, 'Protecting Human Rights: Charting the Way Forward', Address to the 2004 Annual Meeting of the Heads of Human Rights Field Presences, 22 November 2004.

follow that up with scrutiny of the nature of the international responses and interventions? I am not so sure. I am constantly struck, for instance, by the extent to which UN human rights operations, when it comes to their day to day operations, seem to be able to operate free of any public gaze—be it of the local and global civil society or of anyone else. Except when some specific scandal erupts, such as of sexual abuse, there is a sense that they can do as they want. The situation is only marginally better when it comes to the human rights protection work of the humanitarian and development communities. As a result, there is little motivation for the international programmes to become more effective or to take responsibility for their failures; in short, to be publicly accountable. Foreign national human rights organisations in could set a very valuable precedent if they were to find an appropriate way to undertake such monitoring—maybe concentrating on countries which are in receipt of their country's assistance or where peacekeeping missions contain their military or police components. Alternatively, useful work could be done in partnering and supporting local NGOs in conflict-affected countries to themselves do the monitoring whereby they can promote local accountability.

More generally, I think it would be very helpful for foreign national organisations to consider how they could further develop their partnerships with civil society in war affected countries. There are many such support gaps at the international level. For instance, there are far too few experts that can be called on to do human rights skills development work in post-conflict situations. And here again the need is probably best addressed by the foreign NGOs finding ways to help local and regional organisations to themselves develop their own skills and capacities in these areas.

Finally, I have an appeal for those who are from the academic world or otherwise committed to action-oriented research. Their work is urgently needed in support of efforts to protect civilians. Far too little is known about the impact of war, how best to provide human rights protection and the roles of the various international humanitarian and human rights actors. I have referred to the lack of understanding regarding the human rights of the aged, of children; as well as of the gaps in doctrine, method and codes for human rights field work. These are just the tip of the iceberg in terms of knowledge gaps. What is more, much of the research which is underway seems—at least to me—to stop just short of what is most needed—the practical guidance that can make a difference in the field. Research, in order to develop those sorts of outputs, needs to tackle much broader subject areas and be conducted on the basis of exchange and cooperation between academics, policy makers and practitioners.

In the course of this analysis, I have only barely sketched an outline of the crisis of war-affected civilians and the multiple ways in which we fail them. There was the possibility to no more than hint at what they need and are entitled to demand from us. I hope though that I have provoked some thought on where we might go from here. The challenge is vast. So too are the possibilities—that is, as long as we never lose sight of the goal—which is the protection of the human rights of the most vulnerable people on this planet.

CHAPTER THREE

THE PROTECTION OF CIVILIANS

Mark Bowden[1]

Introduction

This chapter will set out some of the achievements and challenges when it comes to the protection of civilians in crises and conflicts. We begin with a discussion of environment in which protection needs to take place.

I. *A Changing Environment*

Despite their protected status, civilian populations are intentionally and illegally targeted by warring parties throughout the world for both strategic tactical reasons. Civilians are also indirectly and negatively affected by the political and military decisions made by parties to conflict.

It's often claimed that this is a new or worsening situation. It's argued that conflict today is no longer waged according to the rules of war. Internal conflicts are proliferating and parties to conflict are no longer trained national armies. Sometimes they are merely, and tragically, drugged children with no cause, no ideology and no other way to make a living.

Compared to the warfare of the last century between large national armies, these claims may be true. The situation may be growing worse. In retrospect however, the years of nation-state warfare with clearly defined militaries may have been the aberration, rather than the norm. Moreover, even then the protection of civilians was more often theory than fact, as Nanking, Dresden and the eastern front in Russia can attest.

What has changed perhaps is the degree of tolerance for crimes against civilians. This may be due to a spreading acceptance and appreciation for the rule of law. The rise of the global media has also put far off events in places like Rwanda and Congo and now Darfur in the living rooms of people all over the world in a way media could never display recent massacres or those of the wars of colonialism.

[1] The views expressed are those of the author in his personal capacity.

Bertrand G. Ramcharan (Ed.), Human Rights Protection in the Field, 59–69.

The end of the Cold War has also facilitated a decreasing acceptance for attacks against civilians. In the Cold War the practices visited by tyrants and thugs against their civilian populations were dismissed or justified as necessary in the interest of the wider ideological struggle. Now this is no longer necessary. During the Cold War, local conflicts were also frequently tamped down to prevent any local struggle from blossoming into a full superpower confrontation.

It is also now much more clear that chaos in one place can aid and abet tragedy elsewhere and threaten international peace and security—a point first brought home by the waves of refugees from Southeast Europe and Rwanda in the 90's and later, by the events of 9/11.

II. *The UN Response*

Compared to our colleagues in civil society, the United Nations has not been at the forefront of efforts to foster changing attitudes, and then transform these into changed practice. Equally however, it has not been wholly absent from these efforts. When the Secretary-General launched the present reform agenda in 1997, he and that agenda insisted that the United Nations put the individual—his or her security and well-being—at the centre of everything we do.

Today, at its request, the Security Council receives a briefing every 6 months on the protection of civilians in armed conflict, and a report of the Secretary-General on emerging protection issues every 18 months. These reports have resulted in two Security Council Resolutions and produced a set of recommendations for action drawing on Human Rights, Refugee, and International Humanitarian Law. The recommendations subsequently served as a basis for two important tools. First came the Aide Memoire—a checklist of priority protection issues and principles adopted by the Council to help it consider protection needs when formulating resolutions and designing or reviewing peacekeeping mandates.

After the Aide Memoire came the Road Map. In June 2001, the Security Council asked the Secretariat to reorganize the forty-four recommendations contained in the first two protection reports into different groups, with the aim of clarifying responsibilities, enhancing cooperation and facilitating their implementation by the Council. It was from this request that the Road Map evolved. The Road Map was also intended to facilitate a comprehensive UN system-wide approach to protection issues and to promote practical implementation of the Secretary-General's 54 recommendations.

Unfortunately, the Road Map exercise proved to be extremely cumbersome and labour intensive. At his December 2003 briefing, therefore, the USG for Humanitarian Affairs sketched for the Security Council a "Ten Point Platform on the protection of civilians in armed conflict." The Platform distils many of the key issues set out in the broader protection framework and provides a less-complicated framework for monitoring and reporting on protection of civilians issues. Subsequent protection of civilians briefings and reports have used the "Ten Point Platform" rather than the "Road Map" as their analytical framework.

III. *Present Issues*

All targeted violence against civilian populations is in itself abhorrent. Some forms of violence however, have a particularly devastating effect on the bonds that hold societies together and the economic basis of societies, thereby destabilizing these communities making them a potential threat to peace and security. The 10 Point Platform focuses on these.

1. *Sexual violence against women*

Problem

a. Sexual violence against women undermines and destroys community cohesion, bonds, and structures. Women are therefore, purposefully targeted for sexual violence as a means to destroy communities.
b. High prevalence of HIV/AIDs, means many survivors of sexual violence will become infected, removing key breadwinners from poor societies, undermining long-term economic prospects.

What needs to be done

a. Prevent abuse from occurring through peacekeeping deployments.
b. Mitigate effects by, i) changing cultural attitudes that lead to ostracism of survivors and their children, ii) better treatment of HIV/AIDs, including increased availability of advanced medicines.

Constraints

a. Peacekeeping operations are frequently deployed after abuse has occurred.
b. Particular needs of survivors and their communities are not well understood by peacekeepers, nor is it well understood that reducing ostracism can help stabilize communities and increase stability and should therefore be a goal of peacebuilding efforts.

2. *Violence against children*

Problem

a. Children's socialization is incomplete. They are therefore easily indoctrinated making them attractive conscripts.
b. Conscripting children and directing them to carry out atrocities against members of their community also undermines and destroys community cohesion. Children are therefore purposefully targeted for violence and recruitment.

What needs to be done

a. Prevent abuse from occurring through peacekeeping deployments.
b. Mitigate effects by changing cultural attitudes that lead to ostracism of survivors.
c. Re-education and livelihood opportunities needed to provide survivors with viable alternatives to a life of violence.

Constraints

a. Peacekeepers are frequently deployed after abuse has occurred.
b. Particular needs of survivors and their communities not well understood by peacekeepers, nor is it well understood that reducing ostracism can help stabilize communities and increase stability and should therefore be a goal of peacebuilding efforts.
c. Support for longer-term reintegration programs, and livelihood programs that would support reintegration, are typically underfunded.

3. *Violence against IDPs and Refugees*

Problem

a. The increased vulnerability of IDPs and refugees due to their dislocations from their homes, livelihoods and support networks, make them an attractive target to armed groups in need of recruits and support.
b. The protected status of IDPs and refugees also make these populations attractive source of cover.
c. Both these factors lead to camp and community infiltration. Violence is then frequently employed as a mean of control and conscription.
d. The presence of armed or partisan groups in turn makes the IDP and refugee camps and communities a target to opponents.
e. The presence or armed or partisan groups and the resulting increase in violence can lead to resentment from host communities.

f. Increased insecurity can also lead to decreased humanitarian access, which may in part be the aim of violence.

What needs to be done

a. Prevent infiltration from occurring through peacekeeping deployments, the dispatch of monitors, and the early engagement of skilled humanitarian organization.
b. Design and negotiate minimum standards for camps and areas hosting displaced with armed groups and governments.

Constraints

a. Slow deployment of peacekeepers, monitors and humanitarian staff.
b. Poor camp management skills facilitate infiltration and violence—e.g. lack of registration, inappropriate location and layout, lack of adequate water and sanitation forcing women to leave camps and exposing them to attack; alternative community structures not encouraged and built.

Efforts to address these attacks on civilians are undermined by three trends, also the focus of the 10 Point Platform:

1. *Limited Access*

Problem

a) A lack of access for humanitarian staff is one of the main impediments to protecting civilian populations in armed conflict. Without access humanitarian workers can not provide material assistance to which people have a right, nor can they prevent, mitigate and respond to protection needs.
b) Access is purposefully denied through violence as well as administrative and bureaucratic obstacles by parties to conflict that do not want humanitarians present because their presence would keep them from carrying out attacks on civilians which may be part of their political and military strategy or tactics, or because the humanitarians would bear witness to such attacks.
c) Access is also indirectly denied as a consequence of insecurity, or poor infrastructure.

What needs to be done

a) Humanitarian organizations need to build closer relations with community early so the community can press for better access.
b) Make improved, open, consistent access a provision or focus of

facilitated discussions or negotiations between parties. Stressing these supposedly non-political issues can have benefits on political discussions by building confidence. Also successful access negotiations, by putting monitors and witnesses on the ground can lower levels of violence and increase prospects for peace.

Constraints

a) Carrying out or supporting access negotiations, and building closer relations with communities requires a different and deeper sort of analysis than humanitarians typically carry out. Unlike objective assessment of needs it requires thorough political analysis—understanding the motivations, strategies, tactics, weaknesses, and leverages of various parties to the conflict, communities, community leaders and other actors such as donors.

2. *Targeting of Humanitarian Staff*

Problem

a) As noted, humanitarian staff are sometimes purposefully targeted for violence to prevent access.
b) Staff are targeted in order to disrupt relief and recovery programs that might conflict with the ideological, religious, political or military aims of a party to a conflict.
c) Staff are also sometimes targeted for economic gain.
d) Staff are also sometimes simply in the wrong place at the wrong time.

What needs to be done

a) Better dialogue, relations, understanding with communities can lead to a better understanding of risks; early warning of risks, and can also increase the political costs for would be targeters, reducing the benefit of attacks and making them less likely.

Constraints

a) Poor understanding of local communities on the part of humanitarian staff.
b) Association with peacekeeping operations, political missions, and military forces can lead to perception that humanitarians are partisan, decreasing their acceptance.
c) International community does not make distinctions between humanitarians and military sufficiently clear when militaries carry out assistance and hearts and minds campaigns.

3. *Impunity*

Problem

a) Pervasive impunity is the biggest impediment to protecting civilians.
b) The consequences for targeting civilians, constraining access and targeting humanitarian staff are insufficient to curb these actions.

What needs to be done

1) More aggressively build local capacities for rule of law at the first sign of tension and through the lifespan of conflicts.
2) Member states and international organizations should make participation in peace and political negotiations and participation in future governments contingent on good treatment of civilians, support for access, support for humanitarian assistance and prosecution of violations.
3) Member states should make political, military, and economic support for armed groups, political factions, governments and individual leaders more contingent on protection of civilians, support for access and treatment of aid workers.
4) Make protection of civilians and support for access and humanitarian assistance a feature of military aid and training programs.
5) Make greater use of targeted sanctions against individuals and parties that repeatedly target civilians, deny access and encourage attacks against aid workers.
6) Prosecute individuals responsible for attacks on civilians and aid workers in third countries claiming jurisdiction and in the International Criminal Court.

Constraints

1) Preventive local capacity building poorly funded.
2) Member states and international organizations traditionally reluctant to link protection and inclusion, however, (i) desire for respect and legitimacy is frequently strong, (ii) setting conditionalities for achieving respect can be effective, and (iii) better treatment of civilians (with less destruction to society and economies) leads to more stable and enduring peace.
3) Difficulty in targeting sanctions.
4) Humanitarian organizations have not adequately demonstrated links between protection and peace and security and interests of member states; nor have they adequately identified specific

ways member states could use their leverage to help humanitarian organizations protect civilians.

5) Actions when they are taken are frequently ill coordinated. Use of leverage by member states and activities by humanitarian organizations need to be well coordinated. Structured mechanisms for such coordination may be needed.
6) Humanitarian organizations have made ineffective use of media to pressure member states into applying their leverage.
7) Monitoring and reporting needed to support individual prosecution are frequently lacking.

IV. *The Rights Forum*

Even limiting ourselves to these three protection issues and these three impediments to improved protection, when in fact, as the Aide Memoire lays out, there are considerably more, it is clear that translating decreased acceptance for protection violations into actual decreases in occurrence and severity must involve peacekeeping operations, humanitarian actors, donor governments and member states. Changes are needed in the design and focus of peacekeeping and peace building operations. Humanitarian organizations need to improve their management of camps, their negotiating skills, their engagement with communities, and the targeting of their requests for support from member states. Improvement in information gathering, political and contextual analysis and intelligence are needed to undermine these other improvements. Donors need to increase timely support for rule of law capacity building, reintegration and restoration of livelihoods. Relief is not enough. And member states need to make better and more frequent use of their leverage with parties to conflict and increase the costs of failure to comply with international standards and norms.

These various efforts can be done separately, but in fact, to be most effective, such reforms should be undertaken in a complementary fashion, What is the right forum however, to coordinate these efforts? Both the Security Council and ECOSOC have proven to be difficult fora to fashion and implement more than vague agendas of support as seen with the Road Map. The Peace Building Commission and Peacebuilding Support Office proposed by the recent High Level Panel may offer a suitable alternative.

V. *Protection on the Ground*

On the ground, the issue of coordination has become similarly acute. Among NGOs and civil society operating in conflict zones, protection is now being viewed as something broader than we have understood in the past, encompassing more than a defence against political and physical violence. Full and free expression of political rights and a lack of physical violence only go so far in the face of war and conflict. Since the Second World War, and especially since the end of the Cold War, more civilians have died from war, than in war—from deprivation rather than direct physical violence. Most people who die during armed conflict do so because of the hunger, disease, and exhaustion that results from the impoverishment, displacement and destitution that war forces upon them.

Protection is now generally believed to include many inter-connected activities including, for example, efforts to improve physical security, provide humanitarian assistance, support human rights, extend rule of law and nurture transitional justice. Indeed, the most widely held definition—refined through a series of workshops led by ICRC involving more than fifty organizations—describes protection as: *"all activities aimed at ensuring full respect for the rights of the individual in accordance with the letter and the spirit of the relevant bodies of law, i.e. human rights law, international humanitarian law and refugee law."* This can entail:

i) ensuring that harm doesn't occur
ii) ameliorating or repairing the damage of past violence or deprivation
iii) mitigating the worst consequences of continuing violations
iv) contributing to the prevention of further violations; and
v) ensuring judicial and social redress for past abuses.

For many humanitarian agencies, this broader view of protection has prompted them to explicitly re-conceive and redesign their entire range of programs as a means of helping individuals attain certain human rights—the rights based approach. For other agencies, the broader view of protection has prompted them to launch advocacy campaigns alongside their existing material assistance efforts. In addition to building health posts and water points, for example, these agencies will advocate that local authorities invest more in basic social services, pointing to the government's obligations under various international covenants. For still other humanitarian organizations, the broader view of protection has meant, stepped-up efforts to 'Do No Harm', to consider the potential impacts of their material assistance programs on protection. A poorly designed IDP camp, for example, can put children and women at increased risk of sexual exploitation and abuse if the latrines or water points are put in dark areas of the camp with little foot traffic.

If protection is broader it is also a shared responsibility. Although some organizations like ICRC, OHCHR, and UNHCR do have protection-specific mandates, no agency has a mandate so comprehensive as to encompass all the various activities needed to improve the protection of civilians in armed conflict. Similarly, no one agency has the capacity to address all development, humanitarian, human rights, and peace-building work that may be needed to create more protective conditions on the ground. At the same time, mandates, organisational focus and comparative advantages sometimes overlap. For example, four mandates pertain to unaccompanied children: those of UNICEF, UNHCR, The SRSG for Children and Armed Conflict and ICRC. Given this reality—multiple mandates and roles, no comprehensive mandate or capacity, overlapping mandates—there is growing acceptance that collective, collaborative or, at the very least, complementary action is needed among various actors if protection for civilians is to be fully realized. Currently, however, lessons from the field clearly demonstrate that sufficient complementarity is not happening.

Protection gaps and duplications exist in most conflicts. As the approach to protection has broadened therefore, a debate has started to emerge. What is the right forum for bringing protection efforts together on the ground? Has a new role emerged and is this one that OCHA is well suited to fill: helping the Humanitarian Coordinator to ensure and facilitate complementary action that will help close the protection gap. Ensuring collective, collaborative or complementary action is precisely the reason that the Humanitarian Coordinator, OCHA and its antecedents were created. The Humanitarian Coordinator and OCHA work with their humanitarian partners to ensure there are strategies and mechanisms in place to fill gaps in the assistance effort. OCHA could do the same for protection. It could work to effectively promote and support the preparation and implementation of strategic protection plans for civilians, including IDPs, and ensure the complementarity of protection players' efforts. OCHA could serve as the secretariat for the collective effort to ensure that international legal standards and their accompanying humanitarian responsibilities are clearly identified, communicated and addressed as strongly as possible by those with specific protection responsibilities and capacities. It could also promote and work for a strong, people-centred protective capability within the humanitarian community.

Conclusion

Unfortunately, time may not be on our side. Already the window is closing on our opportunity to institutionalize the decreasing tolerance for violence against civilians in the same way previous changes in attitude were codified in the Geneva Conventions and the creation of the ICRC. Although 9/11 made clear that instability anywhere in this world has a very long reach, it has also renewed the Cold War willingness to make protection of civilians an early and expedient, if unfortunate casualty of efforts to root out and destroy terrorists. Already we see counter-terrorism measure enacted in established and recent democracies alike that do not always comply with human rights obligations.

CHAPTER FOUR

OPERATIONALISING THE PROTECTION OF CIVILIANS

Elissa Golberg[1]

Introduction

It has now been five years since Canada first proposed that the United Nations Security Council acknowledge and address the protection of civilians as an issue that was central, not tangential, to its responsibilities for maintaining peace and stability.[2] Canada argued then, and still argues today, that if the Council is to maintain its legitimacy, its decisions must better account for the reality that attacks against civilians are often a war aim in contemporary armed conflict. It must also have the courage to take necessary political action. And for such political action to be effective, the Council must have at its disposal a range of tested non-coercive and coercive tools that can be utilized.

On balance, the Security Council has made important progress. A normative framework has been established, and has been buttressed by practical strategies, which should enable it to take concrete initiatives in response to situations where the safety of civilians is at risk. Leaders in numerous fora have endorsed this framework, including the G7, the Millennium Declaration, the Constitutive Act of the African Union, the Commonwealth and the Francophonie.

In addition, regional institutions, national governments, UN country teams, human rights and humanitarian actors have pursued complementary efforts. And yet, while we have made substantial headway in advancing the rhetoric of civilian protection, implementation and capacity remain key challenges, if not obstacles. In some instances, terminology—including clarifying precisely what is meant by civilian protection—has been a barrier. For this agenda to have lasting affect on the global public peace and security policy, we must better understand the limitations inherent in pursuing such an agenda while seeking to build on good practice.

[1] The views presented in this paper are those of the author and do not necessarily reflect those of the Canadian Government.

[2] Canada made advancing the Protection of Civilians a key priority during its 1999–2000 Security Council tenure, during which time resolutions 1265 (1999) and 1296 (2000) on civilian protection were adopted.

Bertrand G. Ramcharan (Ed.), Human Rights Protection in the Field, 71–78.

I. *Progress*

As noted, important progress has been made on the Protection of Civilians (POC) Agenda since 1999. There has been a significant increase in global awareness, knowledge, advocacy, and normative development. The protection of civilians and related issues—conflict prevention, children and armed conflict, women, peace and security are firmly on the international peace and security agenda.

The Security Council regularly uses the language of human rights, humanitarian and refugee law in addressing country situations. The Council now routinely calls for unhindered humanitarian access, and has expressed concern about insecurity in camps for displaced persons and attacks against aid workers, including in Afghanistan, DRC, Liberia and Burundi.[3] The Council is increasingly sensitive to the humanitarian and development implications of conflict and post-conflict contexts and the need to consolidate peace. Complex links between small arms proliferation, DDR and war economies have been recognized by the Security Council and efforts have been proposed to address such circumstances.[4]

The protection of civilians is increasingly reflected in the mandates of peacekeeping operations. Since 1999, six peace support operations have included express provisions under Chapter VII for peacekeepers to use force to protect civilians "under imminent threat of physical violence" within their areas of deployment and capabilities. This is a significant development. It meant, for instance, that the Uruguayan battalion felt empowered to protect compounds where civilians had gathered in the Ituri region from attack in 2003.[5] Contrast this with the early 1990s in Bosnia and Rwanda, where peacekeepers argued they were constrained by their mandates from protecting civilians at risk. The civilian components of multidimensional peace support operations also reflects these concerns, with child, gender ad HIV/AIDS advisors now regularly included.

Concern for civilian protection has also been evident in the design and implementation of new sanctions regimes. Having learned from its previous use of broad-based sanctions, the Council is expressly including human-

---

[3] See, generally, B.G. Ramcharan, The Security Council and the Protection of Human Rights. Kluwer, 2002.

[4] For instance, the UNSC has called for cooperation among UN missions in Liberia, Sierra Leone and Cote D'Ivoire. In addition, the UNSC mandated peace support missions in Burundi and DRC are cooperating on small arms proliferation and DDR of former combatants. Finally, at the UNSC's request, expert panels have explored the illicit exploitation of natural resources in DRC and Liberia.

[5] See DPKO Lessons Learned Unit report on DRC.

itarian exemptions in order to mitigate any unintended humanitarian impacts. Other innovations are also apparent. In addition to the expert panels on war economies, there is now also the prospect of naming and shaming those who use child soldiers.[6] The Security Council has undertaken fact-finding missions to better engage and understand the complex issues before it. In addition, increasing advances are being made on rule of law issues, with the importance of addressing impunity through national and international mechanisms noted in Council resolutions, such as the tasking of a Commission of Inquiry for Darfur, the findings of which were submitted by the Council to the International Criminal Court for action.[7]

Finally, nowadays, reporting by the Secretariat to the Council also includes better analysis of specific impact of conflict on civilians, including reference to humanitarian access, human rights promotion and protection, child protection, sexual violence, and impunity. This is key for encouraging and influencing Council decision-making.

It is also important to note that important developments have also taken place on the Protection of Civilians agenda beyond the UN Security Council, with initiatives such as:

- Development of UN Guidelines on Disarmament, Demobilisation, Relief and Rehabilitation (DDRR) and on the Humanitarian impact of Sanctions;
- Normative work on the separation of armed elements in refugee camps and capacity building initiatives with host governments to reduce insecurity in refugee camps;
- Establishment of Protection Working Groups (e.g. Angola, Colombia, Darfur) and Child Protection Networks at field level;
- Regional meetings where Protection of Civilian priorities are identified;
- Establishment of Country-Specific civilian protection strategies involving the government concerned, UN country teams and NGOs; and
- Friends groups created to advance progress in capitals and in New York on the Protection of Civilians, Children and Women, Peace and Security agendas.

II. *Pitfalls*

In spite of impressive advances, we know however that the implementation of the protection of civilian's agenda is uneven, and faces numerous

[6] See UNSC resolution 1379. Resolution 1539 tasks UN country teams to develop specific action plans on child protection.

[7] See UNSC resolution 1593 (2005).

obstacles to its effective pursuit. It would be fair to argue that some of our key advances have been more in what the Security Council says than what it has done. Even there, we face limitations because there are some contexts where the Council is engaged but it is reluctant to use Protection of Civilians language, for example in the Occupied Palestinian Territories; where it takes a long time to get the Council engaged despite evidence of a threat/link to peace and security (Sudan/Darfur; Colombia); or where the Council has not engaged because of interests of a Permanent Member (Chechnya).

Several factors are at play in such situations, and eight key issues should be highlighted in this regard:

First, the make-up of the Council, individual Council members' perceived interests and allegiances, and political realities (including the receptivity of parties to conflict) sometimes limits the effectiveness of the Council in this area with consequent negative impacts for the protection of civilians on the ground.

Second, the absence of a consistent champion in the Council can be an obstacle. The Council often needs to be specifically guided to take action, which requires consistent briefings by the Secretariat and by NGOs. For this reason, it has often been the case that leadership to promote the POC agenda has been assumed by non-permanent members of the Council, and depending on Council make-up it is not always evident a candidate will appear.

Third, there is the issue of the continued weakness of the conflict prevention agenda. It has become a truism to say that preventing conflict and serious violations of human rights and humanitarian law is the best way to enhance the legal and physical safety of civilians. However, beyond hortatory statements by the Council and a presidential statement and thematic resolution, it rarely engages in preventive diplomatic action. This is true for a number of reasons, not least because of political sensitivities and the Council's continued reactive approach, which has proved difficult to overcome.

Fourth, there is sometimes a lack of political will, consensus, and resources/capabilities to effectively pursue Council decisions that relate to the protection of civilians. Darfur is a case in point. In July 2004, the Council adopted a robust resolution on Darfur, which included specific demands that violence against civilians be stopped and the adoption of an arms embargo against those perpetrating these actions. However, it would be another eight and half months before the Council would agree on the creation of a monitoring mechanism for the arms embargo, on benchmarks for measuring progress by the Government of Sudan regarding Janjaweed, and on the importance of increasing the number of human rights monitors that should be deployed.

Fifth, the means are sometimes limited to enforce decisions of the Council. In the first instance, UN Country Teams lack capacity to pursue and advance the protection of civilians agenda.[8] In addition, there have been particular challenges when it comes to peacekeeping operations that have expressly been given Protection of Civilians mandates. Central to this question is whether such missions have the means and capabilities to fulfil the range of tasks they are being assigned. To date, often the answer is "no", and it is useful to explore this in some further detail.

Unfortunately, mission planning is weak, including intelligence on parties to a given conflict, their capabilities and intent. This failure is partly due to the fact that many member States are reluctant to allow the UN to have an independent intelligence capacity. In addition, there is an absence of common doctrine and inter-operability for robust civilian protection missions. In most contexts, there is also an inadequate number of troops or equipment to fulfil mandates being assigned.

Importantly, there is often likewise an absence of a common understanding of what it means to have a Protection of Civilians mandate. Indeed, it is often unclear how the protection problem is understood in each case, and two different troop contributors to the same mission may interpret such questions differently as may the Force Commander. Moreover, there is debate about whether clear doctrine is required for peacekeepers on when and how to use force to protect civilians or of adequate rules of engagement and understanding of tasks at hand.

Decisions about the protection of civilians tend to assume a common understanding as to the nature and scope of the agenda but in practice there may be a diversity of conceptions when debated. There is also uncertainty of how to interpret the language of "within means and capabilities", which has increasingly been included by UNSC members in relation to POC mandates for peace support operations. Currently, there is considerable latitude among troop contributors to interpret mandate, which relates to capabilities, professionalism, and national mindsets.

There are other problems in practice. Pre-deployment training often doesn't include specific Protection of Civilians elements, explanations or tools. Troop Contributing Countries have first responsibility for ensuring their troops are adequately prepared for and understand their mission, and there is a need for greater collaboration among troop contributors in this area. Member States must also be clear about what they can and can't offer in support of such missions.

The UN Department of Peacekeeping Operations also has a role to play in developing doctrine for multidimensional and robust peace support

[8] "Protect or Neglect" OCHA, Brookings-SAIS Project on Internal Displacement, 2004.

operations and drafting mission standard operating procedures. At the same time, we need to be careful about having a boiler plate for country specific Protection of Civilians mandates. In some instances, it is creating confusion about roles and responsibilities.

The sixth set of issues that can act as an obstacle to the effective pursuit of the POC agenda is that, notwithstanding the existence of mandates that include provision for use of force to protect civilians, there remains a lack of consensus around criteria for such deployments and use of force guidelines. The recent report of the High Level Panel on New Threats, Challenges and Change and the Secretary-General's report on "In Larger Freedom" seek to respond to this issue by proposing that the Security Council adopt use of force criteria.

Seventh, a key absence of systematic analysis of what is and is not working in terms of Protection of Civilian missions and initiatives at the country level is a critical inhibiting factor. There have been insufficient lessons-learned exercises pursued on POC mandates. There is also a need to assess the experience of child and gender protection advisers.

An eighth and final cluster of issues relates to the continued distinctive pursuit of protection of civilians, women, peace and security, children and armed conflict agendas, and the pursuit of separate initiatives by advocacy groups in this regard without sufficient explicit recognition of overlap. For instance, competing 'friends' groups on these issues by advocacy NGOs and States has mitigated the identification and pursuit of synergies.

III. *Prospects*

It is easy to become discouraged if one focuses only on the obstacles to making progress. However, we must recall that only five years ago, the Security Council focused not on the protection of people but of convoys and facilities. It also paid very little attention to the particular rights, needs and vulnerabilities of women and children. That has changed fundamentally.

Much of this agenda is achievable and practical. Many of the challenges identified can be overcome, but it will require concerted political action, continued norm development and operational implementation, monitoring, assessment and adjustment. There are a number of concrete initiatives that must be pursued.

First, it is essential that better-defined trigger mechanisms for action by the Security Council be developed for countries where civilians are clearly at risk, but where the Council has hitherto not been formally seized. This includes criteria around the use of force.

Second, the Security Council should adopt specific and time-bound measures in responding to country situations where civilians are at risk. In addition to the obvious tool kit of sanctions and peace support operations, other tools should be better exploited such as: Fact-finding missions; Commissions of Inquiry; Expert panels; Letters; and Security Council envoys. The Council must be able to respond better to the "so what next" question, when problems occur (e.g. when parties implicated in a UNSc resolution don't respond to hortatory resolutions or arms embargoes). There must also be increased emphasis on preventive action. The Security Council should show greater willingness to draw on the UN's human rights and humanitarian mechanisms for early warning, promote preventive deployments and diplomatic initiatives, and be more vigilant in post-conflict contexts. Here the Secretariat should be more pro-active, particularly in bringing options to the UNSC's attention where it may take constructive actions.

Third, the Security Council, Troop Contributing Countries, Secretariat entities, Special Representatives of the Secretary-General and UN Country Teams, drawing on information from NGOs, should regularly assess the implementation of Protection of Civilians missions. Good practices should be identified and disseminated. Different scenarios should be gamed and options identified. In this context, States, DPKO and regional organizations need to inquire about pre-deployment training (e.g. ask troops who have been deployed to POC missions to clarify what kind of training would have assisted them to fulfil the POC tasks). Attention must also be given to whether more robust missions might be done under the framework of coalitions of the willing.

Fourth, where Protection of Civilians mandates are to be given, much greater emphasis needs to be given to appropriate mission planning and intelligence; appropriate resources, configuration, equipment and support for forces, including identification of reserves; guidance for Troop Contributing Countries on the use of force; better briefings, training, and preparation of Force and Contingent commanders; enhanced Protection of Civilians training for Troop Contributing Countries, including with real life situation exercises; clarifying different roles and capacities as regards the military and civilian police roles in the protection of civilians; and clarifying how the protection of civilians fits in with integrated missions planning.

Fifth, there should be strengthened enforcement and monitoring of arms embargoes, asset seizures, travel bans and other coercive measures, with due attention to humanitarian impact as per the OCHA guidelines.[9]

---

[9] See Annex I to this book.

Sixth, UN Country Team capacity to lead and coordinate on protection issues must be prioritised and strengthened. There should be greater commitment by the Security Council to provide political backing to UN Country Teams efforts vis-à-vis governments and non-state actors. Here again, we need to identify good practices and ensure their wide dissemination.

Seventh, there is need for greater clarity on the roles expected to be played by regional organizations on the protection of civilians, their accountability with respect to the Security Council and ways to build this capacity and implement lessons learned.

Eighth, there is need for continued attention to cross-border and regional dimensions to protection challenges. Recent experiences in West Africa on small arms, the transit of armed actors, and exploitation of natural resources will be important to asses in this regard.

Ninth, there is need for continued strengthening of other measures, such as the development of guidelines on: DDRR; the separation of armed elements from refugees and displaced persons, particularly in camp contexts; and the development of codes of conduct regarding issues such as the identification of ombudspersons and dealing with hate media.

Tenth, we must create better synergies in the agendas for the Protection of Civilians, Children and Armed Conflict, Women and Peace and Security. The Secretariat must continue to provide solid analysis and recommendations for action by the Security Council.

IV. *Conclusion*

This agenda is urgent, particularly in an international context where the death and displacement of civilians are often a deliberate war aim of combatants. The actions identified however will also demand a medium and long-term perspective. It is no longer acceptable for the international community to allow situations to spin out of control, leading to regional instability, and serious violations of human rights and humanitarian law. Failure by our global peace and security mechanisms to respond to such challenges undermines their credibility with the public. More importantly, failure to address such circumstances has devastating consequences for conflict affected women, men, boys and girls which we can not afford to ignore.

CHAPTER FIVE

THE PROTECTION OF REFUGEES AND DISPLACED PERSONS

Kamel Morjane[1]

Introduction

UNHCR is a protection agency. Its mandate is clear: a person fearing persecution who flees across an international border deserves international protection because he or she cannot avail himself or herself of the protection of his/her Government. But what happens when those who have sought protection from one group or state entity and enjoyed asylum in a foreign country find themselves again at risk? What can we do for the doubly threatened, for the refugee who has escaped one terrible situation, only to find himself or herself again under attack? And what of those civilians who have not been able to cross a border, but whose security is under threat and have the same fear of persecution? And how does UNHCR cooperate and coordinate with other agencies which have a protection mandate to guarantee protection to those who are in need? These are some of the issues UNHCR deals with daily and which I shall address in this essay.

I shall briefly outline the nature of the problem from UNHCR's perspective, and then describe some of the measures and initiatives we are involved in to alleviate the problem. My focus is on refugees, as they are of most immediate concern to UNHCR, but I will raise a few other questions representing gaps in the protection of civilians.

The Problem

Six months ago, a refugee transit centre in Gatamba, Burundi, was attacked. Some 160 Congolese refugees died and many more were severely wounded during the course of one unimaginable, horrific night. Both Burundi and Rwanda threatened to invade the DRC to pursue the assailants, but would that really help protect the refugees?

[1] The views expressed are those of the author in his personal capacity.

Bertrand G. Ramcharan (Ed.), Human Rights Protection in the Field, 79–85.

In northern Uganda in 2004, attacks by the Lord's Resistance Army resulted in hundreds of civilian deaths, including 30 refugees, and large scale displacement. What could have been done to protect these people?

A humanitarian presence is one means of providing protection to civilians caught-up in an armed conflict situation. As a matter of fact, we cannot think of any protection without a presence. But the humanitarian law and the refugee law principles are not always respected. *Humanitarian access* is either denied or obstructed in about 20 conflicts around the world, leaving some 10 million people worldwide in need of protection, but also of food, water, shelter, medical care and the basic means of survival without recourse to the humanitarian community. And we witness intimidation, physical threat and direct attack against humanitarian personnel as they attempt to carry out their mandate—as demanded by the international community—in conflict and post-conflict situations. In Afghanistan, Iraq, Chechnya, Côte d'Ivoire, Liberia, Somalia, Sudan, Indonesia and elsewhere, humanitarian staff have lost their lives in the line of duty. In as much as the fate of threatened populations depends upon the presence of humanitarian workers, their security begins with the security of humanitarian workers.

UNHCR's *mandate* in providing international protection to refugees, and assisting States in identifying and delivering solutions to refugees' problems clearly brings us into the realm—and the international agenda—of the protection for civilians in armed conflict. Those with no other option but to seek safe refuge away from their home where conflict rages have often been denied the most basic of human rights. Yet as we have witnessed in many refugee and IDP settlements, the protection they sought has not always been guaranteed.

Attacks on refugee camps and attempted infiltration by militia groups not only threaten the lives and security of refugees, but undermine the very notion and institution of asylum.

Action and Activities

In order to address the physical insecurity of people of concern to the Office, UNHCR has promoted and applied a number of *actions and activities* in partnership with States, members of the donor community, other international agencies, operational partners and refugees themselves.

For example, the problem of refugee camp security was first brought to the attention of UNHCR's Executive Committee in 1979, in the context of attacks on refugee camps in the southern Africa region. In 1983, the then High Commissioner Poul Hartling stated that without close cooperation with the political organs of the United Nations and close consultation with the Secretary-General, UNHCR was neither able—nor indeed competent—to undertake effective action in case of armed attacks on refugee camps.

Consultations were initiated and have borne fruit much later. It is not rare to see the High Commissioner addressing the Security Council in a special session on refugees. Of particular relevance to UNHCR are *Security Council Resolutions 1208 (November 1998) and 1296 (April 2000)*. The former calls upon African States to further develop institutions and procedures to implement the provisions of international law relating to the status and treatment of refugees and the provisions of the OAU Convention. It makes specific reference to the location of refugees at a reasonable distance from the border of the country of origin (according to the OAU principles, a reasonable distance means a minimum of 50 kms) and the separation of refugees from other persons who do not qualify for international protection afforded refugees or otherwise do not require international protection. Resolution 1296 invites the Secretary-General to bring to the attention of the Security Council situations where refugees and internally displaced persons are vulnerable to the threat of harassment or where their camps are vulnerable to infiltration by armed elements and where such situations may constitute a threat to international peace and security.

A second example: in 1998, former High Commissioner Sadako Ogata presented a conceptual framework of possible measures to be considered in situations of refugee insecurity. Known as the 'ladder of options', and based upon consultations with the Under-Secretary-General for Peacekeeping operations, the framework describes the "soft", "medium" and "hard" measures (or options) that can be undertaken to address the prevailing security environment.

The 'soft' option includes preventive measures by States and UNHCR such as limiting the size of camps, ensuring their location at a reasonable distance from the border to the country of origin, and including refugees in camp management decisions. Under this 'soft' option, governments should already consider the separation of armed elements, while the international community could provide assistance to national law enforcement authorities. The 'medium' option might include the use of dedicated security teams, the deployment of multi-national civilian observers or an international police force to support national law enforcement efforts. And finally, as a measure of last resort, the 'hard' option refers to the use of a UN Peacekeeping Operation or that of a multi-national or regional force under Chapter VI of the UN Charter, or even Chapter VII, in case there is no consent by States for external intervention.

Another development took place in December 2000, when UNHCR *Global Consultations on International Protection* were launched. It engaged States and other partners in a broad-ranging dialogue to explore how best to revitalize the existing international regime for the international protection of refugees while ensuring flexibility for addressing new challenges and problems. In the resulting *Agenda for Protection*, one goal (number 4) aims at effectively addressing refugee security-related concerns through resourcing States for securing the safety of refugees and for the separation of armed elements from refugee populations; informing the Secretary-General and the Security Council of security issues; preventing military recruitment of refugees; and preventing age-based and sexual and gender-based violence.

In 2002 UNHCR's Executive Committee adopted Conclusion N° 94 on the Civilian and Humanitarian Character of Asylum. It calls upon UNHCR and States to facilitate a process leading towards the elaboration of measures for the disarmament of armed elements and the identification, separation and internment of combatants. In June last year, UNHCR convened a 'Meeting of Experts' from governments, international organizations and other actors (including DPKO) with the intention of developing practicable operational guidelines, which are to be finalized shortly.

UNHCR continues to assist States in enhancing national law enforcement capacities with the aim of strengthening refugee camp security mechanisms. The '*security package*' model most often cited was developed with the Tanzanian Government eleven years ago. UNHCR has since adopted a similar approach to camp security in a number of other countries; most recently in Chad, but also in Kenya, Ghana, Sierra Leone, Liberia and Nepal.

In some situations, this was not possible because there was no state or no authority—the case of the Kivu in 1994, a territory with exiles from Rwanda and no real authority on the Zairian side. Secretary-General Boutros Ghali asked for forces but the situation was complex. One possible answer was: Zairian soldiers under the command of foreign officers—a very special situation where. Without any mandate from the Security Council but with the agreement of the Zairian Government, UNHCR did it.

Here, let me make special mention of a very proactive—and in many ways a pioneering—collaboration in refugee camp security undertaken in 2003–2004 with the Government of Canada, reflecting that country's resolve to help UNHCR and States 'operationalize' the previously mentioned 'ladder of options' framework. The *Royal Canadian Mounted Police* deployed experienced officers to assist and advise Guinean police in maintaining law and order within refugee camps throughout the country. I am hoping that we can draw lessons from this that may help in the further development of effective approaches to the protection of civilians.

In the years since the Security Council adopted its first resolution on the protection of civilians in armed conflict, peacekeeping mandates have broadened and assumed a stronger protection focus. UN mission mandates have been complemented by timely deployments of peacekeeping troops to avert immediate crises and to restore order. There have also been strong efforts at the regional level to address the protection of displaced persons and other civilians, particularly in Africa. This is encouraging, and UNHCR is ready to play its part in supporting such efforts.

To this effect, one year ago UNHCR and DPKO entered into an 'agreement' and a commitment to enhance cooperation in the areas of Refugee Security; Rule of Law; Mine Action; DDR; and Technical Support. It is expected that a staff exchange between the two organizations will facilitate this important effort.

While I have indicated some areas in which UNHCR is active, it is clear that the primary responsibility for the protection of refugees and civilians lies with States themselves. There are situations—especially when national security has been compromised—that expose the limit of UNHCR's capacity, competence and mandate.

One way for UNHCR to assist States in ensuring their responsibilities under international refugee law and to help address any violations by States in the security of refugees may be UNHCR's supervisory role as defined in *Article 35 of the 1951 Refugee Convention*. Discussions with Governments on how best to enhance this role as guardians of the Convention are ongoing. This is absolutely necessary as UNHCR can face restrictions when fulfilling this particular responsibility. For example, there isn't a compulsory reporting mechanism and no process by which States can be held accountable for their failure to respect the Convention, except maybe at an indirect level when they present their periodic report to the Human Rights Committee. Wherever the recommendations on our enhanced supervisory role will take us, it goes without saying that both with respect to identifying violations, but especially when engaging in the search for solutions, the unwavering support of the international community is essential.

The Security Council has adopted a comprehensive framework and agenda for the protection of civilians. Resolutions 1265 and 1296, the Aide Memoire, the "roadmap" and the Secretary-General's ten-point platform all reflect the commitment of the Security Council. This framework must now become the benchmark for holding the Council and its member-States accountable for action.

IDPs and Coordination

I have focused so far on the plight of refugees in need of additional protection, as these people are of core concern to UNHCR, but would like to mention outside the refugee area three issues:

(1) As is well known, the group of civilians that is perhaps at greatest need of protection are the *internally displaced.* Their protection needs may be as acute as those of refugees, but their plight is more precarious because of the lack of smoothly functioning and predictable arrangements to deal with them. The 'Benn proposals', highlight many important issues including the lack of institutional responsibility for IDPs, and suggests that we should look for ways ahead. Hilary Benn is certainly correct in his analysis of the problem, and his identification of gaps and poor coordination. He suggests a strengthened Humanitarian Coordinator system in severe emergencies. I am sure that concerned groups will find interest in discussing and having some thoughts on this issue and these proposals. If the responsibility and the accountability in a refugee situation are primarily with UNHCR (Chad/Darfur), when it comes to the IDPs at the heart of the problem of their protection lies the question of coordination, amongst the UN and also with sister agencies like ICRC as well as NGOs, in what is known as the collaborative approach.

(2) This is certainly a real improvement compared to the previous situation but it is not enough. We need a *more efficient way to protect IDPs and more accountability*. The world is changing with more focus by the international community on good governance and human rights (Darfur, Togo, etc.). In the conflicts to come—as per the trend during the last few years—there will be more IDPs and less refugees, and it will not be acceptable to have a distinction in the treatment and the protection between members of the same group, victims of the same mistreatment and persecution, the distinction made only on the fact that they have or they have not crossed an international border. One structure or one agency should be in charge of IDPs.

(3) My third question or issue where I can see a serious gap: *when a group of refugees has been excluded from the benefit of the international legal instrument conceived to protect refugees with the ambition of being universal.* I want here to address briefly an issue which during my entire career has been a headache for me: the fact that the Palestinian refugees cannot avail themselves of the 1951 Geneva Convention, just because they are registered (and sometimes without being registered) with UNRWA. To be excluded from the UNHCR mandate, this is normal, but not to benefit from the basic principles of refugee law—I would say even general principles—this, I cannot understand. Let me clarify here that it was the Arab States present in Geneva in the plenipotentiary conference which adopted the Convention who asked for the non-inclusion of the refugees who are receiving protection or assistance from another UN agency than UNHCR (political reasons).

Conclusion

Innocent civilians still constitute the majority of victims in areas of armed conflict, and while progress has been made, much still needs to be done to fully 'operationalize' the UN framework for their protection.

UNHCR will continue to work to ensure that the 'doubly threatened', the refugees, are more effectively protected and will continue to do whatever it can for the IDPs whenever it is asked to do so.

The establishment of a wider 'culture of protection' remains a distant but achievable goal, but I do hope that we will be able, in the future, to more clearly define some of the steps we might follow to make this a reality.

CHAPTER SIX

IMPLEMENTING INTERNATIONAL HUMANITARIAN LAW: OLD AND NEW WAYS

Michel Veuthey[1]

1. *Introduction: From Celebrations to Challenges and Reflections*

The end of the 20th century was marked by a series of celebrations pertaining to human rights and humanitarian law: bicentennial of the American Declaration of Independence (1776), bicentennial of the French Revolution (1789), fiftieth anniversary of the United Nations Charter (1945), of the Universal Declaration on Human Rights (1948), and of the four Geneva Conventions of 12 August 1949 on the protection of war victims. The adoption of the Statute of the International Criminal Court, in Rome in July 1998, was also part of this series of events, which, after the fall of the Berlin Wall, led ua to believe that humankind was entering a new era of international cooperation.

The beginning of the 21st century brought more realism: the United Nations Millennium listed what still needs to be done.[2] And the 11 September shifted priorities of many countries from freedom to security.

Implementation is only one of the seven following stages in the struggle for the respect of legal norms protecting human life and dignity. We should include all of them in considering how to improve the implementation of international humanitarian law:

a) codification
b) ratification
c) application
d) implementation
e) sanction of violations
f) reparation
g) reconciliation.

---

[1] Doctor of Laws (Geneva), Associate Professor, Institut du Droit de la Paix et du Développement, University of Nice, Vice-President, International Institute of Humanitarian Law. E-mail of the author: mveuthey@mac.com

[2] See the UN Millenium Development Goals (MDG) online: www.un.org/millenium-goals/

Bertrand G. Ramcharan (Ed.), Human Rights Protection in the Field, 87–117.

Each stage of the *codification* of international humanitarian law was the result of a post-war shock wave in public opinion and governments, a collective painful process of learning. These codifications occurred as follows:

- The battle of Solferino (1859)[3] between Austrian and French armies was the impetus for the First Geneva Convention, in 1864, protecting military wounded on land;
- The naval battle of Tsushima (1905) between Japanese and Russian fleets prompted adjustment of the Convention on war at sea, in 1907, extending protection to military shipwrecked;
- World War I brought about the two 1929 Conventions, including a much broader protection for prisoners of war;
- World War II led to the four 1949 Conventions,[4] an extensive regulation of the treatment of civilians in occupied territories and internment. The 1949 Geneva Conventions—with the UN Charter in 1945, the Universal Declaration on Human Rights in 1948—are the result of the tragedies of millions of civilians and prisoners victims of total war and genocide in Europe and in Asia. The survivors pushed for the adoption of international instruments in order to avoid the repetition of such tragedies;
- The decolonization of African colonies and the Vietnam War preceded the two 1977 Additional Protocols,[5] which brought written rules for the protection of civilian persons and objects against hostilities;
- A worldwide campaign by Governments, United Nations agencies, the Red Cross and Red Crescent Movement and NGOs in a full partnership, which stressed the human suffering and socio-economic costs caused by anti-personnel mines resulted in the total ban on anti-personnel landmines signed in Ottawa on 4 December 1997;[6]
- A similar worldwide coalition[7] provoked the adoption of the International Criminal Court Statute in Rome in 1998.

---

[3] See: Henry DUNANT: A Memory of Solferino, Geneva: ICRC.

[4] Geneva Convention for the Amelioration of the Condition of the Wounded and Sick in Armed Forces in the Field, Aug. 12, 1949; Geneva Convention for the Amelioration of the Condition of the Wounded, Sick and Shipwrecked Members of the Armed Forces at Sea, Aug. 12, 1949; Geneva Convention Relative to the Treatment of Prisoners of War, Aug. 12, 1949; Geneva Convention Relative to the Protection of Civilian Persons in Time of War, Aug. 12, 1949.

[5] Protocol Additional to the Geneva Conventions of 12 August 1949, and relating to the Protection of Victims of International Armed Conflicts (Protocol I); Protocol Additional to the Geneva Conventions of 12 August 1949, and relating to the Protection of Victims of Non-International Armed Conflicts (Protocol II).

[6] See Kenneth ANDERSON, "The Ottawa Convention Banning Landmines, the Role of International Non-Governmental Organizations and the Idea of International Civil Society", EJIL, Vol. 11, (2000) No. 1, full text available online: http://www.ejil.org/journal/Vol11/No1/art8.html

[7] The Coalition for the International Criminal Court. See http://www.iccnow.org/

As for the issue of *ratification*, the universal ratification of the 1949 Geneva Conventions is a fact. More ratifications are needed for the 1977 Additional Protocols as well as for the 1998 ICC Rome Statute.

The decisions on the *application* of the 1949 Conventions and 1977 Additional Protocols are the key to their implementation, with the legal status of conflicts, territories, categories of persons, individuals.[8]

We shall deal with the topic of implementation along the following lines:

- existing legal mechanisms of international humanitarian law;
- recent developments;
- proposals.

Implementation includes the *sanction* of violations, even *reparation* (indemnities to victims). As we shall see, it should be extended to *reconciliation* in order to prevent recurring conflicts and violations of international humanitarian law.

2. *Legal Mechanisms*

The mechanisms provided for in the 1949 Geneva Conventions on the protection of war victims are:

1. The *States Party*, which undertakes to "respect and ensure respect" for the Conventions in all circumstances."[9] "Respect" clearly refers to the individual obligation to apply it in good faith from the moment that it enters into force.[10] "To ensure respect", according to the ICRC Commentary to the 1949 Conventions, "demands in fact that the States which are Parties to it should not be content merely to apply its provisions themselves, but should do everything in their power to ensure that it is respected universally."[11]

[8] See the INTERNATIONAL COURT OF JUSTICE (ICJ). *Legal Consequences of the Construction of a Wall in the Occupied Palestinian Territory*. Advisory Opinion. 9 July 2004, paragr. 96–101 on the applicability of the Fourth Geneva Convention of 1949 to all the territories occupied by Israel in 1967. Available online at: http://www.icj-cij.org/icjwww/idocket/imwp/imwpframe.htm

[9] Common Article 1 to the 1949 Geneva Conventions

[10] ICRC Commentary on the Additional Protocols, Geneva, ICRC, 1987, p. 35, para. 39.

[11] ICRC Commentary III, p. 18 (Art. 1). See

- Luigi CONDORELLI and Laurence BOISSON DE CHAZOURNES, « Quelques remarques à propos de l'obligation des Etats de « respecter et faire respecter » le droit international humanitaire « en toutes circonstances », in SWINARSKI, Christophe (Ed.) Studies and essays on international humanitarian law and Red Cross principles, Geneva, ICRC, 1984, pp. 17–35;
- Umesh PALWANKAR. "Measures available to States for fulfilling their obligation to ensure respect for international humanitarian law" IRRC no. 298, pp. 9–25;
- BOISSON DE CHAZOURNES, Laurence, and CONDORELLI, Luigi. "Common Article 1 of the Geneva Conventions revisited: Protecting collective interests", *IRRC*, March 2000, Vol. 82, No. 837, pp. 67–87

This collective responsibility to implement international humanitarian rules[12] often takes the form of bilateral or multilateral measures by States Party. Leaving aside the exceptional meeting provided for in Article 7 of Protocol I of 1977[13] States Party to international humanitarian law treaties have used bilateral or multilateral meetings, at the United Nations, the Non-Aligned Movement (NAM), regional organizations (OAS, AU, OSCE, the European Parliament, the Council of Europe) as well as the Inter-Parliamentary Union (IPU), to manifest their concern that humanitarian law should be respected.[14] "In all circumstances" means in time of armed conflict as well as in time of peace, taking preventive steps, in the form of training[15] or evaluation,[16] and prosecution.[17]

---

[12] The 1949 Geneva Conventions as well as Additional Protocol I, for the States Party to this Protocol. See the ICRC Commentary on the Protocols, ad Art. 1 of Protocol I, pp. 35–38.

[13] Article 7 ("Meetings"): "The depositary of this Protocol [Switzerland] shall convene a meeting of the High Contracting Parties, at the request of one or more of the said Parties and upon the approval of the majority of the said Parties, to consider general problems concerning the application of the Conventions and of the Protocol". Such a meeting was convened by Switzerland on 5 December 2001 in Geneva. ("Conference of the High Contracting Parties to the Fourth Geneva Convention.")

[14] ICRC Commentary on the Additional Protocols, p. 36, paragr. 43.

See also Michel VEUTHEY, « Pour une politique humanitaire » in SWINARSKI, Christophe (Ed.) Studies and essays on international humanitarian law and Red Cross principles, Geneva, ICRC, 1984, pp. 989–1009.

[15] Training is an obligation according to the four 1949 Geneva Conventions: Article 47 of the First Convention states the following: "The High Contracting Parties undertake, in time of peace as in time of war, to disseminate the text of the present Convention as widely as possible in their respective countries, and, in particular, to include the study thereof in their programmes of military and, if possible, civil instruction, so that the principles thereof become known to the entire population, in particular to the armed fighting forces, the medical personnel and the chaplains."

The Second Convention contains a similar provision (Article 48).

Article 127 of the Third Convention adds the following paragraph: "Any military or other authorities, who in time of war asume responsibilities in respect of prisoners of war, must possess the text of the Convention and be specially instructed as to its provisions."

Article 144, 2 of the Fourth Convention reads as follows: "Any civilian, military, police or other authorities, who in time of war assume responsibilities in respect of protected persons, must possess the text of the Convention and be specially instructed as to its provisions."

Additional Protocol I

- reaffirms the duty to disseminate (Article 83—Dissemination); and
- adds the obligation to ensure that legal advisers are available (Art. 82—Legal Advisers in armed forces)

Additional Protocol II, applicable in non-international armed conflicts, simply states that "This Protocol shall be disseminated as widely as possible." (Art. 19—Dissemination).

[16] Article 36 ("New Weapons") of Protocol I reads as follows:

"In the study, development, acquisition or adoption of a new weapon, means or method of warfare, a High Contracting Party is under an obligation to determine whether its employment would, in some or all circumstances, be prohibited by this Protocol or by any other rule of international law applicable to the High Contracting Party."

[17] The four 1949 contain common provisions on the "Repression of Abuses and Infractions":

According to common Article 1 to the four 1949 Geneva Conventions and to Article 1 of Additional Protocol I, all States Parties to these instruments have the obligation *"to respect and ensure respect" for them "in all circumstances"*. This wording has been widely understood as implying a double responsibility for every State Party: for its own duties as well as a collective responsibility for the behavior of other States Parties.[18] The International Court of Justice held that Article 1 had turned into customary law.[19]

2. The *Protecting Power*,[20] which was widely used in Europe during WW II[21] and much less therafter.[22] Additional Protocol I defines the Protecting

---

- First Convention: Art. 49–51
- Second Convention: Art. 50–52
- Third Convention: Art. 129–131
- Fourth Convention: Art. 146–148

Article 85 of Additional Protocol I reaffirms those provisions, adds a few acts to be considered as grave breaches (specially attacks against civilians and civilian objects), and classifies grave breaches of the 1949 Conventions and Protocol I as war crimes. See also Maria Teresa DUTLI and Cristina PELLANDINI "The International Committee of the Red Cross and the implementation of a system to repress breaches of international humanitarian law" IRRC, No 300, May 1994, pp. 240–254.

[18] Jean S. PICTET (Ed.) *The Geneva Conventions of 12 August 1949. Commentary. IV. Geneva Convention relative to the protection of civilian persons in time of war.* Geneva, International Committee of the Red Cross, 1958, pp. 15–17.

[19] INTERNATIONAL COURT OF JUSTICE, *Case concerning the military and paramilitary activities in and against Nicaragua (Nicaragua v. United States of America), Judgement of 27 June 1986 (Merits)*, Vol. 114, Para. 220. The ICJ reaffirmed the importance of Common Article 1 to the 1949 Geneva Conventions in its Advisory Opinion on the *Legal Consequences of the Construction of a Wall in the Occupied Palestinian Territory (2004)*, paragr. 158:

The Court would also emphasize that Article 1 of the Fourth Geneva Convention, a provision common to the four Geneva Conventions, provides that "The High Contracting Parties undertake to respect and to ensure respect for the present Convention in all circumstances." It follows from that provision that every State party to that Convention, whether or not it is a party to a specific conflict, is under an obligation to ensure that the requirements of the instruments in question are complied with." Also see Antonio CASSESE, *International Law*, pp. 6–8 ("Collective Responsibility"), pp. 182 ss. ("State Responsibility") and especially pp. 207–210, and p. 419.

[20] See George A.B. PEIRCE, "Humanitarian protection for the victims of war. The system of Protecting Powers and the role of the ICRC", Military Law Review, Vol. 90, 1980, pp. 89–162 and D.P. FORSYTHE, "Who guards the guardians: Third parties and the law of armed conflict", American Journal of International Law, vol. 70, 1976, pp. 41–61.

[21] H. COULIBALY, "Le rôle des Puissances protectrices au regard du droit diplomatique, du droit de Genève et du droit de La Haye", in: F. KALSHOVEN, Y. SANDOZ, eds., Implementation of International Humanitarian Law, Dordrecht, Martinus Nijhoff, 1989, pp. 69–78.

C. DOMINICE, J. PATRNOGIC, "Les Protocoles additionnels aux Conventions de Genève et le système des Puissances protectrices", Annales de droit international médical, vol. 28, 1979, pp. 24–50.

J.-P. KNELLWOLF, Die Schutzmacht im Völkerrecht unter besonderer Brücksichtigung der schweizerischen Verhältnisse, Dissertation Bern, Bern, Ackermanndruck, 1985.

B. LAITENBERGER, "Die Schutzmacht", German Yearbook of Interntional Law, vol. 21, 1978, pp. 180–206.

[22] It was used in Suez in 1956, in Goa in 1961 and between India and Pakistan in

Power in international humanitarian law as "a neutral or other State not a Party to the conflict which has been designated by a Party to the conflict and accepted by the adverse Party and has agreed to carry out the functions assignated to a Protecting Power under the Conventions and this Protocol."[23]

The role of the Protecting Power is to maintain liaison between two States at war, to bring relief assistance to the victims and protection to prisoners of war and civilian internees.

3. The *International Committee of the Red Cross (ICRC)*, which received mandates from the international community in the 1949 Geneva Conventions:

- to visit and interview prisoners of war[24] and civilian internees;[25]
- to provide relief to the population of occupied territories;[26]
- to search for missing persons and to forward family messages to prisoners of war[27] and civilians;[28]
- to offer its good offices to facilitate the institution of hospital zones[29] and safety zones;[30]
- to receive applications from protected persons.[31]
- to offer its services in other situations[32] and especially in time of non-international armed conflicts.[33]

The First 1977 Additional Protocol mentions two additional mechanisms of implementation:

- The *United Nations*, "in situations of serious violations of the Conventions or of this Protocol" (Art. 89 of Protocol I).

1971. For a more recent example, see the State Department Press Briefing, Thursday, April 1, 1998 p.m.:

"The United States Government is contacting authorities in Belgrade through our Protecting Power, Sweden, in regard to the illegal abduction of three American servicemen who were serving in non-combatant status in Macedonia. There is no basis for their continued detention by the Belgrade authorities. We insist that they be provided any necessary medical assistance and treated humanely and in accordance with all prevailing international agreements and standards. We will hold Belgrade authorities responsible for their safety and treatment." http://www.aiipowmia.com/inter/in040299e.html

[23] Protocol I, Art. 2, letter C.
[24] Third Geneva Convention, Article 126.
[25] Fourth Geneva Convention, Article 143.
[26] Fourth Geneva Convention, Articles 59 and 61.
[27] Third Geneva Convention, Article 123.
[28] Fourth Geneva Convention, Article 140.
[29] First Geneva Convention, Article 23.
[30] Fourth Geneva Convention, Article 14.
[31] Fourth Geneva Convention, Article 30.
[32] Article 9 of Conventions I, II and III; Article 10 of the Fourth Convention.
[33] Common Article 3 to the 1949 Conventions.

– The optional "*International Fact-Finding Commission*" (Art. 90 of Protocol I)[34]

To this day, none of these provisions (Article 89 and 90 of Protocol I) has been invoked.

The implementation mechanisms of international criminal law[35] was significantly developed as the United Nations Security Council established the ad hoc Tribunals on Former Yugoslavia and Rwanda[36] and with the 60th ratification of 1998 Rome Statute of the International Criminal Court[37] on 11 April, and its entry into force on 1 July 2002.

---

[34] The website of the Commission: http://www.ihffc.org

[35] See "International Criminal Law" by Patrick HEALY & Kimberly PROST, McGill University Faculty of Law http://www.law.mcgill.ca/academics/coursenotes/healy/intcrimlaw/ and the following links mentioned there:

Nuremberg Trials London Agreement of August 8th 1945 (http://www.yale.edu/lawweb/avalon/imt/imt.htm).

Charter of the International Military Tribunal (http://www.yale.edu/lawweb/avalon/imt/imt.htm), Judgment of the IMT for the Trial of German Major War Criminals (http://www.yale.edu/lawweb/avalon/imt/imt.htm).

[36] See the following links, quoted by Patrick HEALY & Kimberly PROST: Jurisdiction of the Yugoslavian and Rwandan Ad Hoc Tribunals, Security Council Resolution 827 (1993), 25 May 1993 (http://www.un.org/Docs/sc.htm), Security Council Resolution 955 (1994), 8 November 1994, (http://www.un.org/Docs/sc.htm), Statute of the International Criminal Tribunal for the Former Yugoslavia ("ICTY"), Arts. 6, 8, 9. (http://www.un.org/icty/basic.htm), Statute of the International Criminal Tribunal for Rwanda ("ICTR"), Arts. 5, 7, 8 (http://www.ictr.org), ICTY, Rules of Procedure and Evidence, Rules 7–13 (http://www.un.org/icty/basic.htm), ICTY, Prosecutor V. Dusko Tadic a/k/a "Dule", Appeals Chamber Decision on the Jurisdictional Motion, 2 October 1995, ss. 9–48, 9–64. (http://www.un.org/icty/cases-ae2.htm), Substantive Law and the Ad Hoc Tribunals, Statute of the ICT Y, Arts. 2–5, 21 (http://www.un.org/icty/basic.htm), Statute of the ICTR, Arts. 2–4, 20 (http://www.ictr.org), ICTY, Prosecutor v. Drazen Erdemovic, Appeals Chamber, Joint separate opinion of Judge McDonald and Judge Vohrah, ss. 32–58, 66, 73–91, Separate and dissenting opinion of Judge Cassese, ss. 11–12, 40–51. (http://www.un.org/icty/cases-ae2.htm), ICTR, The Prosecutor v. Jean-Paul Akayesu, Trial Chamber, Summary of the Judgment. (http://www.ictr.org), ICTR, The Prosecutor v. Jean-Paul Akayesu, Trial Chamber, Judgment, ss. 5.5 and 7. (http://www.ictr.org), Evidence, Procedure, and the Ad Hoc Tribunals, ICTY, Rules of Procedure and Evidence, Rules 39–43, 54–61, 89–98 http://www.un.org/icty/basic.htm), ICTY, Prosecutor V. Dusko Tadic a/k/a "Dule", Judgment on evidentiary matters. (http://www.un.org/icty/cases-te.htm), Judgment on Corroboration in section V(c), Judgment on Hearsay in section V(h), ICTY, Prosecutor v. Blaskic, Judgment on the request of The Republic of Croatia for review of the decision of Trial Chamber II of 18 July 1997, ss. 25–60. (http://www.un.org/icty/blaskic/ace14.htm).

[37] See Jurisdiction of the ICC: Trigger Mechanisms and the Exercise of the Court's Jurisdiction (http://www.un.org/icc/backinfo.htm) Rome Statute of the International Criminal Court, Arts 11–15, 17–18. (http://www.un.org/icc).

Substantive Law and the ICC:

Crimes within the Court's Jurisdiction (http://www.un.org/icc/backinfo.htm).

Rome Statute of the International Criminal Court, Arts 5–9, 21, 22–33, 55, 67, 69. (http://www.un.org/icc).

Preparatory Commission for the International Criminal Court: results of working groups on ICC rules of procedure and evidence.

Most recent laws (http://www.un.org/law/icc/prepcomm/docs.htm.)

The International Criminal Court is a milestone in the international community's fight to end impunity for war crimes, genocide and crimes against humanity.

The International Criminal Court will be able to punish war criminals and perpetrators of genocide or crimes against humanity in cases where national criminal justice systems are unable or unwilling to do so. It is vital for the Court's effective functioning that tall States ratify the Rome Statute and that the States Parties rapidly adopt comprehensive implementing legislation in order to be able to cooperate with the Court.[38]

3. *New Developments*

Increasingly, human rights mechanisms, on the international, regional and national level, deal with human rights as well as with international humanitarian law issues:

- *The United Nations* General Assembly (Third Committee), the Commission on Human Rights, the Sub-Commission on the Promotion and Protection of Human Rights, the Human Rights Committee;
- *For the Americas*: the Organization of American States Commission on Human Rights and the Human Rights Court;
- *For Africa*: the African Commission on Human and Peoples' Rights, under the aegis of the African Union (AU). The Commission was established in 1987 in Banjul, The Gambia. The Commission comprises 11 officials, each from a different country. They serve for renewable six-year terms which governments cannot cut short. They also elect their own president and vice-president, and determine their own operational rules. The African Commission's role is more wide-ranging than that of its European counterpart, which is confined to handling complaints. Its missions also include promotion of human and peoples' rights and interpreting the Charter. The Commission may also develop and set out principles and rules for use by African lawmakers, and co-operate with other African or international institutions involved in rights issues. The AU adopted in 1998 a Protocol on the Establishment of the African Court on Human and People's Rights, which is not yet in force.
- *In Europe*: the European Commission, the European Court, the European Committee for the Prevention of Torture and Inhuman or Degrading Treatment or Punishment, all under the aegis of the Council of

[38] International Criminal Court: A reality at last, ICRC, Geneva, 11 April 2002.

Europe,[39] as well as the relevant organs of OSCE[40] and the European Union.[41]

In addition to the formal mechanisms of implementation of international humanitarian law and human rights, there is an increasing role for informal mechanisms, on the international as on the national level:

- good offices[42]
- media, local, regional and international,[43]
- NGOs such as Human Rights Watch[44] or Amnesty International
- ad hoc independent monitors, agreed upon by all parties;[45]
- private diplomacy, including private economy (multinational as well as local);
- spiritual leaders,[46] including mediators such as the Sant'Egidio Community.[47]

---

[39] See the website of the CPT: http://www.cpt.coe.fr/

[40] Elisabeth KARDOS-KAPONYI "The Charter of Fundamental Human Rights in the European Union" p. 139, mentions the Office for Democratic Institutions and Human Rights (ODHIR), the High Commissioner of National Minorities and the Representative on Freedom of the Media. Document available online: www.lib.bke.hu/gt/2001–1–2/kardos-kaponyi.pdf

[41] Ibidem, pp. 140–170.

[42] The ICRC can offer its good offices to facilitate the establishment of hospital zones (according to Article 23 of the First 1949 Convention) and safety zones (Art. 14, First Convention). Other institutions or persons could offer their good offices. See B.G. RAMCHARAN. Humanitarian Good Offices in International Law: The Good Offices of the United Nations Secretary-General in the Field of Human Rights. The Hague: Martinus Nijhoff, 1983.

[43] See Roy W. GUTMAN, "Spotlight on violations of international humanitarian law. The role of the media" IRRC no 325 (December 1998), pp. 619–625, Urs BOEGLI, "A few thoughts on the relationship between humanitarian agencies and the media" ibidem, pp. 627–631, and, more generally, DANIELI, Yael (Ed.), *Sharing the Front Line and the Back Hills. International Protectors and Providers: Peacekeepers, Humanitarian Aid Workers and the Media in the Midst of Crisis,* Amityville, NY, Baywood Publishing, 2002, 429 p.

[44] See the open letters sent to public officials in Washington DC and in Europe after the 11 September 2001 in order to promote the application of international humanitarian law and fundamental human rights guarantees.

See also the open letter sent to the Revolutionary Armed Forces of Colombia-People's Army (FARC-EP) on 8 May 2002 denouncing the use of indiscriminate weapons (gas cylinder bombs) as contrary to international humanitarian law. A copy of the letter sent to Commander Marulanda can be found at http://www.hrw.org/press/2002/05/colombia0508.pdf

[45] See the following Human Rights Watch appeals:

- Israel/Palestinian Authority: Protect Civilians, Allow Independent Reporting (HRW Press Release, April 3, 2002) at http://hrw.org/press/2002/04/isr-pa040302.htm
- Jenin: War Crimes Investigation Needed (HRW Press Release, May 3, 2002) at http://hrw.org/press/2002/05/jenin0503.htm

[46] See Daniel L. SMITH-CHRISTOPHER (Ed.) *Subverting Hatred. The Challenge of Nonviolence in Religious Traditions.* New York, Orbis Books, 1998, 177 p.

[47] See http://www.santegidio.org/ and Andrea RICCARDI, *Sant'Egidio, Rome et le monde,*

4. *Proposals for a Better Respect of International Humanitarian Law*

We would like to develop the following proposals:

- reinforce existing mechanisms of international humanitarian law (IHL);
- make a better use of mechanisms of other legal systems;
- be more creative in using remedies.

4.1. *Reinforce Existing International Humanitarian Law Mechanisms*

4.1.1. *States Parties to the Geneva Conventions*

The individual duties of each State Party in preventing and repressing violations of international humanitarian law are clearly defined in the 1949 Conventions and 1977 Protocols.

As for their collective responsibilities, there is still much to be done to clarify the extent of Common Article 1 to the 1949 Geneva Conventions. The international community of States Party to the 1949 Geneva Conventions should reaffirm their collective responsibility according to Article 1, common to all four Conventions and to Protocol I. According to this provision, "*The High Contracting Parties undertake to respect and to ensure respect for this Convention in all circumstances*". Should measures[48] be limited to diplomacy, adoption of resolutions or rather the use of sanctions[49] and peace-enforcement operations in order to stop genocide and arrest war criminals? A number of Security Council resolutions, including those on anarchic conflicts, call upon all parties to respect international humanitarian law and reaffirm that those responsible for breaches thereof should be held individually accountable.

Existing rules and mechanisms could certainly be used more effectively on the domestic as well as on the international level. National implementing regulations as well as the criminal prosecution of violations by domestic courts could be improved. The role of regional organizations (African Union, Arab League, Council of Europe, OSCE, Organization of American States) to "ensure respect" for international humanitarian law "in all circumstances" could be enhanced.

Beauchesne éditeur, Paris, 1996 and Philippe LEYMARIE, "Les bâtisseurs de paix de Sant'Egidio", *Le Monde Diplomatique*, Septembre 2000, pp. 16–17.

[48] See Umesh PALWANKAR, "Measures available to States for fulfilling their obligation to ensure respect for international humanitarian law" IRRC, no. 298, pp. 9–25.
http://www.icrc.org/Web/Eng/siteeng0.nsf/iwpList113/35289C31F0187A41C1256B6600591427

[49] Such as the U.S. Foreign Assistance Act, which forbids security assistance to any government that "engages in a consistent pattern of gross violations of internationally recognized human rights" [22 U.S.C. Secs. 2034, 2151n].

In its Advisory Opinion of 7 July 2004, the International Court of Justice reaffirmed that

> "[. . .] every State party to that Convention, whether or not it is a party to a specific conflict, is under an obligation to ensure that the requirements of the instruments in question are complied with"[50]

This obligation can take different forms:

> "Given the character and the importance of the rights and obligations involved, the Court is of the view that all States are under an obligation not to recognize the illegal situation resulting from the construction of the wall in the Occupied Palestinian Territory, including in and around East Jerusalem. They are also under an obligation not to render aid or assistance in maintaining the situation created by such construction. It is also for all States, while respecting the United Nations Charter and international law, to see to it that any impediment, resulting from the construction of the wall, to the exercise by the Palestinian people of its right to self-determination is brought to an end. In addition, all the States parties to the Geneva Convention relative to the Protection of Civilian Persons in Time of War of 12 August 1949 are under an obligation, while respecting the United Nations Charter and international law, to ensure compliance by Israel with international humanitarian law as embodied in that Convention."[51]

4.1.2. *Switzerland as the Depositary of the Geneva Conventions*

Is the role of the Depositary limited to registering ratifications or a more dynamic one?

On 5 December 2001, Switzerland, as the Depositary of the 1949 Geneva Conventions, reconvened a Conference of High Contracting Parties to the Fourth Geneva Convention.[52] The Swiss Department of Foreign Affairs took this opportunity to explain its position in this regard:

> In its capacity as the Depositary of the Geneva Conventions, Switzerland acts within the attributions of a Depositary, as foreseen by international law; its

[50] 2004 Advisory Opinion, paragraph 158. Also see paragraph 157:
57. With regard to international humanitarian law, the Court recalls that in its Advisory Opinion on the *Legality of the Threat or Use of Nuclear Weapons*, it stated that "a great many rules of humanitarian law applicable in armed conflict are so fundamental to the respect of the human person and 'elementary considerations of humanity' . . .", that they are "to be observed by all States whether or not they have ratified the conventions that contain them, because they constitute intransgressible principles of international customary law" (*I.C.J. Reports 1996 (I)*, p. 257, para. 79). In the Court's view, these rules incorporate obligations which are essentially of an *erga omnes* character.

[51] 2004 Advisory Opinion, paragraph 159.

[52] Conference of High Contracting Parties to the Fourth Geneva Convention on measures to enforce the Convention in the Occupied Palestinian Territory, including Jerusalem, at Geneva on 15 July 1999; Conference of High Contracting Parties at Geneva on 5 December 2001. Documents available online at [Accessed 30 May 2005]: http://www.eda.admin.ch/eda/e/home/foreign/humsec/hupomi/4gc.html

tasks are mainly to provide services of "notarial" nature (to inform, to consult).

The humanitarian tradition of Switzerland and its policy of "good offices" lead Switzerland to facilitate the emergence of a consensus as broad as possible between States Parties, in order to find appropriate responses on questions related to international humanitarian law.

[. . .]

A clear distinction has to be drawn between the role and action of Switzerland in its capacity as the Depositary, on one side, and those of Switzerland as State Party on the other side. As well as all other States Parties, Switzerland undertakes "to respect and to ensure respect" for these Conventions "in all circumstances" (common art. 1 of the Geneva Conventions).

As almost the whole international community, Switzerland considers that the IVth Geneva Convention is applicable de jure to all Territories occupied by Israel. Thus, the Jewish settlements established in the Occupied Palestinian Territories represent a flagrant violation of the IVth Convention. Other practices, as the disproportionate and indiscriminate use of force (e.g. terrorism), collective punishment (e.g. closures) or reprisals are also prohibited by international humanitarian law. Its respect, in particular the respect of the IVth Geneva Convention, is of crucial importance in the context of the present crisis in the Middle East.

In this region as elsewhere in the world, Switzerland is strongly committed to ensuring respect of international humanitarian law and uses different instruments, as e.g.:

- financial and political support to institutions providing protection or humanitarian relief (ICRC, UNRWA),
- financial support to NGOs providing legal aid or promoting respect of international humanitarian law or of human rights,
- application of the federal legislation on the export of weapons and other military equipment,
- diplomatic demarches with regard to violations of the IVth Geneva Convention,

public statements and co-sponsoring of resolution of the UN Commission of Human Rights, etc.[53]

4.1.3. *The International Committee of the Red Cross (ICRC)*

The ICRC's role as a neutral intermediary and independent humanitarian institution should be reinforced and accepted by all parties to today's armed conflicts, Governments and Non-State actors.[54] The ICRC needs to "take new initiatives to reach out to all actors that can obstruct its operations".[55]

[53] http://www.eda.admin.ch/eda/e/home/foreign/hupol/4gc.html

[54] See Pierre KRÄHENBÜHL, ICRC Director of Operations, "The ICRC's approach to contemporary security challenges: A future for independent and neutral humanitarian action", IRRC, September 2004, Vol. 86, No. 855, pp. 505–513.

[55] Speech by the ICRC's Director-General, Angelo Gnaedinger, to the Donor Retreat

The ICRC should be able to promote "special agreements" between parties to conflicts, according to Common Article 3, without any consequence on the status of the conflict, the parties or the territories.

Special agreements were concluded through ICRC delegates in the Spanish Civil War (for the application by both the Madrid Government and the Burgos Junta of the two 1929 Geneva Conventions),[56] in Palestine in 1948,[57] in the Yemen Civil War in 1963[58] as well as in the Civil War in Nigeria[59] in 1969. Both sides accepted to abide by the four 1949 Geneva Conventions. In Afghanistan, the Soviet Union on one side and the Afghan mujahideens on the other side both signed the same agreement with the ICRC in order to ease the plight of prisoners: the Soviets let the ICRC visit prisoners in the Puli-Charki jail in Kabul and the mujahideens handed over their Soviet prisoners to the ICRC for a two-year internment in Switzerland before being repatriated to Mother Russia. In former Yugoslavia, numerous special agreements were concluded in Geneva and elsewhere under the auspices of the ICRC.[60] The status of the conflicts was on purpose left unclear—whether international or non-international—in order not to jeopardize ICRC's activities on the spot. In Somalia, ICRC was allowed to visit a US POW in the hands of General Aidid, thanks to such a special agreement.

In addition to the general applicability of the Geneva Conventions to a conflict and to the improvement of the treatment of prisoners on both sides, the establishment of protected areas was achieved by ICRC thanks to special agreements in Jerusalem in 1948, in Dacca/Dhakka in 1971, in Nicosia in 1974, in Jaffna in 1990, in Dubrovnik and Osjek in 1991. The rejection by the UN Security Council of such a procedure for Srebenica—and the creation of the so-called "safe areas" instead—paved the way for the massacre of thousands of civilians.[61]

---

on the Consolidated Appeals Process and Coordination in Humanitarian Emergencies (Montreux, Switzerland, 26–27 February 2004).

[56] See Dr. Marcel JUNOD, *Warrior Without Weapons*. Translated from the French *"Le Troisième Combattant"* by Edward Fitzgerald. London, Jonathan Cape and New York, Macmillan, 1951, 318 p.

[57] See Jacques de REYNIER, *1948 à Jérusalem*, Geneva, Georg, 2002, 175 p. (First and second editions published by the Editions de la Baconnière, Neuchâtel, 1950 and 1969). On this conflict and other special agreements, see Michel VEUTHEY, Guérilla et droit humanitaire, Geneva, ICRC, 1983 (Second edition), pp. 50–51.

[58] See K. BOALS, "The Internal War in Yemen" in Richard A. FALK (Ed.) *The International Law of Civil War*, Baltimore, Johns Hopkins Press, 1971.

[59] ICRC, *Rapport d'activité 1967*, p. 37, and John STREMLAU, *The International Politics of the Nigerian Civil War*, Princeton, NJ, Princeton University Press, 1977.

[60] See Jean-François BERGER, *The humanitarian diplomacy of the ICRC and the conflict in Croatia (1991–1992)*. Geneva, ICRC, 1995, 70 p.

[61] See the UN and the Dutch official reports on Srebrenica:

The need for an active bilateral[62] and multilateral[63] humanitarian diplomacy remains as great as ever.

4.1.4. *The Protecting Power*
The role of the Protecting Power could be rediscovered, not only in international conflicts but also in civil wars.

4.1.5. *The Fact-Finding Commission*
The Fact-Finding Commission should be more pro-active, offer its services, including in non-international armed conflicts.[64]

4.1.6. *Impartial humanitarian organizations*
The 1949 Geneva Conventions—especially Common Article 3—mention "an impartial humanitarian body, such as the International Committee of the Red Cross, may offer its services to the Parties in conflict", other humanitarian organizations might use this provision.

4.1.7. *United Nations*
The role of the UN, mentioned in Article 89 ("Co-operation") of Additional Protocol I, needs to be clarified.

- *The fall of Srebrenica.* A/54/549, 15 November 1999, available [Accessed 30 May 2005]: http://www.hri.ca/fortherecord1999/documentation/genassembly/a–54–549.htm
- NETHERLANDS INSTITUTE FOR WAR DOCUMENTATION (NIOD) Srebenica. Een "veilig" gebied. Reconstructie, achtergronden en analyses van de van een Safe Area ("Srebrenica. A 'safe' area. Reconstruction, background, consequences and analyses of the fall of a safe area"). Summary and order form of the Dutch original and English translation available at http://www.srebrenica.nl/ [Accessed 30 May 2005]

[62] See Angelo GNAEDINGER, Jean de COURTEN, Nicolas SOMMER. *Golfe 1990–1991. De la crise au conflit. L'action humanitaire du CICR.* Genève, CICR, Août 1991, 47 p., and Michel VEUTHEY. "De la Guerre d'Octobre 1973 au Conflit du Golfe en 1991: Les Appels du CICR pour la protection de la population civile." In DELISSEN, Astrid J.M. and TANJA, Gerard J. (Eds.) *Humanitarian Law of Armed Conflict. Challenges Ahead.* The Hague, Martin Nijhoff, 1992.

[63] Michel VEUTHEY. "The Humanitarian Network. Implementing Humanitarian Law through International Cooperation" *Bulletin of Peace Proposals.* Oslo. 18 (2), 1987, pp. 133–146.

[64] See the Report of the International Humanitarian Fact-Finding Commission (1997–2001), p. 2:

> "The armed conflict in Colombia represented the only situation in which the Commission almost became concretely involved. Between 1995 and 1999, repeated contacts with the government and one armed opposition group led to a stage in which the two parties were on the verge of signing an agreement to submit selected cases to the Commission. A change in the political landscape brought the process to an end."

This document is available online at: http://www.ihffc.org/en/documents/Report–2001–en.pdf

Respecting fundamental human values belongs to the framework of the maintenance and re-establishment of international security.[65]

The international humanitarian law dimension should be included in peacekeeping operations. Peacekeeping forces should be trained, monitored in order to respect fully their obligations towards civilians, prisoners, wounded.[66]

The legitimacy of military actions, including peacekeeping operations, depends on the behavior of troops.[67] Civilian casualties, allegations of ill-treatment, torture and execution of prisoners that stained various wars, and even peacekeeping operations, did bring them to an end, due to the reaction of public opinion against torture,[68] killing of civilians[69] and mistreatment of prisoners.[70]

There is a need for clearer mandates for UN troops, including the prevention of war crimes, the protection of civilian populations and humanitarian workers, and the search for and arrest of persons suspected of war crimes. And without adequate resources even the clearest mandates cannot be fulfilled.

We need to exert better targeted bilateral and multilateral sanctions, diplomatic, economic and adequate military pressures against violators, in accordance with the UN Charter and international humanitarian law.[71]

---

[65] See Michel VEUTHEY "The Contribution of the 1949 Geneva Conventions to International Security", *Refugee Survey Quarterly*, Vol. 18, Nr. 3, 1999, pp. 22–26.

[66] See
- PALWANKAR, Umesh, "Applicability of international humanitarian law to United Nations peace-keeping forces", *International Review of the Red Cross*, n° 294, 1993, pp. 27–240;
- SHRAGA, Daphna. "UN Peacekeeping Operations: Applicability of International Humanitarian Law and Responsibility for Operations-Related Damage" *AJIL*, Vol. 94, No. 2, April 2000, pp. 406–412.

[67] On peaceekeeping operations and international humanitarian law, see
- Robert KOLB. *Droit humanitaire et opérations de paix internationales*. Genève/Bâle/Munich/Bruxelles, Helbing & Lichtenhahn/Bruylant, 2002, 125 p.
- Daphna SHRAGA, "UN Peacekeeping Operations: Applicability of International Humanitarian Law and Responsibility for Operations-Related Damage" *AJIL*, Vol. 94, No. 2, April 2000, pp. 406–412.

[68] The French War in Algeria was not lost militarily but because of reactions from the Algerian and French population, as well as from international public opinion, mostly against torture. See among others Henri ALLEG, *La question*. Paris, Pauvert, 1965, 121 p., P. VIDAL-NAQUET, *La torture dans la République. Essai d'histoire et de politique contemporaines (1954–1962)*. Paris, Editions de Minuit, 1972, 202 p. and John TALBOTT. *The War Without a Name: France in Algeria, 1954–1962*. New York, Knopf, 1980, 320 p.

[69] Such as in Vietnam, by the air bombings in the North and killings like the My Lai massacre in the South.

[70] Such as in Somalia, where Belgian, Canadian and Italian troops where prosecuted for mistreatment of prisoners and civilians.

[71] See Anna SEGALL. "Economic sanctions: legal and policy constraints" *IRRC* December 1999, Vol. 81, No. 836, pp. 763–784, and Claude BRUDERLEIN, "U.N. Sanctions Can

4.2. *Better Use of Implementation Mechanisms of Other Legal Systems*

International humanitarian law mechanisms need to be complemented by the implementation mechanisms of other legal systems: human rights, refugee law, the prohibition of torture, the prohibition of genocide, the protection of the natural environment, the protection of cultural objects, disarmament and arms control, the prohibition of illicit trafficking (arms, diamonds, drugs, human beings), compensation and reparation (civil liability).

4.2.1. *Human Rights*

Human Rights mechanisms, at the national, regional and universal level, should be used more in monitoring, reporting, preventing and repressing international humanitarian law violations.

As the International Court of Justice stated, the application of international humanitarian law does not exclude the application of human rights:

> "More generally, the Court considers that the protection offered by human rights conventions does not cease in case of armed conflict, save through the effect of provisions for derogation of the kind to be found in Article 4 of the International Covenant on Civil and Political Rights. As regards the relationship between international humanitarian law and human rights law, there are thus three possible situations: some rights may be exclusively matters of international humanitarian law; others may be exclusively matters of human rights law; yet others may be matters of both these branches of international law. In order to answer the question put to it, the Court will have to take into consideration both these branches of international law, namely human rights law and, as *lex specialis*, international humanitarian law."[72]

4.2.2. *Refugee Law*

Refugee status, according to Refugee Law instruments, should never be granted to war criminals. Former Liberian President Charles Taylor, who

---

Be More Humane and Better Targeted" *Public Affaius Report*, University of California, Berkeley, Vol. 41, No. 1, January 2000.

(http://www.igs.berkeley.edu/publications/par/Jan2000/Bruderlein.html)

Arthur C. HELTON and Robert P. DeVECCHI, "Human Rights, Humanitarian Intervention & Sanctions" http://www.foreignpolicy2000.org/library/issuebriefs/IBHumanRights.html and H.C. Graf SPONECK, "Sanctions and Humanitarian Exemptions: A Practitioner's Commentary" *European Journal of International Law*, Vol. 13, Issue 1, 2002, pp. 81–87—Full text available at: http://www3.oup.co.uk/ejilaw/current/130081.sgm.abs.html.

[72] INTERNATIONAL COURT OF JUSTICE (ICJ). *Legal Consequences of the Construction of a Wall in the Occupied Palestinian Territory*. Advisory Opinion. 9 July 2004, paragr. 106. Available online at: http://www.icj-cij.org/icjwww/idocket/imwp/imwpframe.htm

See also the last sentence of paragraph 137:

"The construction of such a wall accordingly constitutes breaches by Israel of various of its obligations under the applicable international humanitarian law and human rights instruments".

has been granted refugee status in Nigeria, should be surrendered to the Special Court for Sierra Leone.[73]

4.2.3. *Prohibition of Torture*

The prohibition of torture belongs to the hard core of international humanitarian law (Common Article 3 to the 1949 Geneva Conventions) as well as to underogable rights.

Its national, regional and universal mechanisms could definitely complement and reinforce the work of the International Committee of the Red Cross pertaining to the protection of prisoners.[74]

4.2.4. *Prohibition of Genocide*

Lessons need to be learned from the Holocaust, Cambodia and Rwanda, among other genocides. ICRC President Jakob Kellenberger highlighted the following at the Stockholm International Forum, organized by the Swedish Government on 26–28 July 2004:

- Genocide, like armed conflict of a certain dimension, does not erupt from one day to the next. It is the result of a combination of factors: a lack of dialogue, a failure to respect others and an absence of shared values being among the important ones. It is difficult to anticipate the critical moment at which genocide will begin or the scope that the massacre will take. Greater efforts must therefore be made to interpret the warning signs and respond to them adequately. This should not be too difficult. Genocide needs organizers. It is also most useful to distinguish at an early stage what comes from below and what from above.
- More information on the causes of tensions and injustice, and a proper analysis of this information, are of critical importance in forestalling violence.

The ICJ had similarly stated in its earlier Advisory Opinion on The Legality of the Threat or Use of Nuclear Weapons, on 8 July 1996, paragraph 25:

"The Court observes that the protection of the International Covenant of Civil and Political Rights does not cease in times of war, except by operation of Article 4 of the Covenant whereby certain provisions may be derogated from in a time of national emergency".

[73] See AMNESTY INTERNATIONAL. *Special Court for Sierra Leone: Statement to the National Victims Commemoration Conference, Freetown, 1 and 2 March 2005* (AI Index: 51/002/2005), 1 March 2005.

[74] See the March 2005 issue of the *International Review of the Red Cross* (Vol. 87, Nr. 857) and especially the articles by
- Edouard DELAPLACE and Matt POLLARD. "Visits by human rights mechanisms as a means of greater protection for persons deprived of their liberty", pp. 69–82. Available online at: http://www.icrc.org/Web/eng/siteeng0.nsf/htmlall/review-857-p69/$File/irrc_857_Delaplace_Pollard.pdf
- Alfred de ZAYAS. "Human rights and indefinite detention", pp. 15–38. Available online at: http://www.icrc.org/Web/eng/siteeng0.nsf/htmlall/review-857-p15/$File/irrc_857_Zayas.pdf

However, the inability of the international community to prevent genocide cannot be explained solely by a lack of information or a poor understanding of the situation. Alarm bells ring for those who are listening. There is another, far more worrying factor in play, and that is the lack of will to act, or the lack of power to take the necessary preventive measures.

- Keeping alive the memory of past acts of genocide is an effective way of stiffening the resolve to act early on should threats of genocide appear again in any context. Holocaust Memorials are extremely important. It is imperative that the genocide that occurred in Rwanda 10 years ago, and indeed all other acts of genocide, be remembered. We must not forget nor should we accept that geographical distance implies moral distance, thus weakening our resolve to act when genocide looms.[75]

His conclusion was:

> There is no alternative to strengthening our respect for the dignity of each individual human being if we want to prevent future threats of genocide. The various preventive measures that are needed, from short-term emergency interventions to long-term education, will require different time frames and involve the work of many. The ICRC stands ready to play its part.

Article 8 of the 1948 Genocide Convention reads as follows:

> "Any Contracting Party may call upon the competent organs of the United Nations to take such action under the Charter of the United Nations as they consider appropriate for the prevention and suppression of acts of genocide or any of the other acts enumerated in Article 3."

Its wording is very similar to Article 89 ("Cooperation") of the First Additional Protocol I of 1977. States Parties to both instruments could certainly make more use of them in the future.

Only under intense pressure from civil society will Governments act on behalf of victims of genocide.[76]

4.2.5. *Protection of the Environment*

The protection of the natural environment is closely linked to international humanitarian law.

---

[75] Available online at: http://www.icrc.org/web/eng/siteeng0.nsf/iwpList98/9B5A0983ED60D6D3C1256E2B0039EA98

[76] See
- Martin GILBERT. *Auschwitz and the Allies.* New York, Holt, Rinehart and Winston, 1981
- Samantha POWER. *A Problem from Hell. America and the Age of Genocide.* New York, Basic Books, 2002
- Samantha POWER. "Bystanders to Genocide. Why the United States Let the Rwandan Tragedy Happen", *The Atlantic Monthly*, September 2001 http://www.theatlantic.com/issues/2001/09/power.htm
- Gerard PRUNIER. *The Rwanda Crisis: History of a Genocide*, New York, Columbia University Press, 1997, 389 p.

In its 1996 Advisory Opinion on Nuclear Weapons, he International Court of Justice considered a number of international instruments protecting the environment:

> These included Additional Protocol I of 1977 to the Geneva Conventions of 1949, Article 35, paragraph 3, of which prohibits the employment of "methods or means of warfare which are intended, or may be expected, to cause widespread, long-term and severe damage to the natural environment"; and the Convention of 18 May 1977 on the Prohibition of Military or Any Other Hostile Use of Environmental Modification Techniques, which prohibits the use of weapons which have "widespread, long-lasting or severe effects" on the environment (Art. 1). Also cited were Principle 21 of the Stockholm Declaration of 1972 and Principle 2 of the Rio Declaration of 1992 which express the common conviction of the States concerned that they have a duty "to ensure that activities within their jurisdiction or control do not cause damage to the environment of other States or of areas beyond the limits of national jurisdiction".[77]

4.2.6. *Protection of Cultural Objects*

Cultural objects could be the heart and soul of nations. The Second Protocol to the 1954 Hague Convention for the Protection of Cultural Property in the Event of Armed Conflict provides useful complements for a better respect of cultural objects, and of measure to take in time of peace and of armed conflict.[78]

4.2.7. *Disarmament and Arms Control*

Not only weapons of mass destruction but small arms and light weapons[79] could be causes of massive violations of international humanitarian law. Monitoring arms transfers, beginning with light weapons,[80] and promoting

---

[77] INTERNATIONAL COURT OF JUSTICE. *Legality of the Threat or Use of Nuclear Weapons*, paragr. 27.

[78] See Jean-Marie HENCKAERTS. "The significance of the Second Protocol to the 1954 Hague Convention for the Protection of Cultural Property in the Event of Armed Conflict". IRRC, No 835, pp. 593–620.
Available online at: http://www.icrc.org/Web/Eng/siteeng0.nsf/iwpList74/DFE2EF4C9B065770C1256B66005D898C

[79] See among others:
– INTERNATIONAL COMMITTEE OF THE RED CROSS (ICRC)
Arms Availability and Violations of International Humanitarian Law and the Deterioration of the Situation of Civilians in Armed Conflicts. Expert Group Meeting. Report. Oslo, Norway, 18–20 May 1998, Oslo, Norwegian Red Cross, 1998, 87 p.
– UNITED STATES DEPARTMENT OF STATE Arms and Conflict in Africa
Bureau of Intelligence and Research Bureau of Public Affairs July 1999.

[80] See William HARTUNG "The New Business of War: Small Arms and the Business of Conflict" Ethics & International Affairs Annual Journal of the Carnegie Council on Ethics and International Affairs, Vol. 15, No 1 (2001). The author's argument is the following: The proliferation of internal conflicts fueled by small arms poses a grave threat to

innovative disarmament approaches, such as "weapons for food" or "weapons for development".[81]

4.2.8. *Prosecution of Illicit Trafficking (Arms, Diamonds, Drugs, Human Beings)*
The prosecution of illicit trafficking of arms, diamonds, drugs and human being is a necessary complement to the prevention and prosecution of violations of humanitarian law. Violations of IHL and drug- and arm-trafficking[82] frequently go hand in hand.[83]

4.2.9. *Compensation and Reparation*
Compensation is mentioned both in Article 3 of The Hague Convention Concerning the Laws and Customs of War on Land of 1907 and in Article 91 ("Responsibility") of the First Additional Protocol of 1977:

> "A Party to the conflict which violates the provisions of the Conventions or of this Protocol shall, if the case demands, be liable to pay compensation. It shall be responsible for all acts committed by persons forming part of its armed forces."

The link between implementation and reparation is clearly explained by the International Court of Justice in its 2004 Advisory Opinion:

> "As regards the legal consequences for Israel, it was contended that Israel has, first, a legal obligation to bring the illegal situation to an end by ceasing forthwith the construction of the wall in the Occupied Palestinian Territory, and to give appropriate assurances and guarantees of non-repetition.

---

peace, democracy, and the rule of law. The weapons of choice in today's conflicts are not big-ticket items like long-range missiles, tanks, and fighter planes, but small and frighteningly accessible weapons ranging from handguns, carbines, and assault rifles on up to machine guns, rocket-propelled grenades, and shoulder-fired missiles. In conflict zones from Colombia to the Democratic Republic of the Congo, picking up a gun has become the preferred route for generating income, obtaining political power, and generating "employment" for young people, many no more than children, who have little prospect of securing a decent education or a steady job. Ending the cycle of violence fueled by small arms must become a top priority for the international community. No single treaty or set of actions, however, will "solve" the problem of light weapons proliferation. What is needed is a series of overlapping measures involving stricter laws and regulations, greater transparency, and innovative diplomatic and economic initiatives.

[81] See G. MUGUMYA. Exchanging Weapons for Development in Cambodia: An Assessment of Different Weapon Collection Strategies by Local People. Geneva, UNIDIR, April 2005, 132 p.

Other projects have been conducted in Albania, Mozambique and South Africa, among other places.

[82] See Ahmed RASHID, "The Taliban: Exporting Extremism" *Foreign Affairs*, Nov./Dec. 1999, pp. 22–35: *"The drug trade will expand. Those are the costs that no country—not Afghanistan, the United States, its allies, China or Iran—can hope to bear"*.

[83] See SALON.COM "Genocide, and drug-trafficking too", by Frank SMYTH http://www.salon.com/news/1999/03/05news.html

> It was argued that, secondly, Israel is under a legal obligation to make reparation for the damage arising from its unlawful conduct. It was submitted that such reparation should first of all take the form of restitution, namely demolition of those portions of the wall constructed in the Occupied Palestinian Territory and annulment of the legal acts associated with its construction and the restoration of property requisitioned or expropriated for that purpose; reparation should also include appropriate compensation for individuals whose homes or agricultural holdings have been destroyed.
>
> It was further contended that Israel is under a continuing duty to comply with all of the international obligations violated by it as a result of the construction of the wall in the Occupied Palestinian Territory and of the associated régime. It was also argued that, under the terms of the Fourth Geneva Convention, Israel is under an obligation to search for and bring before its courts persons alleged to have committed, or to have ordered to be committed, grave breaches of international humanitarian law flowing from the planning, construction and use of the wall."[84]

Other legal remedies against violations of international humanitarian law could include:

- asking for compensation by way of civil liability claims;[85]

---

[84] Paragraph 145. Also see:

152. Moreover, given that the construction of the wall in the Occupied Palestinian Territory has, *inter alia*, entailed the requisition and destruction of homes, businesses and agricultural holdings, the Court finds further that Israel has the obligation to make reparation for the damage caused to all the natural or legal persons concerned. The Court would recall that the essential forms of reparation in customary law were laid down by the Permanent Court of International Justice in the following terms:

–60–

"The essential principle contained in the actual notion of an illegal act—a principle which seems to be established by international practice and in particular by the decisions of arbitral tribunals—is that reparation must, as far as possible, wipe out all the consequences of the illegal act and reestablish the situation which would, in all probability, have existed if that act had not been committed. Restitution in kind, or, if this is not possible, payment of a sum corresponding to the value which a restitution in kind would bear; the award, if need be, of damages for loss sustained which would not be covered by restitution in kind or payment in place of it such—are the principles which should serve to determine the amount of compensation due for an act contrary to international law." (*Factory at Chorzów, Merits, Judgment No. 13, 1928, P.C.I.J., Series A, No. 17*, p. 47.)

153. Israel is accordingly under an obligation to return the land, orchards, olive groves and other immovable property seized from any natural or legal person for purposes of construction of the wall in the Occupied Palestinian Territory. In the event that such restitution should prove to be materially impossible, Israel has an obligation to compensate the persons in question for the damage suffered. The Court considers that Israel also has an obligation to compensate, in accordance with the applicable rules of international law, all natural or legal persons having suffered any form of material damage as a result of the wall's construction.

[85] John F. MURPHY "Civil Liability for the Commission of International Crimes as an Alternative to Criminal Prosecution", *Harvard Human Rights Journal*, Vol. 12 (Spring 1999), pp. 1–56.

• introducing claims against private companies[86] that support[87] groups that commit violations[88] in countries where they operate.[89]

4.2.10. *Traditional customary mechanisms (such as* "gacaca"*)*
Traditional customary mechanisms—not mentioned in international law instruments—are sometimes a very useful approach to relieve over-burdened legal mechanisms.[90] Those approaches often fill the gap between the sanction of violations and reconciliation, especially in non-international armed conflicts.

The ethics deficit[91] is not only in the denial of the fundamental dignity of others or in the denial of justice for too many victims of war crimes, crimes against humanity and genocide. It is also to be seen in the excessive emphasis on an impossible justice, and on the denial of forgiveness and reconciliation.

The South African Truth and Reconciliation Commission (TRC)[92] was set up by the Government of National Unity to help deal with what happened under apartheid. The conflict during this period resulted in violence and human rights abuses from all sides. No section of society escaped these

---

"Because of the resistance of governments, progress toward greater civil liability for international crimes will depend upon the efforts of non-governmental actors to bring pressure to bear on governments". In an analogous context, see Jordan J. PAUST, "Suing Saddam: Private remedies for War Crimes and Hostage-Taking," 31 Virginia Journal of International Law 351–380 (1991).

[86] Fabrice WEISSMAN, "Liberia. Can Relief Organizations Cope With The Warlords?" in Médecins Sans Frontières/Doctors Without Borders, World in Crisis. The politics of survival at the end of the 20th century, London/New York, Routledge, 1997, pp. 100–121:

"Until it faces up its responsibilities, the international community could at least impose an embargo upon the private companies which continue to exploit the country's resources for the sole benefit of the warlords" (p. 121, conclusion).

[87] See this statement by the US Committee for Refugees (http://www.refugees.org/help/diamond_action.htm):

"Some of the worst refugee crises in Africa are fueled in part by the flow of illicit diamonds and other valuable natural resources. In countries like Sierra Leone, Angola, and Congo "diamonds are a rebel's best friend." Illegal diamond deals are the primary source of revenue in this region and allow combatants to purchase weapons and ammunition at alarming levels".

See the Report, available online, "The Heart of The Matter: Sierra Leone, Diamonds & Human Security", by Ian Smillie, Lansana Gberie and Ralph Hazleton, Partnership Africa Canada, Ottawa, January 2000, http://www.web.net/pac/pacnet-l/msg00009.html.

[88] One case is this of security measures taken by oil companies in Colombia which led Human Rights Watch to issue the following statement: ("Colombia: Human Rights Concerns Raised By The Security Arrangements Of Transnational Oil Companies (April 1998) http://www.hrw.org//advocacy/corporations/colombia/Oilpat.htm

[89] See by analogy Gary LEECH, http://www.salon.com/news/feature/2000/09/07/oil/.

[90] See Laura OLSON. "Mechanisms complementing prosecution". *International Review of the Red Cross*, Geneva, March 2002, Vol. 84, No. 845, pp. 173–189, especially pp. 185–187.

[91] Provide footnote text.

[92] See Alex BORAINE, *A Country Unmasked: Inside South Africa's Truth and Reconciliation Commission.* New York, Oxford University Press, 2001, 448 p.

abuses.[93] The TRC was the result of a compromise settlement between one side asking for a Nuremberg-like trial[94] and the other side for a blanket amnesty. It was an original combination of African tradition *("ubuntu")* and Christian sacramental approach *("penance")*.[95]

The Chaiman of the TRC, Archbishop Desmond Tutu, in his Freword to the Final Report, quotes Judge Marvin Frankel:

> "A nation divided during a repressive regime does not emerge suddenly united when the time of repression has passed. The human rights criminals are fellow citizens, living alongside everyone else, and they may be very powerful and dangerous. If the army and police have been the agencies of terror, the soldiers and the cops aren't going to turn overnight into paragons of respect for human rights. Their numbers and their expert management of deadly weapons remain significant facts of life . . . The soldiers and police may be biding their time, waiting and conspiring to return to power. They may be seeking to keep or win sympathisers in the population at large. If they are treated too harshly—or if the net of punishment is cast too widely—there may be a backlash that plays into their hands. But their victims cannot simply forgive and forget."[96]

Less elaborate approaches of "Truth and Reconciliation Commissions" have been considered and experimented as tools of mending societies torn apart by war in Argentina, Bolivia, Bosnia, Brazil, Chad, Chile, East Timor, El Salvador, Ethiopia, Germany, Guatemala, Honduras, Northern Ireland, Morocco,[97] Paraguay, Peru, Philippines, Rwanda, Sierra Leone,[98] Uruguay,

---

[93] See the official website of the South African TRC: http://www.doj.gov.za/trc/ [Accessed 30 May 2005].

The full report is available online at: http://www.info.gov.za/otherdocs/2003/trc/ [Accessed 30 May 2005].

A printed version (5 volumes and a CD-ROM) was published in March 1999 by MacMillan (London, UK).

[94] Apartheid has been declared a grave breach of international humanitarian law in Protocol I, (Art. 85, 4, c).

[95] Michael Jesse BATTLE and Desmond Mpilo TUTU Reconciliation: The Ubuntu Theology of Desmond Tutu, Cleveland, OH, The Pilgrim Press, 1997.

[96] Marvin FRANKEL, Out of the Shadows of the Night: The Struggle for International Human Rights.

[97] Susan SLYOMOVICS, "A Truth Commission for Morocco", Middle East Report 218, Spring 2001 http://www.merip.org/mer/mer218/218_slymovics.html

[98] See the 2000 Report of the UN Office of the High Commissioner for Human Rights to the General Assembly (A/55/38, paras. 37–45) http://www.hri.ca/fortherecord2000/vol2/sierraleonega.htm

> "The report notes that the OHCHR provided technical assistance to the government in drafting the law on the Truth and Reconciliation Commission (TRC). The OHCHR also developed a project for the preparatory phase of the Commission. The resumption of hostilities in May 2000 caused the Security Council to reconsider the role of UNAMSIL as well as other justice issues, including the establishment of a court to try human rights and humanitarian law abuses related to the conflict. The High Commissioner stated that these issues are crucial for the proper functioning of the TRC. The ongoing armed conflict, however, has delayed the implementation of the preparatory phase of that Commission".

Zimbabwe.[99] It certainly is a painful process,[100] and a healing one, which should not be exceptional.[101]

4.3. *Explore New Approaches*

4.3.1. *Reaffirm fundamentals and rules applicable in all circumstances (Common Article 3 and underogable Human Rights)*

We need to underline the common values, to move beyond the celebrations of the 20th century of the 50th anniversary of the UN Charter, of the Universal Declaration on Human Rights, of the 1949 Geneva Conventions, of the 1951 Convention on Refugees among others to reaffirm the universality of fundamental values.

There are divergences of opinion between American and European allies (on the death penalty, for example). There are differences of emphasis between civil and political rights on one hand and social and economic rights on the other. There are also differences between other countries on importance of individual and group rights.[102]

We therefore need to reaffirm a common core of human values, in discovering what makes them universal beyond cultural differences:

- The right to life
- The right to personal security and religious freedom
- The right to family life
- The right to health care, adequate nutrition and shelter
- The principle of non-discrimination

---

[99] Priscilla B. HAYNER "Fifteen Truth Commissions" Human Rights Quarterly Vol. 16, n. 4, Nov. 1994, pp. 597–655, Mike KAYE "The Role of the Truth Commissions in the Serarch for Justice, Reconciliation and Democratisation: Salvadorean and Honduran Cases" J. Lat Amer. Stud. 29, pp. 695–716; Neil J. KRITZ (Ed.) Transtional Justice: How Emerging Democracies Reckon with Former Regimes, Washington DC, USIP, 1995, 3 vol., José ZALAQUETT, "Moral Reconstruction in the Wake of Human Rights Violations and War Crfimes" in Jonathan Moore (Ed.) Hard Choices, Lanham, Rowman & Littlefield, 1998, pp. 211–227 and the website of the USIP http://www.usip.org/library/truth.html as well as: http://www.beyondintractability.org/m/truth_commissions.jsp

[100] See Priscilla B. HAYNER, Unspeakable Truths: Confronting State Terror and Atrocity New York, Routledge, 2001, 340 p.

[101] See this prayer by Archbishop Tutu:

"We pray that wounds that may have been re-opened in this process have been cleansed so that they will not fester; that some balm has been poured on them and that they will now heal."

http://www.macmillan-reference.co.uk/PandH/TRCforeword.htm

[102] "Human rights is a complex idea with differing emphases even as between various Western societies. Only with appropriate humility and self-doubt can true dialogue be encouraged." Stephen J. Toope, Cultural Diversity and Human Rights (F.R. Scott Lecture) http://collections.ic.gc.ca/tags/cultural.html

– The prohibition of torture, inhuman or degrading treatment or punishment.[103]

The International Court of Justice, in the Nicaragua Case, considered Article 3 of the 1949 Geneva Conventions as *"elementary considerations of humanity"* binding all:

> "The Court considers that the rules stated in Article 3, which is common to the four Geneva Conventions, applying to armed conflicts of a non-international character, should be applied. The United States is under an obligation to "respect" the Conventions and even to "ensure respect" for them, and thus not to encourage persons or groups engaged in the conflict in Nicaragua to act in violation of the provisions of Article 3. This obligation derives from the general principles of humanitarian law to which the Conventions merely give specific expression".[104]

It reads as follows:

> "In the case of armed conflict not of an international character occurring in the territory of one of the High Contracting Parties, each Party to the conflict shall be bound to apply, as a minimum, the following provisions:
>
> (1) Persons taking no active part in the hostilities, including members of armed forces who have laid down their arms and those placed hors de combat by sickness, wounds, detention, or any other cause, shall in all circumstances be treated humanely, without any adverse distinction founded on race, colour, religion or faith, sex, birth or wealth, or any other similar criteria. To this end the following acts are and shall remain prohibited at any time and in any place whatsoever with respect to the above-mentioned persons:
> (a) violence to life and person, in particular murder of all kinds, mutilation, cruel treatment and torture;
> (b) taking of hostages;
> (c) outrages upon personal dignity, in particular, humiliating and degrading treatment;
> (d) the passing of sentences and the carrying out of executions without previous judgment pronounced by a regularly constituted court affording all the judicial guarantees which are recognized as indispensable by civilized peoples.
>
> (2) The wounded and sick shall be collected and cared for.

[103] Paul GROSSRIEDER, "Humanitarian Standards and Cultural Differences" in ICRC, Seminar for non-governmental organizations on humanitarian standards and cultural differences. Summary Report, ICRC & The Geneva Foundation to Protect Health in War, Geneva, 14 December 1998. Text available online:
http://www.people.virginia.edu/~hc3z/ICRC-culture.htm

[104] International Court of Justice, *Case concerning the military and paramilitary activities in and against Nicaragua (Nicaragua v. United States of America), Judgement of 27 June 1986 (Merits)*, Vol. 114, Para. 218. On this case, see: Rosemary ABI-SAAB, "The 'General Principles' of humanitarian law according to the International Court of Justice", *International Review of the Red Cross*, July–August 1987, pp. 367–375.

> An impartial humanitarian body, such as the International Committee of the Red Cross, may offer its services to the Parties to the conflict.
>
> The Parties to the conflict should further endeavour to bring into force, by means of special agreements, all or part of the other provisions of the present Convention.
>
> The application of the preceding provisions shall not affect the legal status of the Parties to the conflict."

Renaissance literally means re-birth, renewal, return to the source. We need to research the roots of fundamental values in all civilizations, in order to move beyond the superficial universality of legal instruments, too often perceived as imposed by Western powers, and poorly implemented in too many cases.

As the ICRC survey conducted in 1999 for the 50th anniversary of the 1949 Geneva Conventions demonstrated, the local spiritual values are often the only efficient, convincing factor, which motivate the compliance with humanitarian rules in warfare.[105]

4.3.2. *Research factors influencing application and implementation. Draw lessons from best and worst practices in past and recent history.*

> *"Above all, we need detailed study of the pressures and factors that are persuasive for humanitarian law observance. It must not be assumed that courts, prison and firing squads are the sole mechanisms of enforcement"* wrote G.I.A.D. Draper.[106]

The following factors, which could influence the behaviour of parties to a conflict in a positive should be considered:

1. *reciprocity* (mutual interest);
2. *military efficacy* (not contradictory with humanity);
3. *reprisals* (neither helpful nor permissible);
4. *economy* (the need to save resources);
5. *public opinion* (a question of image);
6. *return to peace* (which is the normal state of human relations);
7. *ethics* (religious, moral, political legitimacy);

---

[105] See the Global Report and the Parallel Report (Country Reports) of the "People on War Project" at:

http://www.icrc.org/Web/Eng/siteeng0.nsf/iwpList74/4145CC3D8B377429C1256EB400268 0BD

All reports in PDF format are available online. The data of the survey carried out by the ICRC in 17 countries are available online at SIDOS (Swiss Data Online for the Social Sciences):

http://www.sidos.ch/data/projects/pow/default.asp?lang=e [Accessed 30 May 2005]

[106] G.I.A.D. DRAPER, *The Implementation and Enforcement of the Geneva Conventions of 1949 and of the two Additional Protocols of 1977*, Recueil, des Cours, 1979, III, The Hague, p. 1.

8. *the human factor* (the role of individuals);
9. *preservation of civilization* (a common interest of every human being);
10. *synergy* (as the result of combining different approaches).

Reciprocity is inherent in all fields of law. There is no law without reciprocity. Thus treating prisoners humanely can influence the fate of the prisoners on the other side of the front, as well as the enemy's attitude towards civilian populations and the means and methods of warfare employed.

It must nonetheless be pointed out that in the 1949 Geneva Conventions[107] and in the 1969 Vienna Convention on the Law of Treaties *reciprocity is no longer a legal condition* for application of humanitarian law.[108]

The principle of humanity, the cornerstone of humanitarian law, has frequently been in opposition to military necessities. Nevertheless, these two essential factors are not necessarily contradictory. On the contrary, humanity and military effectiveness are often complementary; and the best approach is indeed to highlight the mutual military, political and economic benefits of recognizing the enemy—civil or combatant—as a human being with the same dignity as oneself. The surrender of the enemy may be more easily obtained if the enemy appreciates that it will be treated humanely. Moreover, attacks against the civilian population, far from reducing it into submission, more often incites it to resistance.

Additionally, discipline of its own troops must incorporate the respect of humanitarian restraints. History shows that when combatants are given free rein to kill and destroy indiscriminately or commit acts of savagery against the enemy are more inclined to turn against their own leaders and to act ruthlessly against their own population. To assure that humanitarian principles are respected and implemented at this most basic level, credible

[107] The four Geneva Conventions of 12 August 1949 on the protection of war victims do not recognize reciprocity, the only exception, contained in Article 2 common to all four Conventions, being a Power not a Party to the Convention; they provide for the inalienability of rights (Art. 7 of the First, Second and Third Convention; Art. 8 of the Fourth Convention) and prohibit reprisals (First Convention, Art. 46; Second, Art. 47; Third, Art. 13, and Fourth, Art. 33).

See on this subject: PICTET, *Commentary*, I, p. 28; PICTET, *Red Cross Principles*, p. 87; PINTO, R. *Les règles du droit international concernant la guerre civile*, Recueil des Cours, The Hague, 1965, I, p. 530.

[108] Art. 60, paragraphs 1 and 5:

"1. A material breach of a bilateral treaty by one of the parties entitles the other to invoke the breach as a ground for terminating the treaty or suspending its operation in whole or in part."

[. . .]

"5. Paragraphs 1 to 3 do not apply to provisions relating to the protection of the human person contained in treaties of a humanitarian character, in particular to provisions prohibiting any forms of reprisals against persons protected by such treaties."

See Paul REUTER, *La Convention de Vienne sur le droit des traités*, Paris, 1970, p. 47.

instruction and rigorous training are essential. To this end, it is important that the these rules be disseminated simply and clearly and that they be coupled with a system of disciplinary sanctions guaranteeing their observance.[109]

Violations of the Geneva Conventions represent a serious threat to international security, at the regional level and worldwide. Thus, international humanitarian law is increasingly becoming an essential part of global security issues, on the national, regional and international levels. Security today, however, also means human security, solidarity in peace and restraints in conflict that safeguard the common humanity.

The *economy* is another factor conducive to the implementation of humanitarian law. It is obviously more costly to strike indiscriminately than to limit one's attacks to military objectives. It is better for forces intent on liberating or conquering civilians, not to endanger their very survival by completely disorganizing their economic life or to create more displaced persons than can be sheltered and fed. Donor countries could use their economic leverage to put pressure on parties in internal conflicts to abide by humanitarian standards. In the same way, private companies could also play a role in this process.

No Government and no group of insurgents can be indifferent to *public opinion* (domestic and international). In order to preserve their legitimacy, political systems must either incorporate what is humanitarian or disappear for lack of humanity. Public opinion therefore is an important factor in implementing fundamental values. Its effects can be *negative* (calling for reprisals) or *positive* (asking for restraints and humanity).

The contribution that respect for humanitarian law can make to *peace* is an important political factor that is often overlooked. Just as respecting human rights facilitates the maintenance of peace, so the restoration of peace is largely facilitated by humanitarian acts. Such acts (release of prisoners, for example) are like seeds of dialogue that foster dialogue and reconciliation. Humanitarian gestures are the first step towards peace.

---

[109] See the Military Courses organized by the Institute of International Humanitarian Law in San Remo (Italy) www.iihl.org and

- Cees DE ROVER, 'Police and Security Forces. A new interest for human rights and humanitarian law' *International review of the Red Cross*, no. 835 (September 1999) pp. 637–647.
- Cees DE ROVER, *To Serve and to Protect. Human Rights and Humanitarian Law for Police and Security Forces*, ICRC, Geneva, 1998.
- Dieter FLECK (Ed.), *The Handbook of Humanitarian Law in Armed Conflicts*, Oxford, Oxford University Press 1995, 589 p.

Ethics is the fundament of political legitimacy. As Nobel Prize Albert Camus wrote during the Algerian War: *"To fight for a truth without destroying it by the very means used to defend it."*[110]

4.3.3. *Use new approaches to change the behaviour of parties to conflicts*
New approaches are needed to influence parties to conflicts.

4.3.4. *Use new technologies to monitor the conduct of hostilities in order to prevent and prosecute violations*
New technologies are available to monitor the conduct of hostilities. If they would be used more widely, they could contribute to the prevention and repression of violations: the monitoring of radio- and telephone communications are available practically exclusively to Governments, which could make known to belligerents that they are monitoring their instructions and would not remain indifferent to orders incompatible with international rules of the laws and customs of war, fundamental human rights or the prohibition of genocide. Until recently, satellite pictures were the monopoly of intelligence services. Commercial satellites now routinely provide NGOs such as Amnesty International, Human Rights Watch and Physicians for Human Rights with pictures of burned down villages in an African civil war. Could Governments Parties to the Geneva Conventions make an even better use of the sharper images they could retrieve, day and night, and release some of them?[111]

4.3.5. *Approach new actors, and make them accountable*
Non-State actors[112] play an increasing role in armed conflicts. Engaging them to abide by humanitarian rules and principles[113] is needed, not only

[110] Albert CAMUS, *Actuelles III. Chroniques algériennes (1939–1958)*, Paris, Gallimard, 1958, p. 24 *"Se battre pour une vérité en veillant à ne pas la tuer des armes mêmes dont on la défend"*.

[111] See the 2004 high-resolution satellite images of destroyed villages in the Darfur on the USAID website:
http://www.usaid.gov/locations/sub-saharan_africa/sudan/satelliteimages.html [Accessed 30 May 2005]

[112] See Rainer HOFMANN (Ed.)/Nils GEISSLER (Assistant Ed.): Non-State Actors as New Subjects of International Law. International Law—From the Traditional State Order Towards the Law of the Global Community. Proceedings of an International Symposium of the Kiel Walther-Schücking-Institute of International Law, March 25 to 28, 1998. Berlin 1999. Duncker und Humblot. 175 p.
Daniel BYMAN, Peter CHALK, Bruce HOFFMAN, William ROSENAU, David BRANNAN.
Trends in Outside Support for Insurgent Movements, Washington, DC, Rand, 2001.

[113] See the "Guidelines for Engaging Non-State Actors in a Landmine-Ban"
http://www.icbl.org/wg/nsa/library/draft%20guidelines.html

by the ICRC,[114] but also by Governments, international organizations,[115] NGOs[116] and civil society, including diasporas.[117]

4.3.6. *Reach individuals*

Lawyers tend to see only Governments, institutions, and mechanisms.

Throughout history, individuals appealed to the public conscience, and changed history: Las Casas on behalf of the human dignity of Amerindians, Cesare Beccaria and Voltaire against torture, Victor Hugo against the death penalty, Emile Zola against bigotry in the Dreyfus Case. In the 20th century, Gandhi in South Africa and India, Martin Luther King in the United States, Mgr Romero in El Salvador, Dom Helder Camara in Brasil, Mgr Carlos Belo in East Timor all spoke out against injustices that mobilized the public conscience.

We need to reach individuals, at all levels, to exert an influence, from near and far, on parties to conflicts. Former Heads of State, like Nelson Mandela, can—and did—certainly exert an influence. In a similar way, artists, actors and athletes, among others, could be used to bring a humanitarian message. The International Committee of the Red Cross (ICRC), for example, asked musicians to write songs against excessive violence ("So Why" and "Woza Africa").[118]

---

and Claude BRUDERLEIN, "The Role of Non-State Actors in Building Human Security: The Case of Armed Groups in Intra-State Wars." *Policy paper for the Centre for Humanitarian Dialogue*, Geneva, Switzerland (prepared for the Ministerial Meeting of the Human Security Network in Lucerne), May 2000. www.hdcentre.org/NewsEvents/1999/Policy%20paper.doc.

[114] See Michel VEUTHEY. "Learning from History : Accession to the Conventions, Special Agreements, and Unilateral Declarations" in COLLEGE OF EUROPE. *Proceedings of the Bruges Colloquium. Relevance of International Humanitarian Law to Non-State Actors. 25–26 October 2002*. Collegium, Bruges (Belgium), No. 27, Spring 2003, pp. 139–151.

[115] Such as UNICEF in the Sudan in 1995 and OCHA in the Congo (DRC) in 1998.

[116] Such as the "Geneva Call", an international humanitarian organisation dedicated to engaging armed non-state actors (NSAs) to respect and to adhere to humanitarian norms, starting with the ban on antipersonnel (AP) mines. Geneva Call provides an innovative mechanism for NSAs, who do not participate in drafting treaties and thus may not feel bound by their obligations, to express adherence to the norms embodied in the 1997 antipersonnel mine ban treaty (MBT) through their signature to the "Deed of Commitment for Adherence to a Total Ban on Anti-Personnel Mines and for Cooperation in Mine Action" [PDF File]. The Government of the Republic and Canton of Geneva serves as the guardian of these Deeds. http://www.genevacall.org/home.htm

[117] The Tamil communities abroad had a moderating influence on the "Tamil Tigers" of the LTTE in Sri Lanka.

[118] "WOZA AFRICA" Project by the ICRC in 1997. See the following document online: http://www.icrc.org/Web/eng/siteeng0.nsf/iwpList75/644CDEA605D33696C1256B66005AD038

4.3.7. *Mobilize public conscience*

Public conscience extends beyond the individual's moral sense. It refers to values that are shared within a community, be it a family, a tribe, a nation, a religious or professional group, a region (Africa, Latin America, North America, Western Europe, Eastern Europe, North Africa and the Near East, Oceania, South-East Asia, etc.) a group of nations (industrialized or developing), and even all humankind.

> Public conscience is related to the concepts of natural law[119] and the law of nations *("jus gentium", "droit des gens", "Völkerrecht")* in their original meaning of common values among all civilized peoples and customary values of all human civilizations, including spiritual values, humanitarian principles, professional ethics (military, medical). It forms a safety net of fundamental principles found in various part of international law (laws of war, humanitarian law, human rights, international law protecting the environment, among others) linked to the survival and fundamental dignity of humankind. Even if the core of public conscience is universal, it is adjustable to cultures, situations and circumstances. Public conscience can indeed take different forms in different places and different times. It can even take the form of a negotiated compromise between justice and forgiveness. Public conscience can indeed take different forms in different places and different times.

Public conscience could also be considered as the principles that are widely recognized as advancing the universal common good, not limited to individual rights. Changes in the public conscience that promote inclusion that represent a widening of rights are progressive, and those that create exclusion are regressive. The notion of individual rights may be a Western concept, but the ethic of fairness is not. According to Erich Fromm, there are *"Life-Affirmative Societies"*[120] among primitive tribes, in which the main emphasis of ideals, customs and institutions is the preservation and growth of life in all its forms. In these societies we find a minimum of hostility, violence, or cruelty among people, no harsh punishment, hardly any crime, and the institution of war is absent or plays an exceedingly small role.

We need a renaissance, to move from a *Code of Enmity* to a *Code of Amity*, from confrontation to cooperation.

---

[119] Paolo BENVENUTI, "La clausola Martens e la tradizione classica del diritto naturale nella codificazione del diritto dei conflitti armati" in *Scritti degli allievi in memoria di Giuseppe Barile,* Padova, CEDAM, 1995, pp. 173–224.

[120] Eric FROMM *The Anatomy of Human Destructiveness,* New York: Holt, Rinehart and Winston, 1973, p. 168.

CHAPTER SEVEN

PROTECTION IN THE FIELD: HUMAN RIGHTS PERSPECTIVES

OHCHR Staff

Introduction

The *Secretary-General's Programme of Reform*, launched in late 1997, states that human rights cut across each of the four substantive fields of the UN Secretariat's work programme (peace and security; economic and social affairs; development cooperation; and humanitarian affairs) and human rights should be fully integrated into all UN activities. Human rights were made a core component in the mandate of the four Executive Committees.

In 1999 the Executive Committee on Peace and Security (ECPS) adopted *Principles for Integration of Human Rights into United Nations Activities for Conflict Prevention, Peacemaking, Peace-keeping and Peace-building*, which were developed by a ECPS Task Force, chaired by the editor of this volume, consisting of OHCHR, OCHA, DPA, DPKO and UNDP. Among other things, it was agreed that OHCHR must be integrally involved in the design of human rights components managed by DPKO or DPA and "humanitarian emergency responses need to take into account human rights violations that may be at the root of crises and should strive for respect of international human rights norms".

As a part of the reform OHCHR is actively involved together with humanitarian and development partners on ongoing work on *transition*, in order to strengthen the role of human rights as a common denominator providing a bridge between relief and development.

The Security Council discussion on protection of civilians in armed conflict as a humanitarian imperative was introduced by the Secretary-General's report on the Situation in Africa in 1998.[1] In February 1999 the Security Council requested that the Secretary-General provide recommendations on ways the Council could improve the "physical and legal protection of civilians in armed conflicts". Since then the Secretary-General has presented a series of reports to the Security Council on the issue.[2] The Security Council has

[1] S/1998/318.

[2] S/1999/957, S/2001/331, S/2002/1300, S/2004/431.

Bertrand G. Ramcharan (Ed.), Human Rights Protection in the Field, 119–125.

passed two resolutions, in 1999 and 2000,[3] and issued four Presidential Statements.[4] The High Commissioner for Human Rights made a statement in the Security Council open meeting on the issue in 1999 and 2001, but the general trend has been to task OCHA to brief the Council on Secretary-General's behalf.[5]

At present the Security Council framework under this theme *includes the following areas*:[6] security for displaced persons and host communities; access to vulnerable populations; safety and security of humanitarian and associated personnel; security and the rule of law; DDRR; small arms and mine action; effects on and contribution of women; effects on children; justice and reconciliation; training of security and peacekeeping forces; media and information; natural resources and armed conflicts; and humanitarian impact of sanctions. The Security Council framework of protection of civilians goes beyond a strict timeframe of an armed conflict (includes activities for prevention and post-conflict) and it includes a wide spectrum of activities, some of them not carried out by humanitarian relief agencies.

A UN internal process under the Security Council framework on protection of civilians is led by OCHA. In the beginning of 2003 a working-level ECHA Implementation Group was established to develop a consolidated interagency approach to the actions required and to support the development of key materials and activities for implementation. The New York Office of OHCHR has been actively involved in this process. Further, OHCHR has contributed to other OCHA activities with Member States under this framework, like regional workshops and roundtable discussions.

The humanitarian community (including actors outside the UN) is increasingly concerned about the "humanitarian identity" becoming blurred, advocating for further separation from political, military, and human rights actors. Some humanitarians feel that in many parts of the world their acceptance and safety is endangered due to the perceived blurring of roles. They acknowledge that there are several reasons for this, but express particular *concern over the UN's concept of integrated missions*, which is seen by some as creating further constraints on humanitarian space and access. This issue was discussed in the IASC Principals' and Working Group meetings, as well as the July 2004 ECOSOC Humanitarian Affairs Segment. While the

[3] S/RES/1265, S/RES/1296.

[4] S/PRST/1999/6, S/PRST/2002/3, S/PRST/2002/41, S/PRST/2003/27.

[5] The selection of actors providing briefings to the Security Council in its open sessions on the item has had interesting variations: In Feb. 1999 ICRC, UNICEF, and SRSG CAAC; in Sept. 1999 SG and HCHR; in April 2000 SG and ICRC; April 2001 DSG and HCHR; Nov. 2001 OCHA; March 2002 OCHA; Dec. 2002 SG, OCHA and ICRC; June 2003 OCHA; Dec. 2003 OCHA; June 2004 OCHA.

[6] Themes are in accordance to the revised Aide Memoire of 15 December 2003.

impact of integrated missions on humanitarian assistance is being reviewed by OCHA, humanitarian colleagues are aware that that the integrated mission approach is central to the Brahimi reforms, as is the mainstreaming of human rights in peace missions.

At the same time, the humanitarian community, represented by OCHA, has made increasing *efforts to raise directly before the Security Council both political issues and human rights related to protection of civilians*, acknowledging on several occasions that while humanitarian action provides immediate relief, the root causes of a conflict and human rights violations must be addressed for sustainable solutions.

Most recently, in cooperation with the Office of Legal Affairs, OCHA initiated a treaty event called "Focus 2004: *Treaties on the Protection of Civilians*" to take part at HQ during the GA. The "treaties on the protection of civilians" put forward by the event and its publications are in fact human rights treaties together with IHL, IRL and ICL treaties.

I. *Conceptual Issues*

There is *no common, system-wide (or ECHA) understanding of the concept "protection."* This has given rise to problematic inconsistencies in both usage and practice. For its part, OCHA considers "humanitarian protection" to be a wider umbrella that includes but is distinct from human rights. From OHCHR's point of view human rights protection is a wider concept, including not only civilians but all individuals in time of peace and war. OHCHR emphasizes, as well, obligations of promotion, alongside protection. OHCHR's approach to protection is based on the provisions of international human rights law, international humanitarian law, international criminal law, and international refugee law. Our approach is informed by the full range of internationally agreed human rights standards, as well as the Vienna Declaration, the mandate of the High Commissioner for Human Rights and the Secretary-General's reform programme. Notably, key humanitarian agencies, OCHA among them, did agree in the ECPS context, to the "Principles for the Integration of Human Rights into UN Activities for Conflict Prevention," Peacemaking, Peace-keeping and Peace-building, which themselves do much to define a framework for rights-based protection.

The IASC definition of protection, developed in an ICRC[7]-led process with active OHCHR participation, provides a useful and rights-sensitive understanding of the term. It defines the concept of protection as encompassing

[7] "Strengthening Protection in War", 2001, ICRC.

"all activities aimed at ensuring full respect for rights of the individual in accordance with the letter and the spirit of the relevant bodies of law, i.e. human rights, humanitarian law and refugee law," holds that "human rights and humanitarian actors shall conduct these activities in an impartial manner" and that this shall not be "on the base of race, national or ethnic origin, language or gender." Protection activities were defined as "any activity—consistent with the abovementioned purpose—aimed at creating an environment conducive to respect for human beings, preventing and/or alleviating the immediate effects of a specific pattern of abuse, and restoring dignified conditions of life through reparation, restitution and rehabilitation".

Within the Security Council framework the concept of protection of civilians in armed conflict is essentially undefined. The Secretary-General's 2001 report says it is a *process that depends on the circumstances and stages of a particular conflict.* Relevant activities might include the delivery of humanitarian assistance, monitoring and reporting on human rights; institution building, governance and development programmes; and deployment of peacekeeping troops. However, in the report of 2004, reference is made to the importance of "maintaining a clear and common understanding of protection", based on the Secretary-General's call for a system-wide approach. Nevertheless, no common UN definition has been yet proposed or agreed.

II. *Institutional Issues*

While the first two reports to the Council on protection of civilians in armed conflicts (1999 and 2001) were strong in addressing impunity and ensuring compliance with human rights, IHL and refugee law, we have perceived a *recent shift towards emphasizing issues that humanitarian actors are "more comfortable" with,* like access for and security of humanitarian personnel. One recent indication of this has been an attempt to promote a restricted focus on an ill-defined (and rather selective) concept of "restorative justice," in lieu of the full spectrum of transitional justice options and objectives. These more narrow approaches have important potential implications for the content of Council resolutions and the structure and functions of mandated missions.

We believe that the concept or objectives of *"protection of civilians in armed conflict" cannot be directly transferred to a discrete structural component in a peace operation.* Nevertheless, since the autumn of 2003, several attempts have been made to promote the setting up in peace missions of "civilian protection components" in place of human rights components, or the deploying of "protection specialists" alongside or instead of human rights officers. When pressed for justifications, no clear or compelling arguments on the comparative added value or distinct purpose of such entities has been provided by their proponents. Instead, references have been made mainly to the need to provide better support to the humanitarian coordinator on access negotiations, etc. (Given that the Humanitarian Coordinator is now typically integrated in the PKO structure, it is hard to see the added value even for these purposes). Nor have clarifications been offered for how they are to fit into the existing integrated mission structures. Some observers have expressed the concern that these recent initiatives may not be based on actual experience or needs on the ground, but rather on pressures on OCHA to demonstrate to the Security Council their involvement in protection of civilians at the field level. Furthermore, there are good reasons to fear that a shift to such "protection" entities could be done at the expense of the human rights agenda, and provide a convenient opportunity to avoid dealing with "hot" human rights issues considered to be politically sensitive or otherwise "compromising" to the humanitarian identity. Indeed, cases where humanitarian actors have demanded that human rights issues should not be raised in certain situations of humanitarian emergencies are not uncommon.

For the purpose of understanding the humanitarian interface, the following overview of recent *institutional arrangements in missions* can be identified:

1) *Human Rights component,* an explicit human rights component of a peacekeeping operation, taking several forms, in accordance with the OHCHR/DPKO MOU and usual practice (for example in Sierra Leone, DRC, and Afghanistan). The unit usually also supports the work of the DSRSG, who in humanitarian emergencies normally is the humanitarian coordinator. The mandate covers human rights protection of all individuals, including civilians.
2) *Human Rights component with a Protection Adviser in DSRSG's Office* (Burundi). This was a compromise solution, which was not favoured by OHCHR. The role of the protection adviser is to support the humanitarian coordinator. It is not clear why this person is not therefore a "humanitarian adviser", if that is what is needed.
3) *Human Rights and Protection component* (Liberia). This too was compromise language, following an attempt by OCHA to have the human rights component entirely deleted and replaced with a civilian protection component. No additional activities are included that a traditional human rights unit would not carry out. Attempts were made by OCHA to have such a unit also established in Haiti and Burundi, without any policy discussion or a concept paper.

4) Human rights officers/protection officers *as a part of the humanitarian office*: (UNOHCI-Iraq deployment in spring 2003 during the conflict, before the establishment of UNAMI; Sudan/Darfur; and Angola following the evolution of the situation and the dissolution of the peacekeeping mission to the Technical Unit under RC/HC). This approach has usually been taken when there is no existing human rights mandate. A portion of activities are usually directed toward integration of human rights into humanitarian action. Difficulties have been faced with monitoring and reporting on human rights abuses under humanitarian mandate.
5) *Protection groups* are often established for wider field coordination (including government representatives, local NGOs, international NGOs, etc.). These are often lead by a human rights officer (Cote d'Ivoire, Sierra Leone, Liberia, and Iraq) or by OCHA (Sudan, where there is a separate human rights group).
6) A *stand alone Human Rights Office*, with a varying degree of cooperation with the peacekeeping operation and/or humanitarian community.

The issue of a "protection gap" has resurfaced recently in connection with assistance to *internally displaced persons* (*IDPs*). Members of the Senior Network on IDPs concluded that the focus should be on the gap in monitoring and reporting on the human rights of IDPs that, in their view, stemmed from the limited operational capacity of OHCHR.

We note that various institutional arrangements also exist on *protection of the rights of the child*:

(1) Establishment of *child protection officers* as a part of a human rights component, including a child protection adviser to SRSG.
(2) Having a separate *child protection component and a human rights component*, as in MONUC.
(3) *Child protection adviser posts filled by SGSR CAAC within the human rights component.*

In our view, vulnerable groups should not be preconceived, but must be determined on a basis of a thorough *needs assessment*, which should be built upon in the mission planning. The humanitarian system often responds automatically to the vulnerability of children, without regard to other vulnerable groups on the ground, such as minorities, migrants, prisoners, etc.

A key consideration, where other (non-human rights specialist) actors are involved in human rights protection, is the assurance of *quality control in the interpretation, observation and application of human rights standards and methodologies.* OHCHR should exercise collegial leadership in this regard.

Conclusion

OHCHR should *analyze existing policy and practice for institutional arrangements in missions* (e.g., the 1999 ECPS paper on principles of human rights integration, the Secretary-General's reform, the Brahimi report, the OHCHR-DPKO MOU, etc.), as well as language options for SC mandates for human rights components, with a mind to formulating a standard policy on preferences for such institutional arrangements. Elements for consideration will include:

- *Mandates*: What is the relationship between OHCHR's global mandate for the promotion and protection of all human rights on the one hand, and the individual human rights mandates of individual Peacekeeping Operations on the other?
- *Roles, responsibilities and tasking*: Who does what within the mission on human rights related issues? What is the appropriate interface between the various roles?
- *Delegation*: What mandated OHCHR responsibilities might be "delegated" to others within a mission?
- *Reporting*: How should mission reporting lines on human rights issues be defined (Double reporting lines to SRSG and HC?).
- *Placement in the mission*: Where should the senior human rights staffer sit within a mission? Highest level reporting to the SRSG. Part of the "cabinet"? Within a pillar? Dotted line relationships to the pillars?
- *Resources*: What is our position on resources for "getting the job done"? What dedicated resources are needed? In what ways and areas can the resources of other parts of the mission be used for HR tasks? What should come from assessed (PKO) contributions? From extra-budgetary sources? From OHCHR?
- *Staff identification, recruitment and deployment*: How can OHCHR play its role in this regard more effectively, efficiently, and quickly?

CHAPTER EIGHT

HUMAN RIGHTS FIELD OPERATIONS: A NEW PROTECTION TOOL

William G. O'Neill

Introduction

The end of the cold war and the disintegration of the Soviet Union made the world increasingly safe for violent, non-nuclear conflicts. As superpower intervention and the chance for escalation to a larger, potentially nuclear war diminished, existing conflicts intensified and new ones emerged. At the same time, the outside sponsors of many conflicts lost interest because they were no longer of strategic importance. Perversely, the belligerents now fought with greater desperation knowing that their old superpower godfather was unlikely to ride to their rescue.

The intensity and ensuing brutality of conflicts in the 1990s was not the only surprise. Wars were fought to control power and resources in a single state and were not usually between states; civilians, not armed combatants, became the intentional targets of violence. Wars in the Former Yugoslavia, Africa, the Caucasus and Latin America saw huge numbers of civilian casualties compared to those killed and wounded in either the regular armed forces of a state or in the ranks of insurgents. This led to large flows of people on the move to escape fighting. Armies and insurgents burned crops, destroyed farmland, planted thousands of landmines, wrecked schools and hospitals and looted shops.

Despite their intensity, several conflicts became ripe for resolution. Some UN officials in the early 1990s sensed an opportunity to use human rights and international humanitarian law to begin a peace process. This idea and the subsequent initiatives originated in UN headquarters in New York, in particular the Department of Political Affairs (DPA). The DPA proposed to deploy specialists in human rights and the laws of armed conflict if possible alongside traditional UN military peacekeepers. The UN Mission to Namibia in the late 1980s was an early prototype of this model, and included a contingent of international police to monitor and report on compliance by local forces, and to train a Namibian police force.

Bertrand G. Ramcharan (Ed.), Human Rights Protection in the Field, 127–140.

Human Rights Field Operations: The El Salvador Precedent

The first full-blown human rights field presence came a few years later in El Salvador. As part of the efforts to end a conflict that had extended over two decades and had killed over 70,000 people, UN negotiators proposed sending a team of unarmed civilians to El Salvador to monitor compliance with human rights and humanitarian law by both the state security forces and the FMLN guerrillas. The two sides agreed, primarily because each did not trust the other and believed that independent monitors would verify their opponents' violations. The UN exploited this opening, and the 1991 San Jose Accords created the first major UN human rights field operation, the United Nations Observer Mission in El Salvador, known by its Spanish acronym "ONUSAL."

ONUSAL constituted a remarkable departure for both the UN and member states. Traditionally, the notion of state sovereignty has frustrated UN efforts to garner compliance with human rights standards. Many member states have relied on Article 2(7) of the UN Charter to deflect any criticism of a state's treatment of its residents, asserting that this is 'essentially within the domestic jurisdiction' of the state and thus outside the purview of the UN. ONUSAL breached the wall of state sovereignty. Deployed even before the parties had agreed to a cease-fire, the 42-member team had a far-reaching mandate, highly intrusive and unprecedented for a UN mission. ONUSAL could move freely and had the right to set up offices anywhere in El Salvador. Its members could visit all places of detention, unannounced if they so chose. They could speak to anyone they wished in the course of their monitoring; the Government and the FMLN promised not to harm anyone who met with ONUSAL or provided information to the mission. ONUSAL's offices and correspondence were immune from search. The mission was also mandated to report periodically to the Secretary-General on the parties' observance of human rights and the laws of armed conflict.

The ongoing presence of a team of international observers—roaming around the country, asking difficult questions, observing trials, reviewing police files, visiting prisons, interviewing victims of and witnesses to abuses, writing reports and establishing contacts with leading NGOs—constituted a major advance in the UN's efforts to seek greater observance of human rights and to protect people. ONUSAL was a qualitative leap from the somewhat hidebound and passive UN human rights procedures based in Geneva. ONUSAL was active, on the ground, persistent and had the wonderful virtue of being able to follow up its inquiries regularly; its findings could not be easily ignored or dismissed. Unlike other initiatives, ONUSAL also had staying power: its presence in El Salvador did not end until May 1995, when it was reduced in size and the UN responsibility for the Mission passed from the Security Council to the General Assembly. This longevity ensured that inquiries did not flame out and key cases or issues were neither ignored nor forgotten.

Cambodia, Haiti and Guatemala: Developing the Model

Once the ONUSAL precedent was established, other human rights field missions soon followed. These missions were sometimes part of broader peacekeeping operations with military and police components; in a few cases a human rights mission was deployed alone. The host state usually consented to the presence of the human rights field office, often under great pressure from the peace negotiators; in a few cases, East Timor and Kosovo for example, the state's consent was lacking and the mission entered under a Chapter VII mandate from the Security Council.

The UN Transitional Authority in Cambodia (UNTAC) followed the El Salvador mission. Created as a result of the Paris peace negotiations in 1991, UNTAC had sweeping powers amounting to what some experts saw as a new form of UN trusteeship. While the human rights component of the Mission was relatively small, it monitored the human rights situation throughout the country and helped start projects with a longer-term impact, such as judicial reform and helping to create and then reinforce Cambodian NGOs. UNTAC even had its own prison, prosecutors and judges, and participated in drafting new laws for post-Khmer Rouge Cambodia.

The OAS/UN International Civilian Mission in Haiti (MICIVIH) began its work in 1993. Guatemala was next with the UN Verification Mission (MINUGUA) starting in 1994. These were both large operations that emerged from negotiations led by DPA personnel from New York. These missions had no input from the-then Center for Human Rights in Geneva or its successor, the Office of the High Commissioner for Human Rights (OHCHR).

The OHCHR finally entered the fray in mid-1994 after the beginning of the genocide in Rwanda that April. The first High Commissioner, José Ayala-Lasso, visited Rwanda and promised to send several hundred human rights observers. This represented a radical shift for the Geneva office, which had no experience in recruiting for, training or mounting a large field operation in a war zone. This deficiency became clear as the mission started slowly and its staff, while well-meaning, were poorly organized and equipped, had received no training, committed some fundamental errors and sometimes alienated the very people they had come to protect.

The rest of the 1990s and the first years of the 21st century saw a dramatic increase in UN-sponsored human rights field missions. The picture grew more complicated as the High Commissioner, despite inexperience and budget limits requiring these missions to be funded by voluntary contributions from member-states, established field operations in Bosnia and Herzegovina, Colombia, Cambodia, Burundi, Croatia, Indonesia, the Federal Republic of Yugoslavia and the Sudan (Darfur). The Department of Peacekeeping Operations (DPKO) in New York also became a player. The DPKO incorporated a human rights department in most of its operations, including Liberia, Sierra Leone, the Central African Republic, Cote d'Ivoire, Angola, East Timor, the Democratic Republic of the Congo, Afghanistan and Kosovo.

Regional organizations have also mounted human rights field operations, especially the Organization for Security and Cooperation in Europe (OSCE). The OSCE has large human rights missions in Bosnia (42 international field officers) and Kosovo (71 international officers). It has smaller operations in numerous states of the former Soviet Union (Tajikistan, Kazakhstan, Kyrgyzstan, Belarus, Moldova, the Ukraine) and has a joint human rights office with UN/DPKO in Abkhazia/Georgia. The European Union (EU) was a joint-sponsor of the mission in Rwanda until 1997 while the OAS co-sponsored the mission in Haiti until June 1999.

This explosion of human rights field operations in just 14 years is a welcome advance. Deploying human rights professionals on the ground for extended periods to investigate and follow-up allegations, report publicly, and intervene with local officials to request corrective action secures an improvement in human rights more quickly and decisively than by holding periodic meetings in Geneva and New York, or issuing reports and resolutions that few people ever read. This ongoing presence permits human rights officers to participate in projects that can embed human rights in national institutions, and to work closely with the all-important local NGO community and burgeoning state institutions like Ombudspersons and National Human Rights Commissions.. Human rights field operations provide an opportunity for meaningful, realistic and practical programs addressing the actual abuses that will lead to real protection for real people.[1]

Humanitarian Actors

As the conflicts of the 1990s and early 21st century exploded, so too did the number of innocent civilians who were in dire need of humanitarian

[1] Kenneth L. Cain, 'The Rape of Dinah: Human Rights, Civil War in Liberia, and Evil Triumphant', *Human Rights Quarterly* 21 (1999), p. 297. The author strongly criticizes several international human rights groups for advocating "abstract, ideal standards . . . and articulat[ing] aspirational human rights goals that had no hope of actually being implemented in the real world.' He called this 'human rights cheerleading."

assistance. One barometer of the changing nature of these conflicts became the huge number of the internally displaced, who soon surpassed the number of refugees. The Secretary-General, recognizing this new phenomenon, requested the Commission on Human Rights to create a new post, the Special Representative of the Secretary-General on the Internally Displaced (IDPs) in 1992. Simultaneously, the United Nations High Commissioner for Refugees (UNHCR), the Department of Humanitarian Affairs (later renamed the Office for the Coordination of Humanitarian Affairs, "OCHA"), other UN bodies and international non-governmental organizations began to dedicate expertise and resources to confront the challenges and needs of the millions of internally displaced forced to flee their homes due to violence. In addition, the various humanitarian agencies realized they needed to adapt to the new challenges facing everyone in these war zones, displaced or not.

An important evolution in the approach to humanitarian action resulted from the changing nature of conflict post-Cold War. The focus shifted from purely providing humanitarian assistance to new approaches involving advocacy, dissemination of standards, monitoring and reporting on violations, emphasizing rights and adopting an international law-based approach. This was new and jolting to many humanitarian organizations. For example, the OCHA Field Manual says that it is important to emphasize that IDPs are not merely victims needing assistance, but holders of rights to whom duties are owed by both the national authorities and the international community. The Inter-Agency Standing Committee reinforced this message by adopting a broad definition of "protection" for IDPs: "The concept of protection encompasses all activities aimed at obtaining full respect for the rights of the individual in accordance with the letter and the spirit of the relevant bodies of law (i.e. HR [human rights], IHL [international humanitarian law], refugee law)."[2]

An increasing attention to protection, in addition to providing material assistance, reflects the experience of many who worked in the conflicts of the 1990s and first half-decade of the 21st century where it was not nearly enough to deliver assistance to unarmed civilians caught in bloody conflicts, targeted by the warring parties; the "well-fed dead" syndrome haunted and challenged humanitarian and human rights actors to do more. Human rights and humanitarian professionals, gingerly at first, have had to develop protocols and methods for working more closely than they ever had in the

---

[2] OCHA Inter-Agency Standing Committee, Policy Paper Series, No. 2, "Protection of Internally Displaced Persons" (2000), p. 4, quoting from a background paper prepared for the Third Workshop on Protection, ICRC (7 January 1999).

past, but with one joint goal in mind: maximizing protection. An Afghan relief worker expressed the challenge most clearly:

> "The power of [material] humanitarian assistance is not sufficient . . . international organizations have to focus on rights that Afghans want to realize . . . Security—national and individual—is about physical security from war, execution, detention, loss of shelter, losses of dignity."[3]

Many UN agencies, especially UNICEF, have adopted a "rights-based approach to their humanitarian and development work. Rejecting the old model that used concepts like "needs" and "charity," organizations like CARE, Save the Children and OXFAM now ground their work in the main human rights treaties and emphasize rights the "citizens" of a state have and the "duties" the state must fulfill in respecting, fulfilling and protecting people's rights. This has led to a major shift in the way these organizations work with a resulting premium on protection.[4]

Protection in Action: Haiti: The Early Days of MICIVIH (1993–95)

Armed with broad Terms of Reference, MICIVIH's field observers roamed all over Haiti seeking information on the human rights situation. This was, during 1993–94, a complicated job, since the military ruled Haiti and barely tolerated the Mission's presence. For the first time in Haitian history, international observers observed and reported week after week, month after month, on how the Haitian military treated the population; judges and lawyers were assessed on whether they were upholding Haitian law while police behavior was being observed and scrutinized.

MICIVIH's goal was to improve compliance with human rights standards. To achieve this goal, Mission observers sought information from reliable sources on the current human rights situation. Every day, Haitians would visit MICIVIH's regional offices and tell their stories; some were victims of abuse, others had witnessed violations or had information about specific incidents. After taking down the essentials, field officers would seek corroboration of the information by visiting the site, cross-checking information with other sources or reviewing documents. Once the human rights

---

[3] Inter-Agency Standing Committee, *Growing the Sheltering Tree: Programmes & Practices Gathered from the Field* (2002), p. 5. This study compiles numerous examples of "protection practices" by humanitarian agencies and collaboration between them and human rights specialists.

[4] For more on the rights-based approach *see* William G. O'Neill, "The Rights-Based Approach to Development, *InterAction Newsletter*, December 2003, available at www.interaction.org.

field officers had obtained sufficient confirmation, they would raise the case with local military officials, the police or the judiciary. The most serious cases were referred to headquarters for action to be taken at a higher level. These cases often appeared in the regular reports sent to UN and OAS headquarters in New York and Washington.

MICIVIH officers visited Haitian prisons and detention centers. When possible, they did so without prior notice. Sometimes Haitian military authorities, in violation of the Terms of Reference, refused entry. Once inside, MICIVIH personnel would check the prison register, though in many cases the prison kept no register so no one—not even the head of the prison—knew who was in the facility or the number of prisoners. Observers would supply the prison with a notebook and pens and then show the officer how to maintain this new register and what kind of information was to be included. On follow-up visits, the field officers would check the register to see whether it was accurate. The observers interviewed prisoners and assessed the conditions of detention. Haitian prisons were miserable places, with no running water, toilets or showers; relatives had to bring food since the prison provided none. Medical care was non-existent. Observers alerted other UN and humanitarian agencies who tried to fill these gaps. MICIVIH field officers often found that the detainees had been in prison for months, in some cases years, without being charged, let alone tried. Many had been beaten. MICIVIH raised these cases with the authorities, requesting that they respect national and international law. In many cases, the Mission's intervention led to the release of prisoners who were being illegally detained.

In response to the findings made during these prison visits and from observing the virtual collapse of the Haitian judicial system, MICIVIH created two initiatives. The first was to assign the doctors in the Mission the task of creating an emergency medical unit, in collaboration with Haitian medical professionals, to treat torture victims and prisoners. This unit successfully treated dozens of Haitians, and also documented cases of torture and mistreatment for possible future use in trials against their abusers. This task was dangerous. The military and police knew that their abuses were now being uncovered and recorded; the Haitian doctors and nurses took great risks in doing this work, but they saved lives and probably deterred further torture and mistreatment. The "cover" let alone the resources from MICIVIH aided their work. In just four months in 1993, the unit treated 85 victims of human rights violations, including knife, machete and gunshot wounds, beatings, and one case of torture by electric shocks.[5]

[5] William G. O'Neill, 'Human Rights Monitoring vs. Political Expediency: The Experience of the OAS/UN Mission in Haiti', *Harvard Human Rights Law Journal* 8 (1995), p. 115.

The second project was the creation of a Haitian Legal Aid network. With financing from two donor countries, the MICIVIH Legal Department identified Haitian lawyers willing to take cases referred to them by the Mission. MICIVIH paid these lawyers a fee and they represented torture victims and others detained illegally. Again, this was a potentially life-threatening job. Yet some brave Haitian lawyers went to court and argued, for the first time in Haitian history, that the military was acting illegally. These lawyers secured the release of numerous people. They also made Haitian judges and prosecutors apply the law and thus improved the functioning of the judicial system. MICIVIH field officers observed these court hearings and this also exerted pressure on the judiciary to do its job and this in turn could protect the judges from subsequent criticism or worse by the military, who were unhappy with this sudden concern for applying the law. Judges could tell the military that they had to enforce the law because the international human rights mission would report right away if they did not. According to one Haitian judge:

> At least [the military and the *macoutes*][6] were a little afraid that the members of the international community were observing them. Whenever they arrested someone or tortured him, members of the mission turned up to demand that the victim be released or to give him medical attention. That is to say, the presence of the mission has caused a certain decrease in cases of human rights violations.[7]

This strategy of constant presence, follow-up and intervention is the hallmark of a human rights field operation. By showing up every day in court, by continually meeting with local government authorities, by returning to the same prisons and police stations each week for months, by offering on-going training to local human rights advocates, defense lawyers and journalists, MICIVIH secured improved compliance with human rights law and greater protection for Haitians. A MICIVIH report noted that

> the Mission has seen an increasing willingness by judges to apply the law on arrest and detention, and a marked increase in granting provisional liberty to detainees. Prisoners have been processed through the system faster and some now even receive a hearing within 48 hours after arrest, as is required by the Constitution but was exceedingly rare before the presence of the Mission.[8]

---

[6] A Haitian paramilitary force created by long-time dictator Francois Duvalier in the late 1950s.

[7] *Haiti: Learning the Hard Way*, p. 57.

[8] *See* Note by the Secretary-General, The Situation of Democracy and Human Rights in Haiti, Report of the International Civilian Mission in Haiti, UN Doc. A/48/532 (1993), pp. 28–9.

Rwanda: Protection Challenges after a Genocide

The UN Human Rights Field Operation in Rwanda (HRFOR) adopted a fairly hard-nosed approach to its work starting in 1995. In mid-1997, after numerous internal meetings, HRFOR adopted 'program-based planning and assessment'. Each unit and regional office was required to craft a quarterly work plan. These plans described the objective of every initiative, the 'client' or target group, the time-frame, the amount of resources (personnel, equipment and money) required, constraints and, most importantly, means to verify the impact or success of the project. The teams identified three or four projects for each quarter and then met with the Head of Mission and other concerned senior managers who signed off on the plans following discussion.

For example, one regional office identified overcrowding in the local prison as a serious human rights problem. Most of the prisoners had no case files or '*dossiers*' which violates Rwandan law. The office decided to make this a priority issue and aimed to reduce the number of prisoners without *dossiers* in detention. Their goal was a 20% reduction in the next three months, with priority given to those who had been in detention for up to three years without charge. The team responsible for the prison went to the prison's director, explained Rwandan and international law and offered to provide training for police investigators responsible for creating the *dossiers*. They also offered to help the prison administration set up a review panel, with the aim of granting provisional release to those who had been in detention the longest, unless credible evidence emerged that they were implicated in a serious crime or human rights violation. HRFOR officers even provided transport to police investigators and prosecutors so that they could interview witnesses and victims in far-flung villages to gather evidence. The government had often used as an excuse for failing to create dossiers that they had no means to visit the scenes of violations or to interview eyewitnesses. The mission removed this excuse by taking police and prosecutors in mission vehicles. HRFOR also provided paper, pens and files to the ill-equipped investigators.

At the end of the first three months, the team noted a 10% decrease in the number of persons in detention without a *dossier*. The goal for ensuing quarters was a further reduction in the prison population among those with no case files.

Another example of HRFOR protection-focused work that rigorously identified and sought to achieve concrete performance measures concerned the indiscriminate use of force by Rwanda's army in its fight against Hutu extremists and militias. Violence intensified in 1997, resulting in several large massacres in the northwest; many women and children were killed, allegedly caught in the 'cross-fire' between the militias and the Rwandese Patriotic Army (RPA). When Mission officers visited the sites of some massacres and interviewed survivors, however, there was no indication of 'cross-fire' or a battle. All evidence indicated that the shooting was from one direction only: the RPA's. Despite several meetings with senior officers, no progress occurred on the issue. HRFOR felt compelled to document the most severe cases and to issue a public report in the face of consistent government resistance and denial. Following the public report, although angry, senior RPA officers agreed that some 'excesses' might have been committed. The chief military prosecutor launched investigations, using information provided by HRFOR, and several military officers were arrested. The prosecutor also asked HRFOR for assistance in training his staff in investigating violations of the Geneva Conventions and in training senior RPA officers in the provisions of the Geneva Conventions and Protocols which the Mission did, in conjunction with the International Committee of the Red Cross. The combination of training and strict oversight that could result in criminal prosecutions led to improved performance by the RPA which in turn meant greater protection for innocent civilians.

Bosnia and Herzegovina: Greater Protection for Civil and Political and Economic, Social and Cultural Rights

The OSCE's Human Rights Department (OSCE/HRD) in Bosnia and Herzegovina has deployed over 40 field officers throughout the country; since the 1995 Dayton Accords, it has focused on both civil and political and economic and social rights. Because the Office of the High Representative (OHR), the senior civilian official in Bosnia and Herzegovina, has the power to remove government officials for malfeasance or non-cooperation, the OSCE/HRD has an unusually strong capacity to enforce compliance with international norms.

Property rights are crucial to the human rights situation in Bosnia-Herzegovina, and an important indicator of the state of human rights is whether an ethnic group can return to an area in which it is a minority. The OSCE/HRD established several programs to encourage and monitor 'minority returns' in the late 1990s and 2000–2003. First, it launched an intensive campaign to inform pre-war occupants of their right to return to their homes, and how to file a claim to repossess their property. By April 2000, 190,000 such claims had been filed.[9] Secondly, the OSCE/HRD

[9] OSCE Human Rights Department, 'Examples of Impact of Human Rights Officers in the Field', April 2000 (on file with the author).

and other groups helped establish "Double Occupancy or Property Commissions," charged with identifying cases where pre-war occupants should receive authorization to repossess their property.

Next, OSCE drafted police guidelines for evictions. It distributed these guidelines to the police, including the International Police Task Force (IPTF) and discussed the human rights components of an eviction from property. The Guidelines were incorporated into training and exercises used by the Bosnian police (in both entities—Republika Serbska and the Bosnian-Croat Federation) and the IPTF. Before these guidelines were developed, police presence at evictions had been rare, resulting in violence, recriminations and failure to enforce judicial orders. Police started to attend evictions regularly to ensure that they are carried out lawfully. The OSCE/HRD now can assess its impact in the property rights area by measuring the effectiveness of the claims procedure, police presence and willingness to enforce eviction orders and the number of people able to return to their pre-war homes, thus providing an important measure to assess its work. Moreover, each of the 42 international Human Rights Officers in the HRD and all its units in Headquarters adopted quarterly work plans to identify priorities, goals and performance measures, especially those related to property issues.

Seemingly mundane, administrative matters can be very important in Bosnia- Herzegovina, and the OSCE/HRD, along with UNHCR, have recognized this and acted. OSCE human rights field officers and UNHCR protection officers noticed that people without ID cards could not receive essential municipal services. So the OSCE/HRD and other international agencies helped create a new Bosnia-Herzegovina ID card that will allow access to services, without specifying the bearer's ethnic identity.

Kosovo: Post-War Protection when Reconciliation Remains a Pipe-Dream

The protection challenges in Kosovo underscore the importance of creating strong working relations across the new multi-dimensional peacekeeping playing field. Human rights is too important to be left to human rights officers alone; protection is now everyone's business.

In Kosovo, the security threat on any given day ranges from rampant common crime, to mortars launched from hills, to new land mines being planted, to increasingly violent organized crime involving the drug trade, trafficking in women and stolen cars, to planned provocations by Serb extremists in northern Mitrovica and cross-border insurgencies with Macedonia and southern Serbia-proper. And all may involve the same perpetrators or people closely linked. NATO's Kosovo Force (KFOR), the UN's international civilian police (CIVPOL), human rights officers from the OSCE, the UN and protection officers from UNHCR and UNICEF all must work together to control these threats.

Close coordination exists on intelligence matters. Most of the violence in Kosovo stems from organized groups. In many cases there is an overlap between the former insurgents and organized crime on the Albanian side and between the former security forces and political hard-liners on the Serbian side. KFOR intelligence services, working with CIVPOL special investigators and INTERPOL, have cracked several criminal enterprises.

A good example of collaboration occurred in November 2000 when, following close surveillance, a joint CIVPOL/KFOR operation broke up a trafficking in women network and prostitution ring in Fushe Kosova/Kosovo Polje. Seven men were arrested, including several believed to be former Kosovo Liberation Army members. Twelve women from Moldova were freed from what amounted to sexual slavery; after giving statements to the local judiciary they were offered the chance to go home.[10] Ironically, the trafficking and prostitution scheme required considerable collaboration between local Albanian and Serbian pimps which shows that inter-ethnic cooperation exists in some matters. The successful raid followed the creation of a specialized CIVPOL unit focusing on trafficking in women and prostitution which have become major problems in Kosovo following the 1999 conflict.

Human rights officers, CIVPOL and KFOR have adopted creative protection strategies for ethnic minorities. Unannounced and random foot patrols and checkpoints keep the perpetrators of violence off-balance. Searching vehicles, especially those without proper registration plates or papers, has yielded many weapons; KFOR and CIVPOL immediately search the residences of people in such vehicles which has yielded even more weapons. KFOR and CIVPOL have opened emergency hot-lines and provided phones for minorities in their enclaves, improving both the reality and the perception of security. Putting in speed bumps in the roads that go near or through minority enclaves or go past the remaining Serbian Orthodox churches and monasteries has helped deter attacks. British KFOR have built new roads by-passing Albanian villages to link Serbian enclaves. Reinforced steel doors for minority-occupied apartments have also helped. And in a few cases, 24-hour/7-days-a-week sentries have guarded the residences of some minorities in Pristina, Podujevo and a few other towns.

The most compelling example of protection in action has been the UN Mission in Kosovo's (UNMIK) Joint Task Force on Minorities. The Joint

[10] Nicholas Wood, "Kosovan sex slave ring is smashed," *The Guardian*, Nov. 18, 2000.

Task Force included in 1999–2000 its joint chairs: OSCE and UNHCR, and representatives from KFOR, CIVPOL, OHCHR, ICRC, UNICEF, UNMIK's Pillar Two (Civil Administration) and the Senior Advisor on Human Rights to the SRSG. The Task Force has published numerous reports on the situation for minorities in Kosovo, each a wealth of detail and revealing an on-going climate of fear, danger and a growing self-segregation for the sake of survival among Kosovo's remaining minorities. It is the most effective example of inter-agency cooperation and protection that I have ever seen in a peacekeeping operation.

For example, OSCE human rights officers and UNHCR protection officers had identified a serious problem in the Zupa Valley northeast of Prizren town in the fall of 1999. Men and women, predominantly Serb, but also including Muslim Slavs, over 65 years-old, were targeted in several villages in the valley. KFOR sent patrols to these villages which were greatly appreciated but not sufficient. The Task Force decided to send me to the area to collect facts about the attacks and report back to it with a proposed plan of action.

I visited several of the villages on October 21, 1999 accompanied by staff from OSCE/Human Rights' Prizren office. We met with several elderly Serbian women who were completely terrified and with good reason. Two of them had recently been severely beaten. One woman's face was still swollen badly and she had black and blue marks on her neck, ten days after the beating. A 96 year-old man was beaten to death in one of the villages on 15 September; his body was found in his house with his hands tied behind his back and a strap tied across his mouth. Everyone we met with begged for more KFOR protection. They feared for their lives. In some cases the alleged perpetrators were arrested, but were later released and were seen again in the area soon after.

We met a German KFOR patrol and the soldiers said they wanted to do more to protect the villagers. So far, they could only patrol and everyone knew that the perpetrators of these crimes and human rights violations only waited for the patrols to leave and they then returned to terrorize, beat, kill and steal. In one village we came upon three men who were stealing bees, hives and honey from beehives; this is not trivial, as honey production is one of the few income-producing activities left in the area. We were able to stop them, get the license plate number of their truck and alert KFOR who came and questioned the men.

Following this visit I wrote a memo to the SRSG explaining the situation and recommended that KFOR place a check-point on the one road leading to and from the villages. The Deputy SRSG for Humanitarian Assistance (Dennis McNamara) also visited the villages within days and delivered a similar recommendation to the SRSG. The Principal Deputy

SRSG then met with KFOR Commander who agreed to allow Turkish KFOR to erect a checkpoint. German KFOR increased their mobile patrols and varied the timing to make them unpredictable. The attacks stopped. This was an example of Task Force action yielding real results which led to increased protection for a population at risk. This is an excellent example of how human rights officers and their military and police counterparts can combine expertise, resources and influence to yield something greater than their individual efforts ever could.

Conclusion

Protecting human rights has evolved enormously since 1948 when Eleanor Roosevelt and her colleagues introduced the Universal Declaration of Human Rights to a new organization, the United Nations in a world still smoldering from the fires and holocaust of World War II and where roughly one-half the world's population lived in colonies with no right to self-determination yet.

Over the next 40 years the UN excelled at creating human rights standards and generated dozens of treaties, conventions and procedures which while essential, had limited impact on protecting people from abuses.

Since 1991, the UN and regional bodies have adopted a more active stance to protect rights and to prevent further violations. Presence on the ground has proven to be an effective protection and preventive tool. Moreover, the growing understanding among humanitarian and development officers of their role in promoting and protecting human rights, combined with increased participation by military peacekeepers and UN international civilian police has had a multiplier effect far beyond what the limited resources of the UN's OHCHR could ever have hoped to accomplish.

Yet the horrendous abuses in Darfur, eastern Congo, Colombia, Sri Lanka and Nepal, to name just a few, remind us that while the advances have been real and substantial, no one should relax. The human rights field officers and their allies in other disciplines must constantly improve their strategies and tactics while solidifying their alliances because the human rights abusers have not surrendered.

CHAPTER NINE

THE PROTECTION METHODS OF HUMAN RIGHTS FIELD OFFICES

Bertrand G. Ramcharan

Introduction

Human rights field offices are on the cutting edge of human rights protection. They are a significant new addition to the armoury of international protection—as William O'Neill has demonstrated in the preceding chapter. Protection, however, is a difficult and challenging business. How is it done in practice? What are the good practices that can be identified in the operations of the field offices to date? There is little in the literature on this issue of methods of protection. That will be the subject of this chapter.

Fortunately, there is public documentation that gives a good window into the methods of protection in use by some of the human rights field offices. Of particular significance in this regard are the reports submitted on their operations to the Commission on Human Rights and reports of the Secretary-General to the Security Council. In 2004, for example, reports were submitted to the Commission on Human Rights on the operations of field offices of the Office of High Commissioner in Cambodia and Colombia and on the operations of human rights sections of United Nations peace operations in Timor Leste and Sierra Leone. The coverage of these reports gives a reasonable idea of the protection role and methods of these four operations. It is instructive to look at this coverage.

I. *Range of Activities of Human Rights Field Offices*

A. *Cambodia*

The report on the OHCHR field office in Cambodia provides information on general objectives, the protection of human rights through monitoring, investigation and reporting; election-related activities; the issue of impunity; land rights; human rights in development, including economic, social and cultural rights; the rule of law framework; the activities of a

Bertrand G. Ramcharan (Ed.), Human Rights Protection in the Field, 141–151.

regional office in Battambang; treaty reporting obligations and implementation of recommendations made by treaty monitoring bodies; educational, technical assistance and public information programmes; assistance to the Special Representative of the Secretary-General on human rights in Cambodia; and cooperation and coordination with the United Nations system, donors and the diplomatic community. As will be seen later in this chapter, the protection-related activities are quite substantial.

The report on the activities of the OHCHR field office in Colombia covers the national context and dynamics of the internal armed conflict; state policies and follow-up of international recommendations; breaches of international humanitarian law by armed actors; the human rights situation; the situation of particularly vulnerable groups; and has various annexes, one of them giving 'Representative Cases of human rights violations and breaches of international humanitarian law'. Without a doubt, it is a major protection document in and of itself, for Colombians.

B. *Sierra Leone*

The report on Sierra Leone covers the human rights situation in Sierra Leone and the Human Rights Activities of the United Nations in Sierra Leone. As far as the UNAMSIL Human Rights Section is concerned, it provides information on its activities in the districts, monitoring of the courts, police stations and prisons. It also provides information on issues of training; capacity-building, technical cooperation and advocacy; the national human rights commission and the Office of the Ombudsman; the Truth and Reconciliation Commission; and the Special Court. Significant protection activities by the UNAMSIL Human Rights Section are related, as will be seen later in this chapter.

C. *Timor Leste*

The report on Timor Leste covers the justice system, prisons, the national police, the defence forces, the ombudsman, accession to international human rights instruments, the Commission for Reception, Truth and Reconciliation, the investigation and prosecutions of serious crimes, the Ad Hoc Human Rights Tribunal, women, children, refugees and illegal immigrants, and separated Timorese children. The investigation and prosecutions of serious crimes is particularly instructive.

The documentation on these four situations is ample. There is additional information available on other field offices of OHCHR in the Annual Appeals for voluntary contributions issued by the Office of High Commissioner for Human Rights. These provide information, for example on OHCHR field offices that have operated in Angola, Bosnia and Herzegovina, Burundi, Democratic Republic of the Congo and Palestine. Reports submitted by the Secretary-General to the Security Council have provided information on the human rights sections of other UN peace operations, for example in Burundi, Cote d'Ivoire.

Based on the information available, it is possible to offer a presentation of the methods of protection being applied by human rights field offices. We shall employ a framework of analysis we have advanced elsewhere, namely preventive protection, mitigatory protection, and remedial or justice-related protection.

II. *Preventive Protection*

In the nature of things, human rights field offices are usually established in the aftermath of conflict or of gross violations of human rights and are therefore mostly involved in containment or remedial mode. At the same time, prevention must be on their radar screen, particularly where there is a threat to specific population groups. The land project of the OHCHR Cambodia Office would seem to fall into this category.

A. *Prevention in Colombia*

The report on Colombia submitted to the Commission on Human Rights in 2004 discussed the situation of particularly vulnerable groups including human rights defenders, ethnic groups, women, children, journalists, communities at risk, and other vulnerable groups. The report contained specific recommendations by the High Commissioner for "prevention and protection", including the following:

"105. The High Commissioner encourages the Government to strengthen coordination between the Early Warning System (SAT), established in the Office of the Ombudsman, and the Inter-Institutional Early-Warning Committee (CIAT), following up on the actions taken by authorities in areas identified by risk reports. The Committee ought also to include the Office of the Ombudsman, the Social Solidarity Network and the Ministry of Justice and the Interior's Programme for protection of human rights defenders

"106. The High Commissioner encourages the Government to ensure that the programmes for the protection of human rights defenders and other groups, for which the Ministry of the Interior's Human Rights Department is responsible, operate with the necessary coverage and effectiveness. The Ministry, together with other State institutions, ought to search for new mechanisms aimed at reducing risk factors and at acting preventively against them.

"107. The High Commissioner encourages the Social Solidarity Network, together with other government and State institutions. to put into practice, as soon as possible, preventive and protective actions and programmes that have been agreed upon with the communities at risk. With respect to displacement, the United Nations Guiding Principles should be strictly applied.

"108. The High Commissioner exhorts the Government and Congress to ensure inclusion in the national budget of funds required to provide the Procurator General's Office and the Office of the Ombudsman with the necessary means to establish themselves in localities in which they are currently absent, especially in areas with a high proportion of indigenous, Afro-Colombian and displaced persons. The High Commissioner also recommends that the Procurator General's Office and the Office of the Ombudsman comprehensively include Municipal Ombudsmen in their activities and programmes related to human rights protection and promotion.

"109. The High Commissioner encourages the Procurator General to carry out, during the first semester of 2004, the pending review of military intelligence records concerning human rights defenders and organizations. This review ought to be carried out at least once a year.

"110. The High Commissioner recommends the State Procurator's institutions (Ministerio Publico) and senior officials to comply with their duty to take disciplinary action against any State employees who through their declarations, actions or omissions in any way discredit or jeopardize the work of human rights defenders.

"111. The High Commissioner encourages the Minister of Defence to develop, on the basis of the results of an independent study, in a comprehensive, systematic and operational way, the training in human rights and international humanitarian law of all members of the security forces."

The emphasis on prevention in these recommendations is striking. The Colombia Office of the Office of High Commissioner for Human Rights is a veritable laboratory in the quest for human rights protection and, as the High Commissioner at the time, I was proud to advance these preventive recommendations.

B. *The Land Project of the OHCHR Cambodia Office*

According to the report submitted to the Commission on Human Rights in 2004, the OHCHR Office in Cambodia continued its study of large-scale agricultural plantations. The OHCHR study had sought to identify the extent to which land concessions had contributed to the development and economic and social well-being of the Cambodian people as a whole, specifically in terms of their contributions to overall State revenue and to the livelihood of affected local communities including both land concessions and rubber plantations operated by the State, to identify their effect on the human rights of people living within or close to their boundaries. The OHCHR Office researched, reported, analysed and monitored the situation of the human rights of local populations. It conducted field work in selected areas and investigated and documented the situation of human rights in four land concessions in Phnom Srouch district, Kompong Speu province, owned by several companies, one land concession in Kompong Chhnang province (Pheapimex) and in the Tumring rubber plantation.

Fieldwork had been conducted thus far in nine land concessions and one rubber plantation. Detailed research had been undertaken in three of these locations, including semi-structured qualitative interviews with local populations, activists, authorities and concession company representatives. OHCHR staff had also conducted open interviews with non-governmental organizations at national and provincial levels, and met regularly during the course of the study with those involved in land policy and administration in Cambodia, including relevant government officials at both national and provincial levels, civil society and international agencies.

The Office had collected data about existing concessions, and assessed compliance by concessionaires with both the Land Law of 2001 and the terms of the concession contracts. The Office had also sought to contribute to the process of drafting sub-decrees essential to implement the Land Law, most specifically the sub-decrees on the procedures for granting land concessions for economic purposes, and on the reduction and specific exemptions of land concessions exceeding 10,000 hectares.

In undertaking its study, OHCHR staff had experienced considerable difficulty in obtaining information relating to land concessions although this information concerned matters of significant public interest that should be in the public domain (such as the process for granting new land concessions, fees, contracts, shareholders, payment of deposit, fees and maps). Even where the Office was able to obtain access to the contracts, individual shareholders of relevant companies could not be identified. The difficulties in accessing this information had "highlighted the urgency for more open administrative practices and policies to enable informed debate about land in Cambodia and better decision-making in the administration of land the development of policy." There was "also a need for a consultative process with local populations and a regulatory environment effective in monitoring the activities of the companies and ensuring compliance with the law and the terms of the contracts."

The long range preventive significance of this kind of activity in Cambodia is inestimable.

C. *The Anti-Trafficking Activities of the OHCHR Officer in Bosnia and Herzegovina*

The OHCHR Office in Bosnia and Herzegovina has its antecedents in the conflict that took place in that country in the 1990s. It began life to support the activities of the then Special Rapporteur on human rights in the Former Yugoslavia. As it evolved, the Office came to take on a lead role in combating trafficking and prostitution in the Balkans.

The Office, and especially its current Chief, Madeleine Rees, courageously denounced the engagement of members of the United Nations police contingent in Bosnia in consorting with trafficked women and prostitutes. The role of the office helped bring the spotlight on a problem that was assuming large proportions among United Nations peacekeepers.

The Bosnia Office also engaged in a concerted campaign to denounce trafficking in young women in Bosnia and Herzegovina and in the Balkans at large. It collaborated in a study on Trafficking in South-Eastern Europe and has undertaken follow-up action subsequently. These anti-trafficking activities undoubtedly will have long-range preventive effect and rank among the significant prevention efforts of human rights field offices.

III. *Mitigatory Protection*

There is a great deal of mitigatory protection activities to be found in the operations of human rights field offices, as the following examples will demonstrate.

A. *Crisis Response*

The Regional Representatives of the Office of High Commissioner for Human Rights have only recently begun to function and are not strictly speaking human rights field offices of the kind being discussed in this book. But in the area of crisis prevention and response they can and do play an important role. The Regional Representative for Asia-Pacific, for example, in a note on activities during the period January 2002 to December 2003, reported the following:

> The Regional Representative has made interventions with authorities on individual cases or patterns of violations in Nepal, Thailand, and Pakistan. The work on countries in conflict—Nepal and Indonesia (Aceh)—has been firmly aimed at the protection of civilians and other non-combatants. The office also refers people to appropriate mechanisms in individual countries, such as national human rights commissions, and to UN special procedures. An important part of the Office's work is to alert Geneva to serious cases or patterns of violations of human rights and human rights crises, provide analysis of the situation, if necessary by carrying out a mission and making recommendations for interventions, including by special procedures. In such situations we also contact and work with the Resident Coordinator to encourage appropriate UN Country Team action (e.g. in Laos, Indonesia, Nepal, Malaysia). We provide whatever advice and support is possible before and after special procedures visit the region, especially those in 2002–2003 to Myanmar and Thailand. We have developed a table to track planned and completed visits to the regions by special procedures.[1]

B. *Monitoring, Investigation and Reporting*

OHCHR/Cambodia continued to monitor the human rights situation throughout the country, to investigate reports involving serious violations of human rights and document patterns of such violations. It regularly brought its concerns to the attention of local and national government authorities, and proposed means of redress. The Office also remained in regular communication with the judiciary, non-governmental organizations and the international community on these issues.

During the reporting period, the Office gave particular attention to investigating human rights violations in the context of the National Assembly elections of July, 2003. In particular, it investigated a number of murders of persons affiliated with political parties. It also monitored restrictions on freedoms of assembly and association in the post-election period, and other reports of serious human rights violations.

OHCHR Cambodia continued to receive complaints from the public about human rights violations, and took up serious cases, including cases of violence and intimidation of political activists: land disputes and land grabbing: torture and cruel, inhuman or degrading treatment in places of detention: and serious breaches of criminal process guarantees. Staff also followed the progress of cases involving those charged with offences relating

[1] OHCHR Regional Representative for Asia-Pacific. Principal Initiatives and Resources: January 2002–December 2003, pp. 2–3.

to the anti-Thai riots of 29 January 2003 who were eventually tried in September, 2003. The Office followed up on previous work on street retribution (mob killings) and prison conditions, continued to investigate unresolved cases and assisted human rights non-governmental organizations in the effective commission of their work. It also assisted human rights defenders facing threats to their safety.

The Office also investigated and documented disputes over land and other natural resources. They often involved disputes between local populations or fishermen and those with political and economic influence, including military officers and business interests. Detailed study of these cases had helped to document and raise recurring problems both in the management of natural resources and the mechanisms for dealing with land disputes and related violations of human rights.

With the guidance and support of OHCHR, the UNAMSIL Human Rights Section continued to implement its mandate through monitoring and reporting on the situation in police stations and prisons, the functioning of the judicial system and the state of national human rights institutions, documenting war-related violations; and organizing training and capacity-building activities for members of the judiciary, law enforcement officials, local human rights non-governmental organizations and civil society organizations.

During the reporting period, the UNAMSIL Human Rights Section stepped up its prison monitoring activities, extending them to all provincial penitentiary facilities. Eight human rights officers assisted by a number of national staff have been deployed in 8 districts where they monitor and report on the developments in conditions throughout the 12 districts of Sierra Leone.

Reports from the field offices in Sierra Leone, particularly in the first half of the year, contained recurrent themes with regard to detention facilities, prisons and police outposts throughout Sierra Leone. These included: overcrowding, prolonged detention without trial, escapes, deplorable detention conditions and understaffing. Lactating mothers were often detained with their babies under living conditions that might threaten the health of both mother and baby. A constant feature in all detention centres was the persistent practice of locking up juveniles with convicted adult criminals or adults accused of serious criminal offences.

C. *Field Missions*

During 2003, 168 field missions were carried out in Colombia and 44 complaints were received, of which 936 were admitted. Field missions and the permanent presence in the branch offices in Cali and Medellin, enabled the office in Colombia to follow up on the regional and local situation as well as to provide advice to the authorities and institutions of civil society in the field of human rights and international humanitarian law while accompanying local processes undertaken in the areas included in the mandate. In order to facilitate this work, the office planned to open a new branch office in Bucaramanga.

Additionally, although it was difficult to measure their impact, field missions fulfilled the purpose of promoting preventive and protective measures for the communities. These visits, carried out mostly with the Colombian authorities, are made to zones in which the presence of the State has been traditionally weak or non-existent.

D. *Regional Sub-Office*

The report on the Cambodia Office provided a good indication of the contribution of a regional office. The regional office in Battambang, Cambodia, covers the provinces of Battambang, Banteay, Meanchey and Oddar Meanchey, as well as the municipality of Pailin, working under the supervision of the Phnom Penh office. During the reporting period, staff monitored and investigated complaints of violations of human rights related to the elections, making regular interventions with local and provincial authorities. The work was undertaken in close cooperation with non-governmental organizations. The office remained in regular contact with provincial authorities, such as the courts, police and military, throughout the reporting period.

The Office investigated sensitive cases involving alleged violations in isolated areas which local human rights groups had difficulties in accessing, and in areas with systemic or widespread breaches of human rights. They also carried out routine monitoring in districts still dealing with the transition from military to civilian rule, linking this work with education and training efforts.

The Office also investigated and joined efforts to resolve disputes involving conflicts over natural resources, such as a long-standing land dispute in Koh Kralor district, and a conflict involving the Prek Chas fishing community, whose representatives faced imprisonment and fines after confiscating illegal fishing equipment from a local merchant. The case was taken to the court of appeal. During the reporting period, staff conducted several one-day training courses in economic, social and cultural rights for villagers and the local authorities, particularly in those districts affected by land disputes.

IV. *Remedial and Justice-Related Protection*

Human Rights field offices can be seen pushing for remedies and for justice for the victims of gross violations of human rights as will be seen in the examples below.

A. *Investigation and Prosecution of Serious Crimes*

The Serious Crimes Unit (SCU) was established in Timor Leste in 2000 and is responsible for the investigation and prosecution of all serious crimes (including genocide, war crimes, crimes against humanity, murder, sexual offences and torture) that took place in Timor Leste between 1 January and 25 October 1999. Early in its existence it was decided to concentrate resources initially on the prosecution of 10 priority cases relating to the specific incidents and 5 cases that showed a widespread pattern of serious crimes.

As at the time of writing, 79 indictments had been filed, including indictments relating to the 10 priority cases. Some 367 individuals had been charged, with 308 suspects alleged to have committed crimes against humanity, including murder, sexual offences, torture, inhumane acts, persecution, deportation and unlawful imprisonment. In July 2003, the Acting Deputy Prosecutor-General filed the Maliana indictment charging 57 people with crimes against humanity, including murder, torture and persecution. This indictment related to the *Tentara Nasional Indonesia* (TNI) (Indonesian National Army) and militia attack on the Maliana Police Station, in which at least 13 people were murdered; 13 others who fled the attack were tracked down and murdered the following day. Members of TNI, Indonesian police and militia groups are among those charged in this indictment.

The Special Panels for Serious Crimes of the District Court of Dili, composed of international and Timorese judges, had convicted 38 accused persons. There were more than 50 accused persons part-way through or awaiting trial in Timor Leste. A number of interlocutory and final decisions had been appealed in the Court of Appeal, although five appeals from 2001—four from the prosecution and one from the defence—remained pending.

B. *Battling Impunity*

The OHCHR Office in Cambodia started a project in November, 2003 to review and follow up on human rights violations that were the subject of action by the United Nations Transitional Authority in Cambodia in 1992 and 1993, as well as by the Office of the Special Representatives during the subsequent decade. On the basis of this review and an analysis of relevant political and legal developments, a report containing recommendations was being prepared. The Office planned to develop a long-term strategy on how to effectively address impunity.

Conclusion

This chapter has shown that human rights field offices are a new pillar of protection and are taking the human rights endeavour to new vistas. There is a rich experience of methods of prevention, mitigation, and remedies/justice. In the view of the author of one of the chapters of this volume, a new profession is emerging: the human rights field officer, a courageous crusader for human rights protection.

CHAPTER TEN

THE HUMAN RIGHTS COMPONENTS OF UN PEACEKEEPING AND PEACEBUILDING OPERATIONS, AND THE FIELD OFFICES OF UNDP AND THE OFFICE OF HIGH COMMISSIONER FOR HUMAN RIGHTS

OHCHR Staff

Editor's introduction

In order to give an idea of the experiments underway for the protection of human rights in the field we include below the gist of the principal human rights components of UN Peacekeeping Operations and of the Office of the High Commissioner for Human Rights. The information is compiled from materials obtained from the website of the Office of High Commissioner, with slight editing in places.

I. *Abkhazia (Georgia) (OHCHR/OSCE)*

Terms of Reference/Legal Authority

The Human Rights Office in Abkhazia, Georgia (HROAG) was established on 10 December 1996 following Security Council Resolution 1077 (1996) of 22 October 1996. As mandated by that resolution, the Office is jointly staffed by OHCHR and the OSCE, in accordance with a Memorandum of Understanding signed between the two organizations on 29 April 1997. The Human Rights Office forms part of the DPKO United Nations Observer Mission in Georgia (UNOMIG), under the authority of the Head of Mission of UNOMIG.

Functions/Mandate

HROAG's mandate was approved by the UN Security Council and spelled out in the Programme for the Protection and Promotion of Human Rights in Abkhazia (Annex 1 to the Secretary-General's report to the Security Council regarding the situation in Abkhazia, Georgia dated 15 April 1999, S/1996/284).

Bertrand G. Ramcharan (Ed.), Human Rights Protection in the Field, 153–210.

The mandate of the Human Rights Office is to monitor the human rights situation in Abkhazia and to protect the human rights of the population of Abkhazia, Georgia, in the spirit of the Universal Declaration of Human Rights, to promote the respect for human rights and to contribute to a safe and dignified return of refugees and internally displaced persons, to establish direct contacts in Abkhazia so as to improve the human rights situation and to report on human rights developments.

Main Activities

HROAG carries out monitoring of human rights in order to help strengthen the rule of law in Abkhazia, Georgia, and to support the return of internally displaced persons under safe and dignified conditions. Monitoring done by the Office includes collection of first-hand information directly from witnesses and other reliable sources, analysis of the development of the legal system, and key institutions for the protection and promotion of human rights.

In addition, monitoring of the human rights situation is carried out through HROAG's office in mid-town Sukhumi and by regular visits of HROAG staff throughout Abkhazia, Georgia and in particular to the Gali district adjacent to the cease-fire line. The Office addresses the relevant authorities in order to redress the violations, whenever appropriate.

Donations of HR publications are made to libraries through Abkhazia, Georgia, as is distribution of publications identified for HR depository libraries.

Regular meetings are held with the Georgian authorities in Tbilisi as well as with the Abkhaz *de facto* authorities related to the human rights situation.

The work of the Office included the implementation of the OHCHR Technical Co-operation Project, which was completed in February 2002. Activities planned under the project included the translation of the International Bill of Human Rights into the Abkhaz language; training courses on UN human rights teaching in higher education; establishment of two human rights depository libraries; training courses on teaching in the area of administration of justice; training courses on human rights and capacity development for NGOs mass media; scholarships for officials, educators, NGO and mass media representatives for further in-depth study of human right.

Recent Activities

Since one of the major objectives of HROAG is to contribute to a safe and dignified return of internally displaced persons and refugees through improvement of the human rights situation in the Gali district, HROAG has increased its activities in that district. Thus, HROAG actively worked from Sukhumi to address the needs for human rights protection of the Gali population and support local NGOs by carrying out regular visits on a weekly basis. In operative paragraph 18 of its res. 1554 (2004) adopted on 29 July 2004, the Security Council "call[ed] again upon the Abkhaz side to agree to the opening as soon as possible of the Gali branch of the human rights office in Sukhumi and to provide security conditions for its unhindered functioning".

Ongoing and upcoming programmes include the following:

- Human rights training programme for the local law enforcement agencies offered for implementation in the Sukhumi militia school;
- Legal advisory services to the local population and monitors court trials and pretrial detention facilities;
- Human rights awareness and capacity-building through the implementation of the OHCHR Assisting Communities Together programme aimed at the nongovernmental sector;
- Facilitation of a number of projects sponsored by other international donors and governments;
- Human rights training for school children;
- Broadcast of television programmes on human rights;
- Management training for local NGOs dealing with human rights;
- Production of a puppet theatre show based on Abkhaz legends, with human rights elements incorporated, targeting children.

II. *Human Rights Field Presence in Afghanistan (UNAMA) (DPKO)*

Terms of Reference

Under the terms of the Bonn Agreement, the United Nations is charged with responsibility for human rights investigation, advice, education and institution building. The Bonn Agreement, signed by the parties on 5 December 2001 and endorsed by Security Council resolution 1383 of 6 December 2001, acknowledges the centrality of human rights and calls upon the United Nations to assist Afghanistan in the advancement of human rights promotion and protection. The Agreement contains several explicit references to human rights, and calls for assistance and support from the United Nations and the international community.

Human rights is central to the purposes and functions of the mission. Under the terms of the Bonn Agreement, the United Nations is responsible for assisting with the establishment of an independent human rights commission, investigating human rights violations, recommending corrective action, and implementing a programme of human rights education. The mission was also be expected to fully integrate human rights into its humanitarian, reconstruction and political activities, to assist in the building of sustainable domestic institutions of human rights and the rule of law, and to provide technical and advisory support to transitional justice initiatives.

Mandate and Functions

UNAMA has sought to integrate a crosscutting capacity for human rights. Unlike in previous operations, where human rights capacities were concentrated in a single part of the mission, UNAMA adopted an approach designed to bring the full range of mission assets to bear on the human rights mandate. Thus, a human rights component, as such, was not be established. Rather, a Senior Human Rights Adviser in the Office of the SRSG, with dedicated resources and full-time human rights staff, works with relevant staff located in the mission's main operational pillars. The Adviser has terms of reference to advise the SRSG and to coordinate all relevant mission activities, including monitoring, investigations and community liaison carried out under Pillar One, and human rights education, institution building, and humanitarian protection activities carried out under Pillar Two. Designated staff in both pillars regularly report on human rights developments to the Advisor, who is responsible for the consolidation and analysis of that information, and for recommending appropriate action to the SRSG. The Senior Human Rights Adviser also reports to the High Commissioner for Human Rights.

The Adviser and the human rights unit also serve as the principal contact point for the independent human rights commission, and works with the Office of the High Commissioner for Human Rights in managing the joint UNAMA/OHCHR technical cooperation project in support to the two-year work programme of the Human Rights Commission.

III. *Human Rights Field Presence in Angola (UNCT)*

Terms of Reference and Legal Authority

The United Nations human rights presence in Angola developed through a number of phases. The first phase was the attachment of a small contingent of international human rights officers to the United Nations Verification Mission in Angola (UNAVEM II) in 1996, which was expanded in 1997 as UNAVEM III and then became the United Nations Observer Mission in Angola (MONUA) that included a Human Rights Division (HRD).

While the peace process unraveled towards the end of 1998, the HRD began to work with a view to strengthening the capacity of the government and the civil society to promote respect for human rights. MONUA's mandate ended on 26 February 1999. At the request of the Angolan Government, the United Nations Security Council, in an unprecedented resolution (No. 1229 of February 1999), directed the HRD to continue its activities during MONUA's liquidation period. Thus, the HRD focussed on some essential components of a peace-building process such as strengthening government/state human rights institutions and raising awareness of human rights standards.

On 4 April 2002, taking into account the developments after the death of Mr. Jonas Savimbi, leader of UNITA, in February 2002, as well as the commitment of both the Government and UNITA to implement the Lusaka Protocol, the Security Council adopted resolution 1433 authorizing the establishment, as a follow-on mission to UNOA, of the United Nations Mission in Angola (UNMA) for an initial period of 6 months until 15 February 2003. According to the resolution, the mandate of UNMA included, inter alia, providing assistance to the Government of Angola in "the protection and promotion of Human Rights and in the building of institutions to consolidate peace and enhance the rule of law". The Security Council also approved the deployment of 16 additional International Human Rights Officers, including 6 UN Volunteers.

After the withdrawal of UNMA in mid-February 2003, the HRD has been integrated into the Technical Unit established under the supervision of the Resident/Humanitarian Coordinator, to implement the residual tasks of the UNMA, including human rights. The HR section of the Technical Unit reports to the High Commissioner for Human Rights who guides its substantive human rights work, through the Resident/Humanitarian Coordinator.

Mandate and Objectives

In the line of the SG's report to the Security Council (S/2002/834) and its mandate in operative paragraph 3, section B of resolution 1433 (2002), the continued role of the Division consists in the protection and promotion of human rights; in the building of institutions to consolidate peace and enhance the rule of law and democracy; and in child-protection. It calls for the nationwide support for the exercise of rights, the promotion of not only knowledge of rights but training in how to use the law to protect, as well as the establishment of mechanisms of protection and reconciliation wherever necessary.

Main Activities

The Human Rights Division:

- Assists the National Assembly and other relevant institutions to carry out constitutional and legal reforms in conformity with international human rights standards.
- Provides training to members of the justice system in data collection, planning and monitoring to reinforce institutional capacity.
- Provides training to civil society organisations and networks to strengthen their capacity to protect human rights.
- Supports the creation of para-legal associations at the community level and helps to link these associations to protection networks within civil society.
- Facilitates the creation of national human rights institutions in accordance with the Paris Principles.
- Established a Forum on Peace and Human Rights to facilitate dialogue between key individual actors on peace and a culture of human rights.
- Conducts media campaigns related to civil society participation and protection mechanisms.
- Continues the FAA training programme and expands activities to include the Angolan National Moral and Civic Education Police.
- Conducts quantitative and qualitative human rights surveys on citizen perceptions of human rights and the justice system in Angola, as a follow-up to similar surveys conducted in 2000.
- Assists the Government of Angola in the development of a National Human Rights Action Plan.

IV. *Human Rights Field Presence in Bosnia and Herzegovina (OHCHR)*

Terms of Reference

The context in which OHCHR operates in Bosnia and Herzegovina (BiH) is unique. It is a country which has undergone a devastating conflict with appalling violations of human rights and humanitarian law; it is a country in transition from an ostensibly socialist to a capitalist economy and it is still an emerging state with ethnic tensions and a powerful influence of organized crime and corruption, in part left over from the war period.

The framework that has been created is, in theory, comprehensive: the Dayton Peace Agreement (DPA) ensured that the highest level of internationally recognized human rights protections would apply by, inter alia, making the European Convention for Human Rights and Fundamental Freedoms directly applicable. In addition the DPA gave mandates to a wide range of international agencies to assist in the realization of its terms, creating the Office of the High Representative to oversee its implementation.

The role of OHCHR in BiH is to bring expertise commensurate with the changing needs of the country—to serve as catalyst in respect of the promotion and protection of human rights and the rule of law, with a particular focus on those aspects not directly addressed through the mandates of others—and to ensure human rights promotion and protection becomes nationally sustainable. To achieve this, the Office utilizes the following approach:

To identify the situation on the ground in critical human rights areas of concern; To analyze the legislative and policy framework relating to the issue in light of relevant human rights standards; To work toward human rights compliance, including legislative and policy reform, and implementation.

Therefore, OHCHR serves as a catalyst for the international community to incorporate international human rights protections, with a particular emphasis on ensuring a gender analysis and non-discrimination. To ensure the sustainability in the promotion and protection of rights, the Office works with the government and the NGO community, thus moving towards the stage where human rights protection is advocated at the national level by government and civil society.

OHCHR has operated in Bosnia and Herzegovina on the basis of Annex 6 of the General Framework Agreement for Peace, where the Parties invited the OHCHR to closely monitor the situation of human rights in BiH and committed themselves to providing full and effective facilitation, assistance and access in the conduct of OHCHR's duties.

Mandate/Functions & Main Activities

OHCHR is reorienting its activities in South-Eastern Europe from predominantly country-specific programs towards five issues of region-wide concern, namely: trafficking/smuggling/organized crime; impunity, including missing persons; refugees/IDP and vulnerable categories of migrants; human rights education and promotion; and rights-based approaches to development. This will result in OHCHR field offices in BiH an the Federal Republic of Yugoslavia taking a common and unified approach to issues, based on expertise developed through its long-term presence in former Yugoslavia.

The regional approach will subsume the priorities on which OHCHR BiH continues to focus: (1) gender mainstreaming, (2) economic and social rights, (3) protection of minorities and vulnerable groups, and (4) human rights assessments at the municipal level, cross-cutting all priorities of the Office. Further, OHCHR services the Special Representative of the Commission on Human Rights in carrying out his mandate.

Gender

Through the provision of technical expertise, OHCHR has prioritized increasingly the Government's capacity to integrate a gender perspective into its policy development and legislative reform process. Further, the Office collaborates with national civil society to develop its expertise in utilizing international laws and standards in protecting and promoting women's rights.

To combat trafficking comprehensively, OHCHR addresses its causes and consequences, emphasizing the rights of the victim, State responsibility, and appropriate law enforcement. Efforts to ensure coordination and collaboration have sought an integrated approach incorporating prevention, law reform, gender, social and economic rights, migration issues, and the rule of law.

On a regional level, OHCHR BiH is part of the expert coordination group of the Stability Pact Task Force, coordinating responses in South-Eastern Europe. In June 2002 OHCHR, together with UNICEF and OSCE/ODIHR, released an extensive report on trafficking in human beings in South-Eastern Europe. The Office is using the OHCHR Human Rights Principles and Guidelines on Human Trafficking as the basis for implementing a regional program on trafficking.

Social and Economic Rights

OHCHR has been at the forefront in integrating human rights and non-discrimination into social and economic reform processes, in particular, labour, health and social protections.

OHCHR has been working with the Government and civil society on the Poverty Reduction Strategy processes to ensure human rights are integrated. The office is focusing on the process, emphasizing broad participation and identifying gaps in human rights protection. Further, OHCHR provides guidance on the strategy to sectors of society previously excluded from the process, such as trade unions, women's organizations, families of the missing, and children.

Discrimination and Protection of Minorities

In addressing the protracted situation of refugees and internally displaced persons, OHCHR focuses on sustainable solutions that emphasize genuine choices in decisions to return or locally integrate. In so doing, the Office underlines the absolute necessity to protect and promote all human rights for all displaced persons regardless of their status.

As BiH overhauls its migration framework, OHCHR is providing expertise on human rights standards applicable to aliens within the country. This assistance targets protection of vulnerable categories of aliens, such as torture victims, the stateless, smuggled migrants, and victims of trafficking in persons, as well adherence to other treaty obligations. In addition, the Office has been working to ensure that measures to combat terrorism are compatible with human rights standards and the rule of law.

Human Rights at the Municipal Level

Through a joint program with the UN Develop Programme, the Office is implementing the Rights-based Municipal Assessment Programme (RMAP) to comprehensively assess protection of all human rights at the municipal level. Through rights-based assessments, the RMAP provides reports including analyses, baselines, and indicators specifically relevant to the municipality, against which progress can be measured and targeted programming designed and implemented.

V. *Human Rights Field Presence in Burundi (OHCHR)*

Terms of Reference/Legal Authority

Since their inception in 1994, technical cooperation activities have been the object of successive agreements signed between the OHCHR and the Government of Burundi respectively in 1995, 1996, and 1997.

Following a statement by the Chairman of the Security Council in March 1995 and the 1995/90 resolution of the Commission on Human Rights, emphasizing the need to take preventive action through the presence of human rights experts and observers throughout Burundi, the High Commissioner decided to carry out a visit to the country. In April 1995 there was an exchange of letters between the High Commissioner and the Government of Burundi, which was followed by an agreement of co-operation signed in November 1995. Within the framework of the a Mission of Observation was established in Burundi.

Functions and Mandate

The outcome of the Arusha peace process, the prospects for a real cease-fire, and the capacity of the country to address long-lasting unsolved issues were elements taken into account in the identification of OHCHR's priorities in Burundi. The 10 year old conflict in Burundi has shown deep divisions and gaps in the national community. In this context, OHCHR Burundi plays an important balancing role. Its independence, expertise and neutrality make it a reliable and a trustworthy partner for the government, the civil society and the UN agencies. In 2002, two consecutive evaluation missions were conducted by the Department for International Development (DFID) and OHCHR. Civil society, government and donors representatives as well as the beneficiaries, made recommendations requesting the continuation and the strengthening of the activities and the assistance provided by OHCHR Burundi. The Office is trying to provide an appropriate response to these recommendations, subject to the availability of human and financial resources.

Achievements of OHCHR in Burundi include: In the area of protection—release of illegally detained persons; shortening of pre-trial detention periods; reinforced national capacities for investigation and follow-up of human rights violations. In the area of administration of justice—decrease of the occurrence of arbitrary arrest and lengthy periods of detention without trial; legal assistance to more than 2000 detainees and plaintiffs with regard to the 1993 events: In the area of human rights promotion—establishment of a human rights culture in Burundi; establishment of network of human rights associations; human rights training of magistrates, lawyers, members of the armed and security forces; women leaders and youth.

Main Activities

A. *Technical Co-operation*

Technical cooperation activities focuses on:

- Strengthening the judiciary system in Burundi
- Contributing to the revision of internal laws with a view to harmonizing their provisions with international instruments on human rights
- Training the military, the police and the gendarmerie in the field of human rights
- Building capacity and supporting human rights organizations, civil society, and in particular to national media and NGOs
- Providing training and education sessions

- Promoting human rights culture and providing documentation on human rights

B. *Mission of Observation*
The main activities under this component are:

- Investigation of allegations of serious human rights violations, including the right to life, enforced or involuntary disappearances and illegal arrests, arbitrary detention coupled with torture and other inhuman and degrading treatments.
- Collection of testimonies in the field from local and provincial civil and military authorities regarding violations of human rights.
- Visits to the main detention centres of the country, with a focus on individual and private interviews, and regular assessment of detention conditions.
- Judicial assistance to the detainees in order to speed up the judicial process.
- Field visits to regroupment camps, visits of injured victims of human rights violations in hospitals.
- Monitoring of compliance with the provisions of Human rights treaties signed by Burundi.
- Pursuing of a dialogue with the Government authorities and monitoring of the protection process, including the Government's responsibility in ensuring long term improvements through the high level inter-ministerial committee, recently renamed National Commission on Human Rights.
- Reports (weekly and monthly).

C. *Legal Assistance Programme*
The main activities under the Legal Assistance programme are:

- Provision of lawyers working as consultants with a view to providing legal assistance to those accused of criminal responsibility for acts committed in the aftermath of former President Ndadaye's assassination and of assisting related civilian parties and families of victims.
- Confidence-building with regard to the judiciary.
- Indirect contribution to the reduction of the number of death sentences or in the speeding up of the judiciary process for pity criminals and those proved innocent.

D. *Promotion of Human Rights*
The main activities are the provision of support to community based organizations through the OHCHR ACT program as parts of OHCHR efforts to reinforce the local NGOs, civil society, the media on human rights.

E. *Other*
OHCHRB actively contributes to the preparation and venue of the missions of the Special Rapporteur on the situation of human rights in Burundi, while providing pertinent information on a regular basis.

VI. *Human Rights Field Presence in Cambodia (OHCHR)*

Mandate and Functions

The Cambodia office was established as an operational presence in Cambodia in October 1993 at the end of the United Nations Transitional Authority in Cambodia. Its mandate and that of the Special Representative of the Secretary-General for human rights in Cambodia are set down in Commission on Human Rights Resolution 1993/6, and elaborated upon in subsequent Commission and General Assembly resolutions. They combine monitoring, protection and public reporting functions with technical assistance and advisory services. Both the office and the Special Representative have reported each year to the Commission on Human Rights and the General Assembly on the human rights situation and the role and achievements of the office.

Implementing Arrangements

OHCHR/Cambodia operates through its main office in Phnom Penh and a small regional office in Battambang. The management structure consists of the chief's office, a technical cooperation programme, a protection programme, and the administrative unit.

The chief's office is responsible for overall policy and management, including coordinating support to the Special Representative of the Secretary-General, preparing reports, and undertaking activities to foster an enabling environment for human rights work in Cambodia.

The technical cooperation programme helps to develop the institutional capacity, laws, policies, and practices that are necessary to implement Cambodian Law and international human rights agreements and instruments, and to implement human rights standards in development programmes.

The protection programme is responsible for safeguarding human rights through monitoring, research and analysis, and reporting on the human rights situation.

The Administrative Unit provides personnel, administrative, financial, and logistical support, and serves as the security focal point.

The office receives funding through the regular budget which covers a core staff of seven professional international staff and 18 national general service staff. Project expenses are funded under the Trust Fund for Human Rights Education Programme in Cambodia, established by the United Nations Transitional Authority in Cambodia (UNTAC) and transferred to OHCHR in 1993.

Coordination

OHCHR Cambodia works with the executive, legislative, and judicial branches of the Government, is a member of the UN country team, and cooperates with the international financial institutions and other multilateral and bilateral donors and development agencies on issues of common concern. OHCHR's office coordinates closely with NGOs in all areas of its work.

VII. *Central Africa:* *Sub-regional Center for Human Rights and Democracy (OHCHR)*

Terms of Reference/Legal Authority

The Sub-regional Center for Human Rights and Democracy in Central Africa has been established as a field office of OHCHR in Yaounde, at the request of the Economic Community of Central African States (ECCAS) and after the approval of the UN General Assembly (res. 53/78 of 4 December 1998 and res. 54/55 of 1 December 1999).

Functions/Mandate

As provided for by the resolution adopted by the ECCAS Member States, during the 4th Ministerial Conference of the United Nations Standing Advisory Committee on Security Questions in Central Africa in Yaounde on 8 April 1994 and relevant subsequent resolutions adopted by the UN General Assembly, the mandate of the Sub-regional Center for Human Rights and Democracy includes:

- Training staff engaged in administering human rights matters;
- Extending support to the establishment or strengthening of national human rights institutions;
- Assisting in the dissemination and public awareness of international human rights instruments;

- Developing and carrying out activities at the sub-regional level with a view to strengthening sub-regional networks in support of human rights, democracy and the rule of law;
- Building national and sub-regional capacities in the fields of integrating human rights into peace-keeping, peace-building and peace-making operations; and,
- Assisting the human rights field operations deployed in the sub-region in developing training materials and in implementing training sessions.

Main Activities

The Sub-regional Center started its activities in March 2001, by organizing a Workshop on human rights education in Central Africa, in close cooperation with the UNDP and the Institute of International Relations of Cameroon (IRIC). The participants in the Workshop adopted the "Yaounde Declaration", which recommended, inter alia, the implementation, by the Sub-regional Center of a plan of action The Center established a documentation center in November 2001. The Center also publishes a Newsletter on Human Rights and Democracy: The Centre is the subject of a separate chapter of this book.

VIII. *Human Rights Field Presence in the Central African Republic (DPA)*

Terms of Reference/Legal Authority

On 22 October 1999, the Security Council adopted resolution 1271 by which it welcomed the Secretary General's proposal to deploy a multi-disciplinary team (DPA, DPKO, UNDP, OHCHR) to Bangui, to explore, in consultation with the Government and other national and international stakeholders, the possibility of maintaining a United Nations political presence after the withdrawal of MINURCA. The mission took place from 15 to 19 November 1999. Based on the recommendations of that mission, a new UN political office was put in place, the "United Nations Peace Building Support in Central Africa Republic", comprising political, military and civilian police and a human rights component. The Latter was to be composed of 2 to 3 human rights officers. The main activities of the human rights component has been to strengthen national human rights capacities by organizing human rights training for NGOs, civilian and military authorities; ensuring dissemination of human rights instruments, providing support for non-governmental and governmental human rights projects and following the human rights situation closely.

The UN political office in CAR was established on 16 February 2000. BONUCA's Human Rights Section was entrusted with the mandate to build upon MINURCA'S accomplishments and to strengthen national human rights capacities. The plans of the human rights component included: Institution-building; strengthening of the civil society; implementation of human rights education programmes; and human rights promotion and public awareness campaigns. While MINURCA's Human Rights Section was administered by DPKO on the basis of an MOU between DPKO and OHCHR-BONUCA Human Rights Section is presently supported by DPA. United Nations human rights monitors will be able to operate throughout the countryside, and the peace-building support office will provide judicial assistance to human rights victims. The office will also play an active role in promoting the disarmament of combatants as well as for providing guidance for the implementation of BONUCA's human rights programmes.

Functions and Mandate

The main functions of the Human Rights Section are the following:

1) to provide expertise and assistance to the Representative of the Secretary-General on human rights, including monitoring of the human rights situation in the mission area;
2) to provide advice and technical assistance with regard to legal reforms;
3) to observe human rights trends in the country;
4) to implement human rights training programmes for law-enforcement officials, and security forces.

Main Activities

Under MINURCA the following activities have been carried out by the human rights component since its establishment in June 1998:

- Human Rights training sessions for the National Police: The training sessions focused on human rights and law enforcement and included topics such as the evolution of human rights, police investigation of human rights abuses, arrest and detention procedures respectful of human rights, the use of force by police in a state of emergency and armed conflict, etc.
- Human Rights training sessions for the National Gendarmerie: the Human Rights Section, in collaboration with the civilian police of MINURCA, participated in several training sessions for Officers of the gendarmerie. The training focused on human rights and law

enforcement and the role of the National Gendarmerie in the promotion and protection of human rights and the role of security forces during elections.

- Institution-Building: One of the most important initiatives was the organization of a conference entitled "Human Rights and National Re-construction" held in June 1999 and attended by over 200 participants, representatives of Governments and different sectors of civil society. A series of recommendations developed during the meeting were used to advance the formulation of a "National Plan of Action on Human Rights".
- Human Rights Public Awareness: The Human rights section is broadcasting human rights programmes on radio MINURCA (2 million listeners). Extensive promotional activities are organized on Human Rights Day, including an essay writing contest in the school of Bangui, debates, theatre presentations, among other activities. Numerous publications of international and national human rights standards have been distributed widely.

Since 1999, BONUCA's Human rights Section has given emphasis to the judiciary and has already organised a number of seminars including:

- Seminar on human rights within the national reconstruction strategy;
- National seminar on the respect of provisions and principles of human rights standards within the administration of justice;
- National seminar on the role of justice in the consolidation of peace and the rule of law.

Beside the organization of various seminars for law enforcement officials, BONUCA's human rights Section has adopted the strategies aimed at:

- Reinforcing national capacities through participation of judicial personnel to attend training sessions at The Institut International de l'Administration Publique, training Centre for Magistrate of Porto-Novo, International Institute of Human Rights to enable them to broaden their experience with colleagues from other countries;
- Reforming legal documents in light of international human rights standards;
- Supporting victims of human rights violations through advocacy of 2 national lawyers, recruited by BONUCA for legal assistance;
- Creating a human rights library to enable researchers, students, interns, members of NGOs to conduct research in the field of human rights in the country.
- Additionally, a documentation centre on human rights has been established and will allow students to have access to case-laws of national and international courts. Moreover, BONUCA' s Human Rights Section

contributed to the translation of human rights instruments into the local language.

- Placing human rights issues in the work plan of all of the five substantive commissions during the national Dialogue forum, and assisting in drafting the final and general reports on the National Dialogue.

IX. *Central Asia Sub-Regional Office*

Terms of Reference/Legal Authority

The initiative of OHCHR in Central Asia arises from the UN Secretary-General and the High Commissioner's emphasis on the development of regional strategies focusing on national capacity building, as well as the call by the UN Inter-agency Framework Team on Conflict Prevention for attention to human rights in the Ferghana Valley region in Central Asia. The resulting project, based on a thorough needs assessment process, was finalized with Governments in the region.

The needs assessment process included missions, fielded between December 2001 and April 2002, to Kazakhstan, Kyrgyzstan, Tajikistan, and Uzbekistan, following invitations from these respective Governments; and the submission of recommendations for technical cooperation to an Expert Panel on Central Asia for considerations and comments.

A Regional Project for Central Asia was developed focusing on Human Rights Education and foreseeing the establishment of an OHCHR Regional Advisor in the region.

A formal exchange of letters between OHCHR and the above mentioned Governments was the basis for agreement on the project.

Functions and Mandate

OHCHR's Regional Project for Central Asia foresees activities both at the regional and national levels.

The objectives of the project are to:

- Provide widespread access on human rights information to the general public and relevant target sectors.
- Increase capacities of educators of future teachers, as well as of teachers, in the field of human rights, civic education, democracy and rule of law.
- Establish national and regional dialogues and networks of policy makers, experts, educators, international organizations and donors active in the areas of human rights and human rights education.

- The establishment of an OHCHR Regional Advisor, based in the region, will ensure that a high level of human rights expertise is available in the region for the state and civil society, from a non adversarial source.

The Regional Advisor's activities in the field of public information and policy development contributes to the dissemination of human rights information as well as to the mainstreaming of human rights throughout government policies and legislation, and in the work of UN country teams.

Main Activities

The high-level regional advisor deployed to the region conducts several workshops on human rights for government officials and policy makers, local government officials, civil society organizations and others. The regional advisor also produces commentaries and articles on relevant human rights topics. These are disseminated through newspaper articles and radio broadcasts in Russian and/or local languages.

- The Regional Advisor works closely with United Nations agencies to mainstream human rights into their work.
- The Regional Advisor provides widespread access to the general public and relevant target sectors to human rights information: will disseminate articles and presentations on specific human rights topics published in national newspapers or journals and broadcasts on national radio stations by the OHCHR Regional Experts. Short publications by the OHCHR Regional Advisor on specific topics related to human rights, rule of law and democracy are being published, printed, translated (as appropriate), and distributed.
- The Regional Office for Central Asia is establishing national and regional dialogues and networks of policy makers, experts, educators, international organizations and donors active in the areas of human rights and education; is convening group meetings on specific human rights topics held at the provincial and local levels, under the aegis of the Regional Advisor and with the participation of local authorities, grassroots organizations and movements; High level roundtable meetings at the national level to discuss specific topics and policy issues relevant to human rights, rule of law and democracy are held under the aegis of the Regional Advisor and with the participation of governmental officials, policy makers, and others as appropriate.

The Regional Advisor for Central Asia also serves as a resource person for the Human Rights Education related activities of the Regional Project for Central Asia.

X. *Human Rights Field Presence in Colombia (OHCHR)*

Terms of Reference/Legal Authority

In April 1996, the President of Colombia invited the High Commissioner for Human Rights to open an office in Bogotá. After extensive negotiations between the OHCHR and the Government of Colombia, an agreement was signed in November 1996 establishing a field office in Bogotá with six international staff. The agreement has been extended and modified on various occasions. In February 2000 the Government relaxed the restriction on the number of international personnel allowed to work in the country and in September 2002, at the request of President Uribe, the office's mandate was extended until October 2006.

Functions and Mandate

The mandate of the Office in Colombia includes:

- observing respect for human rights and international humanitarian law in the country;
- advising Government authorities and civil society on formulating and implementing policies, programmes and measures to promote and protect human rights;
- providing technical assistance that supports the formulation and application of those policies, programmes and measures.
- Each year the office prepares an analytical report on the country's human rights situation and respect for international humanitarian law which the High Commissioner submits to the United Nations Commission on Human Rights.

For the period 2004 to 2006, the office will focus its efforts in four areas: observing respect for human rights and humanitarian law, advising national authorities and institutions, civil society and the United Nations system on human rights issues; providing technical cooperation and assistance to strengthen national institutions and to mainstream human rights into the United Nations system; and disseminating information and promotional materials on human rights. The office will also continue to provide technical support in designing projects and verifiable indicators of results and impact, and will cooperate with any United Nations efforts related to resolving the armed conflict.

- In 2004, it will open a third regional office in Bucaramanga, to cover the north-eastern part of Colombia.

Main Activities

As part of its integral strategy, the office has strengthened and further improved its communications and relationship with Government bodies, as well as with other state or civil society institutions, in order to contribute to an adequate implementation of the High Commissioner's concrete recommendations contained in the report on the human rights situation in Colombia. Furthermore, the office has provided analysis and advice on policies, programmes and draft laws, and its observations were disseminated among the Government, Congress and civil society.

The consolidation of the sub-offices in Cali and Medellín enabled the office in Colombia to strengthen its visibility at the regional level, as well as developing a coherent and articulated working relationship with regional and local governmental and non-governmental bodies. The increase in the number of missions (175 field missions were held in 2003) generated a stronger visible presence and a better knowledge of local situations.

Technical cooperation and training activities continued to contribute to the strengthening of the capacity of national institutions involved with human rights and made them more aware of the importance for Colombia to implement international recommendation in this field. In particular the Office of the Ombudsman, the Office of the Attorney General, members of Congress and municipal representatives, were the main recipients of such training. At the end of the 2003, more than 1000 municipal representatives were trained in human rights and international humanitarian law. This was possible through a joint effort with the European Community.

During 2003, more than 117.000 publications published and distributed by the office were disseminated to different target groups, such as schools, media, attorneys, public prosecutors, ombudsmen, municipal representatives, university professors, opinion makers, journalists, human rights defenders, NGOs, government officers, public libraries and also to illegal armed groups. The office conducted 10 workshops in human rights and international humanitarian in 2003 and a total of 160 journalists were trained. The office prepared 26 press statements, held 7 press conferences, and appeared in more than 700 newspaper notes and 1100 T.V. and radios broadcaster notes.

XI. *République Démocratique du Congo (OHCHR)*

Le Cadre Légal de l'Intervention du HCDH en RDC

Conformément à la résolution 1995/69 de la Commission de Droits de l'homme du 9 mars 1995, des négociations ont été initiées avec le

Gouvernement et le Haut Commissaire, établissant un Bureau du HCDH à Kinshasa.

Le Bureau du Haut Commissariat aux Droits de l'Homme en la République Démocratique du Congo a été établie le 21 août 1996. Le protocole d'accord a été modifié le 3 octobre 2000 permettant ainsi l'ouverture des bureaux ou locaux auxiliaires sur le territoire de la République Démocratique du Congo.

Le Mandat du Bureau

Le mandat du Bureau, tel que résultant du protocole d'accord modifié du 3 octobre 2000, est axé sur deux orientations principales:

- L'observation de la situation des droits de l'Homme, en vue, d'une part d'informer le Haut Commissaire de l'évolution de la situation des droits de l'Homme à travers le pays, et d'autre part, d'assister le Rapporteur Spécial dans l'accomplissement du mandat que lui a confié la Commission des Droits de l'Homme;
- La coopération technique: conseiller et assister le Gouvernement et les ONG dans le domaine de la protection et de la promotion des droits de l'Homme.

Activités Exécutées

Les activités réalisées par le bureau sur terrain du HCDH depuis son ouverture tournent autour des deux volets de son mandat.

A. *Dans le domaine de l'observation de la situation des droits de l'homme*
Les activités exécutées par le Bureau dans le domaine de l'observation de la situation des droits de l'homme concernent notamment la collecte d'informations sur des cas de violations des droits de l'homme (le suivi de ces cas, l'observation des procès, les visites des lieux de détention, les missions d'enquêtes), l'appui aux mécanismes de la Commission des droits de l'homme (mécanismes thématiques des droits de l'homme et le Rapporteur spécial) et la poursuite de la coopération avec les mécanismes judiciaires nationaux et internationaux.

B. *Dans le domaine de la coopération technique*
Les activités mises en œuvre en 2003 comprennent des cycles de formation (à l'intention des officiers des forces armées, des femmes, des animateurs des mouvements associatifs, des ONG des droits de l'homme), l'introduction de l'enseignement des droits de l'homme dans le cursus scolaire, le renforcement des capacités opérationnelles de la société civile et

des organes nationaux de promotion et de protection des droits de l'homme, des campagnes sur la culture de la paix et la résolution pacifique des conflits. Des émissions radiophoniques sur les droits de l'homme, la résolution pacifique des conflits et la paix sont produites et diffusées dans les provinces septentrionales de la RDC depuis mai 2001. En outre, des spots et des émissions portant sur le rôle, les mécanismes et l'importance des institutions citoyennes pendant la période de transition sont diffusés sur 6 chaînes de radio et 5 chaînes de télévision. Cette activité est réalisée en partenariat avec l'Unité de Production des Programmes d'Education Civique (UPEC) qui est une ONG des droits de l'homme.

C. *Centre de documentation*
Grâce aux financements de l'Ambassade de la Grande Bretagne, du Haut Commissariat des Nations Unies aux Droits de l'Homme et de l'Union Européenne fut créé en avril 1999 le Centre de Documentation ayant pour objectifs:

- le renforcement des capacités des questions relatives aux droits de l'homme tant par les institutions publiques que par la société civile;
- la promotion et la vulgarisation des instruments nationaux régionaux et internationaux relatifs aux droits de l'homme.

Dans le cadre du mainstreaming des droits de l'homme dans les activités des autres organismes des Nations Unies, le Bureau du HCDH en RDC participe pleinement à tous les programmes dans les domaines de la paix, de la sécurité et des affaires humanitaires. Depuis, le Bureau tient des réunions mensuelles de concertation et de coordination sur les questions des droits de l'homme avec les services de coopération des Ambassades, les agences du Système des Nations Unies, les ONGs Internationales et d'autres partenaires impliquées dans les droits de l'homme. Dans ce même contexte, il coordonne aussi des réunions du groupe thématique droits de l'homme et justice.

Le HCDH tient à l'amélioration de la situation des droits de l'homme et à l'avènement d'un Etat de droit en RDC. A cet égard, il continuera:

- à promouvoir l'application des conventions des droits de l'homme ratifiées par la RDC;
- à vulgariser les informations sur ces conventions et à encourager la ratification de nouvelles conventions et protocoles additionnels;
- à renforcer les capacités des institutions gouvernementales des ONGs des droits de l'homme ainsi que d'autres organisations de la société civile;
- à entretenir une étroite et fructueuse coopération avec la section Droit de l'homme de la MONUC, dans le cadre du M.O.U qui lie les deux structures.

– Dans le cadre du processus de paix, le HCDH a apporté son appui à la mise en place de l'Observatoire national des droits de l'homme, au processus de mise en place de la Commission Vérité et Réconciliation et à l'organisation d'une mission d'évaluation du système judiciaire.

XII. *Eritrea/Ethiopia (DPKO)*

Terms of Reference/Legal Authority

The United Nations Mission to Ethiopia and Eritrea (UNMEE) was established on 31 July 2000 by Security-Council resolution 1312 (2000) and following the signature of the Cessation of Hostilities Agreement in June 2000. UNMEE is mandated to monitor the cessation of hostilities and assist in the implementation of the Peace Agreement signed in December 2000. Resolution 1320 (2000) of 15 September 2000 called on UNMEE to "coordinate the Mission's activities in the Temporary Security Zone (TSZ) and areas adjacent to it with humanitarian and human rights activities of the United Nations and other organizations in those areas". In his report dated 18 September 2000, the Secretary-General announced his decision to include a small Human Rights Component within UNMEE. The Human Rights Office (HRO) was established in May 2001. The Human Rights Office is composed of a chief, who serves as Human Rights Advisor to the SRSG, and a ten human rights officers deployed in five offices within the mission area.

UNMEE reports through the Chief of Mission to the UN Department of Peace-Keeping Operations (DPKO). Reports of the Human Rights Component to the SRSG are copied to the OHCHR. OHCHR provides, as requested, substantive support and advice to the HRO. The HRO is funded through the UN regular budget.

Functions/Mandate

The mandate of the Office focuses on addressing human rights concerns resulting from the Ethiopia/Eritrea conflict.

The Algiers Peace Agreement of 12 December 2000 committed the parties to provide "humane treatment to each other's nationals and persons of each other's national origin within their respective territories." Paragraph 2(i) of Security Council Resolution 1320 dated 15 September 2000 mandates UNMEE "to coordinate the Mission's activities in the Temporary Security Zone (TSZ) and areas adjacent to it with humanitarian and human rights activities of the United Nations and other organizations in those areas."

Since the 13 April 2002 ruling by the Ethiopia and Eritrea Boundary Commission (EEBC), the HRO has been paying special attention to the situation of resident populations of areas which will be subject to a change of sovereignty as a consequence of demarcation, and IDPs who would like to return to these areas, to ensure that their basic rights are protected. An UNMEE/UNCT Task Force was established in that regard to assess the possible human rights and humanitarian consequences of the transfer of territory, and formulate strategies to address these.

Main Activities of the Human Rights Office

The main activities of the human rights component are:

- Monitoring the situation of civilians affected by the conflict, in particular the situation of Eritrean nationals and persons of Eritrean origin in Ethiopia, and of Ethiopian nationals and persons of Ethiopian origin in Eritrea;
- Investigating allegations of cross-border incidents, detentions and disappearances, and other human rights violations within those areas;
- Advising the Ethiopian and Eritrean Governments of its findings and propose remedial action;
- Monitoring repatriations of each other's nationals, under ICRC auspices;
- Monitoring the release and repatriation of prisoners of war and all civilians detained as a result of the conflict;
- Establishing and chairing a joint UNMEE/UN Country Team Human Rights Forum for the regular exchange of information and coordination of activities and programs;
- Advising the SRSG, the Force Commander, and other UNMEE components on matters related to human rights;
- Providing human rights training for military and civilian staff of UNMEE.

XIII. *Human Rights Field Presence in the Former Yugoslav Republic of Macedonia (OHCHR)*

Terms of Reference/Legal Authority

The Technical Cooperation Programme Office in Skopje (OHCHR Skopje), established in July 2002, has as its primary responsibility to facilitate the implementation of a Comprehensive Technical Cooperation Programme in the field of Human Rights. OHCHR Skopje also provides support to

OHCHR ad-hoc Technical Cooperation activities and has a role to represent OHCHR through contacts and coordination with international agencies, Government, donors and civil society on the ground.

Functions/Mandate

The OHCHR office in Skopje is mandated to facilitate implementation of the Comprehensive Technical Cooperation programme agreed upon with the Government in early 2002. Subject to periodic implementation reviews, the overall programme will last between three and five years and will cover the following initial areas:

- human rights education in schools;
- strengthening of civil society;
- development of national human rights action plan;
- support to human rights institutions; and
- strengthening of the Government capacity in the field of human rights.

The programme is implemented in close cooperation and consultation with partners in the Government, among international organisations and the civil society in the country. The main OHCHR function is to coordinate the work of these partners, and provide monitoring, evaluation and coordination of project activities and reporting.

In addition to its primary function, OHCHR Skopje participates in OHCHR regional and sub-regional technical cooperation activities and programmes and facilitates the implementation of country projects carried out within the worldwide Assisting Communities Together—ACT Project.

Within the general OHCHR human right mandate, OHCHR Skopje supports and makes available human rights information and documentation to wide range of beneficiaries from the authorities, civil society, and various international and national organizations.

The Office is managed by one national staff member.

Main Activities

Technical Cooperation

In the initial phases of implementation of the Comprehensive Technical Cooperation Programme in the country, OHCHR Skopje activities are focused on the following priority areas:

- Human Rights Education—establishment and effective functioning of a national consultation mechanism to evaluate achievements in formal and informal education to date; defining a concept and draft content

of human rights education textbooks for primary and secondary schools, teacher training and pilot-tests of the concept;
- Strengthening of Civil Society—development of training modules to be applied in up to 10-12 human rights workshops for civil society members; development of a certification programme at a national University and mentoring and fellowship programmes abroad as well as organising consultation meetings between civil society and relevant Government departments;
- Strengthening of the Government Capacity in the Field of Human Rights—including funding of two posts, IT equipment and in service-training in Treaty Body reporting and establishment of a human rights documentation centre in the Human Rights Unit of the Ministry of Foreign Affairs. Support to other human rights activities and initiatives

OHCHR Skopje participates in the work of the UN Country Team and several human rights related working groups and co-chairs with OSCE the Human Rights Institution/Capacity Building co-ordination group.

XIV. *Human Rights Field Presence in Guatemala (OHCHR)*

Terms of Reference/Legal Authority

The Office was established as part of a technical co-operation project signed by OHCHR with the Government of Guatemala in 1996.The office's mandate concluded in September 2000. A final evaluation mission was carried out in June 2000. A new project document was signed with the Government of Guatemala in August 2001. The project was revised in 2002 and in 2003. In December 2003 an agreement was signed with Government of Guatemala to establish a new office with a monitoring mandate.

Functions and Mandate

The project has five main components:

(1) assistance to the Government of Guatemala in developing and implementing a system of participatory monitoring and reporting with regard to the international human rights treaties ratified by Guatemala;
(2) assistance to the Ombudsman, the Ombudsman for Indigenous Women and NGOs in coordinating efforts with the international human rights mechanisms
(3) assistance in the mainstreaming of human rights into the activities of the UN country team and MINUGUA.

(4) support to the promotion of indigenous rights and multiculturalism, and for the elimination of ethnic and racial discrimination.
(5) training of judges and magistrates in international human rights instruments, and the mechanisms for applying these principles in the domestic judicial process.

Main Activities

The project has five main components:

Component 1: The issue of assistance in strengthening the national capacities and developing and implementing a system of participatory monitoring and reporting with regard to the international human rights treaties ratified by Guatemala has been followed by a national project staff, which hosted several meetings with civil society, the office of the Ombudsman and the Presidential Commission for Human Rights (COPREDEH), to evaluate the implementation of the Government's obligation in the field of human rights and to report to competent international mechanisms. OHCHR gathered two staff from COPREDEH, one staff from the Ombudsman's Office, one staff from a leading NGO umbrella organization, and two staff from the UN Country Team and trained them for two weeks on the elaboration and presentation of reports to UN human rights mechanisms, as well as on the follow-up to recommendations from these mechanisms. Now the project is establishing a coordinated programme for COPREDEH to prepare Guatemala's overdue reports on the Convention Against Torture and the Convention on the Elimination of Racial Discrimination, through a participatory process that would include the Ombudsman's Office and leading NGOs.

Component 2: The issue of assistance to the Ombudsman, the Office of Defence for Indigenous Women (DEMI) and NGOs in coordinating efforts with the international human rights mechanisms has been followed directly by the Project Coordinator, who has carried out several trainings and conferences for civil society, the national human rights institution, the Government and the UN agencies, on how to channel communications and reports to relevant human rights mechanisms. In coordination with MINUGUA, the project has also elaborated a Draft Manual for the Verification of Human Rights Violations and a more specific Draft Manual for the Verification of Violations Against Indigenous Peoples, both of which are now being finalized. The manuals is about how to report human rights abuses before local, national and international mechanisms, and will soon be published and distributed by OHCHR, which is also organizing trainings on how to use the manual. OHCHR is also organizing discussions to follow the recent visits to the country by the Special Rapporteurs on the Rights of Indigenous Peoples and on Human Rights Defenders to inform the public of the content of their reports, and to analyze adequate follow-up to their recommendations.

Component 3: The issue of providing assistance and advice to the UN system on human rights related matters, in particular through participating actively in the process of transfer of MINUGUA's tasks to the UN system has been carried out jointly by an international project staff, and the Project Coordinator. Through this work, OHCHR has been supporting the process of transfer of MINUGUA's tasks to the UN system and to strengthen the UN system's capacities in the field of human rights. The project staff has regularly reviewed activities by the UN Country Team to ensure the mainstreaming of human rights is integrated into the work of the different agencies and programmes working in the country, taking a lead role in several processes such as the review of the Common Country Assessment (CCA/UNDAF), the elaboration of Millennium Development Goals (MDG), and others. Not only has OHCHR been integrated into the inter-agency working groups on Indigenous Peoples' Issues (GRUTIM) and has reactivated the Inter-Agency Group on Justice and Security (GIJUS) but it has also been active in other inter-agency working groups (Gender, Communications), as well as in bilateral work with several agencies such as UNDP, UNICEF, and the ILO.

Component 4: The issue of strengthening national capacities of verification of indigenous peoples' rights and to promote multiculturalism has been undertaken by two national project staff with expertise on indigenous rights. Through their work, OHCHR has collaborated with MINUGUA in the preparation of manuals and guidelines on the human rights for the indigenous peoples of Guatemala, and in conducting workshops for indigenous communities and NGOs on human rights and indigenous peoples, in the capital and in the interior of the country. OHCHR and MINUGUA have also been providing technical support for the formation of a comprehensive umbrella organization for indigenous organizations, which has now been denominated National Indigenous Council (CNI), and has encouraged better coordination among civil society, especially between non-indigenous NGOs and their indigenous counterparts, through joint activities aimed specifically at promoting knowledge of instruments and mechanisms for the promotion and protection of indigenous peoples' rights. OHCHR has also assisted the DEMI in analyzing the situation of indigenous women in Guatemala with regards to their rights, a study of their situation, which is now reflected in the DEMI's Annual Report.

Component 5: The issue of support to the mainstreaming of human rights into the curricula of the Judicial School or UCI has been followed by national project staff with expertise on human rights and national law. OHCHR has been coordinating with the UCI to prepare a Guide of Indigenous Peoples' Rights with a select number of national case studies to serve as examples of how to integrate indigenous peoples' rights into judicial arguments, decisions and sentences. A document elaborated by OHCHR containing recommendations on integrating multiculturalism in the new Procedural Code was also presented to the UCI. With regard to training, a roster of national experts which could be used by trainers was compiled for UCI, and a first training module for the people in this roster was implemented in various parts of the country with the participation of Community Peace Judges, legal auxiliaries, administrative staff (including translators) and members of the community. As a follow-up activity, a diagnosis of the knowledge, attitudes and practices of judges with regards to multiculturalism, based on a questionnaire form that they completed, was carried out. The deficiencies in each of the themes were discussed with authorities from the UCI.

XV. *Human Rights Field Presence in Guinea Bissau (DPA)*

Terms of Reference/Legal Authority

The Security Council, in its resolution 1233 of 6 April 1999, supported the decision of the Secretary-General to establish a Post-Conflict Peace-Building Office in Guinea-Bissau (UNOGBIS) under the leadership of a Representative of the Secretary-General (S/1999/233). Currently the mandate of UNOGBIS is to:

(1) Help create an enabling environment for the consolidation of peace, democracy and the rule of law and for the organization of free and transparent elections;
(2) Actively support national efforts, including those of civil society, towards national reconciliation, tolerance and peaceful management of differences;
(3) Encourage initiatives aimed at building confidence and maintaining friendly relations between Guinea-Bissau, its neighbours and its international partners;
(4) Seek the commitment of the Government and other parties to adopt a programme of voluntary arms collection, disposal and destruction;
(5) Provide the political framework and leadership for harmonizing and integrating the activities of the United Nations system in the country.

The OHCHR and the United Nations Department of Political Affairs (DPA) decided to create a small Human Rights Unit (HRU), to work on human rights issues within UNOGBIS with a view to creating an environment for consolidating peace, democracy and the rule of law. The HRU has two international Human Rights Officers and one national Human Rights Officer.

UNOGBIS reports on human rights issues through the Representative of the Secretary General, Head of Mission, and the Office of the High Commission for Human Rights provides guidance to the human rights Unit.

Objectives

Although UNOGBIS' mandate does not mention specifically human rights, it has given a broad interpretation to its mandate and to the concepts of Peace, Rule of Law and Democracy to enable it to carry out its human rights mandate, including monitoring and reporting responsibilities.

The HRU aims at facilitating the formulation of a National Human Rights Action Plan. It also provides technical assistance on human rights in order to reinforce the national capacity building of various institutions. Other project components include human rights monitoring; radio programmes, training of former combatants; training for parliamentarians; dissemination of human rights publications in Creole, and organization of special events during national and United Nations human rights days.

Main Activities

The Human Rights Unit has been implementing a programme aiming at strengthening national capacity in the field of human rights by providing technical assistance, especially training, to various entities. OHCHR and DPA/HRU jointly carried out a project focused on the realization of two main goals:

- The setting-up of an Inter-ministerial Committee on human Rights, and the implementation of a National Plan of Action in the field of human rights.
- Preparation and implementation of a comprehensive training programme for Law enforcement officials which would include the holding of a number of seminars and the creation of a follow-up mechanism.
- Providing training on human rights and the Rule of Law (a) for the National Assembly, including its specialized commissions (b) for Governors and local administrators, (c) for judges, prosecutors and the lawyers.
- Enhancement of civil society organizations, including women in the field of human rights. The HRU cooperates with other UN agencies

present on the ground, particularly with UNDP in the context of the UN country team and the elaboration of the United Nation Development Assistance Framework (UNDAF), and the monitoring of allegations of human rights violations and abuses.

XVI. *Guyana*

In June 2004, a Human Rights Adviser was appointed to work in the Social Cohesion Unit of the United Nations Country Team (UNCT) under the Resident Coordinator. The HRA 1 supports human rights related initiatives in Guyana to be carried out by the UNCT in close cooperation with the Government and civil society organizations. In her initial activities, she will be assisted by an OHCHR consultant, specifically tasked to assist the Government in the establishment of a mechanism to prepare reports to UN treaty monitoring bodies.

XVII. *Haiti*

Security Council Resolution 1529 stressed the need to create a secure environment that enables respect for human rights, and requested the Secretary-General to establish a United Nations Programme of Action to assist the constitutional political process and to promote and protect human rights, as well as the development of the rule of law. In this regard, the OHCHR has sought to provide substantive and methodological support in all phases during the elaboration and implementation of the above-mentioned programme.

An OHCHR international human rights adviser has been advising the Resident Coordinator, the UNCT and the Task Force Group on human rights issues. He is also expected to discuss with the Government the initiation of an OHCHR project of technical cooperation in the field of human rights.

Advice is also being provided on tailored programs and activities aimed at enhancing national capacities for the protection and promotion of human rights and assistance is being provided to relevant institutions such as the Judicial School and the Office of the Ombudsman (OPC). The activities are being implemented in coordination with UNDP and the Special Mission of the Organization of American States in Haiti. An OHCHR proposal has been included in the Flash Appeal for Haiti.

XVIII. *Human Rights Field Presence in Liberia (DPKO)*

Terms of Reference/Legal Authority

UNMIL was established pursuant to Security Council resolution 1509 (2003) of 19 September 2003. The Mission has the overall mandate to support the implementation of the Comprehensive Peace Agreement signed in Accra on 18 August 2003 between the Government of Liberia, the Liberians United for Reconciliation and Democracy (LURD), Movement for Democracy in Liberia (MODEL) and the political parties. To that end the Security Council's mandate requires UNMIL to:

- Support the implementation of the Ceasefire Agreement;
- Support humanitarian and human rights assistance; and
- Support security reform.

With the establishment of UNMIL the mandate of the erstwhile United Nations Office in Liberia (UNOL) was terminated and its major functions transferred to UNMIL as proposed in the Secretary-General's letter of 16 September 2003 addressed to the President of the Security Council.

Functions and Mandate

The human rights and protection component of UNMIL is responsible for implementing the human rights mandate of the Mission, which includes the following tasks:

- To contribute towards international efforts to protect and promote human rights in Liberia, with particular attention to vulnerable groups including refugees, returning refugees and internally displaced persons, women, children and demobilized child soldiers, within UNMIL's capabilities and under acceptable security conditions, in close cooperation with other United Nations agencies, related organizations, governmental organizations, and non-governmental organizations.
- To ensure an adequate human rights presence, capacity and expertise within UNMIL to carry out human rights promotion, protection and monitoring activities.
- The Human Rights and Protection Component also provides human rights training, assistance in capacity building for government and civil society and in collaboration with OHCHR technical cooperation activities.
- Provides leadership and a forum for international and national advocacy on human rights and protection issues on Liberia.

Main Activities

The Human Rights and Protection Component initiated and led advocacy activities that culminated in the ratification of the following human rights treaties by the Government of Liberia:

- The Rome Statute of the International Criminal Court;
- The International Covenant on Economic, Social and Cultural Rights;
- The International Covenant on Civil and Political Rights and its First Optional Protocol.

The Human Rights Component also undertook joint human rights training activities with UNDP under its human rights and protection programme and has developed joint technical assistance projects with OHCHR and UNDP in the area of human rights training and investigations; It participated as an observer and human rights resource in the Joint Monitoring Committee (JMC) established to monitor the implementation of the Ceasefire Agreement.

The Human Rights and Protection Component also endeavours to:

- Facilitate, in collaboration with civil society organizations and the government, the establishment of the Truth and Reconciliation Commission and Independent National Commission for Human Rights—provided for in the Comprehensive Peace Agreement;
- Support the establishment of human rights societies in all fifteen counties of Liberia;
- Support the establishment of a human rights and documentation centre in Monrovia;
- Provide training in human rights for government officials and representatives of civil society organizations;
- Provide training in reporting on human rights treaties and implementation of recommendations of treaty bodies to relevant government officials and representatives of civil society organizations;
- Conduct investigations of past violations of human rights and humanitarian law so as to provide support for the work of the Truth and Reconciliation Commission and any other justice mechanism that may be established in the future.

XIX. *Human Rights Field Presence in Mexico (OHCHR)*

Terms of Reference/Legal Authority

On 1 July 2002, the OHCHR and the government of Mexico signed an agreement: for the establishment of an OHCHR office in Mexico. The office in Mexico is composed of a Representative, two human rights officers, and two assistants. The above staff is responsible for the implementation of the project activities. The project also hires national and international consultants for specific activities.

The first phase of a predecessor technical cooperation programme completed in September 2001, included 4 components in the areas of the administration of justice and national initiatives on human rights and indigenous rights, with all four being developed jointly with governmental institutions at national and local level, human rights institutions, NGOs, indigenous organizations and the academic sector.

According to the evaluation of the first phase conducted by an independent expert: "On balance, it can be concluded that the first phase provided an historic opportunity for an international presence in the defense and observation of human rights in Mexico. The role assigned to Mexican civil society and to the international community is a substantial achievement which marks a significant shift from former Mexican Governments´ approaches and should be an example to other countries in the Latin American region".

All of the actors involved in the first phase agreed on the need to continue the technical co-operation programme. The second phase is the result of a wide and inclusive exercise by the Mexican government, OHCHR and other UN agencies established in Mexico, CNDH and NGOs, making it possible to formulate a new programme that will have the active support of all the different parties.

In October 2001, a Mexican delegation visited OHCHR headquarters in order to identify the priorities of the technical co-operation for the next 12 months 2002–2003. As a result of the consultations, the parties reached several understandings that served as a basis for the design of this project.

Functions and Mandate

OHCHR is now implementing the second phase of the project, which has the objectives of assisting the Government in launching national initiatives on human rights, strengthening Mexico's National Commission on Human Rights the fight against impunity and securing indigenous rights.

The project is expected to run three more years; activities for each year will be agreed upon annually by OHCHR and the Government.

Main Activities

The Project reflects those areas identified as priorities in the current Mexican context, which were also the subject of several recommendations issued by UN monitoring and thematic mechanisms as well as regional human rights institutions:

In a general context, the specific objectives and the expected results are as follows:

Component 1
Activity a) Diagnosis of the human rights situation in Mexico

Objective
Development of the diagnosis of the human rights situation and fundamental freedoms in Mexico.

Outputs

- The Diagnosis identified the political, legal, economic and social needs for the improvement of the human rights situation in Mexico. This took into account the recommendations issued by UN treaty monitoring bodies and thematic mechanisms to the Mexican State.
- The Diagnosis identified the political, economical, legal, social and cultural actions/issues/institutions, which contribute to the respect for human rights in the country as well as the means for enacting UN monitoring and thematic mechanism recommendations given to the Mexican State.
- A diagnosis provides the basis for a new National Programme on Human Rights.

Activities
The activities of the Office in Mexico include:

- To evaluate the political, legal, economic, social and cultural situation in Mexico with regard to the respect for human rights.
- To identify the legal, political, economic, social and cultural obstacles, which are preventing Mexico from fully respecting human rights and to give efficient internal execution of the recommendations offered to the Mexican State by the UN monitoring and thematic mechanisms.

- To analyze through a transparent and participatory process, in order to achieve a legitimate diagnosis validated by all actors involved.
- To organize a national forum for the presentation of the Diagnosis.
- Public presentation of the diagnosis.

The diagnosis was launched on 10 December 2003

Activity b) National Programme on Human Rights

Objective
Elaboration of the National Programme on Human Rights.

Outputs

- A new National Programme on Human Rights, which identifies, coordinates and coherently develops actions to be implemented by the executive, legislative and judicial powers, as well as by the human rights institutions, will be integrated.
- The autonomy and independence of federal and state commissions for human rights, as well as the coordination and participation of civil society in the design, execution, follow up and evaluation of the National Programme, will be assured through clear mechanism.
- An adequate mechanism for the follow up and evaluation of the National Plan of Action, with the full participation of the Mexican authorities, at national and local levels, state autonomous organisms, human rights institutions and civil society, will be developed.

Activities

- To elaborate a new National Programme which will coordinate actions to be implemented by the Mexican authorities at national and local levels, and the human rights institutions, all of them in collaboration with Mexican NGOs, and which establishes a state policy in the matter.
- To organize a national forum for the presentation the National Programme on Human Rights by all actors involved.
- To identify the adequate mechanisms to follow up and evaluate the National Programme through a transparent and participatory methodology.
- Public presentation of the National Programme on Human Rights.

Component 2
Strengthening of the National Commission for Human Rights (CNDH)

Objectives

- To strengthen the institutional capacity of the CNDH to meet its mandate (including strengthening of the complaints handling process of the CNDH).
- To increase public awareness on human rights standards and norms, effective dissemination of lessons learned and best practices as well as public advocacy of human rights principles in the country.
- Strengthening the documentation centre.

Outputs

- Strengthening of the complaints handling process.
- To increase public awareness on human rights standards and norms, effective dissemination of lessons learned and best practices as well as public advocacy of human rights principles in the country.
- Improvement of the Commission's Documentation Centre.

Activities

- Review of the Process to determine, procure and install appropriate software for the monitoring and complaints handling systems.
- Development of a complaints-handling manual for use by staff of the CNDH assisted by a short-term consultant.
- Improvement of the monitoring and complaint handling processes, including receiving complaints, reviewing complaints, investigation, decision and action, resolution and follow-up, assisted by (a) short-term consultant(s) experienced in handling complaints and monitoring by national human rights institutions.
- Arrange a study tour for one or two senior staff members with responsibility for complaints to gain experience in the complaints and monitoring functions of other national human rights institutions.
- Undertake the training of selected staff of CNDH in "training of trainers" (TOT techniques) by an international and a national consultant.
- Undertake the training of selected staff of CNDH in TOT techniques by an international and a national consultant
- Provide a short-term study award or other assistance to enable CNDH staff to be trained in TOT or human rights education techniques at internationally accredited training centers or with other well-established national human rights institutions.
- To evaluate the necessities of the CNDH' documentation center.

Component 3
Training Courses on Medical and Forensic Examination of Torture

Objective
To provide Mexican authorities at national and local level, autonomous organisms, human rights institutions, NGOs and the academic sector with the capacity to apply and properly disseminate the model procedures adopted during Phase I.

Outputs

- Presentation of training manuals on the medical and forensic examination of cases of torture.
- Health professionals, judges and lawyers (150) specialised on the model procedures concerning the medical and forensic examination of cases of torture, respectively.
- Work plans for the adequate dissemination of model procedures on medical and forensic examination of torture to be implemented in 2003.

Activities

- Adoption of the Official norms on the medical and forensic examination of cases torture (activity conducted by the Government).
- Elaboration of training manuals on the medical and forensic examination of torture.
- To integrate working plans for the dissemination of the standard procedures (activity conducted by the beneficiaries of this component).
- Conduction of three training courses (2 for medical examination and 1 for forensic examination) on the model procedures adopted in Phase I.

Partners: International Rehabilitation Center for Torture Victims (medical examination) and Argentine Forensic Anthropology Team (forensic examination)
Duration: 5 days per training course

Component 4
Course on UN Human Rights Mechanisms Addressed to Indigenous Representatives

Objectives
Strengthen the capacity of indigenous organizations and representatives in their knowledge of human rights and on their use of UN human rights mechanisms.

Outputs
- 80 indigenous representatives trained on human rights and the use of UN human rights mechanisms.

– Compilation of proposals to improve the situation of the indigenous peoples in Mexico to be considered during the integration of the National Plan of Action.

Activities
To carry out two regional training courses addressed to indigenous representatives on human rights and the use of UN human rights mechanisms.

XX. *Human Rights Field Presence in Nepal (OHCHR)*

Terms of Reference

Following a request by UN Resident Coordinator (RC) in Nepal, OHCHR has appointed a Senior Human Rights Officer (SHRO) to work with the UNCT in Kathmandu, Nepal in March 2003.

Mandate and Functions

According to terms of reference, the SHRO stimulates discussions in Nepal on ways to address the human rights issues during the peace process and carries out advocacy on immediate and longer term measures, advises and acts as a resource person for the UNCT.

The SHRO carries out his tasks in close coordination with the NHRC and in a manner that recognizes and builds the capacity of the NHRC to play a leading role in the protection and promotion of human rights. The SHRO acts as a resource for the NHRC and UNDP's project of support for the NHRC.

The SHRO advices the UNCT by keeping them up to date on human rights developments and proposing strategies for the various Agencies to promote and protect human rights.

Main Activities

The main activities of the SHRO are:

– To integrate human rights as an essential component of any peace process and/or any peace-building efforts.
– To expand the capacity of the UNCT to address human rights issues, as part of the coordinated and integrated peace-building efforts of the UN system.
– To provide Human rights expertise to the UNCT.
– To Advise and act as a resource for the RC and the UNCT on human rights in the conflict and during any peace process.

- In consultation with the RC, to convene meetings as necessary of the UN and other agencies to agree on coordinated action on human rights issues.
- To advisee on Human rights issues the NHRC to carry out its mandated role in the peace process.
- To provide practical ways to address human rights during the conflict and as part of any sustainable peace.
- To keep the RC and the OHCHR (Geneva, New York and Bangkok) closely informed of human rights and related developments and to make recommendations for further action on human rights by OHCHR and other UN agencies.

XXI. *Occupied Palestinian Territories (GAZA and the West Bank)*

Terms of Reference/Legal Authority

In April 1996, following a request by the Palestinian Authority (PA), and pursuant to the call of the UN Commission on Human Rights, the OHCHR signed a programme of technical assistance and advisory services with the PA. The agreement provides for the implementation of a comprehensive technical cooperation programme in the field of human rights in the Gaza Strip and the West Bank, and is based on the outcome and recommendations of needs assessment missions conducted by the Office of the High Commissioner for Human Rights (OHCHR) and on broad consultations with Palestinian government officials and civil society organizations, UN agencies and donors active in the Occupied Palestinian Territories (OPT). The current project covers activities planned up to July 2004.

In November 1996 OHCHR established an office in Gaza and in 2000 a sub-office was established in Ramallah. At present there is one international staff and three national Human Rights Officers.

Functions and Mandate

The programme aims to (a) strengthen capacity in the area of rule of law and administration of justice, (b) strengthen the Palestinian Independent Commission on Citizen's rights; (c) strengthen human rights awareness and education; and, (d) mainstream human rights. These aims are approached through working to establish a legal framework consistent with human rights standards, and through supporting Palestinian institutions and organizations in the conduct of legal analysis work. The national human rights action plan would provide a framework for developing capacity, institutions and a culture of human rights as well as an official human rights policy.

Main Activities

Activities carried out under the technical assistance programme include the following:

Legal framework: Several Palestinian laws have been reviewed by the PICCR and Palestinian NGOs in close consultation with official institutions, as well as with other civil society organizations. OHCHR supported this process through expert advice, participation in workshops and funding of research.

Development of the National Human Rights Action Plan:

OHCHR Gaza worked with the Palestinian Ministry of Planning and International Cooperation (MOPIC) to develop the method and approach for the formulation of the National Plan of Action. OHCHR's role has been to support the integration of both PA and civil society efforts to identify their common human rights goals. In that process, OHCHR supported research, consultative workshops, information services and technical input in six key sectors—housing, environment, health, education, social welfare and the administration of justice. The Plan was completed and launched in 2001 and signed by the President of the PA in 2002.

National structures:

Police—OHCHR-Gaza has worked with the Police Training Directorate to strengthen the capacity of the Palestinian Policy and to develop a human rights curriculum for law enforcement officers. A group of Palestinian Police who participated in an in-depth training as well as a 60 hour-long train-the-trainers course is now engaged in providing human rights training on an extensive basis to the various branches of the Palestinian Police. OHCHR continues to support such initiatives, by providing human rights sessions both in courses organized by the Police Training Directorate and the various police branches, and in courses organized by bilateral donors.

Training for senior level police and security officers has supported developing operational guidelines consistent with human rights standards. OHCHR Gaza trained a core group of police officials in human rights standards relating to juvenile justice.

Also, OHCHR Gaza organized courses in human rights training for prison guards and members of the Palestinian Legislative Council (PLC). The office initiated the development of a unified code of conduct and standing orders for Palestinian security forces and provided technical assistance in the drafting of standing orders for prison officials.

A Pocket Guide on Human Rights Standards for the Palestinian Police, containing a summary of international norms relevant to police functions and duties, was produced in 12,000 copies and distributed to police officials. Human rights documentation, training equipment and materials have been provided to the Training Directorate.

PICCR: In addition to the activities mentioned above in the law reform area, OHCHR has supported PICCR in strengthening its field capacity and increasing accessibility to and knowledge of PICCR within the communities it serves.

Palestinian Legislative Council (PLC): OHCHR Gaza provided human rights training to members of the PLC's Committee on Human Rights and Public Monitoring and its secretariat. Fellowships were granted to two members to observe the work of another parliamentary human rights committee in another Arab country. OHCHR Gaza also assisted the PLC in purchasing human rights documentation.

NGOs: Assistance was provided to the Palestinian Centre for Human Rights (PCHR) to support the establishment of a Women and Group Rights' Unit, the work of which focuses on legal research and legal advocacy and assistance to women groups and individuals. OHCHR has supported a similar effort in the West Bank within the organization LAW. Assistance provided to al-Mezan Centre for Human Rights, which focused on economic and social rights, to strengthen its fieldwork unit. OHCHR, Gaza is also assisting other non-governmental organizations to conduct work in the law reform area.

OHCHR, Gaza conducted training sessions for NGOs on human rights, humanitarian law, the functioning of UN human rights treaty bodies, strategic planning and housing rights. It participated and provided technical input in numerous human rights seminars organized by NGOs on a wide number of subjects, including human rights education, women, and others. Human rights documentation has been widely distributed to NGOs in Gaza and the West Bank.

Lawyers: OHCHR Gaza organized training courses on international human rights standards relating to the legal profession and the judiciary. Assistance was provided to the newly established Palestinian Bar Association to purchase human rights documentation.

Assisting Communities Together (ACT) Projects: Within the framework of the ACT project, OHCHR, Gaza and UNDP's Program of Assistance to the Palestinian People, disbursed five small grants to Palestinian community-based organizations working at the grass-root level for human rights advocacy, education and training. Funded activities have focused on women, children and youth, disability and the environment, and have included community theatre.

XXII. *Regional Representatives of OHCHR (Addis Ababa, Bangkok, Beirut, Santiago) (OHCHR)*

Main Activities/Responsibilities

Under the supervision of OHCHR, in regular coordination with the Regional Coordinators, and, where relevant-the Executive Secretaries of the Economic and Social Commissions for Asia-Pacific (ESCAP), Latin America and the Caribbean (ECLAC), Western Asia (ESCWA) and Africa (ECA) regions and UN Country Coordinators in these regions, the regional representatives are responsible for the following:

- Advising OHCHR regarding its regional strategy and activities as well as regional developments which may have human rights policy and operational implications and participation in implementation of frameworks for regional technical cooperation;
- Providing advice to ESCAP/ECLAC/ESCWA/ECA regarding human rights related aspects of their activities, otherwise assisting them in addressing issues of human rights relevant to their mandate and acting as a liaison between them and OHCHR;
- Developing strategic relationships with UN country teams of the regions, advising and lending support as required, especially within the framework of rights-based planning and programming initiatives such as the CCA and UNDAF;
- In collaboration with relevant units of OHCHR, including the Methodology Team and the Right to Development Team, identifying and contributing to the development and implementation of best practices, particularly those relating to promotion of a rights-based approach to planning and programming, coordination mechanisms and inter-agency cooperation;
- Promoting targeted pilot methodologies for the mainstreaming of human rights within the United Nations programming at both the country and regional levels;
- Developing, widening and enhancing OHCHR's network of partners and contacts in the region, identifying potential areas of cooperation for OHCHR;
- Promoting the ratification and implementation of international human rights instruments;
- Providing advice and assistance as requested by Governments;
- Participating as resource persons in human rights seminars, workshops and other activities in the region, as appropriate;
- In coordination with other UN and regional actors, following human

rights developments in the region, with a view to keeping OHCHR informed and advising on timely measures for OHCHR to take in order to contribute to the respect for human rights;
- Upon request, undertaking representational responsibilities on behalf of OHCHR and otherwise undertaking assignments or missions within the regions; and,
- Maintaining ongoing contacts with the High Commissioner's Regional Advisors and with the OHCHR Human Rights Regional Advisors.

XXIII. *Human Rights Field Presence in Sierra Leone (DPKO)*

Terms of Reference

UNAMSIL was established by Security Council resolution 1270 (1999) on October 1999 as a successor to the previous United Nations Observer Mission in Sierra Leone (UNOMSIL).

Functions/Mandate

The human rights mandate of UNAMSIL is wide-ranging and includes monitoring, reporting, technical assistance, training, capacity building, sensitization, and advocacy. Its major tasks have included facilitating the establishment of the National Human Rights Commission, and the Human Rights Documentation, Information and Training Centre as well as supporting the Office of the Ombudsman and the Lawyers Centre for Legal Assistance pursuant to OHCHR's technical co-operation project.

Additionally, the Human Rights Section has supported the preparatory process of the Sierra Leone TRC including support to investigations, identifications of sites.

Its work has also included the provision of support for the effective implementation of the human rights elements of the Lome Peace Agreement, including the Truth and Reconciliation Commission. The "Sierra Leone Human Rights Manifesto" signed on 24 June 1999 by the then High Commissioner for Human Rights, the Government, the representatives of civil society and the UN Special Representative of the Secretary-General, provides an additional framework for human rights activities.

UNAMSIL implements its human rights mandate within a collaborative framework, working as a partner with the Government, National Institutions, UN agencies, human rights and humanitarian non-governmental organisations, both national and international, the inter-religious communities and other members of civil society. In this regard it provides ongoing support to the Human Rights Committees of Sierra Leone. Training sessions on human rights monitoring, reporting and advocacy as well as other forms of technical assistance is provided to the Sierra Leone human rights community.

The existing linkages to the humanitarian emergency allow UNAMSIL to access donor support for its human rights programme through the Consolidated Inter-Agency Appeal for Sierra Leone.

The periodic reports of the Secretary-General to the Security Council on UNAMSIL's activities include a section on human rights, international humanitarian law, women rights, gender issues, rights of the child. UNAMSIL monthly human rights reports are also shared with the UN system, the Government and the diplomatic/donor communities.

Currently, UNAMSIL is assisting OHCHR in implementing activities to support the Sierra Leone Truth and Reconciliation Commission.

UNAMSIL provides technical assistance to non-State entities regarding applicable human rights and humanitarian standards including through education of youth and the provision of information to fighting factions.

UNAMSIL has established regional offices in various parts of Sierra Leone to provide human rights services, including monitoring, training and capacity building.

Main Activities

The main activities include:

- Under the guidance of OHCHR, technical assistance to the Truth and Reconciliation Commission and establishment of a legal aid project;
- Facilitation of and support to a programme of implementation of the human rights elements of the Lomé Peace Accord;
- Expert support for the establishment of a National Human Rights Commission;
- Monitoring and reporting of the human rights situation, including on violations of international humanitarian law;
- Monitoring of the conditions of detention;
- Assessment of the post-conflict environment from a gender perspective, including facilitation of programmes to address the specific needs of women and girls affected by the war;
- Monitoring and technical advice on child rights;
- Needs assessment and technical assistance towards re-establishment of the rule of law, in the field of human rights in the administration of justice;
- Mainstreaming human rights into the activities of the humanitarian community;

- Support to the Sierra Leone Human Rights Committees;
- Institutional support to national human rights NGOs under the umbrella of the National Forum for Human Rights;
- Provision of human rights training to human rights activists, police, the Sierra Leone Army, government officials, and UN peacekeepers, military observers and civilian police, religious and traditional leaders, judicial staff;
- Human Rights education and reconciliation initiatives for youth and the local communities;
- Promotion of human rights standards and applicable humanitarian law principles through UNAMSIL radio broadcasts.

XXIV. *Southern Africa Regional Human Rights Office (OHCHR)*

Terms of Reference/Legal Authority

The Southern Africa Regional Office was created under a Memorandum of Understanding concluded on 4 March, 1998 between UNDP and OHCHR as part of an overall strategy aimed at supporting UNDP Country Offices and UNCTs to follow up on the recommendations of the UN Secretary General's reform and address common concerns in the field of human rights for the countries of the Southern Africa sub-region.

Functions and Mandate

The Office is part of the overall OHCHR regional strategy and of the emerging regional strategy for Africa, and thereby aims to address common concerns for the southern Africa sub-region. It seeks to respond to the long-term objective of enhancing the capacity of African sub-regional organizations and governments, national institutions and civil society to promote and protect human rights. The Office covers fifteen countries in the Region namely: Angola, Botswana, Comoros, Lesotho, Madagascar, Malawi, Mauritius, Mozambique, Namibia, Seychelles, South Africa, Swaziland, Tanzania, Zambia and Zimbabwe.

Supporting Governments and civil society in the region to strengthen good governance, democracy and the rule of law and mainstreaming human rights in programmes and policies are equally important objectives of the Office. Assistance is also made available to United Nations Country Teams (UNCTs) in their efforts to develop a rights based approach to development. The location of the secretariats of the Southern African Community for Development (SADC) and the Common Market for Eastern and Southern

Africa (COMESA) respectively in Botswana and Zambia extends the Office's mandate to working with these regional organizations.

Main Activities

Under joint supervision of OHCHR and the United Nations Resident Coordinators of the participating countries, the Office:

a) Provides human rights training, technical advice and support to governments on treaty ratification, national human rights plans of action, national human rights institutions, treaty body reporting and the incorporation of international human rights standards into national legislation
b) Provides human rights training and support for UN field staff
c) Strengthens sub-regional networks through consultations with sub-regional organisations, facilitating exchanges among human rights experts and practitioners in the region, as well as implementing human rights workshops, seminars and training courses at the sub-regional level for specific target groups.

Under the former project, the Regional Office was conceived to support UN capacity in implementing a rights based approach and to respond to increasing requests for assistance by states in the sub-region. Thus, its response was targeted at training, advice and provision of human rights materials.

The Office facilitated or participated in training activities on integrating human rights into programming in the following countries: Zambia, Mauritius, Lesotho, Zimbabwe, Mozambique and Malawi. It also facilitated or assisted human rights training activities in Namibia, Mozambique, Botswana and Malawi. It was also implemented an adjunct training programme for the Southern African Regional Police Chiefs' Cooperation Organization (SARPCCO).

XXV. *Human Rights Field Presence in Serbia and Montenegro (including Kosovo) (OHCHR)*

Terms of Reference

OHCHR established its Field Presence in the, then, Federal Republic of Yugoslavia (FRY) in March 1996, initially as support to the mandate of the Special Rapporteur of the UN Commission on Human Rights (CHR). Events in the region underlined the need for a broad OHCHR mandate of human rights monitoring, reporting, promotion and protection, which was formalized through a status agreement concluded with the FRY in November 1998. With the transformation of FRY into the State Union of Serbia and Montenegro in January 2003, an additional Memorandum of Understanding was signed between the Council of Ministers of the State Union and OHCHR on 18 March 2003, which reaffirmed the terms of the earlier agreement [1] OHCHR continues to operate as one mission throughout the country, with offices in Serbia (Belgrade), Montenegro (Podgorica) and Kosovo (Pristina).

Functions and Mandate

The context of the OHCHR's work in Serbia and Montenegro is a complex one which demands a broad range of functional human rights activities. Following the significant political changes that took place in the Federal Republic of Yugoslavia in October 2000, much of the focus of the OHCHR's work within Serbia and Montenegro has therefore shifted from monitoring of individual human rights abuses to supporting the efforts of the newly-elected democratic government to carry out substantial reform of its institutions. Confidence-building measures such as training, promotion and education in basic human rights at the community level also serve a critical function both in developing national human rights capacity and in the prevention of future conflict.

OHCHR's medium term objectives in Serbia and Montenegro are to monitor, promote and support the effective implementation of international human rights standards as the "transition" governments undertake institutional reform programs. These objectives were pursued through a strategy of practical cooperation on human rights issues with relevant government authorities, international agencies, ethnic groups and representatives of civil society at the community level.

In the short-run, because of the assassination of Serbia's Prime Minister, the imposition of the State of Emergency and related events, OHCHR was very focused on ensuring that the government authorities understood the limits to derogation from international standards and that the behavior of the police and other state security bodies was being carefully monitored.

OHCHR is the only agency with a human rights based mandate in Serbia and Montenegro. Other actors concentrate their efforts on broad institutional reform and often incorporate human rights into their work. OHCHR has a key role to complement this work through its "arms length" monitoring and analysis (including skills in interviewing victims) of human rights violations and by serving as a link/bridge to the UN human rights mechanisms, particularly the Special Representative of the Commission for

Human Rights. OHCHR provides an objective and transparent "reality check" on the progress being made in the reform process—which is crucial because the process is often presented in unrealistically positive terms.

In Serbia and Montenegro, OHCHR coordinates activities with OSCE, Council of Europe, the UNCT, Government ministries, the Human Rights Contact Group, with NGOs engaged in human rights, development and humanitarian work and with embassies. In Kosovo OHCHR coordinated with UNMIK, KFOR and the Provisional Institutions of Self-Government (PISG), as well as with NGOs, other international agencies and embassies.

Main Activities

In 2003, OHCHR reoriented its activities in Southeast Europe from predominantly country-specific programs towards issues of region-wide concern. The Stabilization and Association Process of the European Commission (EC) provides the framework for preparing the countries of the region for a closer relationship with the European Union. In particular, these countries are required to meet a list of standards, including respect for democratic principles, sustainable returns and economic development. The majority of these requirements involves the adoption of new legislation. While there has been obvious progress in passing necessary legislation throughout the region, it is also common knowledge that effective implementation of these new laws has been highly deficient for different reasons, including weak judiciaries, insufficient access to justice, an absence of witness protection, inefficient police structures, lack of civil society participation, non-functioning administrative structures and weak national human rights protection institutions. This failure to effectively implement new legislation and policy standards has been the principal roadblock to longer-term stability, the development of democratic government institutions and respect for human rights.

While the Field Presences and Technical Cooperation Offices continue to protect and promote human rights within their respective mandate and country, priorities provide a framework for closer cooperation between offices, the allocation of resources, the selection of tasks and the definition of benchmarks and exit strategies.

The office strives to support the cooperation of governments and civil society within the region in its efforts to find sustainable solutions for the human rights challenges related to the following five priority areas:

(1) Impunity and the rule of law
(2) Human rights frameworks for development including poverty reduction strategies

(3) Human trafficking, gender and gender-based violence, exploitation and discrimination
(4) Human rights frameworks for the movement of people, including durable solutions for refugees and IDPs
(5) Human Rights Education and Promotion, including the strengthening of civil society

Training and Capacity-Building

OHCHR has developed a training and promotional package for government ministries to ensure timely and quality reporting to the 6 human rights treaty bodies. These cover ministries at the Federal level and both Republics. In parallel, OHCHR has developed a training package for NGOs in the FRY region to strengthen their knowledge and capacity to use the treaty mechanisms, including shadow reporting and joint advocacy/lobbying strategies.

OHCHR further participates in joint training with OSCE, the Council of Europe and local NGOs to ensure the international human rights standards are presented and understood. OHCHR also undertakes "stand alone" training activities, particularly at the grass roots/community level to ensure that international human rights and norms are fully integrated into national training activities of a broad range of actors.

Support of the UN Human Rights System

OHCHR has unique expertise and role as a "two-way" facilitator between the UN human rights mechanisms and national actors (government and civil society). The office supports treaty bodies and mechanisms of the Commission on Human Rights (e.g. CAT, Working Group on Arbitrary Detention, Special Rapporteur on Human Rights Defenders etc). Through its field presence, OHCHR is able to ensure that UN Committees and Experts get effective access to information and organizations in Serbia and Montenegro and, reciprocally, that local actors understand and establish effective contacts with the human rights mechanisms. OHCHR's Role in Kosovo.

OHCHR has unique monitoring and advisory role in Kosovo that is "arms length" from the UNMIK and KFOR structures. It monitors the human rights situation in Kosovo and makes concrete conclusions and practical recommendations to the governing authorities (UNMIK, KFOR and the new local assembly). Since mid-2002, OHCHR has participated as a member of a 2-tier human rights monitoring mechanism established by UNMIK—the Human Rights Oversight Committee (HROC) and the

Human Rights Working Group (HRWG). The Office also cooperates with the Government of Finland in a substantial human rights promotion and education project.

Vulnerable Groups and Minorities, including Refugees, IDPs and Roma

The human rights dimensions of problems involving IDPs, Refugees and Roma are often overlooked or misunderstood. At a time when these issues are attracting a good deal of public and political debate, OHCHR has a crucial role to play in ensuring that these vulnerable groups are treated as stakeholders and owners of human rights. To this end, OHCHR: (i) reviews and supports efforts at the national level to integrate human rights into national strategy plans for the alleviation of poverty (PRSP) for vulnerable groups—in particular to improve the socio-economic situation of Roma. (ii) chairs a human rights contact group to look at the human rights dimensions of these issues (iii) participates in an OCHA-led working group dealing with IDPs, (iv) reviews and comments on the FRY national strategy plans for refugees and IDPs and the UNMIK (ORC) Strategy for returns to Kosovo to ensure compatibility with human rights norms, including the IDP Guiding Principles; (v) provides independent analysis and recommendations and public reports that highlight the human rights dimensions of the issues and, where necessary, raises public awareness through the media.

Role within the UN Country Team

OHCHR offers practical advice to members of the UN Country Team (UNCT) to ensure that human rights are understood and better integrated into common policy, strategic and programmatic initiatives, including UNDAF, CAP and CCA processes. OHCHR works for example with the UN Country Team (UNCT) in Southern Serbia to ensure that human rights dimensions of humanitarian and development work are fully integrated in the policy, planning and programmes of the members of UNCT, including the CCA/UNDAF.

Southern Serbia

Since early 2001, OHCHR has played a practical role in Southern Serbia to ensure that the terms of peace negotiated between the authorities and Albanian leadership contained suitable human rights guarantees. Since then OHCHR has maintained a full time human rights officer in Southern Serbia to monitor progress in implementing the peace plan, working with the UNCT, OSCE, and local Albanian leadership on a broad range of human rights issues. This unique role of monitoring, and confidence-building on human rights issues is shaped to complement the programmes of other actors in that region. OHCHR carried out field missions to the Sandzak region (both Serbia and Montenegro sides) to identify critical human rights issues that require specific attention and that need to be taken into account in broader institutional reform efforts of other actors such as OSCE etc.

Monitoring and Reporting on Impunity

OHCHR has a particular role and expertise in monitoring, analysing and reporting the extent to which impunity exists in Serbia and Montenegro. This involves trial monitoring, interviewing witnesses and victims of serious human rights violations (especially by police) and analyzing the effectiveness of prosecutors, investigating judges and trials. The purpose of individual case monitoring is to identify and analyze systemic trends/problems and to make recommendations to relevant actors to take remedial action. This role is not undertaken by any other international actor and is uniquely performed by OHCHR. It provides important empirical evidence and human rights analysis against which the broader process of reform can be assessed and modified. National Human Rights institutions/Ombudsman

OHCHR works in close collaboration with OSCE and the Council of Europe to create national human rights institution(s) in Serbia and Montenegro and also supports the work of the Kosovo Ombudsman. Each agency has brought its own expertise to the process in a mutually-reinforcing way. This cooperation has resulted in coherent advice from the international community and a nascent institution that meets basic human rights criteria as to mandate and independence.

Human Rights Co-ordination and Creation of a Human Rights Resource Centre

The Office created and steers the Belgrade Human Rights Contact Group (made up of national NGOs and main international actors, including OSCE, the Council of Europe and members of the UNCT) and chairs thematic working groups on human rights issues such as Roma and IDPs. This venue also serves to strengthen the network between human rights NGOs in Serbia and Montenegro. This model is being replicated by OHCHR's Sub-Office's in Kosovo and Montenegro.

OHCHR is developing a project to create a Human Rights Resource Centre in Belgrade that will serve as a common and neutral resource for many local agencies working in Serbia. It will become the repository for human rights information and resource materials from national, regional and international sources and be a community-owned venue where human rights can be promoted and disseminated among civil society.

Human Rights Education and Promotion

OHCHR has a 2-pronged approach to human rights education. At the community level, it has developed small but sharply focused projects to encourage local NGO capacities. These projects also provide data and material on human rights education that can be collated and used for broader educational reform at the central level. At the central level, the Office uses the empirical results of these community activities to encourage central education authorities to make changes in the way human rights are treated in school curricula and in the methodology of teacher training.

Specifically, the State Union indicated its wish to avail itself of advisory services and technical support "to strengthen national capacities and institutions for the protection and promotion of human rights," which were described in greater detail in an annex on "Agreed thematic areas of technical cooperation." The listed themes have included: assisting the State Union in meeting its reporting obligations under the UN treaties; supporting the establishment of effective national human rights institutions; promoting respect for the rule of law with particular reference to reform of the judiciary, police, media, and armed forces; integrating human rights standards into development and the poverty reduction strategies, with particular reference to such marginalized groups like the Roma, the elderly, persons with disabilities and internally displaced persons; support for efforts to combat trafficking and criminality; promoting awareness of human rights in civil society and the introduction of human rights into formal education; and promoting the human rights dimensions of refugees and internally displaced persons.

XXVI. *Human Rights Field Presence in Sudan (OHCHR)*

Terms of Reference/Legal Authority

On 29 March 2000 the Government of the Republic of the Sudan and the OHCHR signed an Agreement for the provision of technical cooperation in the field of human rights. The agreement followed the adoption of Commission on Human Rights resolution 1999/15, which reflected a request for technical cooperation in the field of human rights put forward by the Government of the Sudan. In the follow-up to this agreement, an

OHCHR advisor on human rights was sent to Sudan in March 2001. The OHCHR advisor has been posted in the framework of the UNDP office in Khartoum with the task of advising the Government of the Sudan on the development of national capacity to promote and protect human rights.

Functions/Mandate

The project aims at strengthening the human rights capacities of the Government of the Sudan (hereinafter GOS) and civil society institutions, by focusing on training programs for governmental and non-governmental institutions. A phased approach has been planned to deliver assistance in terms of providing advisory services to the GOS and the civil society on the development of national capacities to promote and protect human rights. The scope of the assistance is evaluated on the basis of its potential in improving the actual human rights situation on the ground.

Main Activities Carried Out as of March 2003

The first phase of the project, from March to September 2001 focussed on the formulation of projects in cooperation with the GOS and other local counterparts. Following wide consultations, concrete project proposals were formulated in the following fields: administration of justice, legislative reform and human rights education.

The second phase (October 2001 through March 2002) marked the implementation of a number of human rights training seminars. Three initial project activities, including human rights training seminars for national NGOs, the police, and security officers as well as government officials on reporting obligations were carried out.

The third phase, ongoing until March 2003, focuses on the provision of more in-depth training for groups already targeted during the previous phase, as well as the provision of new sessions for new groups (including the Advisory Council for Human Rights, religious groups, prison officers, media operators, parliamentarians and judges) and/or on new topics (such as ratification of CAT, accession to CEDAW, national institutions).

An evaluation of the project took place in mid 2003. As a result, the project will be implemented more closely with the UNCT Sudan.

As part of the UN action plan for Darfur, OHCHR has deployed some of human rights observers since mid-August, 2004. At the same time, OHCHR is working closely with UNAMIS as well as UN humanitarian and development agencies and programmes (in particular UNHCR, OCHA and UNDP) in order to contribute to enhancing the level of protection for affected people in Darfur. The human rights observers are currently deployed in the three States in Darfur (El Fashir, Nyala and El Geneina) so as to promote and protect human rights and follow up on cases with the relevant national authorities.

XXVII. *Sri Lanka*

In June 2004, a Senior Human Rights Advisor attached to the UN Country Team, arrived in Colombo, Sri Lanka. The senior adviser, Mr. Rory Mungoven, works closely with the Resident Coordinator and UN agencies to advise and support strategies to protect human rights and build the human rights capacity of local institutions, civil society and UN itself, particularly in the context of Sri Lanka's evolving peace process.

XXVIII. *Human Rights Field Presence in Tajikistan (DPA)*

Terms of Reference/Legal Authority

The Republic of Tajikistan declared its independence in September 1991. Following the outbreak of a ivil war in the country, the UN Mission of Observers in Tajikistan (UNMOT) was established in 1994. UNMOT assisted the process of negotiations between the conflicting parties and in 1997 the General agreement of peace and national reconciliation in Tajikistan was signed under the UN auspices. It laid the basis for parliamentary elections in February 2000. The mandate of UNMOT expired in May 2000.

1 June 2000, the UN Tajikistan Office of Peace-building (UNTOP) was established with a small international staff under the authority of the DPA. Its objectives are to consolidate the peace, mobilize international resources and assistance for national recovery and reconstruction, coordinate and focus the efforts of the UN country team in matters related to peace-building, promote the rule of law and strengthening democratic institutions and provide support for local human rights initiatives.

A human rights officer was included in the staffing table of UNTOP and deployed in Dushanbe in April 2001. The HRO reports monthly to the OHCHR through the RSG. Local legal officer works with the human rights officer.

Functions and Mandate

Following a request by the Government of Tajikistan for assistance from the OHCHR in July 1999, the OHCHR conducted a mission in order to assess the technical cooperation needs in the area of reporting under human rights treaties in May 2000, as the country had failed until then to fulfil its reporting obligations under the main human rights instruments. The mission recommended providing support in setting up appropriate mechanism to coordinate the reporting responsibilities of the country, carrying out capacity building activities for government structures and NGOs and human rights awareness raising campaign for the general public. The Technical cooperation mission also expressed readiness to provide advice and support to the process of developing and implementing a national program for human rights education.

The human rights officer designed two projects, which received funding by the German Government in 2002–1) on enhancing country's capacities in implementing its treaty reporting obligations and 2) on capacity development in human rights education. In 2003–2004. Follow-up projects received funding respectively by SIDA and the British Government.

In March 2002 Tajikistan was visited by delegation of experts of the OHCHR within the Central Asia HR Needs Assessment Mission. The country has beene included in the Central Asia Regional project of the OHCHR.

Main Activities

Activities carried out in Tajikistan so far include the following:

- Seminars on the objectives and mechanism of human rights reporting—In 2002 they focused on ICCPR and CEDAW, and in 2003–2004 CERD, ICESCR and CAT seminars will follow. Participants include members of the Government Commission in charge of treaty reporting, which was established in 2002, as well as experts and NGOs, engaged in the drafting of the reports.
- Four weeklong trainings were held June-August 2003 on human rights education strategies and techniques, targeting teachers and NGOs in support of the implementation of the Government Programme on Human Rights Education adopted in June 2001.
- In-service training was held in the Academy of Re-training of educational staff in Moscow for the best participants selected from the four trainings in June-August 2003.
- Competitions for the best essays on the subject "Human Rights and You" for secondary school children were organized as well as competition for teachers and NGOs on small projects of human rights lessons in schools.
- Two training exercises and a competition for best articles on human rights for journalists, were carried out in 2003 and 2004, aimed at

raising public awareness and better understanding of human rights.

- A Human Rights Information Centre was opened, providing access to the Internet and printed materials on human rights education and treaty reporting for the public and for the members of the Government commission on treaty reporting. The Centre maintains a HRE website www.tjhr.info

In 2002, a newspaper on human rights education as an attachment to the Teachers Gazette started publishing, and is distributed to all schools in the country and local administration bodies dealing with education. The office provides human rights training for judges and defence lawyers carried out within UNDP supported project of the NGO Legal Education Centre.

The HR office activities include, as well, handling of individual complaints and providing legal advice to visitors. The office maintains contacts with the relevant authorities aimed at redressing cases of HR violations.

XXIX. *Human Rights Field Presence in Timor-Leste (DPKO)*

Terms of Reference

The United Nations Mission of Support in East Timor (UNMISET) was established by Security Council resolution 1410 (2002) of 17 May 2002 for an initial period of 12 months, starting on 20 May 2002, to succeed the United Nations Transitional Administration in East Timor (UNTAET), with the following mandate:

- To provide assistance to core administrative structures critical to the viability and stability of East Timor;
- To provide interim law enforcement and public security and to assist in the development of a new law enforcement agency in East Timor, the East Timor Police Service (EPTS)
- To contribute to the maintenance of the external and internal security of East Timor.

The Security Council also requested UNMISET to give full effect to the three Programmes of the Mandate Implementation Plan as set out in the report of the Secretary-General of 17 April 2002:

- Stability, Democracy and Justice
- Public Security and Law Enforcement
- External Security and Border Control

UNMISET is composed of a civilian component, a police component and a military component. The civilian component includes an Office of the

SRSG, a Directorate of Administration, a group of 100 experts to provide critical assistance to the emergent Government and a Serious Crimes Unit to assist in the conduct of serious crimes investigations and proceedings. The Human Rights Unit (HRU) was established as part of the civilian component and is located in the Office of the Special Representative of the Secretary-General. In its current form, there are 10 East Timorese human rights officers and 14 international human rights officers.

Mandate and Functions

The main areas of focus of the HRU are providing information and advice on the human rights situation and on mechanisms to guarantee full respect for human rights and maintaining liaison with the Reception, Truth and Reconciliation Commission; the Unit also provides human rights training for United Nations and East Timorese officers, in particular police and personnel. The HRU also participates in ongoing activities to ensure a vibrant human rights community will remain after the departure of UNTAET.

Main Activities

The main activities are:

- Advising on the human rights situation to the SRSG and OHCHR
- Advising the government on human rights including needs for protection of human rights
- Developing and publishing relevant human rights materials in local languages
- Providing human rights training to members of the Timor-Leste Police Service and the Prisons Service
- Providing training and support to human rights NGOs
- Supporting the Commission on Reception, Truth and Reconciliation
- Assisting the strengthening of the justice system
- Monitoring the development of laws for consistency with human rights standards and providing advice when requested

CHAPTER ELEVEN

ENHANCING PROTECTION OF WOMEN AND GIRLS IN CONFLICT AND POST-CONFLICT ENVIRONMENTS

Comfort Lamptey[1]

Introduction: The Value of a Gender Lens

Protecting civilians in conflict environments requires an approach aimed at meeting the specific and immediate needs of the affected populations with respect and dignity, whilst also investing in building the capacities of civilian populations to better protect themselves in the long-term. In this regard, measures to ensure protection of civilians have to both identify and analyse problems and challenges that are common to the entire civilian populations, as well as those that are specific in nature to different categories of civilians. In the latter case, the application of a gender perspective provides a means for effectively addressing the specific needs of different groups in a community.

In simple terms, a gender perspective requires a commitment to identifying the differential impact of conflicts on the lives of women, men, boys and girls, and proposing practical solutions to respond to the specific needs identified. In most instances a gender-sensitive approach needs to be complemented with targeted support to empower women in conflict situations, whose social, political and economic status in society is oftentimes unequal to those of men, a situation which is further compounded by the dynamics of the conflict situations.

The specific protection challenges that confront women and girls in recent conflict history, is very often linked to gender inequalities that they faced in society prior to the conflict, and which take on expanded proportions during the war. Specific targeting of civilians in conflicts today also means that women and girls may be victimized in different ways to men and boys.

I. *Risks Facing Women and Girls*

The most common threats to the physical protection of women in conflict environments include harassment, extortion, abductions, rape, forced and

[1] The views expressed are those of the author in her personal capacity.

Bertrand G. Ramcharan (Ed.), Human Rights Protection in the Field, 211–223.

early marriage and forced prostitution that they endure at the hands of both armed fighters and other civilians. Sadly, gender-based violence has become an "inevitable" consequence of wars today. Forced family separations, which oftentimes leave women alone to shoulder the responsibility of care for children, the sick and elderly family members, together with the accompanying trauma of this experience, also presents another level of challenge. The increase in the number of female-headed households during and in the aftermath of conflicts due to the desertion, death, abduction or recruitment of male family members into fighting forces, serve to further deepen women's economic insecurity. Moreover, the fact that women are often under-represented in formal decision-making mechanisms—whether at the level of community structures or in political processes for building peace, further undermines their ability to influence and contribute perspectives that will address these challenges in any meaningful way.

Much of the existing literature on the protection of civilians in conflict acknowledges the adverse impact of conflicts on women and children. Such assertions about the vulnerability of women have not generally translated into any intentional commitment to analysing and addressing the causes of women's vulnerability. Nor have they translated into operational measures that recognise and build on women's potential as change agents, with real capacities to contribute to efforts aimed at building peace and security, in spite of the existence of a range of international instruments and agreements specifically targeted to the protection of women and girls in conflict.

II. *International Framework for Protection of Women and Girls*

For over a decade now, there have been increasing calls to recognise and build on women's capacities to contribute to peace and security in conflict situations. These calls have been vocally expressed by women in conflict zones themselves and have found expression in international commitments and instruments for the advancement of women. In 1995, the Beijing Declaration and Platform for Action highlighted the protection of women in conflict as one of the 12 critical areas of concern. The 1998 Rome Statute of the International Criminal Court (ICC) defines a broad spectrum of gender-based violence as crimes against humanity and war crimes. These include rape, sexual slavery, forced pregnancy and sterilization, and gender-based persecution. In 1999, the UN Security Council adopted Resolution 1265 on the Protection of Civilians in Armed Conflicts, which called on the international community to ensure that the special protection needs of women and children are addressed in all peacemaking, peacekeeping and peace-building efforts.

In 2000, the Security Council adopted Resolution 1325, a landmark resolution on Women, Peace and Security, which both acknowledged the need to address the specific vulnerabilities of women in conflict situations, and also to capitalise on the untapped potential of women to contribute to efforts to establish peace and security. The resolution elaborates recommendations which hold the international community accountable for the protection of women at a number of key levels, which include reversing the marginalisation of women's perspectives in processes for building peace and security; addressing the adverse consequences of war on women and ensuring gender justice for victims of gender-based violence crimes; and recognising the leadership potential and further capacitating women as agents of change in rebuilding post-conflict societies. To date, Security Council Resolution 1325 continues to serve as a guiding framework for engaging and drawing on women's contributions to peacemaking processes at all levels.

III. *Impact of Existing International Instruments*

In the 10 years and 5 years since the adoption of the Beijing Declaration and Platform for Action, and Security Council Resolution 1325 respectively, one can point to mixed results in the level of success in ensuring effective protection of women and girls in conflicts.

At one level, the adoption of specific institutional commitments for the protection of women and girls by international actors operating in conflict environments is one area where much success can be cited. Among humanitarian agencies, the United Nations High Commissioner for Refugees (UNHCR), the World Food Programme (WFP) and the Office for the Coordination of Humanitarian Assistance (OCHA) have all adopted specific commitments or policies aimed at ensuring that their operational programmes work to facilitate better protection of women and girls. The United Nations Department of Peacekeeping Operations (DPKO) has also adopted a policy statement and established institutional mechanisms to support integration of gender perspectives in all functional areas of peacekeeping operations. Other multi-lateral and bilateral donor agencies and humanitarian NGOs operating in conflict environments for the most part, all have in place policies and procedures aimed at ensuring better protection of women and girls.

In spite of the existence of policy and institutional commitments by most of the key actors engaged in the protection of civilians, effective protection of women and girls remains a challenge in most conflict environments today. The following will review the manifestation of this challenge at three key levels. The first level pertains to the conceptual flaws that inform how we define and operationise the objective of protection of women and girls in conflicts. The second challenge relates to the problem of gender-based violence against women and girls and how this continues to undermine and threaten effective protection efforts. The third challenge concerns the persisting economic marginalisation and insecurity of women and girls in conflict environments, which serves to increase their vulnerability to a range of other protection threats.

(a) *Protection through Empowerment*

The notion of women and children as vulnerable, and as victims, permeates much of the theoretical and programmatic approaches to the protection of civilians in conflict situations. Whilst it is indeed the case that women are vulnerable to specific forms of victimization in conflict as has been illustrated above, there is a delicate balance to strike between recognising and addressing the specific vulnerabilities of women and girls, and at the same time ensuring that the definition of protection incorporates an empowerment approach. Programmes and initiatives that take as their starting point a definition of women as vulnerable, fail to ensure effective protection for women and girls in the long term, as they inadvertently reinforce gender inequalities and undermine the capacity and ability of women and girls to protect themselves. This latter outcome however, ultimately provides the best measurement of sustainability and success of these programmes.

Protection as empowerment is critical for building on the capacities and strengths of women to contribute to both short and long-term investments for peace and security. Furthermore an empowerment approach ensures effective harnessing of the opportunities that arise to advance women's rights in conflict environments, through the increased responsibilities that they assume at family and community levels. Situating empowerment as a central component of the protection strategies, needs to underpin both conceptual and operational approaches to protection of women and girls in conflict. It requires a commitment to engaging and listening to women and girls and refraining from the trap of only talking to male leaders and representatives in communities affected by conflicts, or to elite groups of women who may have different interests and priorities to those of the wider community of women. Furthermore, it also requires investments in supporting women and girls to define their own priorities and capitalising on the opportunities presented to advance women's economic, political and social rights and to fully harness their potential to contribute to the peacebuilding agenda.

(b) *Preventing the Scourge of Gender-based Violence*

Gender-based violence—including rape, sexual slavery, forced and early marriage and forced prostitution—is one of the most critical protection challenges confronting women and girls in conflict environments today. In spite of the availability and proliferation of literature and documentary evidence on the pervasive nature of this problem—with its sometimes fatal consequences on the lives of women and girls—gender based violence in conflict situations continues unabated. Some individual agencies including the International Rescue Committee, UNHCR and the UN Population Fund (UNFPA) have initiated specific programmes to address this problem, whilst at the inter-agency level, some efforts have been made in a number of countries including the Democratic Republic of Congo and Haiti, to establish national mechanisms to address violence against women. These investments are however insufficient to address the scale of the problem and often focus on addressing its consequences.

There remains to date no effective mechanism for preventing violence against women in conflict situations. Furthermore, the tendency in many quarters to dismiss this problem as an "inevitable" consequence of war, and the culture of impunity that for the most part exists for gender-based violence crimes, has fuelled this acceptance. The resulting situation is one whereby no systematic data on the scope and the scale of the problem exists. Moreover, there remains inadequate medical, psychosocial, economic and legal support for victims and survivors, who suffer in silence and are often subjected to shame and blame at the hands of their own communities. A reversal of this trend requires that the dominant opinion of the international community and leaders of warring factions in conflict environments, collectively reject the notion of "inevitability" of this problem. It also requires instituting sanctions against armed groups that perpetuate such crimes, whilst ensuring that individual perpetrators are prosecuted.

Prevention of gender-based violence crimes can also be further advanced if more men speak out against these acts and actively engage in all efforts to address this problem. Male political leaders in conflict situations, international and regional partners facilitating peace negotiations and peace-building processes, need to raise the issue of gender-based violence as a core element of the peace and security agenda. A preventive regime further requires that the post-conflict peace-building agenda, situates gender-based violence as a clear and pressing priority to facilitate the consolidation of peace and to support national reconstruction efforts, since the threats to women's lives that is posed by this problem serves to weaken social cohesion and thus undermines the peace dividend itself.

(c) *Addressing the Economic Security Challenge*

The third type of protection challenge under review relates to the question of economic insecurity and economic marginalisation of women and girls in conflict environments, a situation which can work to perpetuate other protection risks including forced prostitution and early marriage. The increased levels of financial responsibility that women assume in war-times, coupled with the rise in the numbers of female-headed households, is often set against a background of limited economic empowerment opportunities available to them. In environments where men are better educated and better informed than women, they are better-placed to access available jobs with international humanitarian agencies operating at community and national levels. Moreover, humanitarian actors and institutions in the field often do not give priority to deliberately targeting women for employment opportunities within their agencies, a factor that further perpetuates this problem.

In those instances where women are targeted for livelihood-related activities, these tend to be limited to small-scale, subsistence level activities in a narrow range of sectors, which may not be linked to market demands, and which therefore limits the possibility of lifting women out of economic destitution. This situation is rife in many displaced and refugee situations. Skills training programmes targeted to women and girls are likewise limited in range and scope and are often confined to traditional activities such as soap-making, embroidery and tailoring. By inadvertently defining support to women's economic activities in small-scale terms, generally outside the scope and framework of mainstream national economic regeneration efforts, the potential to fully mobilise women's economic capital towards post-conflict reconstruction efforts is severely curtailed. Moreover, where livelihood support to women fails to adequately respond to their economic insecurity, women who are living on the margins of survival and unable to meet their basic subsistence needs, are in some cases forced to trade their bodies as the only "bargaining chip" they have to supplement their daily subsistence needs.

Investing in women's economic empowerment is thus an effective protection strategy in conflict and post-conflict environments, which holds both short and longer-term benefits. It requires going beyond mere subsistence level activities in traditional sectors of the economy, to ensuring a diversification of economic activities that target women to non-traditional sectors that are linked to the demands of the market economy. Moreover, such support has to form an integral part of mainstream economic reconstruction efforts in post-conflict environments. Building and strengthening women's economic security, stands as one of the most effective protection strategies to prevent the vulnerability of women and girls to forced prostitution and sexual exploitation in conflict environments.

Against this background we turn to the protection of women in peacekeeping environments.

IV. *Protection of Women in Peacekeeping Environments*

In the period prior to October 2000, the international system was in advocacy mode. As a collective, we were missing a framework for addressing the specific concerns of women in conflict environments and for integrating a gender perspective into policy and institutional processes for building peace.

Women's rights groups were advocating, the world over, for greater attention to the role of women in conflict and peace processes. Regional and country-level networks of women's groups were established in Africa, Asia, Europe and the Americas to spearhead this advocacy. The wide-scale reports of crimes against women in the conflicts in Rwanda and the former Yugoslavia, increasing reports of abductions and forced slavery of girls in the wars in Sierra Leone and Liberia, all added to this momentum. A strong force of women's rights activists working on the process for the establishment of the International Criminal Court advocated and succeeded in gaining recognition for rape as a crime against humanity in the context of war, and this success further galvanized the movement and strengthened calls for a systematic review of the role and impact of armed conflicts on women.

Against the backdrop of wide-scale incidences of violence against women in conflict situations, was the sober reality of an absence of women in processes for negotiating peace. Women in Burundi and Liberia had been campaigning, with limited success, for a voice in the peace negotiations in their respective countries. The Dayton Peace Accords for Bosnia and Herzegovina did not include any reference to gender or women, which served as another missed opportunity for women in the implementation of the peace agreement.

The time was ripe for change. There was an important precedent that had been set by the Graca Machel Study on the Impact of Armed Conflict on Children, which had made a significant impact on the international community's response to this issue by providing a framework for concerted response and a monitoring mechanism. This prompted calls for a similar review of the situation of women in conflict and peace processes leading to the adoption of Security Council resolution 1325 on Women and Peace and Security, and indeed culminated in the Report of the Secretary-General on Women, Peace and Security in October 2002.

A number of enabling conditions facilitated the birth of resolution 1325, including the support of some Member States on the Security Council, who forged alliances with United Nations agencies and civil society organisations to introduce the subject of Women, Peace and Security on the agenda of the Council. Also of importance was the commitment of significant resources by some Security Council members to advance the work of United Nations entities and civil society actors in this area of work.

(a) *The Conceptual Pillars of Security Council Resolution 1325*

Security Council resolution 1325 provides a framework for a system-wide response and for ensuring greater responsibility, at political decision-making levels of peace and security, for addressing the impact of conflicts on women. It has reinforced already existing legal frameworks, including the provisions of the Statute of the International Criminal Court, which recognised systematic rape of women in conflict as a war crime and a crime against humanity. It has further reinforced CEDAW and provided a framework for ensuring that the provisions of CEDAW for expanding the participation of women in political decision-making processes equally applies to women's participation in conflict mediation and peace negotiation processes.

The organising theme of the resolution is *Women as actors* in conflict and post-conflict processes. The resolution elaborates recommendations which hold the international community accountable for addressing this theme at a number of key levels:

- reversing the marginalisation of women's perspectives in processes for building peace and security;
- addressing the adverse consequences of war on women and ensuring gender justice for victims of gender-based violence crimes;
- recognizing the leadership potential and further capacitating women as agents of change in rebuilding post-conflict societies.

(b) *The Impact of Resolution 1325*

The impact of resolution 1325 has been mixed: some progress has been made at the high levels of policy-making but it has been slow at the structural and operational levels.

(1) *Political and Institutional Mechanisms*
Progress at this level includes the institutionalisation of this issue as an agenda item for the Security Council on an annual basis. Some Member States have elaborated national plans of action to facilitate implementation of resolution 1325. Within the United Nations, some Departments and Agencies have established programmes to facilitate implementation of resolution 1325 and the Secretary-General is requiring a system-wide action plan for monitoring implementation of the resolution. Within the Department of Peacekeeping Operations, for example, significant steps have been made to ensure that gender components are integrated in the planning of peacekeeping operations and that gender units exist in all multi-dimensional peacekeeping operations. Tools and resources to support gender mainstreaming efforts have, and continue, to be developed.

The Office of the Special Adviser to the Secretary-General on Gender Equality and the Advancement of Women has a dedicated staff capacity to monitor and coordinate system-wide implementation of the resolution. UNIFEM has a full-fledged programme on women, peace and security, and there is an established NGO Working Group on women, peace and security which has been working to ensure continued advocacy with Member States and the UN on implementation of the resolution. In October 2004, the Secretary-General presented a comprehensive report to the Security Council on system-wide progress with implementation of resolution 1325, which reflects some of these successes.

(2) *Impact on Women in Conflict/Post-Conflict Environment*
The real test of the impact of resolution 1325 lies in reviewing the ground reality of women in conflict situations. One should consider how Security Council resolution 1325 has succeeded in integrating the perspectives of women in peace processes; in protecting women from gender-based violence and in mobilising women as agents of change in post-conflict reconstruction processes. The results at all three levels have been mixed and three examples illustrate this.

(3) *Gender Mainstreaming in DDR Processes*
In Liberia, there has been: successful integration of gender concerns in the DDR programme, with acceptance of the concept of the term—women associated with fighting forces (WAFF); successful policy, planning and implementation level interventions; addressing gender issues in DDR procedures and camp layouts; tracking the number of women disarmed and demobilized—over 21,000 to date. The original estimate was for 2000 women. In spite of this, there are those in Liberia who believe that many

female combatants have still been left out of the process. Challenges, however, relate to the absence of female Military Observers on the ground.

In the Democratic Republic of the Congo, gender mainstreaming in the DDR process has been more challenging. Eligibility for access to the DDR programme has not been recognized for WAFF, and women's concerns have been recognized only at the 'R', Relief, stage. The link between SSR and DDR at the 'R' stage and implications of this for addressing gender concerns have not been well-articulated in the operational context, with a key challenge being how to address women's security concerns when ex-combattants are returning to communities where a credible national police and professional army is not in place to assure them of protection. Limited attention to gender in the SSR process will negatively impact on how women participate in other areas of post conflict reconstruction such as elections.

In Haiti, a reverse picture is presented with regards to the link between women's sense of security and the DDR process. A recent assessment of the DDR in Gonaives illustrates this complexity. Here, women are accepting the use of violence by male gang leaders who they see as their protectors and on whom they depend for economic survival as the main providers and are therefore less reluctant to support the DDR process.

In short, gender mainstreaming in the DDR process is not systematized across the board.

(d) *Women's participation in political decision-making processes*

In Afghanistan, women's participation in the political process can be hailed as a success case: 40% female turn-out in the elections of October 2004, a female presidential candidate; integration of gender concerns in the constitutional drafting process, with a constitutional guarantee of 25% seats for women in the Lower House and 17% of seats in the Upper House in the impending Parliamentary elections. The impact of these advances at the political levels is unevenly felt across the country, though 70% of Afghan women are still in rural areas and have experienced limited change in their status.

In the Great Lakes of central Africa, there has been the successful articulation of women's agenda within the conference themes of the Great Lakes Conference and gender considerations are reflected in the Declaration from the summit of Heads of States, though the main gap that persists is the absence of an implementation strategy.

In Haiti and Burundi, women have participated in preparations for elections, seeking to achieve quota for women's candidates in the run-up to the elections.

In Sudan, there was limited participation of women in the peace talks that preceded the signing of the recent peace agreement. Lack of knowledge among parties to the conflict of the provisions of Security Council resolution 1325 and lack of reference to the resolution among international facilitators amounted to a missed opportunity.

(e) *Gender-based violence in conflict/post-conflict situations*

This is, unfortunately, the level at which the process remains limited still, after four years. At the inter-agency level, some efforts have been made to establish national plans of action for addressing violence against women—for example in Haiti and the DRC, though these serve more as mechanisms for strengthening coordinated actions and activities for prevention and support to victims of sexual violence.

Within functional work areas of peacekeeping there is still much work to be done: addressing the capacity of the police sector to deal with crimes against women, through influencing the training curricula of newly-established police units in Haiti, Liberia and Burundi; institutionalising the establishment of crimes-against-women cells in police stations, as has been tried in Sierra Leone and Timor Leste, though these are *ad hoc* initiatives that need to be further strengthened as part of standard peacekeeping support; ensuring that women and girls are protected from gender-based violence through DDR processes—from camp layout to protection of women and girls in receiving communities; strengthening the nexus between protection of women and girls from gender-based violence within the context of HIV/AIDS programming; systematic attention to gender-based violence crimes within transitional justice mechanisms.

Within the broader environment of conflict and post-conflict situations there is little systematic approach to addressing the continuum of violence against women in conflict situations—whether through ensuring systems for documenting crimes, ensuring support for victims/survivors, ending impunity, to the task of reversing women's continued vulnerability to gender-based violence in post-conflict situations. The culture of impunity for gender-based violence crimes continues to be sustained in post-conflict environments in situations where traditional justice systems prevail. In the case of Afghanistan 70–80% of law adjudicated in the country is outside the formal system. In many refugee situations we have seen instances where rape victims are forced to marry the perpetrators, as a way of limiting the embarrassment which the woman or girl supposedly brings on her family.

Turning to sexual exploitation of women and girls by peacekeepers, this is indeed a grave problem which is a manifestation of the continuum of violence against women into post-conflict situations. There is a need to ensure that the problem is addressed within a broad context of "the vulnerabilities of women and girls to gender-based violence in conflict situations", which requires a wider response from different actors. There is a further need to ensure that attention to this aspect of the problem does not usurp or draw attention away from addressing other equally pervasive forms of gender-based violence which are insufficiently addressed in post-conflict situations—domestic violence and forced marriage.

Conclusion

From the foregoing it will be seen that efforts to date for the protection of women and girls in conflict environments has yielded mixed results, and much scope remains for ensuring effective translation of existing international commitments and agreements for equal rights and protection of women and girls in such situations, into practical reality on the ground.

An important step in this direction requires a recognition of the fact that the protection priorities of civilians are not homogenous. Moreover, protection of women and girls requires a move away from seeing them only in terms of their vulnerability in conflict situations, to recognising and investing in their capacities as change agents. Empowerment of women thus represents an effective and sustainable protection strategy in conflict environments for ensuring that women are able to assume their rights and to thus better protect themselves in the long-term. Of equal importance is the need to ensure that a more serious approach to the prevention of gender-based violence is incorporated in all mainstream peacemaking, peacekeeping and peace-building efforts. Today, this problem continues to receive only marginal attention as a core threat to sustainable peace and security in conflict and post-conflict environments. Finally the need to ensure that economic empowerment activities targeted to women in conflict and post-conflict environments are truly empowering and move beyond simple subsistence or recreational activities, is an important and necessary strategy for reducing building an effective protection regime.

One might ask, where would we be without the resolution of the Security Council. Is it possible to imagine that DPKO, for example, would have put in place the institutional mechanisms that currently exist without the resolution? More important is what remains to be done. Success in building broad-based consensus around implementation of resolution 1325 at policy levels and among institutions of the United Nations needs to be matched by an equally strong investment in empowering women in conflict environments to assume that the resolution serves as a tool that they themselves can effectively employ to change their destiny in post-conflict environments. A strategy for supporting women's groups and organizations is needed. Ironically, since the adoption of the resolution, the force of women's networks that were most vocal at regional levels in advocating and monitoring the role and participation of women in peace processes has dissipated.

It is essential to translate the resolution into the work of actors engaged in conflict/peace transitions—from mediators and peace negotiators, to staff working in peacekeeping. This also requires ensuring a gender balance among actors in decision-making, including facilitators of peace talks, SRSGs, uniformed peacekeeping personnel (1% of military personnel and 5% of civilian police are women. We have 2 SRSGs out of 17).

We need to ensure that a broader framework is developed for responding to sexual exploitation and abuse, one that situates this problem within the broader context of gender-based violence in conflict situations, thus ensuring a more balanced response to a very widespread problem. The ongoing response is at the level of the behaviour of peacekeepers. Is this sufficient to facilitate addressing the root causes of the problem? Economic empowerment of women in these environments is crucial. It is also important to provide adequate resources to ensure that gender units in peacekeeping missions are effective in facilitating gender mainstreaming within the work of the missions. Establishing units without resourcing them makes for slow progress.

At the United Nations level, a collaborative framework for the implementation of resolution 1325 is necessary among the various actors: OHCHR, UNDP, DPKO, UNICEF, UNHCR. More active monitoring by the Security Council of the implementation of resolution 1325 would be helpful, going beyond the once-a-year debate. The Council should monitor for example how implementation of the resolution is reflected in all reports of the Secretary-General and continue to engage systematically with women's organizations when they visit countries in conflict.

It would be helpful to broaden the discussion on the implementation of resolution 1325 to include not only the Security Council but also the General Assembly. Regional and sub-regional organizations also have to integrate resolution 1325 into policy and practice within their institutions. The development of research and resources to support implementation and evolution of gender in peace and security frameworks, through stronger partnerships between gender units of peacekeeping operations and academic/research institutions, would help take the process of implementation forward.

Unfortunately, gender mainstreaming is still approached from a protection/victim perspective instead of a rights and change-agent perspective. Male-dominated mission environments make integration of gender mainstreaming concerns difficult in practice. This must be changed urgently.

CHAPTER TWELVE

THE OHCHR KOSOVO EMERGENCY OPERATION: LESSONS LEARNED

OHCHR Staff

Editor's Note

When nearly a million Albanians were pushed out of Kosovo in 1999 the Commission on Human Rights was in session. This was a major human rights and humanitarian crisis. How would OHCHR respond to it? Three decisions were made: to send the Special Rapporteur on Yugoslavia and a special envoy of the High Commissioner to the area; to deploy human rights staff to gather information from the refugees about criminal violations of human rights that had taken place; and to report weekly to the Commission on Human Rights, which was then in session. This was the first time the Office of High Commissioner had undertaken such an emergency response and it proved an important learning experience. In the piece that follows, lessons learned from this exercise are recorded by OHCHR staff. The Editor was Deputy High Commissioner for Human Rights at the time and he was involved in the establishment, operation, and supervision of this exercise, making the most of what was available by way of human and material resources in OHCHR. The piece below is a fair summary of the operation.

1. *Establishment and objectives*

On 31 March 1999, the High Commissioner for Human Rights decided to re-deploy OHCHR-FRY staff—who had left FRY before the NATO bombing began, to the FYR Macedonia, Albania, and Montenegro (FRY) to set up the High Commissioner's Kosovo Emergency Operation (KEO). The High Commissioner also appointed a Personal Representative, Mr. Michel Moussalli, and asked Mr. Moussalli and the Special Rapporteur of the Commission on Human Rights, Mr. Dinstbier, to travel urgently to the region with a view to monitoring the human rights situation. Mr. Moussalli and Mr. Dinstbier visited the region in April 1999. Mr. Dinstbier subsequently carried out a number of other missions.

Bertrand G. Ramcharan (Ed.), Human Rights Protection in the Field, 225–229.

The objectives of the KEO were set forth as follows: to establish a human rights presence as close as possible to the actual developments in Kosovo; to interview refugees and seek impartial verification about alleged human rights violations; to seek to identify patterns and trends in human rights violations; to consult and help coordinate among international partners the assembling and analysis of information relating to human rights violations in Kosovo; to assemble information in reports to the High Commissioner for Human Rights, the Special Rapporteur and other U.N. mechanisms, including the International Criminal Tribunal for the former Yugoslavia; and to explore opportunities for technical cooperation in the future reconstruction and security of the region.

While deployed in FYROM and Albania, OHCHR staff had neither a mandate nor instructions to monitor the human rights situation in these two countries. As mentioned above, the focus of their work was to document human rights violations taking place in Kosovo.

2. *Staffing*

As a first step in the deployment of staff to FYROM, one human rights officer from Geneva HQ was quickly dispatched to Skopje to lay the logistical groundwork for the arrival of additional staff, to open up contacts with partners, to identify sources of information, and to put in place basic administrative support arrangements. Subsequently, two additional staff from Geneva were deployed to FYROM first and then to Albania for a period of five weeks.

Immediately after the outbreak of the crisis, the Swiss and the Norwegian governments offered to contribute to the Kosovo Emergency Operation by providing OHCHR with human rights monitors. OHCHR signed a partnership agreement with the Swiss Government and with NORDEM, whose terms were defined by the Kosovo desk, together with the Administrative Unit, and the Office of Legal Affairs. The agreements provided the legal framework for the engagement of the Swiss and Norwegian experts. According to the terms of the agreements the experts, even though paid by third parties, would be attached to OHCHR Kosovo Emergency Operation and would report directly to the OHCHR team leaders on the ground.

The negotiation of the agreement took almost a month, and the Swiss and Norwegian human rights observes were not deployed until the beginning of May.

3. *Methodology*

The OHCHR Methodology Team was requested to provide guidance on the collection of information which would allow OHCHR staff to produce sound information in a standardized format, coordinate with other relevant actors in the mission area, and positively respond to the request for cooperation by the International Criminal Tribunal for the Former Yugoslavia. Interview forms for victims and witnesses of human rights violations and Guidelines on Interviewing were developed starting from OHCHR standard methodological materials, as adjusted to the context and objectives of the KEO.

At the same time, with the assistance of a Norwegian expert also seconded to OHCHRGeneva, a data-base for the safe storage, organization and transmission of the information gathered in the field was developed. Due to technical problems, information was not fed into the data-base until the end of March.

The Swiss and Norwegian monitors underwent a pre-deployment briefing of a few days in Geneva, including on the Guidelines, the use of the forms, and the functioning of the database. Difficulties in communication and the fact that the other members of the field teams (OHCHR staff previously based in FRY and redeployed to Albania and FYROM) were not provided with the necessary equipment to use the data base and a technical briefing thereon until later, created a situation of unclarity about the purpose and methods of the information-gathering exercise undertaken by OHCHR.

The request for cooperation by the Office of the Prosecutor of the International Criminal Tribunal on the Former Yugoslavia (ICTY) raised a number of policy and methodological issues with regard to procedures for the sharing of information gathered by OHCHR in the performance of its tasks. ICTY requested that OHCHR: provide it with details of eye-witnesses of incidents which could be construed as crimes falling within the ICTY mandate; ascertain whether individual refugees had identification or documentation; and inform it of uniformly consistent versions of events related to practices by Serbian authorities leading to displacement. Following the High Commissioner's general positive response to the ICTY request, guidelines were developed seeking to reconcile various concerns: lending adequate cooperation to the ICTY; preserving OHCHR's ability to carry out its work within the High Commissioner's mandate; preserving the integrity of established human rights information gathering methodology; and respecting promises of confidentiality of information made by OHCHR to witnesses of violations. The extent to which the guidelines were applied varied.

The definition of procedures for cooperation with the ICTY raised issues which will be relevant for OHCHR beyond the specific circumstances of the KEO. In Geneva, efforts were made to adapt the data-base to the needs of the relevant Thematic Procedures of the Commission on Human Rights. However, due to the extreme caution used to guarantee the confidentiality of the information collected, it was impossible, for technical reasons, to guarantee access to the data-base to all Special Rapporteurs.

4. *Reporting*

The dispatch of human rights monitors had much earlier been welcomed by the Commission on Human Rights (resolution 1999/2) which also requested the High Commissioner to report urgently on the situation of human rights and humanitarian crisis relating to Kosovo. The dispatch of the OHCHR's special mission in response to the Kosovo crisis occurred in a very complex situation and under considerable political pressure. OHCHR staff had to redeploy quickly to a region where a number of other international actors, with considerable resources, had already established their presence and were engaged in human rights related activities. In this environment there was an urgent need for the OHCHR to quickly identify and confirm its role among other actors, and not to be seen as duplicating work already done by others.

The OHCHR's credibility demanded a rapid response in the form of timely short statements on the situation, but at the same time the reputation and role of the Office as a provider of considered, well-documented and objective human rights information dictated that systematic and often time-consuming field research be undertaken before a comprehensive and solid report could be issued. Given the time-constraints and pressure to issue quick reports, secondary sources such as daily reports by other agencies could have crept in when keeping track of rapidly unfolding events on the ground. In doing so, the Office sought to take particular care against "recycling" information publicized by others, and thereby lending, sometimes undue, credence to these reports through the authority of the High Commissioner.

The High Commissioner submitted to the Commission five reports on the situation of human rights in Kosovo, none of which, for the reasons explained below, was based on a full analysis of the information collected by the KEO. The High Commissioner on several occasions, including at the daily Kosovo Emergency Task Force video-conference, declared that OHCHR would produce a comprehensive, analytical report on the findings of its operation.

5. *Operating procedures*

The deployment and particularly the practical setting up of operations in the field was very much improvised and based on common sense and personal experience, rather than carefully developed procedures. OHCHR personnel, including secondees, were not provided with any specific terms of reference beyond the objectives of the Mission as described above, the guidelines on interviewing and cooperation with the ICTY, and the pre-deployment briefing (see paragraph 2 above). This circumstance, and the lack of staff in Geneva to provide clear and consistent directions in keeping with evolving policy priorities, created some misunderstanding in the scope and mandate of the operation (especially by the seconded staff) which affected the quality of the information gathering effort.

In order to facilitate the management of all issues related to the KEO, a Kosovo Emergency Task Force was set up in Geneva, which brought together relevant staff from the Front Office, the Geographic Desk, the Methodology Team, Administration and Security. The Task Force met several times a week.

6. *Logistics*

The redeployment of staff to FYROM, Albania and Montenegro was facilitated by the transfer of equipment and other assets evacuated from the FRY. However, only upon return to Kosovo, was OHCHR staff provided with laptops and printers (while the seconded staff had it from the beginning). The Swiss and Norwegian secondees were promptly provided with the necessary logistical assistance from OHCHR staff on the ground. In FYROM in particular, Norwegian monitors were provided, upon arrival, with a car and an interpreter each.

CHAPTER THIRTEEN

PROTECTING HUMAN RIGHTS IN A SITUATION OF HUMANITARIAN CRISIS: THE CASE OF COLOMBIA

OHCHR Staff

Editor's Note

An earlier chapter provided insights into the methods of operations of the OHCHR Office in Colombia. One of the annexes contains the 2004 Annual Report on the Office submitted to the Commission on Human Rights. In the piece below, we reproduce a note prepared by the staff of the OHCHR Office in Colombia on the challenges of protecting human rights in a situation of humanitarian crisis. It speaks through the voice of the staff on the ground in Colombia.

In seeking to ensure respect for human rights in Colombia, including in the context of the ongoing humanitarian crisis, a number of recommendations of the High Commissioner as set out in his report to the Commission on Human Rights on the situation of human rights in Colombia in 2003, and which are pertinent to the humanitarian situation and its effect on the human rights situation, are recalled below.

First, it is the paramount and primary duty of the State to guarantee the respect for human rights of those persons living within the territory of the State without discrimination. The responsibility of civil society and the international community is to assist the State to comply with its international obligations.

Second, in order to guarantee respect for human rights, the State must develop policies aimed at protecting human rights. In order to assist in the taking of preventive actions, there should be a mechanism in place which can comprehensively and effectively monitor the situation on the ground throughout the territory of the country, with a focus on "at risk" areas. In terms of prevention, the Colombian Government has established the Early Warning System (SAT), and the Inter-Institutional Early Warning Committee (CIAT), aimed at improving the State's coordination and response to possible situations of tension and consequent violations. However, the functioning of the System has demonstrated numerous deficiencies in terms of the effectiveness of risk assessment and response. Accordingly, the

B.G. Ramcharan (Ed.), Human Rights Protection in the Field, 231–234.

High Commissioner has encouraged the Government to strengthen coordination between the SAT and the CIAT. The High Commissioner has also recommended that composition of the CIAT be expanded to include the Office of the Ombudsman, the Social Solidarity Network, and the Ministry of Interior and Justice's Programme for protection of human rights defenders in order to ensure that all relevant actors play a key role in the prevention of violations.

Furthermore, to compliment the work of SAT and CIAT, the High Commissioner has encouraged the Social Solidarity Network, together with other Government and State institutions, to put into practice, preventive and protective actions and programmes that have been agreed upon with the communities at risk. With respect to displacement, the United Nations Guiding Principles should be strictly applied.

In addition, the State should understand and publicly be seen to understand the crucial and central role played by independent and vibrant domestic human rights defenders in preventing and protecting violations. Accordingly, the High Commissioner has recommended that the Government ensure that the programmes for the protection of human rights defenders and other groups operate with the necessary coverage and effectiveness required. Moreover, the Ministry of Interior and Justice, responsible for this protection, together with other State institutions, are encouraged to search for new mechanisms aimed at reducing risk factors and at acting preventively against such risk factors.

The work carried out by the local and international humanitarian community, and, in particular, the information received by these organizations through their direct and regular access to civilians, should be further tapped as a mechanism for better understanding the humanitarian and human rights situation. Specifically, though some of these humanitarian organizations may feel reluctant or unable to respond to violations they come across in their work, this information could be shared with, for example, international observers such as OHCHR human rights officers, who may be in a better position to respond to the information provided. Through its active presence on the ground, OHCHR human rights officers play a role both in protecting persons whose rights have been violated, and may, to some degree, actually prevent violations from taking place.

Third, with a view to regulating the manner in which the internal armed conflict is conducted and therefore reducing the scale of the humanitarian crisis, the High Commissioner has issued the following recommendations addressed at guerilla and paramilitary forces: to respect the right to life of all civilians . . . in particular to refrain at all times from attacks on the civilian population, indiscriminate attacks, the unacceptable practice of kidnapping, recruitment of minors, and acts of terrorism; to refrain from any action that may affect the civilian population's enjoyment of human rights and diminish the ability of the Colombian State to fulfil its obligation to protect and safeguard those rights; and to observe, without restriction, the humanitarian principles of limitation, distinction, and proportionality and the general obligation to protect the civilian population, as well as to guarantee humanitarian access to vulnerable populations.

Fourth, in order to counter the effects of impunity and the spiralling effect this has on the continuing circle of violence and therefore the humanitarian situation, the High Commissioner has called upon the 'Special Committee on the conduct of investigations into human rights violations and breaches of international humanitarian law to present concrete results concerning the selected cases and to present quarterly reports to the President of the Republic on the progress achieved in the investigation of these cases.

Fifth, in order to attempt to minimize the consequences of the humanitarian crisis and to seek to guarantee the economic and social rights of the affected population, the High Commissioner recommended that the Government develop a consistent policy, based on updated statistics, to reduce inequality, confront the extreme poverty that exists in the country and ensure that all necessary steps are taken to decrease illiteracy and unemployment rates and improve access to health care, education and housing. Primary education should be free and health services and housing subsidies ought to be guaranteed for the most disadvantaged sectors of the population.

Sixth, though Colombia has all the outward facets of a State that apparently understands and takes seriously its national and international human rights obligations, in reality, much of this is subverted in the pursuit of the Government's policy of "democratic security" and 2 million people cannot go home.

Accordingly, and in order to seek to support the development of a sustainable domestic human rights culture, the High Commissioner has recommended, *inter alia* that the institutions of Government and other organizations of human rights defenders develop and institutionalize stable communication channels, both at the national as well as the regional levels, in order to achieve a greater degree of understanding and improve the promotion and protection of human rights throughout the country. In addition, the High Commissioner has recommended that the Government, prepare a concerted plan of action on human rights and international humanitarian law, to be created in collaboration with broad sectors of society and including an integral gender approach.

How can OHCHR support the UN Country Team's efforts to integrate human rights in its policies and programmes aimed at supporting the State's response to the humanitarian crisis?

In Colombia, the Humanitarian Action Plan (PAH) has as its central pillar the London Declaration of July 2003, in which the Government committed to implement, inter alia, the recommendations of the High Commissioner for Human Rights, in the following ways:

- Analyze the situation faced by IDPs and other affected populations using a rights-based lens.
- Involve both rights holders and duty-bearers in the development of responses using rights-based processes and the international recommendations as the basis for planning and programming.
- Ensure that the responses themselves are rights-friendly.
- Involve rights-holders in the implementation, monitoring and evaluation of responses, e.g. by ensuring that as relates to the health sector the following activities are undertaken:
  - An understanding of the root causes as to why the right to health is not exercised;
  - Responses which are aimed at strengthening the capacity of the rights-holder to claim his/her rights, and strengthening of the capacity of the duty-bearer to guarantee the rights.

CHAPTER FOURTEEN

THE UN CENTRE FOR HUMAN RIGHTS AND DEMOCRACY IN CENTRAL AFRICA

Teferra Shiawal-Kidanekal[1]

Introduction

Even in the midst of conflicts and crises of human rights violations in many parts of the world, the search must go on for ways of advancing the implementation of human rights and of protecting those at risk. The challenges are daunting: how can one advance human rights in the midst of widespread under-development and poverty? How can one prevent gross violations of human rights in countries where the indecencies of tyrants know no bounds? How can one minimize the risks of atrocities in conflict-prone countries or countries? And yet, advancing the implementation of human rights is often the key to tackling these very problems.

Human rights approaches to development and poverty reduction can help promote a sense of justice and fair play in a country that can, in turn, stimulate the development process. Good governance under the rule of law and with respect for human rights is the antidote to dictators. Respecting human rights in conflict-prone societies can help prevent the descent into conflict. Yes, whatever the adversity, the quest for the universal implementation of human rights must go on—as a matter of necessity and as an issue of justice. Advancing human rights is a moral imperative.

Different parts of the human rights movement are making their distinctive contributions to the advancement of human rights. Scholars advance the philosophical and ethical arguments in support of the justice of the human rights cause. Educators are endeavouring to raise a new generation imbued with the spirit of the universality of human rights. Non-Governmental Organizations and journalists expose gross violations of human rights and call for perpetrators of atrocities to be brought before the courts. International, regional and sub-regional organizations contribute to normative development, promote processes of dialogue with Governments

[1] The views expressed are those of the author in his personal capacity.

Bertrand G. Ramcharan (Ed.), Human Rights Protection in the Field, 235–245.

on their efforts, experiences and problems in implementing international and regional norms, provide advisory services, and seek to help Governments strengthen their national infrastructures for human rights protection. This complementarity of efforts within the human rights movement is as it should be. The Universal Declaration of Human Rights was proclaimed in 1948 to the end that everyone, all individuals and all organs of society shall strive to advance its implementation across the globe.

In the light of experience with the implementation of human rights in the nearly six decades after the proclamation of the Universal Declaration, the United Nations is currently giving emphasis to four areas of practical endeavours at the ground level within countries: strengthening the national protecting system of each country; enhancing the implementation of the core international human rights treaties; increasing the synergies between international human rights investigations and the future protection of human rights: and promoting regional and sub-regional cooperation for the implementation of human rights in areas that have experienced conflicts or crises. It is with the fourth area of emphasis that this essay is concerned and, more particularly with an innovative initiative that is little known, the United Nations Centre for Human Rights and Democracy in Central Africa, which has been operating since the beginning of 2001.

I. *Genesis and Significance of the Centre*

What is significant about the origin of the Centre is that the push for it came not from mainstream human rights activists but from those working on conflict prevention, peacemaking and peace-building in the region. In the 1990s Central Africa witnessed conflicts in quite a few countries and those engaged in peace-making and peace-building realized that one of the keys to future prevention of conflict lay in promoting respect for democracy and human rights in the sub-region. It was this realization that led the Economic Community of Central African States (ECCAS) to call for the establishment of the Centre. This call was taken up by African delegations at the United Nations General Assembly, which requested the United Nations Secretary-General to establish the Centre and provided it with funds from the regular budget of the United Nations for this purpose. This regular budget funding was crucial to the survival and sustainability of the Centre. Initially, the General Assembly authorized a sum of one million dollars for the first biennium and has renewed funding at that level subsequently.

The significance of this action by the General Assembly was that it said, essentially: human rights are important to peace and development of this region; thus cooperation for the implementation of human rights must be institutionalized within the sub-region; a permanent center must be established for this purpose; we shall provide a reasonable funding base which could be supplemented through voluntary contributions; and we must stay the course of human rights implementation in this region. In our view this model is particularly important because it could be replicated in other areas of need—and its costs are reasonable to make it sustainable. The model of the Centre is also significant because it represents a different approach from the classical regional human rights arrangements. The African, American, and European conventions on human rights are normative instruments with Commissions or Courts to watch over their implementation. They have their worth. The Central African center seeks to build upwards through groundwork with Government agencies, educators, judges and the legal profession, law-enforcement agencies, the military and other professional groups. It aims to offer a library and research base for educators and human rights promoters. It is intended to deepen the quest for human rights promotion and protection within the region. With these factors in mind, we shall now look at the mandate of the Centre and the strategies it has pursued since its establishment.

II. *Mission of the Centre*

The United Nations Centre for Human Rights and Democracy in Central Africa was first called for by the Fourth Ministerial Meeting of the United Nations Standing Advisory Committee on Security Questions in Central Africa. On 8 April 1994 the Economic Community of Central African States (ECCAS) adopted a declaration recommending that the United Nations create a sub-regional center for human rights and democracy, located at Yaounde, Cameroon, under the auspices of the then United Nations Centre for Human Rights (now the Office of United Nations High Commissioner for Human Rights). ECCAS's call was taken up by the United Nations General Assembly which, on 1 December 1999, allocated a sum of one million dollars for the establishment of the Centre. Over 2000, work was done on the establishment of the Centre, which began operations in March 2001.

The Centre's activities cover eleven countries in the Central African sub-region: Angola, Burundi, Cameroon, Central African Republic, Chad, Congo (Brazzaville), Democratic Republic of Congo, Equatorial Guinea, Gabon, Rwanda, and Sao Tome and Principe.

The original recommendation of the UN Standing Advisory Committee on Security Questions in Central Africa, as endorsed by ECCAS and, implicitly, by the UN General Assembly, was that the center would have the following mission:

(a) Contributing to training personnel responsible for the management of activities relating to human rights and democracy.
(b) Providing support for the creation and/or strengthening of national institutions responsible for human rights and democracy.
(c) Cooperating in disseminating international instruments relating to human rights and democracy.

The mission of the Centre is thus to help strengthen the national human rights capacity of Member States with a view to sustaining the development of a culture of human rights and democracy for the prevention of conflicts and the promotion of sustainable development. In practice, the Centre strives to provide outreach to the work of the Office of High Commissioner in the sub-region through the promotion of human rights, mainstreaming and advocacy. Special emphasis is placed on marginalized and vulnerable groups, notably women, indigenous minority groups and persons living with HIV/AIDS and physical challenges.

The Centre has intensified contacts with partner agencies and institutions and its activities have so far been focused mainly on:

- Capacity building in human rights and democracy.
- Collaboration with and technical support to national human rights bodies
- Making human rights contributions to the UNDAF processes and cooperate with UN country teams
- Working with partner agencies
- Developing a documentation unit as a resource centre

III. *Launching Strategies*

The formal launch of the Centre took place at a conference in Yaounde, Cameroon, in March 2001. The ceremonial launch of the Centre took place time later that year at a Summit meeting of the ECCAS. At the inaugural conference, which was chaired by Bertrand G. Ramcharan, then UN Deputy High Commissioner for Human Rights, there were many strands of opinion and points of view. The United Nations Department of Political Affairs, which had shepherded the peace process that produced the recommendation for a Centre had more of a political perspective, emphasizing cooperation with ECCAS, democracy, and disarmament. The Deputy Executive Secretary of ECCAS, who attended the Conference, saw the Centre as belonging to ECCAS and felt that there should be in-depth political consultations with the leadership of ECCAS before a strategy was launched. The host government, which had its own sensitivities, strongly urged that the Centre was a United Nations entity and should develop as such. It was firmly against any notion that the Centre belonged to ECCAS because it wished to liberate the Centre from sub-regional constraints. UNDP, which took a strong interest in the Centre and supported its launch, wished to see the Centre take off swiftly. Colleagues in the Office of High Commissioner emphasized human rights education.

As Chair of the launching conference the Deputy High Commissioner turned it into a working seminar and asked each of the participants in turn how they would wish to see the Centre develop and what they would wish to see it concentrate on. There was a strong emphasis on educational activities and support to educators in the sub-region. It was felt that by supporting human rights educators the Centre could have the best impact. Another strong point of view was that the Centre should develop a solid documentation and research base that could be drawn upon by researchers and educators. There was a dearth of materials in the sub-region. Educational materials could also be disseminated by the Centre.

Participants strongly urged that the Centre should work with judges and magistrates because one of the greatest threats to human rights in the region stemmed from political pressure on the judiciary. A distinguished Procureur/Attorney-General present at the Conference said capacity building and training was where the region needed to be supported the most. Judges and magistrates must be independent and serve as the bulwark of human rights protection.

It was also strongly advocated to work with law-enforcement and military personnel. Step-by-step, one would have to build up a culture of human rights among the leaders, educators, judges, magistrates, lawyers, police, prison and military personnel.

The concluding document adopted by the Conference reflected these suggestions and helped influence the subsequent activities of the Centre.

IV. *Working with ECCAS*

As indicated in the preceding section, there were sensitivities in the ECCAS about the Centre and OHCHR had to engage in diplomatic efforts at the founding conference to help lay the basis for smooth working relations in the future. This intensive diplomacy helped, and as the first Director of the Centre and a former Ethiopian diplomat, I was fortunate to discharge my responsibilities in building up good working relations with the Executive Secretary of ECCAS. At a subsequent meeting the Deputy High Commissioner accompanied by the author had with ECCAS leadership on the margins of the Summit of the African Union in Mozambique, in 2003, the Secretary General of ECCAS expressed deep appreciation for the close working relations and particularly urged OHCHR to help ECCAS develop activities for the prevention of conflicts. He thought that the work being done by the Centre in the human rights field was crucial for conflict prevention.

The interaction with the ECCAS Secretariat has proved beneficial. The Centre has been associating the ECCAS Secretariat in all its activities and the latter has been positive and supportive. The two institutions have organized joint activities including seminars on capacity building for civil society held in different countries of the sub-region. The Centre has also been working with the ECCAS Secretariat on issues of early warning, conflict prevention, and peacebuilding.

V. *Working with Governments*

Since its establishment the Centre has carried out activities such as the following in helping to develop national human rights capacity and strengthen national human rights institutions:

- Technical assistance for the strengthening of the operational capacity of the Cameroon National Committee on Human Rights and Fundamental Freedoms
- Technical assistance to the Government of Equatorial Guinea
- Technical assistance to the Government of Chad
- Cooperation with ECCAS in the establishment and operation of its Sub-regional Mechanism for Early Warning (MARAC)

VI. *Working with Educators*

The Centre's emerging documentation and library collection is an important resource base for sub-regional educators and researchers. Since its commencement of operations in March 2001, the Centre has assembled some 5000 volumes from various sources. The Centre publishes a trimestrial bulletin. The documentation unit provides services to more than one thousand five hundred visitors per year. It is used mainly by the media, university students, researchers, and the general public. In view of the growing public demand for access to documentation resources, the Centre has initiated a human rights database and started developing country profiles in the field of human rights and democracy in Central Africa.

The Centre's initial foray in the sub-region was on the issue of human rights education. Its inaugural conference, in March 2001, as mentioned earlier, emphasised this topic.

Since its establishment, the Centre has organized seminars or training workshops on issues such as the following:

- Human rights education
- The development of national human rights action plans
- National human rights strategies (NGOs)
- Women's rights and national legislation
- The role of NGOs
- The role of civil society
- The role of women in national legislatures
- Lobbying techniques for civil society
- Civilian-military cooperation during democratic transition
- Training for Civil Servants of the Ministries of Justice and Human Rights
- Human Rights and the fight against HIV/AIDS
- Workshop on military justice
- Media, Human Rights and Democracy

One year after the initial launch of the Centre, in June 2002, the then High Commissioner Mary Robinson presided over a conference of Ministers of Justice and Presidents of Supreme Courts of the Sub-region on the "Submission of Reports with regard to Human Rights Standards". It was well attended and served to advance the advocacy work of the High Commissioner, providing a forum for one on one discussion with key players in the sub-region.

Interns from the sub-region have been spending time with the Secretariat of the Centre in Yaounde for three-months training periods. So far fifteen groups of interns have passed through the Centre. These have included lawyers, magistrates, civil rights activitists, doctoral students and journalists. To date, nearly seventy interns, drawn from the sub-region and half a dozen others from Europe and North America have passed through the Centre.

In the framework of the United Nations Decade for Human Rights Education (1995–2004) a sensitization project entitled, "Human Rights: Progress and Challenges" has been set up. The project is based on projection of videotapes on human rights and democracy issues. The programme targets several groups, including students, researchers, the military, parliamentarians, civil society leaders, lawyers and educators. In October 2003 the Centre started a pilot project in Cameroon to assist in the establishment of human rights clubs in high schools. This experience is intended to extend to the sub-region.

VII. *Working on Democracy and the Rule of Law*

In the troubled Central African sub-region, as elsewhere in the developing world, it is essential to reinforce the rule of law under democratic governance. This has been a priority area of the Centre from its establishment. The democracy programme focuses mainly on the promotion of democracy and the rule of law as a tool for conflict prevention. The Centre has established partnerships with universities, research institutions and civil society organizations in Central Africa and is working closely with the secretariat of the ECCAS as well as UN entities in the sub-region. Institutions such as the US National Endowment for Democracy, the Africa Democracy Forum, the International Peace Academy and the Electoral Institute of South Africa have started working with the Centre.

The Centre organized in Cameroon, in February 2004, a sub-regional workshop on "Civil Society, Human Rights, and the Rule of Law". The objective of the seminar was to sensitize participants on the indivisibility and interdependence of all human rights, as well on the indissoluble links between the promotion and the protection of rights and the consolidation of the rule of law. It also emphasized the role of the judiciary as the pillar of human rights and the rule of law. Continuing its emphasis on the rule of law, the Centre organized in Brazzaville, Congo, in March 2004, a seminar on Women Journalists, Human Rights and the Rule of Law.

VIII. *Working on Peace-Building, with Law-Enforcement Officials and the Military*

The Centre has been mindful that upholding peace in the sub-region is fundamental to advancing the human rights cause. It has therefore sought to work with partners such as the ECCAS on peace-building issues and has been attentive to the role of the military. It organized a workshop on military justice in Central Africa, held in Libreville, Gabon, in January 2003. At the end of the workshop, participants adopted the Libreville Declaration in which they called on the governments which had not done so to ratify various international and regional human rights instruments and to include their provisions in national legislation.

The Centre also organized, in September 2004, a seminar on civilian-military cooperation during democratic transitions. This was carried out in cooperation with various peace-related institutions. Follow up workshops on the same topic are in progress since then.

IX. *Support of the Human Rights Movement*

Since the Centre is quite new it is still largely unknown within the human rights movement. However, the Centre is gradually receiving offers of partnership or requests for technical assistance from civil society organizations, think-thanks and higher institutions of learning within and outside the sub-region. It would be important to publicize the existence and activities of the Centre within the ranks of research and teaching institutions in particular so that they might contribute to it in the form of materials and substantive support.

For its part, the Centre has been seeking to support sub-regional human rights organizations. Two institutions, Association pour la promotion des droits de l'homme en Afrique Centrale, based in Yaounde, Cameroon, and the Faculte de Droit de l'Universite Marien Ngouabi in Brazzaville, Republic of Congo, have been supported with modest grants to support the teaching of human rights.

Within the framework of a programme of the Office of High Commissioner for Human Rights, *Assisting Communities Together (ACT)*, the Centre has awarded a grant of US$5000 each to three NGOs noted for their dedicated activities and working in the field of human rights and peace advocacy in the sub-region.

X. *Constraints and Achievements*

The Centre's Annual Report for both 2003 and 2004 has registered the following administrative and budgetary constraints being felt:

> Expectations are rising in the sub-region in terms of what the OHCHR can do through the Centre. However, shortage of funding for regular and new activities as well as in meeting infrastructural needs of the Centre remains a main subject for concern.
>
> Clearly, there is a deficit in communications, mandatory additions to local staff salaries and other miscellaneous costs since these were not foreseen in the context of the growing demand on the Centre, thus impacting on the resources. Although the regular budget looks big (USD 500,000) it does not stretch very far.

Insufficient staffing is another cause for concern. With staff departures, the number of staff has been reduced to three (a director, a regional democracy adviser and a human rights specialist). This will have to be seen with the context of growing demands and rectified somehow if OHCHR and indeed the international human rights community are to have a stronger field presence at the sub-regional level.

"Notwithstanding the constraints, what has been achieved in the short time since the Centre started its activities in earnest gives hope and confidence for further developments". Thus far the statistics of activities up to the end of 2004 shows:

No. of seminars: 15 (9 regional and 6 national)
No. of workshops: 8 (5 regional and 6 national)
No. of trainees/participants: 930 (540 male and 290 female)
No of Internships: 70

Publications: 34 (including 14 quarterly bulletins; 12 compilations of training materials)
Web site hits: 15,500
Documentation centre users: 3550
High-level visitors: 352 (Civil society leaders, government officials, UN officials and student groups)

Conclusion

The UN Central African center is barely four years old and is finding its feet. It has made a good start in establishing relations with ECCAS, with Governments of the region, and with civil society. Its documentation base is beginning to take shape and human rights organizations inside and outside the region are starting to discover it and to use its services. It has organized a fair number of seminars for judges, law-enforcement personnel, the military, judges, journalists, educators, and civil society. It has made worthwhile grants to local human rights organizations. The Centre has also been cooperating with sub-regional and external institutions working on issues of peace and development in the sub-region.

The Centre is a labour of love in a sub-region that has seen searing conflicts and is wracked by poverty and poor governance. The challenges of taking forward the human rights idea in such a situation are manifold. Still, the Centre has set about these challenges with grit and with conviction. What will count very much is whether educators, professional groups and civil society in the region come to see the Centre as an institution of value. Quality and pragmatism will be decisive. The support of the wider international human rights movement would help greatly. The Centre provides a framework. Those in a position to do so can help with documentation, with interns, with joint programmes, with expertise, and with encouragement. It was with a view to enlisting this support that this essay was written. The Centre has promise. We can all help it realize that promise.

Relevant Sources

Report of the Secretary-General to the General Assembly on the activities of the Centre, 2001, A/56/36/Add.1

Report of the Secretary-General to the General Assembly on the activities of the Centre, 2002, A/57/394

Annual Report on the Work of the Centre, 2003

Report of the Secretary-General to the General Assembly on the activities of the Centre, 2004.

Bulletin des droits de l'homme et de la democratie (12 issues to date)

Annual Work Plan of the Centre, 2004

Centre Report on Activities, January–June, 2004

Rapport Final, Seminaire Sous-Regional de Formation: Societe Civile, Droit de l'Homme et Etat de Droit. Kribi, Cameroon, 2–4 fevrier, 2004

Rapport General, Seminaire Sous-Regional de Formation: Droits de la femme et legislations nationals en Afrique centrale, Kigali, Rwanda, 17–19 mars, 2004

Rapport Final, Seminaire Sous-Regional de Formation: Femmes Journalistes, Droit de l'Homme et Etat de Droit, Brazzaville, Congo, 29–31 mars, 2004

Rapport Final, Seminaire Sous-Regional sur les Relations Civilo-Militaires, 6–8 septembre, 2004

CONCLUSION

This work began with a recognition that the protection of human rights is in crisis in peacetime as well as during conflicts. As far as future strategies for the protection of human rights are concerned, we set out some thoughts that we think might help take us forward in the coming, difficult period.

As far as the protection of human rights during conflicts is concerned, the crisis is similarly a daunting one. Today's conflicts are mostly internal ones, fought not by disciplined armies respectful of international humanitarian law but often by a motley bunch that respects no known norms or values.

The International Committee of the Red Cross is therefore right to place the emphasis on the responsibility of the individual combatant and upon the law. This must lead us to the justice principle, namely that anyone who transgresses the law should be brought to book before a national or international court.

But courts are expensive and the International Criminal Court is in the early stages of its existence surrounded by strong political objections by the pre-eminent power. The Prosecutor of the International Criminal Court is investigating alleged crimes in some situations of conflict and it remains to be seen whether this will have a deterrent effect on combatants elsewhere. We certainly hope so.

This work has reminded us that twenty-five million people are internally displaced, fourteen million have sought refugee abroad, and the number of civilians affected by conflict runs into the tens of millions. The Security Council and other agencies of the international system have put down strategies for protecting these groups of people but it has been, so far, mostly a labour of hope than of results.

There is very little protection of internally displaced persons. There is very little protection of refugees. There is very little protection on the ground of civilians in armed conflicts. Children are still left to fend for themselves as best they can in many situations and women continue to be raped and abused.

This is not to minimize the importance of the policies and strategies developed so far. They are certainly important and we must build further upon them. There have also been heroic efforts in the UN peacekeeping operations, the human rights field offices, and in the field deployment of human rights and humanitarian organizations, particularly non governmental organizations.

Bertrand G. Ramcharan (Ed.), Human Rights Protection in the Field, 247–250.

Protection on the ground is not an easy task and there are no easy answers. The situation in Darfur is a case in point. There are a few human rights observers on the ground but they are surrounded by the most unscrupulous actors. How does one put down a peacekeeping operation in an area the size of France? Aerial policing, in my view, is the answer. The magnitude of the problem requires strong and decisive action by the international community.

Peacekeeping operations are certainly needed in some situations but because of the size, costs and logistics involved, they cannot be injected into every situation where civilians are at risk in conflicts. There are simply too many such situations for formal peacekeeping forces. This is why we think that the concept of rapidly-deployable human rights and humanitarian observers is one that needs to be brought resorted to more frequently. The late Prince Saddrudin Aga Khan, former United Nations High Commissioner for Human Rights advocated the establishment of a corps of humanitarian observers some while back.

The human rights components of United Nations peacekeeping operations are certainly doing a courageous job, as are the field offices established by the Office of the UN High Commissioner for Human Rights. Agencies and organizations such as UNHCR, OCHA, ICRC, and major human rights and human humanitarian organizations have pioneered new approaches to protection on the ground.

It has been the aim of this book to bring out some of the experiments being tried on the ground with a view to the further development of human rights protection in the field.

BIBLIOGRAPHY

Aspen Institute, Honoring Human Rights and Keeping the Peace. Lessons from El Salvador, Cambodia and Haiti (1995)

Aspen Institute, Honoring Human Rights: From Peace to Justice. Recommendations to the United Nations (1998)

Aspen Institute, Honoring Human Rights Under International Mandates. Lessons from Bosnia, Kosovo, and East Timor. Recommendations to the United Nations (2003)

ICRC, Strengthening Protection in War (2001)

T. Howland "UN Human Rights Field Presences as Proactive Instruments of Peace and Social Change: Lessons from Angola", 26 Human Rights Quarterly (2004), pp. 1–28.

K. Kenny, Human Rights Field Operations. Human Rights Trust, Ireland (2000).

OHCHR Handbook for Human Rights Field Officers 2004

M. O'Flaherty, "Sierra Leone's Peace Process: The Role of the Human Rights Community", 26 Human Rights Quarterly (2004), pp. 29–62.

Report of the Commission on Intervention and State Sovereignty: The Responsibility to Protect

Report of the UN High Level Panel on Threats, Challenges and Change (2004)

Stanley Foundation, UN on the Ground. A Report. 2003

UNHCR, Agenda for Protection (2002)

ABOUT THE AUTHORS

Mark Bowden is a Principal Officer in the Office for the Coordination of Humanitarian Affairs, United Nations. He has extensive experience in the practice of humanitarian protection and relief.

Elissa Golberg is a Foreign Service Officer in the Department of External Relations, Canada.

Michael O'Flaherty is a Member of the United Nations Human Rights Committee and Reader in Law at Nottingham University.

Comfort Lamptey is Gender Adviser in the Department of Peacekeeping Operations, United Nations.

Kamel Morjane is Assistant High Commissioner for Refugees, United Nations.

William O'Neill is an Expert in International Human Rights Law who has served in several human rights field operations.

OHCHR staff refers to staff members of the Office of High Commissioner for Human Rights who have collectively contributed materials assembled by the Editor into chapters.

Bertrand Ramcharan has served as Deputy and later United Nations High Commissioner for Human Rights.

Teffera Shiawal-Kidanekal is Director of the United Nations Centre for Human Rights and Democracy for Central Africa.

Michel Veuthey is an Expert in International Humanitarian Law. He had a long and distinguished career in the International Committee of the Red Cross and is currently Vice-President of the International Institute of Humanitarian Law.

ANNEXES

ANNEX I

STATEMENT BY THE PRESIDENT OF THE SECURITY COUNCIL

At the 4882nd meeting of the Security Council, held on 15 December 2003, in connection with the Council's consideration of the item entitled "Protection of civilians in armed conflict", the President of the Security Council made the following statement on behalf of the Council:

> The Security Council recalls its resolutions 1265 (1999) of 17 September 1999 and 1296 (2000) of 19 April 2000 on the protection of civilians in armed conflict, as well as the statements by its President of 12 February 1999 (S/PRST/1999/6), of 15 March 2002 (S/PRST/2002/6) and of 20 December 2002 (S/PRST/2002/41), and reaffirms the need to keep the protection of civilians in armed conflict as an important item on the Council's agenda.
>
> The Security Council also reaffirms its concern at the suffering inflicted upon, and hardships borne by, civilians during armed conflict, and recognizes the consequent impact that this has on durable peace, reconciliation and development. The Security Council strongly condemns all attacks and acts of violence directed against civilians or other protected persons under international law, in particular international humanitarian law in situations of armed conflict, including such attacks and acts of violence against women, children, refugees, internally displaced persons and other vulnerable groups; reaffirms the need for parties to armed conflict to take all possible measures to ensure the safety, security and freedom of movement of United Nations and associated personnel as well as personnel of international humanitarian organizations in accordance with applicable international law; and recognizes that secure humanitarian access and the swift re-establishment of the rule of law, justice and reconciliation are essential components for an effective transition from conflict to peace. The Security Council reiterates its call to all parties to armed conflict to comply fully with the provisions of the Charter of the United Nations and with the rules and principles of international law, in particular international humanitarian, human rights and refugee law, and to implement fully the relevant decisions of the Security Council. The Security Council recalls the obligations of States to respect and to ensure respect for international humanitarian law, including the four Geneva conventions, and emphasizes the responsibility of States to end impunity and to prosecute those responsible for genocide, war crimes, crimes against humanity and serious violations of humanitarian law. The Security Council also notes with interest the proposal presented by the Under-Secretary-General for Humanitarian Affairs at the 9 December open meeting of the Security Council for a '10-point action plan' on the protection of civilians in armed conflict, and looks forward to further discussions and consultations on this issue.

Bertrand G. Ramcharan (Ed.), Human Rights Protection in the Field, 251–268.

"Recalling that on 15 March 2002 the Security Council adopted the Aide Memoire annexed in the Statement by its President (S/PRST/2002/6) as a means to facilitate its consideration of issues pertaining to protection of civilians, and recalling further that in the statement by its President of 20 December 2002 (S/PRST/2002/41) the Security Council expressed its willingness to update annually the Aide Memoire in order to reflect emerging trends in the protection of civilians in armed conflict, the Security Council adopts the updated Aide Memoire contained in the annex to this Presidential Statement. The Security Council reiterates the importance of the Aide Memoire as a practical tool that provides a basis for improved analysis and diagnosis of key protection issues during deliberations on peacekeeping mandates, and stresses the need to implement the approaches set out therein on a more regular and consistent basis, taking into account the particular circumstances of each conflict situation, and undertakes to remain actively seized of the matter."

PROTECTION OF CIVILIANS IN ARMED CONFLICT

Aide Memoire

For the consideration of issues pertaining to the protection of civilians during the Security Council's deliberation of peace-keeping mandates

Protection of Civilians in Armed Conflict is at the core of the work of the United Nations Security Council for peace and security. On 15 March 2002, the Security Council adopted an Aide Memoire (S/PRST/2002/6) as a practical guide for its consideration of protection issues and agreed to update and review and update its contents periodically. This document provides the first update of this important operational tool, adopted as an annex to Presidential Statement S/PRST/2003/27 on 15 December 2003.

In the letter dated 21 June 2001 from the President of the Security Council addressed to the Secretary-General (S/2001/614), the members of the Security Council welcomed the Secretary-General's report of 30 March 2001 (S/2001/331) on the protection of civilians in armed conflict, and were of the view that further advice of the Secretary-General would be useful in the Council's consideration of the issues contained in the report.

In order to facilitate due consideration, whenever appropriate, of issues pertaining to the protection of civilians in its deliberations on the establishment, change, or close of peacekeeping operations, the members of the Council suggested that an Aide Memoire listing those issues that are relevant in this regard be drafted in close cooperation with the Council.

This Aide Memoire is the result of an inter-active consultation between the Security Council and the Secretariat, and comprises the experiences of a wide range of agencies within the United Nations, including the Inter Agency Standing Committee (IASC). The document is based on the Council's previous consideration of these issues, including resolutions 1265 (1999) and 1296 (2000). It highlights primary objectives for Security Council action, offers specific issues for consideration in meeting those objectives, and lists previous Security Council resolutions and presidential statements that make reference to such concerns.

Bearing in mind that each peacekeeping mandate has to be designed on a case-by-case basis, the document is not intended as a blueprint. The relevance and practicality of each issue described has to be considered and adapted to the specific conditions in each situation. As highlighted in the Secretary-General's report "No Exit Without Strategy" (S/2001/394), the Security Council should reach agreement on clear and achievable mandates for peace operations based on a common understanding of the conflict. In this respect, mobilization, from the outset, of necessary funding and adequate resources needs to be an integrated part of the Security Council's overall consideration.

Most frequently civilians are caught in circumstances of dire need where a peacekeeping operation has not been established. Such situations may require the Council's urgent attention. This Aide Memoire may therefore also provide guidance in circumstances where the Council may wish to consider action outside the scope of a peacekeeping operation.

As a practical tool, the Aide Memoire is without prejudice to the provisions of Security Council resolutions and other decisions by the Council. The document is regularly reviewed and updated to reflect the latest concerns pertaining to the protection of civilians in armed conflict, including new trends and measures to address them.

Security for Displaced Persons and Host Communities

Primary Objectives	Issues for Consideration	Precedents*
1. Prioritize and support the immediate protection needs of displaced persons and civilians in host communities through:	• Measures to enhance security for displaced persons, support the location of camps in secure areas, and facilitate return under safe and dignified conditions. • Measures to enhance security for civilians who remain in their communities and for host communities living in or around areas where refugees or internally displaced persons take shelter. • Provision of appropriate and rapid international assistance.	S/RES/1509(2003), OP3j & l, 6 S/RES/1508(2003), OP10 S/RES/1493(2003), OP27 S/RES/1484(2003), OP1 S/RES/1479(2003), OP10 S/RES/1470(2003), OP16 S/RES/1427(2002), OP12 S/RES/1419(2002), OP11 S/RES/1393(2002), OP11 S/RES/1355(2001), OP14 S/RES/1346(2001), OP7, 8, 9 S/RES/1319(2000), OP1 S/RES/1296(2000), OP12, 14 S/RES/1286(2000), OP12 S/RES/1270(1999), OP19 S/RES/1244(1999), OP9c, 11k, 18 S/RES/1208(1998), OP4, 12
2. Prioritize and support the maintenance of the humanitarian and civilian character of camps and settlements for displaced persons through:	• Provision of external and internal security (screening procedures to separate armed elements from civilians; demobilization and disarmament measures; technical assistance and training by international civilian police and/or military observers; location of camps at a significant distance from international border and risk zones; regional and subregional arrangements).	

	• Cooperation with host State in provision of security measures, including through technical assistance and training. • Deployment of multi-disciplinary assessment and security evaluation teams. • Regional approach to massive population displacement, including appropriate security arrangements.	

Access to Vulnerable Populations

Primary Objectives	Issues for Consideration	Precedents*
Facilitate safe and unimpeded access to vulnerable populations as the fundamental prerequisite for humanitarian assistance and protection through:	• Appropriate security arrangements (role of multinational force; safe corridors; protected areas; armed escorts). • Engagement in sustained dialogue with all Parties to the armed conflict. • Facilitation of the delivery of humanitarian assistance. • Compliance with obligations under relevant international humanitarian, human rights and refugee law. • Counter-terrorism measures (legislation, training, enforcement, regional and international cooperation) in full compliance with all obligations under international law, in particular international human rights, refugee and humanitarian law.	S/RES/1509(2003), OP OP3j, 5, 8 S/RES/1502(2003), OP4, 5b S/RES/1494(2003), OP25 S/RES/1493(2003), OP12, 15, 25 S/RES/1479(2003), OP10 S/RES/1456(2003), Annex OP6 S/RES/1405(2002), OP1 S/RES/1419(2002), OP12 S/RES/1417(2002), OP7 S/RES/1445(2002), OP14 S/RES/1379(2001), OP4, 5 S/RES/1378(2001), OP2 S/RES/1314(2000), OP7, 14 S/RES/1296(2000), OP8, 10, 12, 15 S/RES/1286(2000), OP9, 10 S/RES/1279(1999), OP5e, 7 S/RES/1272(1999), OP2d, 10, 11 S/RES/1270(1999), OP8(d&g), 13, 14, 22 S/RES/1265(1999), OP7, 8, 10 S/RES/1264(1999), OP2 S/RES/1244(1999), OP9h **S/PRST/2000/4**

Safety and Security of Humanitarian and Associated Personnel

Primary Objectives	Issues for Consideration	Precedents*
Ensure the safety and security of humanitarian, United Nations and associated personnel through:	• Respect by all parties to the conflict for the impartiality and neutrality of humanitarian operations. • Support for a safe and secure working environment for humanitarian personnel.	S/RES/1509(2003), OP OP3j, 5 S/RES/1502(2003), OP1, 3, 4, 5(a–c), 6 S/RES/1494(2003), OP25, 26 S/RES/1493(2003), OP25 S/RES/1445(2002), OP14 S/RES/1417(2002), OP7 S/RES/1378(2001), OP2, 5 S/RES/1319(2000), OP1 S/RES/1296(2000), OP12 S/RES/1286(2000), OP9 S/RES/1272(1999), OP10 S/RES/1270(1999), OP8d, 13, 14 S/RES/1265(1999), OP7, 8, 9, 10 S/RES/1244(1999), OP9h S/PRST/2000/4

Security and the Rule of Law

Primary Objectives	Issues for Consideration	Precedents*
Strengthen the capacity of local police and judicial systems to physically protect and enforce law and order through:	• Deployment of qualified and well-trained civilians international civilian police as a component of peacekeeping operations, to enhance the capacity of the United Nations and to assist the host State with law enforcement. (ad ref) • Technical assistance for local police, judiciary and penitentiaries (mentoring; legislative drafting; integration of international personnel). • Mechanisms for monitoring and reporting	S/RES/1509(2003), OP3n S/RES/1493(2003), OP7 S/RES/1401(2002), OP4 S/RES/1400(2002), OP7 S/RES/1378(2001), OP3, 4 S/RES/1315(2000), OP4 S/RES/1272(1999), OP2 (a–c, e), 3c, 13 S/RES/1270(1999), OP23 S/RES/1265(1999), OP15 S/RES/1244(1999), OP9d, 11(i–j)

	• Reconstruction and rehabilitation of institutional infrastructure (salaries; buildings; communications). • Mechanisms for monitoring and reporting of alleged violations of humanitarian, human rights and criminal law.	

Disarmament, Demobilization, Reintegration and Rehabilitation

Primary Objectives	Issues for Consideration	Precedents*
Facilitate the stabilization and rehabilitation of communities through:	• Programs for disarmament and demobilization of combatants, including special measures for women, children and dependants (amnesties; weapons buy-back; economic and development incentives). • Programs for reintegration and rehabilitation of ex-combatants within their communities, including special measures for women and children (community service; counselling services; appropriate education/skills training; family reunification; employment opportunities). • Encouragement of full participation of armed groups in disarmament, demobilization, reintegration and rehabilitation programs. • Measures to address the regional dimensions affecting disarmament, demobilization, reintegration and rehabilitation programmes.	S/RES/1509(2003), OP3 (f & g), 17, 18 S/RES/1479(2003), OP3 (para. 6), 9 S/RES/1460 (2003), OP13 S/RES/1445(2002), OP4, 5, 6 S/RES/1417(2002), OP9 S/RES/1400(2002), OP6 SRES/1379(2001), OP11 (c, d, f), 12a S/RES/1376(2001), OP12 S/RES/1366(2001), OP 16 S/RES/1325(2000), OP8a, 13 S/RES/1318(2000), Annex OPV S/RES/1296(2000), OP 16, S/RES/1270(1999), OP 3, 4, 8(b & c), 9, 20 S/RES/1265(1999), OP12 S/RES/1261(1999), OP15 S/PRST/2000/10 S/PRST/1999/28

Small Arms and Mine Action

Primary Objectives	Issues for Consideration	Precedents*
Facilitate a secure environment for vulnerable populations and humanitarian personnel through:	• Mine-action (coordination centres, land-mine clearance; mine awareness training; victim assistance). • Measures to control and reduce the illicit traffic in small arms and light weapons (voluntary moratoria; arms embargoes; sanctions; regional and subregional approaches). • Involvement of ex-combatants and local communities, in particular women, in the collection and destruction of small arms and light weapons and in de-mining and other mine-action activities.	S/RES/1479(2003), OP13 S/RES/1460(2003), OP7 S/RES/1433(2002), OP3B(2) S/RES/1379(2001), OP6, 9d S/RES/1318(2000), OPVI (para. 1) S/RES/1314(2000), OP8 S/RES/1296(2000), OP10, 20 S/RES/1286(2000), OP12 S/RES/1265(1999), OP17 S/RES/1261(1999), OP14, 17a **S/RES/1244(1999), OP9e** **S/PRST/1999/28**

Effects on and Contribution of Women

Primary Objectives	Issues for Consideration	Precedents*
1. Address the specific needs of women for assistance and protection through:	• Special measures to protect women and girls from gender based discrimination and violence, rape and other forms of sexual violence (access to legal redress; crisis centres; shelters; health care; counselling and other assistance programs; monitoring and reporting mechanisms). • Implementation of measures for reporting on and prevention of sexual abuse and exploitation of civilians by humanitarian workers and peacekeepers. • Mainstreaming of gender perspective, including the integration of gender advisers in peace operations.	S/RES/1509(2003), OP11 S/RES/1493(2003), OP9 S/RES/1479(2003), OP5 S/RES/1460(2003), OP10 S/RES/1436(2002), OP15 S/RES/1400(2002), OP14 S/RES/1379(2001), OP4 S/RES/1325(2000), OP1, 4, 5, 8a, 10, 13, 15 S/RES/1314(2000), OP13, 16e S/RES/1296(2000), OP9, 10 **S/PRST/2001/31**

2. Strengthen the role of women as constructive actors in developing and implementing appropriate responses to protecting civilians through:	• Expansion of the representation, role and contribution of women in United Nations Weld-based operations (among military observers; civilian police; humanitarian and human rights personnel). • Increased and more equitable participation of women at all decision-making levels (political processes; organization and management of refugee and IDP camps; design and distribution of assistance; local governance; education; rehabilitation policies).	

Effects on Childre

Primary Objectives	Issues for Consideration	Precedents*
Address the specific needs of children for assistance and protection through:	• Prevention of and putting an end to the recruitment of child soldiers in violation of international law. • Initiatives, where appropriate, to secure access to war-affected children (days of of tranquillity). immunization; temporary ceasefires; days • Negotiated release of children abducted in situations of armed conflict. • Effective measures to disarm, demobilize, reintegrate and rehabilitate children recruited or used in hostilities. • Specific provisions for the protection of children, including where appropriate, the integration of child protection advisers in peace operations. • Implementation of measures for reporting on and prevention of sexual abuse and exploitation of civilians by humanitarian workers and peacekeepers. • Family reunification of separated children.	S/RES/1509(2003), OP9, 10 S/RES/1493(2003), OP13 S/RES/1479(2003), OP15 S/RES/1460(2003), OP3, 9, 10, 12, 13 S/RES/1436(2002), OP15 S/RES/1400(2002), OP14 S/RES/1379(2001), OP2, 4, 8e, 10c, 11(c, d, f), 12a S/RES/1314 (2000), OP 11, 12, 13, 14, 16, 17 S/RES/1296(2000), OP 9, 10 S/RES/1270(1999), OP18 S/RES/1261(1999), OP 2, 8,13, 15, 17a S/PRST/1998/18

Justice and Reconciliation

Primary Objectives	Issues for Consideration	Precedents*
1. Put an end to impunity for those responsible for serious violations of international humanitarian, human rights and criminal law through:	• Monitoring and reporting on the situation of children. • Establishment and use of effective arrangements for investigating and prosecuting serious violations of humanitarian and criminal law, at the local and/or international level (from the outset of the operation). • Cooperation of States for the apprehension and surrender of alleged perpetrators. • Technical assistance to strengthen local capacities for apprehension, investigation, and prosecution of alleged perpetrators. • Exclusion of genocide, crimes against humanity and war crimes from amnesty provisions. • Referral of situations, where possible and appropriate, to international courts and tribunals.	S/RES/1509(2003), OP10 S/RES/1479(2003), OP8 S/RES/1436(2002), OP11, 15 S/RES/1400(2002), OP5 S/RES/1398(2002), OP14 S/RES/1379(2001), OP9a S/RES/1325(2000), OP11 S/RES/1319(2000), OP2, 3 S/RES/1318(2000), Annex OPVI (para. 3) S/RES/1315(2000), OP1–3, 8 S/RES/1314(2000), OP 2, 9 S/RES/1272(1999), OP16 S/RES/1270(1999), OP17 S/RES/1265(1999), OP4, 6 S/RES/1261(1999), OP 3 S/RES/955(1994), OP1, 2 S/RES/827(1993), OP2, 4
2. Build confidence and enhance stability within the host State by promoting truth and reconciliation through:	• Requests for troop-contributing States to investigate and prosecute, when appropriate, their peacekeepers and security personnel suspected of violating criminal law while in a host State. • ***Appropriate locally adapted mechanisms for truth and reconciliation (technical assistance; funding; amnesties for lower level perpetrators; just reinstallation of civilians within communities).*** • Measures for restitution and reparations (trust funds; property commissions).	

Training of Security and Peacekeeping Forces

Primary Objectives	Issues for Consideration	Precedents*
Ensure adequate sensitization of multinational forces to issues pertaining to the protection of civilians through:	• Appropriate training in humanitarian and human rights law, civil-military coordination, codes of conduct, negotiation and communication skills, child protection and child rights, gender and cultural sensitization, and the prevention of HIV/AIDS and other communicable diseases.	S/RES/1460(2003), OP9 S/RES/1445(2002), OP18 S/RES/1379(2001), OP10b S/RES/1325(2000), OP6 S/RES/1318(2000), Annex OPIII (para. 2) S/RES/1308(2000), OP 3 S/RES/1296(2000), OP19 S/RES/1270(1999), OP15 S/RES/1265(1999), OP14 S/PRST/2001/31 S/PRST/2001/16 S/PRST/1998/18

Media and Information

Primary Objectives	Issues for Consideration	Precedents*
1. Counter occurrences of speech used to incite violence through:	• Establishment of media monitoring mechanisms to ensure effective monitoring, reporting and documenting of any incidents, origins and contents that incite "hate media". • Responsive steps to media broadcasts inciting genocide, crimes against humanity and/or serious violations of international humanitarian law, including, as a last resort, consideration of closing down such media broadcasts.	S/RES/1509(2003), OP16 S/RES/1417(2002), OP4, 5 S/RES/1353(2001), Annex I, B – OP 10, 11 S/RES/1296(2000), OP17, 18

2. Promote and support accurate management of information on the conflict through:	• Technical assistance to draft and enforce anti-hate speech legislation. • Establishment of media coordination centres to facilitate accurate and reliable information management on, and awareness of, the conflict. • Establishment and assistance of local and international media and information outlets, in support of peace operations.	

Natural Resources and Armed Conflict

Primary Objectives	Issues for Consideration	Precedents*
Address the impact of natural resource exploitation on the protection of civilians through:	• Investigation of the linkages between illicit trade in natural resources and the conduct of the conflict. • Measures to address the direct or indirect import of natural resources where proceeds are used to fuel conflict (sanctions; regional and subregional approaches). • Measures against corporate actors, individuals and entities involved in illicit trade of natural resources in violation of relevant Security Council resolutions and the Charter of the United Nations (legislation; penalties for dealers; certification and registration systems; embargoes).	S/RES/1509(2003), OP3r S/RES/1493(2003), OP28 S/RES/1460(2003), OP16b S/RES/1436(2002), OP8 S/RES/1417(2002), OP15 S/RES/1379(2001), OP6, 9d S/RES/1376(2001), OP8 S/RES/1318(2000), Annex OPVI (para. 2) S/RES/1314(2000), OP8 S/RES/1306(2000), OP1, 2, 9,19a

Humanitarian Impact of Sanctions

Primary Objectives	Issues for Consideration	Precedents*
Minimize unintended adverse side effects of sanctions on the civilian population through:	• Humanitarian exemptions in sanction regimes. • Targeted sanctions (sanctions limited in scope and targeted at specific individuals, groups, or activities). • Relevant assessment and review of the humanitarian impact of sanctions, and the behaviour of those targeted by the sanctions.	S/RES/1478(2003), OP18, 19 S/RES/1409(2002), OP4, 5, 6 S/RES/1408(2002), OP16 S/RES/1379(2001), OP7 S/RES/1343(2001), OP5(a–d), 6, 7(a&b), 13a S/RES/1333(2000), OP5(a–c), 7, 8(a–c), 10, 11, 12, 14, 15d, 23 S/RES/1325(2000), OP14 S/RES/1314(2000), OP15 S/RES/1298(2000), OP6, 7, 8, 16 S/RES/1296(2000), OP21 S/RES/1267(1999), OP4 S/RES/1265(1999), OP16 S/PRST/1999/28

***Resolution Index:**
S/RES/1509(2003) on the Situation in Liberia
S/RES/1508(2003) on the Extension of the Mandate of the UN Mission in Sierra Leone (UNAMSIL)
S/RES/1502(2003) on the Protection of Humanitarian Personnel and the UN and its Associated Personnel in Conflict Zones
S/RES/1494(2003) on the Extension of the Mandate of the UN Observer Mission in Georgia (UNOMIG)

S/RES/1493(2003)	on the Extension of the Mandate of the UN Organization Mission in the Democratic Republic of the Congo (MONUC)
S/RES/1484(2003)	on the Authorization of Deployment of an Interim Emergency Multinational Force in Bunia, Democratic Republic of the Congo
S/RES/1479(2003)	on the Situation in Côte d'Ivoire
S/RES/1478(2003)	on Measures Imposed to Enforce Compliance with Demands in Resolution 1343 (2001) Concerning Liberia
S/RES/1470(2003)	on the Extension of the Mandate of the UN Mission in Sierra Leone (UNAMSIL)
S/RES/1460(2003)	on Children and Armed Conflict
S/RES/1456(2003)	on Combating Terrorism
S/RES/1445(2002)	on the Peace Process in the Democratic Republic of the Congo
S/RES/1436(2002)	on the Extension of the Mandate of the UN Mission in Sierra Leone (UNAMSIL)
S/RES/1433(2002)	on the Establishment of the UN Mission in Angola (UNMA)
S/RES/1427(2002)	on the Extension of the Mandate of the UN Observer Mission in Georgia (UNOMIG)
S/RES/1419(2002)	on the Support for Transitional Authority in the full implementation of the Agreement on Provisional Arrangements in Afghanistan pending the re-establishment of Permanent Government
S/RES/1417(2002)	on the Extension of the Mandate of the UN Organization Mission in the Democratic Republic of the Congo (MONUC)
S/RES/1408(2002)	on Measures Against Liberia for Non-Compliance With Demands in Paragraph 2 of Resolution 1343 (2001)
S/RES/1409(2002)	on Arrangements for the Sale and Supply of Commodities and Products to Iraq as a Basis for the Humanitarian Programme
S/RES/1405(2002)	on the Initiative for Fact-Wnding Team for Jenin Refugee Camp
S/RES/1401(2002)	on the Establishment of UN Assistance Mission in Afghanistan (UNAMA)
S/RES/1400(2002)	on the Extension of the Mandate of the UN Mission in Sierra Leone (UNAMSIL)
S/RES/1393(2002)	on the Extension of the Mandate of the UN Observer Mission in Georgia (UNOMIG)
S/RES/1379(2001)	on Children and Armed Conflict
S/RES/1378(2001)	on the Situation in Afghanistan
S/RES/1376(2001)	on the Situation in the Democratic Republic of the Congo
S/RES/1366(2001)	on the Role of the Security Council in the Prevention of Armed Conflicts
S/RES/1355(2001)	on the Situation in the Democratic Republic of the Congo and Extension of the Mandate of the UN Organization Mission in the Democratic Republic of the Congo (MONUC)
S/RES/1346(2001)	on the Extension of the Mandate of the UN Mission in Sierra Leone (UNAMSIL)
S/RES/1353(2001)	on the Strengthening Co-operation with Troop-contributing Countries
S/RES/1343(2001)	on the Situation in Liberia
S/RES/1333(2000)	on the Situation in Afghanistan
S/RES/1327(2000)	on the Implementation of the Report on the Panel on UN Peace Operations
S/RES/1325(2000)	on Women, Peace and Security
S/RES/1319(2000)	on the Situation in East Timor

S/RES/1318(2000)	on Ensuring an Effective Role for the Security Council in the Maintenance of International Peace and Security, particularly in Africa
S/RES/1315(2000)	on the Situation in Sierra Leone
S/RES/1314(2000)	on Children and Armed Conflict
S/RES/1308(2000)	on the Responsibility of the Security Council in the Maintenance of International Peace and Security: HIV/AIDS and International Peace-keeping Operations
S/RES/1306(2000)	on the Situation in Sierra Leone
S/RES/1298(2000)	on the Situation in Eritrea and Ethiopia
S/RES/1296(2000)	on the Protection of Civilians in Armed Conflict
S/RES/1286(2000)	on the Situation in Burundi
S/RES/1279(1999)	on the Situation in the Democratic Republic of the Congo
S/RES/1272(1999)	on the Situation in East Timor
S/RES/1270(1999)	on the Situation in Sierra Leone
S/RES/1267(1999)	on the Situation in Afghanistan
S/RES/1265(1999)	on the Protection of Civilians in Armed Conflict
S/RES/1264(1999)	on the Situation in East Timor
S/RES/1261(1999)	on the Children and Armed Conflict
S/RES/1244(1999)	on the Situation in Kosovo
S/RES/1208(1998)	on the Situation in Africa: Refugee Camps
S/RES/955(1994)	on the Establishment of an International Criminal Tribunal for Rwanda
S/RES/827(1993)	on the Establishment of an International Criminal Tribunal for the former Yugoslavia
S/RES/824(1993)	on the Situation in Bosnia and Herzegovina
S/PRST/2002/41	on the Protection of Civilians in Armed Conflict
S/PRST/2002/6	on the Protection of Civilians in Armed Conflict
S/PRST/2001/31	on Women and Peace and Security
S/PRST/2001/16	on the Responsibility of the Security Council in the Maintenance of International Peace and Security: HIV/AIDS and International Peacekeeping Operations
S/PRST/2000/10	on the Maintenance of Peace and Security and Post-conflict Peace-building
S/PRST/2000/4	on the Protection of United Nations Personnel, Associated personnel and Humanitarian Personnel in Conflict Zones
S/PRST/1999/28	on Small Arms
S/PRST/1998/18	on Children and Armed Conflict

** The Security Council also recognized the relevance of GA/RES/55/2(2000) and GA/RES/46/182(1991) in the broader context of protection of civilians and the root causes of conflicts.

ANNEX II

MEMORANDUM OF UNDERSTANDING BETWEEN THE OFFICE OF THE HIGH COMMISSIONER FOR HUMAN RIGHTS AND THE DEPARTMENT OF PEACEKEEPING OPERATIONS

The maintenance of international peace and security and international cooperation in promoting and encouraging respect for human rights and fundamental freedoms for all are purposes of the United Nations as defined by the Charter. Respect for human rights is itself fundamental to the promotion of peace and security, and a unified United Nations approach to these ends is essential to the fulfilment of these two Charter-mandated objectives. The protection and promotion of human rights are also essential elements of United Nations efforts to prevent conflicts, to maintain peace, and to assist in post-conflict reconstruction endeavours and—with due regard to the specific mandate of each peacekeeping operation—due attention to their human rights aspects is instrumental to the success of United Nations work in these areas. United Nations peacekeeping operations are increasingly multi-dimensional, with the frequent inclusion of human rights mandates and components, tasks and duties.

In keeping with the Brahimi Report, DPKO and OHCHR will, through enhanced cooperation, seek to increase the effectiveness of United Nations peacekeeping and human rights activities. To these ends, DPKO and OHCHR, in strengthening and expanding their cooperation, will seek to establish, institutionalize and maximize the mutual exchange of expertise, advice, information, training and support, drawing upon their respective capacities and mandates.

Human rights components of peacekeeping operations should normally combine promotion and protection functions so as to ensure a comprehensive approach to human rights, in accordance with international human rights standards. The Security Council or the General Assembly, after considering recommendations by the Secretary-General, determines the specific mandate of a peacekeeping operation, including tasks relating to human rights. The early involvement of OHCHR in the planning and implementation of human rights activities by peace-keeping operations can contribute to the sustainability of the achievements of peacekeeping operations after their withdrawal. The strengthening of national human rights structures and capacities can be an important element in ensuring the sustain-

Bertrand G. Ramcharan (Ed.), Human Rights Protection in the Field, 269–275.

ability of the achievements of a peace-keeping operation after it withdraws. The early involvement of OHCHR in the Integrated Missions Task Force (IMTF) established for countries, in which a peacekeeping operation is being planned, is thus crucial.

DPKO and OHCHR have agreed to the annexed statement of areas and methods of cooperation, which may be reviewed as required. DPKO and OHCHR will undertake periodic reviews of the implementation of the MOU.

Signature

Sergio Vieira de Mello
United Nations
High Commissioner

Geneva, 22 November 2002

Signature

Jean-Marie Guéhenno
United Nations
Under-Secretary-General for the Department for Human Rights of Peace keeping Operations

ANNEX TO THE MEMORANDUM OF UNDERSTANDING BETWEEN THE OFFICE OF THE HIGH COMMISSIONER FOR HUMAN RIGHTS AND THE DEPARTMENT OF PEACEKEEPING OPERATIONS

A. *Planning, design and establishment of human rights components of peacekeeping operations*

1. In order to facilitate an integrated approach to peacekeeping and human rights at the earliest possible moment, consultations between DPKO and OHCHR shall take place at the planning stage of peacekeeping operations, it being understood that as the lead Department for peacekeeping operations, DPKO is responsible for planning the operation as an integrated whole, in consultation with other departments, offices, agencies, funds and programmes. OHCHR will participate in the IMTF that is normally established for countries in which a peacekeeping operation is being planned or whose possible establishment is discussed, contributing proposals on the function and structure of the human rights component for the Secretary-General's reports to the Security Council on the establishment of new peacekeeping operations, as well as ensuring that human rights concerns are appropriately reflected in the mission as a whole. It will participate in initial assessment and early deployment missions, conducted by DPKO related to the formulation of proposals for the establishment of new operations, where a human rights component may be contemplated. It will also participate in the evaluation and discussion of mandate adjustments and exit strategies as regards the human rights component of an operation. A staff member from the OHCHR office in New York will be invited to participate in the daily management meetings of DPKO.

2. The activities of human rights components of peacekeeping operations shall be based on international human rights standards, as defined in the relevant international treaties, declarations, guidelines and other instruments. In the implementation of their activities, whether of a monitoring or of a technical cooperation nature, and within the framework of their mandate, human rights components of peacekeeping operations will seek to promote an integrated approach to human rights promotion and protection, paying due attention to civil, cultural, economic, political and social rights, including the right to development, and to the special needs of women, children, minorities, internally displaced persons, and other groups requiring special protection. The involvement of other United Nations

agencies and programmes with special focus on these areas shall be sought to facilitate such integrated approach.

3. OHCHR and DPKO have agreed on a new recruitment procedure for Human Rights Officers to serve in peacekeeping operations. The Head of the Human Rights component in a peacekeeping mission shall be selected by the High Commissioner, with the agreement of the SRSG/Head of Mission. Other staff members in the Human Rights component of a peacekeeping operation shall be selected by the Head of the Human Rights component in consultation with the SRSG/Head of Mission, on the basis of lists of candidates cleared by OHCHR and submitted to DPKO, as a result of the advertisement of vacant posts and in accordance with DPKO standard recruitment procedures.

B. *Institutional arrangements for human rights components of peacekeeping operations*

4. Human Rights components of peacekeeping operations shall be under the authority of the SRSG or Head of the operation and shall enjoy the same status as other components, including with regard to participation in the internal policy-making process and access to documentation. They shall receive substantive support and backstopping by OHCHR. This will include provision of relevant training, documentation, materials and methodological tools developed by OHCHR as well as advice as required. Staff of the human rights component of peacekeeping operations should communicate regularly with colleagues at OHCHR in this regard. The SRSG should be kept fully informed of any communication with OHCHR that could have an impact on the mission, bearing in mind paras. 2 and 12 of the Standard Directives for SRSGs dated 31 August 1998 (relevant paragraphs attached).

5. The performance of Heads of Human Rights components of peacekeeping mission shall be evaluated by the SRSG/Head of Mission or his/her Deputy as the first reporting officer and OHCHR as the second reporting officer in accordance with the established procedures of the e-PAS. The performance of other staff members of Human Rights components of peacekeeping operations shall be evaluated by the Head of the Component as the first reporting officer and the SRSG or his/her Deputy and the OHCHR as the second reporting officers.

C. *Reporting and public statements*

6. The Heads of Human Rights components of peacekeeping operations shall, in the fulfilment of their duties, submit periodic and ad hoc reports on the human rights situation and the activities of the component to the SRSG with a copy to OHCHR, using OHCHR formats issued after consultation between OHCHR and DPKO.

7. Human Rights components of peacekeeping operations shall be responsible for drafting the human rights sections of any internal or public reports prepared by the peacekeeping operations including, for example, reports of the Secretary-General to United Nations bodies. OHCHR will be systematically consulted on the draft of public reports before they are published.

8. The SRSG and the High Commissioner for Human Rights will as far as possible consult prior to issuing public statements or public reports on human rights developments in the country of operation. Public statements by the Human Rights component shall be authorized by the SRSG in consultation with OHCHR. The SRSG may bring to the attention of the HCHR situations requiring his/her public intervention and recommend the issuance of statements. The HCHR could likewise bring to the SRSG's attention human rights situations that could benefit from the HCHR or SRSG public intervention.[1]

D. *Administration and funding*

9. When a human rights component is included in the mandate of a peacekeeping operation, funding for that component, including staff costs, travel, training of mission staff, mission mandated activities, as well as other types of office support assistance and logistics, shall be provided from assessed contributions to the peacekeeping operation concerned, for the activities mandated for that operation and subject to the approval of the GA.

10. DPKO and OHCHR may engage in joint fundraising for activities of human rights components of peacekeeping operations, as appropriate. OHCHR shall seek to mobilize resources for technical cooperation activities of human rights components of peacekeeping operations, including through existing agreements with other organizations.

[1] This paragraph should be read in conjunction with paras. 2 and 12 of the Standard Directives for SRSGs dated 31 August 1998.

11. OHCHR may, at times, open offices to follow on the work of a DPKO peace operation. In those circumstances, DPKO will give OHCHR preferential treatment as afforded to other UN organizations, programmes or funds during the liquidation phase for the purchase of vehicles, hand-over of premises and other logistical facilities".

E. *Human Rights Training for staff of peacekeeping operations*

12. The SRSG or Head of the peacekeeping operation shall ensure that all staff of the operation—whether military or civilian—are aware of, and abide by, international human rights and humanitarian law standards. The SRSG or Head of Mission shall issue instructions to this effect.

13. Human rights training—as relevant to their function—shall be provided to all deployed peacekeeping personnel—whether military or civilian.

14. DPKO and OHCHR shall promote the integration of human rights in the training provided by Member States to their peacekeeping personnel. cooperate in the organization of joint training programmes for national trainers of peacekeeping personnel and for other staff of national peacekeeping training institutions. OHCHR and DPKO shall call upon each other to develop/conceive and participate in training activities organized at the national and regional level, including the United Nations Training Assistance Teams (UNTATs).

15. OHCHR shall finalize the production of training materials on human rights for civilian police and military components of peacekeeping operations, which will be made available to DPKO for dissemination. DPKO shall make available to OHCHR its training materials, as necessary. Existing DPKO materials shall be revised with a view to including human rights standards, as appropriate.

16. Within training activities conducted separately, DPKO and OHCHR shall seek to promote and reinforce human rights and peacekeeping principles and standards, respectively.

17. Staff of human rights components of peacekeeping operations recruited in accordance with the procedure under paragraph 3 above shall undergo specific training on human rights as well as be considered to participate in OHCHR inter-field office staff exchange programmes, field-Geneva rotation programmes, staff training, and pre-deployment briefings in Geneva, subject to availability of resources and the SRSG's approval of their absence from the mission area.

F. *Information alert and exchange*

18. OHCHR shall share in a timely manner with DPKO information available from human rights treaty bodies, mechanisms of the UN Commission on Human Rights, and OHCHR field presences, with a view to alerting DPKO and integrating human rights concerns in UN responses to crises and emergencies. DPKO shall share, on a confidential basis, with OHCHR its situation reports as compiled by the Situation Center as well as where possible other documents and communications with HQ, such as memoranda, background notes, as relevant.

19. When an OHCHR human rights presence is not part of a peacekeeping operation, information relevant to the promotion and protection of human rights available to the peacekeeping operation, or its human rights component, shall be shared in a timely manner with the OHCHR presence for advice and/or complementary action, as appropriate and within the framework of the relevant coordination mechanisms in the field. OHCHR and DPKO shall also discuss the TORs of human rights staff deployed by DPKO, so as to enhance their effectiveness and the complimentarity of action with respect to OHCHR staff on the ground.

20. During the liquidation phase of peace operations, DPKO will make special arrangements for the safe handling and separate archiving of documents and files produced by human rights components. The Head of the human rights unit will assess the feasibility of transmission of pending cases and other relevant documentation to OHCHR or other UN human rights offices remaining in the region as a follow on mission.

G. *Joint initiative*

21. DPKO and OHCHR agree to arrange appropriate exchanges of staff at HQ so as to establish an inter-departmental team to work on issues of common concern, and the joint production of public information materials.

ANNEX III

THE GUIDING PRINCIPLES ON INTERNAL DISPLACEMENT

Introduction: Scope and Purpose

1. These Guiding Principles address the specific needs of internally displaced persons worldwide. They identify rights and guarantees relevant to the protection of persons from forced displacement and to their protection and assistance during displacement as well as during return or resettlement and reintegration.

2. For the purposes of these Principles, internally displaced persons are persons or groups of persons who have been forced or obliged to flee or to leave their homes or places of habitual residence, in particular as a result of or in order to avoid the effects of armed conflict, situations of generalized violence, violations of human rights or natural or human-made disasters, and who have not crossed an internationally recognized State border.

3. These Principles reflect and are consistent with international human rights law and international humanitarian law. They provide guidance to:

(a) The Representative of the Secretary-General on internally displaced persons in carrying out his mandate;
(b) States when faced with the phenomenon of internal displacement;
(c) All other authorities, groups and persons in their relations with internally displaced persons; and
(d) Intergovernmental and non-governmental organizations when addressing internal displacement.

4. These Guiding Principles should be disseminated and applied as widely as possible.

Section I—General Principles

Principle 1

1. Internally displaced persons shall enjoy, in full equality, the same rights and freedoms under international and domestic law as do other persons

Bertrand G. Ramcharan (Ed.), Human Rights Protection in the Field, 277–287.

in their country. They shall not be discriminated against in the enjoyment of any rights and freedoms on the ground that they are internally displaced.

2. These Principles are without prejudice to individual criminal responsibility under international law, in particular relating to genocide, crimes against humanity and war crimes.

Principle 2

1. These Principles shall be observed by all authorities, groups and persons irrespective of their legal status and applied without any adverse distinction. The observance of these Principles shall not affect the legal status of any authorities, groups or persons involved.

2. These Principles shall not be interpreted as restricting, modifying or impairing the provisions of any international human rights or international humanitarian law instrument or rights granted to persons under domestic law. In particular, these Principles are without prejudice to the right to seek and enjoy asylum in other countries.

Principle 3

1. National authorities have the primary duty and responsibility to provide protection and humanitarian assistance to internally displaced persons within their jurisdiction.

2. Internally displaced persons have the right to request and to receive protection and humanitarian assistance from these authorities. They shall not be persecuted or punished for making such a request.

Principle 4

1. These Principles shall be applied without discrimination of any kind, such as race, colour, sex, language, religion or belief, political or other opinion, national, ethnic or social origin, legal or social status, age, disability, property, birth, or on any other similar criteria.

2. Certain internally displaced persons, such as children, especially unaccompanied minors, expectant mothers, mothers with young children, female heads of household, persons with disabilities and elderly persons, shall be entitled to protection and assistance required by their condition and to treatment which takes into account their special needs.

Section II—Principles Relating to Protection from Displacement

Principle 5

All authorities and international actors shall respect and ensure respect for their obligations under international law, including human rights and humanitarian law, in all circumstances, so as to prevent and avoid conditions that might lead to displacement of persons.

Principle 6

1. Every human being shall have the right to be protected against being arbitrarily displaced from his or her home or place of habitual residence.

2. The prohibition of arbitrary displacement includes displacement:

(a) When it is based on policies of apartheid, "ethnic cleansing" or similar practices aimed at/or resulting in altering the ethnic, religious or racial composition of the affected population;
(b) In situations of armed conflict, unless the security of the civilians involved or imperative military reasons so demand;
(c) In cases of large-scale development projects, which are not justified by compelling and overriding public interests;
(d) In cases of disasters, unless the safety and health of those affected requires their evacuation; and
(e) When it is used as a collective punishment.

3. Displacement shall last no longer than required by the circumstances.

Principle 7

1. Prior to any decision requiring the displacement of persons, the authorities concerned shall ensure that all feasible alternatives are explored in order to avoid displacement altogether. Where no alternatives exist, all measures shall be taken to minimize displacement and its adverse effects.

2. The authorities undertaking such displacement shall ensure, to the greatest practicable extent, that proper accommodation is provided to the displaced persons, that such displacements are effected in satisfactory conditions of safety, nutrition, health and hygiene, and that members of the same family are not separated.

3. If displacement occurs in situations other than during the emergency stages of armed conflicts and disasters, the following guarantees shall be complied with:

(a) A specific decision shall be taken by a State authority empowered by law to order such measures;
(b) Adequate measures shall be taken to guarantee to those to be displaced full information on the reasons and procedures for their displacement and, where applicable, on compensation and relocation;
(c) The free and informed consent of those to be displaced shall be sought;
(d) The authorities concerned shall endeavour to involve those affected, particularly women, in the planning and management of their relocation;
(e) Law enforcement measures, where required, shall be carried out by competent legal authorities; and
(f) The right to an effective remedy, including the review of such decisions by appropriate judicial authorities, shall be respected.

Principle 8

Displacement shall not be carried out in a manner that violates the rights to life, dignity, liberty and security of those affected.

Principle 9

States are under a particular obligation to protect against the displacement of indigenous peoples, minorities, peasants, pastoralists and other groups with a special dependency on and attachment to their lands.

Section III—Principles Relating to Protection during Displacement

Principle 10

1. Every human being has the inherent right to life which shall be protected by law. No one shall be arbitrarily deprived of his or her life. Internally displaced persons shall be protected in particular against:

(a) Genocide;
(b) Murder;
(c) Summary or arbitrary executions; and
(d) Enforced disappearances, including abduction or unacknowledged detention, threatening or resulting in death.

Threats and incitement to commit any of the foregoing acts shall be prohibited.

2. Attacks or other acts of violence against internally displaced persons who do not or no longer participate in hostilities are prohibited in all circumstances. Internally displaced persons shall be protected, in particular, against:

(a) Direct or indiscriminate attacks or other acts of violence, including the creation of areas wherein attacks on civilians are permitted;
(b) Starvation as a method of combat;
(c) Their use to shield military objectives from attack or to shield, favour or impede military operations;
(d) Attacks against their camps or settlements; and
(e) The use of anti-personnel landmines.

Principle 11

1. Every human being has the right to dignity and physical, mental and moral integrity.

2. Internally displaced persons, whether or not their liberty has been restricted, shall be protected in particular against:

(a) Rape, mutilation, torture, cruel, inhuman or degrading treatment or punishment, and other outrages upon personal dignity, such as acts of gender-specific violence, forced prostitution and any form of indecent assault;
(b) Slavery or any contemporary form of slavery, such as sale into marriage, sexual exploitation, or forced labour of children; and
(c) Acts of violence intended to spread terror among internally displaced persons.

Threats and incitement to commit any of the foregoing acts shall be prohibited.

Principle 12

1. Every human being has the right to liberty and security of person. No one shall be subjected to arbitrary arrest or detention.

2. To give effect to this right for internally displaced persons, they shall not be interned in or confined to a camp. If in exceptional circumstances such internment or confinement is absolutely necessary, it shall not last longer than required by the circumstances.

3. Internally displaced persons shall be protected from discriminatory arrest and detention as a result of their displacement.

4. In no case shall internally displaced persons be taken hostage.

Principle 13

1. In no circumstances shall displaced children be recruited nor be required or permitted to take part in hostilities.

2. Internally displaced persons shall be protected against discriminatory practices of recruitment into any armed forces or groups as a result of their displacement. In particular any cruel, inhuman or degrading practices that compel compliance or punish non-compliance with recruitment are prohibited in all circumstances.

Principle 14

1. Every internally displaced person has the right to liberty of movement and freedom to choose his or her residence.

2. In particular, internally displaced persons have the right to move freely in and out of camps or other settlements.

Principle 15

Internally displaced persons have:

(a) The right to seek safety in another part of the country;
(b) The right to leave their country;
(c) The right to seek asylum in another country; and
(d) The right to be protected against forcible return to or resettlement in any place where their life, safety, liberty and/or health would be at risk.

Principle 16

1. All internally displaced persons have the right to know the fate and whereabouts of missing relatives.

2. The authorities concerned shall endeavour to establish the fate and whereabouts of internally displaced persons reported missing, and cooperate with relevant international organizations engaged in this task. They shall inform the next of kin on the progress of the investigation and notify them of any result.

3. The authorities concerned shall endeavour to collect and identify the mortal remains of those deceased, prevent their despoliation or mutilation, and facilitate the return of those remains to the next of kin or dispose of them respectfully.

4. Grave sites of internally displaced persons should be protected and respected in all circumstances. Internally displaced persons should have the right of access to the grave sites of their deceased relatives.

Principle 17

1. Every human being has the right to respect of his or her family life.

2. To give effect to this right for internally displaced persons, family members who wish to remain together shall be allowed to do so.

3. Families which are separated by displacement should be reunited as quickly as possible. All appropriate steps shall be taken to expedite the reunion of such families, particularly when children are involved. The responsible authorities shall facilitate inquiries made by family members and encourage and cooperate with the work of humanitarian organizations engaged in the task of family reunification.

4. Members of internally displaced families whose personal liberty has been restricted by internment or confinement in camps shall have the right to remain together.

Principle 18

1. All internally displaced persons have the right to an adequate standard of living.

2. At the minimum, regardless of the circumstances, and without discrimination, competent authorities shall provide internally displaced persons with and ensure safe access to:

(a) Essential food and potable water;
(b) Basic shelter and housing;
(c) Appropriate clothing; and
(d) Essential medical services and sanitation.

3. Special efforts should be made to ensure the full participation of women in the planning and distribution of these basic supplies.

Principle 19

1. All wounded and sick internally displaced persons as well as those with disabilities shall receive to the fullest extent practicable and with the least possible delay, the medical care and attention they require, without distinction on any grounds other than medical ones. When necessary, internally displaced persons shall have access to psychological and social services.

2. Special attention should be paid to the health needs of women, including access to female health care providers and services, such as reproductive health care, as well as appropriate counselling for victims of sexual and other abuses.

3. Special attention should also be given to the prevention of contagious and infectious diseases, including AIDS, among internally displaced persons.

Principle 20

1. Every human being has the right to recognition everywhere as a person before the law.

2. To give effect to this right for internally displaced persons, the authorities concerned shall issue to them all documents necessary for the enjoyment and exercise of their legal rights, such as passports, personal identification documents, birth certificates and marriage certificates. In particular, the authorities shall facilitate the issuance of new documents or the replacement of documents lost in the course of displacement, without imposing unreasonable conditions, such as requiring the return to one's area of habitual residence in order to obtain these or other required documents.

3. Women and men shall have equal rights to obtain such necessary documents and shall have the right to have such documentation issued in their own names.

Principle 21

1. No one shall be arbitrarily deprived of property and possessions.

2. The property and possessions of internally displaced persons shall in all circumstances be protected, in particular, against the following acts:

(a) Pillage;
(b) Direct or indiscriminate attacks or other acts of violence;
(c) Being used to shield military operations or objectives;
(d) Being made the object of reprisal; and
(e) Being destroyed or appropriated as a form of collective punishment.

3. Property and possessions left behind by internally displaced persons should be protected against destruction and arbitrary and illegal appropriation, occupation or use.

Principle 22

1. Internally displaced persons, whether or not they are living in camps, shall not be discriminated against as a result of their displacement in the enjoyment of the following rights:

(a) The rights to freedom of thought, conscience, religion or belief, opinion and expression;
(b) The right to seek freely opportunities for employment and to participate in economic activities;
(c) The right to associate freely and participate equally in community affairs;
(d) The right to vote and to participate in governmental and public affairs, including the right to have access to the means necessary to exercise this right; and
(e) The right to communicate in a language they understand.

Principle 23

1. Every human being has the right to education.

2. To give effect to this right for internally displaced persons, the authorities concerned shall ensure that such persons, in particular displaced children, receive education which shall be free and compulsory at the primary level. Education should respect their cultural identity, language and religion.

3. Special efforts should be made to ensure the full and equal participation of women and girls in educational programmes.

4. Education and training facilities shall be made available to internally displaced persons, in particular adolescents and women, whether or not living in camps, as soon as conditions permit.

Section IV—Principles Relating to Humanitarian Assistance

Principle 24

1. All humanitarian assistance shall be carried out in accordance with the principles of humanity and impartiality and without discrimination.

2. Humanitarian assistance to internally displaced persons shall not be diverted, in particular for political or military reasons.

Principle 25

1. The primary duty and responsibility for providing humanitarian assistance to internally displaced persons lies with national authorities.

2. International humanitarian organizations and other appropriate actors have the right to offer their services in support of the internally displaced. Such an offer shall not be regarded as an unfriendly act or an interference in a State's internal affairs and shall be considered in good faith. Consent thereto shall not be arbitrarily withheld, particularly when authorities concerned are unable or unwilling to provide the required humanitarian assistance.

3. All authorities concerned shall grant and facilitate the free passage of humanitarian assistance and grant persons engaged in the provision of such assistance rapid and unimpeded access to the internally displaced.

Principle 26

Persons engaged in humanitarian assistance, their transport and supplies shall be respected and protected. They shall not be the object of attack or other acts of violence.

Principle 27

1. International humanitarian organizations and other appropriate actors when providing assistance should give due regard to the protection needs and human rights of internally displaced persons and take appropriate measures in this regard. In so doing, these organizations and actors should respect relevant international standards and codes of conduct.

2. The preceding paragraph is without prejudice to the protection responsibilities of international organizations mandated for this purpose, whose services may be offered or requested by States.

Section V—Principles Relating to Return, Resettlement and Reintegration

Principle 28

1. Competent authorities have the primary duty and responsibility to establish conditions, as well as provide the means, which allow internally displaced persons to return voluntarily, in safety and with dignity, to their homes or places of habitual residence, or to resettle voluntarily in another

part of the country. Such authorities shall endeavour to facilitate the reintegration of returned or resettled internally displaced persons.

2. Special efforts should be made to ensure the full participation of internally displaced persons in the planning and management of their return or resettlement and reintegration.

Principle 29

1. Internally displaced persons who have returned to their homes or places of habitual residence or who have resettled in another part of the country shall not be discriminated against as a result of their having been displaced. They shall have the right to participate fully and equally in public affairs at all levels and have equal access to public services.

2. Competent authorities have the duty and responsibility to assist returned and/or resettled internally displaced persons to recover, to the extent possible, their property and possessions which they left behind or were dispossessed of upon their displacement. When recovery of such property and possessions is not possible, competent authorities shall provide or assist these persons in obtaining appropriate compensation or another form of just reparation.

Principle 30

All authorities concerned shall grant and facilitate for international humanitarian organizations and other appropriate actors, in the exercise of their respective mandates, rapid and unimpeded access to internally displaced persons to assist in their return or resettlement and reintegration.

ANNEX IV

ANNUAL REPORT OF THE OHCHR FIELD OFFICE IN CAMBODIA (2004)

Summary

The present report describes the role and achievements of the Cambodia Office of the High Commissioner for Human Rights (OHCHR/Cambodia) from July to December 2003 in assisting the Royal Government and people of Cambodia to further the protection and promotion of human rights. It has been prepared pursuant to resolution 2003/79 adopted by the Commission on Human Rights on 25 April 2003.

During the reporting period, OHCHR/Cambodia continued to support the Special Representative of the Secretary-General for human rights in Cambodia in carrying out his mandate, and facilitated his tenth mission to Cambodia from 27 November to 6 December 2003.

An external evaluation of the Cambodia Office was undertaken in late October and early November 2003 to assess the impact and relevance of the Office's programmes, major human rights protection and promotion issues, possible developments as a result of the recent National Assembly election, and the complementarity of the Office's programme with other relevant activities of the United Nations. It was asked to make recommendations for the future role and structure of the Office. The mission concluded that the presence of the OHCHR/Cambodia represents a positive commitment of the international community to Cambodia, and that the continued existence of the Office in Cambodia is essential for fostering respect of human rights until conditions change to a satisfactory extent, and pending the development of effective and independent national human rights institutions. While some areas require more focus and improvement, it found that the Office's programmes contribute significantly to promoting human rights, particularly in the area of protection.

To assist the Government in meeting its international human rights obligations, OHCHR/Cambodia continued to monitor the general human rights situation, to investigate reports of violations of human rights, and to document patterns of such violations. It regularly brought its concerns to the attention of provincial and national authorities, requesting their intervention.

Bertrand G. Ramcharan (Ed.), Human Rights Protection in the Field, 289–309.

Activities of OHCHR/Cambodia's programme in connection with the National Assembly elections of 27 July 2003 over the reporting period included: protection work during the election campaign and in the months following the elections; providing information to the Government and the international community on the situation; working with local non-governmental organizations conducting election-related human rights monitoring and responding to their protection concerns; and assisting in the preparation of public reports issued by the Special Representative, the most recent of which he released in December 2003. The election programme will close at the end of January 2004.

To assist the Government in developing natural resource policies in a manner consistent with Cambodia's international human rights obligations, OHCHR/Cambodia has concentrated on an aspect of land policy about which there is little information in the public domain. The Office continued to study, through fieldwork, research and analysis, the effect of large-scale agricultural plantations on the human rights of populations living within or close to their boundaries, and the extent to which they have contributed to the development and economic and social well-being of the Cambodian people as a whole. Based on the findings, the study will make recommendations to relevant government authorities and to international agencies.

OHCHR/Cambodia continued to contribute to the legislative process and to the process of justice sector reform, through providing comments on draft laws, facilitating discussion amongst interested parties on legal policy issues, providing advice on legal issues, particularly on criminal justice process and procedure, and monitoring trials of concern in the court system. The Office continued its work on legal aid, through a study on legal representation. It has collected data in four courts, and has consulted with organizations providing legal aid in Cambodia in order to prepare a preliminary paper about access to justice for the poor.

OHCHR/Cambodia continued to support and to cooperate closely with Cambodian non-governmental and civil society organizations in carrying out their work in accordance with the Declaration on the Right and Responsibility of Individuals, Groups and Organs of Society to Promote and Protect Universally Recognized Human Rights and Fundamental Freedoms. The Office was also active in the implementation of education and technical assistance and advisory services programmes.

The Office continued its work on economic and social rights. Because of the strong nexus between health and poverty, OHCHR/Cambodia began to undertake consultations and research on the right to health.

OHCHR/Cambodia continued its participation in United Nations and donor coordinating mechanisms, and in activities and meetings of the

United Nations Country Team with a view to integrating human rights into national development processes, including the National Poverty Reduction Strategy, the Millennium Development Goals, and the United Nations Development Assistance Framework.

CONTENTS

	Paragraphs
Introduction	1–6
I. Assistance to the Special Representative of the Secretary-General	7–8
II. Role of the United Nations High Commissioner for Human Rights in Assisting the Government and People of Cambodia in the Promotion and Protection of Human Rights	9–55
A. General objectives	9–10
B. The evaluation mission	11–14
C. Protection of human rights: monitoring, investigation and reporting	15–17
D. Election programme	18–20
E. Study on impunity	21
F. The land project	22–27
G. Human rights in development, including economic, social and cultural rights	28–31
H. Rule of law framework	32–41
I. Regional office in Battambang	42–44
J. Human rights reporting obligations and implementation of recommendations made by treaty monitoring bodies	45–47
K. Educational, technical assistance and public information programmes	48–52
L. Cooperation and coordination with the United Nations system, donors and the diplomatic community	53–55
III. OHCHR/Cambodia Staff and the Financial Situation of the United Nations Trust Fund for a Human Rights Education Programme in Cambodia	56–62

Introduction

1. The Cambodia Office of the United Nations High Commissioner for Human Rights (OHCHR/Cambodia) was established pursuant to resolution 1993/6 of the Commission on Human Rights, which entrusted the Office to:

(a) Manage the implementation of educational and technical assistance and advisory services programmes and ensure their continuation;
(b) Assist the Government of Cambodia, at its request, in meeting its obligations under the human rights instruments to which it is a party, including the preparation of reports to the relevant treaty monitoring bodies;
(c) Provide support to bona fide human rights groups in Cambodia;
(d) Contribute to the creation and/or strengthening of national institutions for the promotion and protection of human rights;
(e) Continue to assist with the drafting and implementation of legislation to promote and protect human rights; and
(f) Continue to assist with the training of persons responsible for the administration of justice.

2. OHCHR/Cambodia also assists the Special Representative of the Secretary-General for human rights in Cambodia in the discharge of his duties, as mandated by resolutions of the General Assembly and the Commission on Human Rights.

3. The present report contains information on the role and achievements of OHCHR/Cambodia from July 2003 to December 2003 in assisting the Government and people of Cambodia in the promotion and protection of human rights. It has been prepared pursuant to Commission on Human Rights resolution 2003/79 adopted on 25 April 2003. Information about the work of OHCHR/Cambodia from January 2003 to June 2003 is contained in the report submitted to the General Assembly at its fifty-eighth session (A/58/268).

4. A memorandum of understanding for the implementation of a technical cooperation programme on human rights was signed by the High Commissioner for Human Rights and the Royal Government of Cambodia in February 2002, for a period of two years. The Memorandum includes the following areas of cooperation: the provision of continuing assistance to the Government in promoting and protecting human rights; the promotion of greater integration of the human rights dimension into education, health and other development programmes; the provision of technical support for the Government's reform programmes, including in the areas

of administration of justice and the legislative process; encouraging the participation of civil society and promoting public education in democracy and human rights, especially in the domains of economic, social and cultural rights; and the provision, upon the Government's request, of technical assistance and advice in fulfilling its responsibilities, including submission of reports to meet its international human rights treaty obligations. During the tenth official visitof the Special Representative of the Secretary-General on human rights in Cambodia, the Prime Minister made a pledge that the Government would renew the existing terms of the memorandum of understanding upon its expiry.

5. The Office's programmes are implemented in cooperation with a number of institutions with human rights responsibilities, including the Supreme Council of Magistracy; the courts; the Office of the Prosecutor General; the Royal School for Training Judges and Prosecutors, the Commissions on Human Rights and Reception of Complaints and the Commissions on Legislation of the National Assembly and the Senate; the Cambodian Human Rights Committee; the Department of Prisons; and with the Ministries of Justice, Interior, Land Management, Agriculture, Forestry and Fisheries, Women's and Veterans' Affairs, and Health. The Office also cooperates with a wide range of non-governmental organizations working on human rights, legal and development issues.

6. An external review of the role of the Office and its future programmes was undertaken in October-November 2003, with a view to making recommendations about the future role and structure of the Office.

I. *Assistance to the Special Representative of the Secretary-General*

7. During the reporting period, OHCHR/Cambodia regularly provided the Special Representative of the Secretary-General for human rights in Cambodia with information on issues of concern, in particular in the areas of: justice sector reform; the National Assembly elections held in July 2003; restrictions on the freedoms of expression, association and assembly; the excessive use of force by police; issues relating to corruption, disbursement and access to information; land and forestry issues; prison conditions and prison reform; impunity; police-court relations; legal aid; a range of criminal justice issues; a human rights-based approach to development and economic and social rights; and compliance with international human rights obligations.

8. OHCHR/Cambodia facilitated the Special Representative's tenth mission to Cambodia carried out in accordance with his mandate: to maintain contact with the Government and people of Cambodia; to guide and

coordinate the United Nations human rights presence in Cambodia; and to assist the Government in the promotion and protection of human rights. The findings of this mission, undertaken between 27 November and 6 December 2003, are summarized in his report to the sixtieth session of the Commission on Human Rights (E/CN.4/2004/105), and a second report issued by the Special Representative on the National Assembly elections in mid-December 2003. The Special Representative's mission focused on the general political climate in the wake of the National Assembly elections, justice sector reform, ongoing problems in the criminal justice system, and the impact on human rights of natural resource policies and practices in Cambodia. He continued to discuss and promote a human rights approach to development, and began consultations on the right to health. The Office prepared comprehensive briefing papers for the Special Representative to facilitate his mission, and assisted him in the preparation of his reports to the General Assembly and the Commission on Human Rights, and his public reports and statements released in Cambodia.

II. *Role of the United Nations High Commissioner for Human Rights in Assisting the Government and People of Cambodia in the Promotion and Protection of Human Rights*

A. *General objectives*

9. The strategy of OHCHR/Cambodia combines a dual approach of working on immediate issues while pursuing the longer-term goal of helping to establish and strengthen institutions to safeguard and ensure future respect for human rights. Working jointly with others, the Office aims to contribute towards a Cambodian society based on respect for human rights under the rule of law, and the presence of a strong civil society that is able to operate in accordance with the provisions of the *Declaration on the Right and Responsibility of Individuals, Groups and Organs of Society to Promote and Protect Universally Recognized Human Rights and Fundamental Freedoms.*

10. Challenges include building an independent judiciary, creating adequate checks on the exercise of the executive power and effective mechanisms of accountability, and confronting long-standing problems of impunity and corruption which continue to impede efforts at reform. In addition to its work with Government institutions, the Office continues to work with non-governmental organizations and other civil society groups to promote policies and practices consonant with Cambodia's international human rights obligations, and to assist in their efforts to secure redress for victims of violations and on broader legal and policy issues with human rights implications.

B. *The evaluation mission*

11. An external evaluation of the Office was undertaken in late October and early November 2003.[1] Its principal aim was to take stock of the activities of the Office in order to assess their impact, relevance and efficiency, as well as to identify major human rights issues and make recommendations for the future role and structure of the Office. The mission met with a range of governmental and non-governmental actors, and representatives from international organizations and the diplomatic community. Field visits were also conducted to the regional office in Battambang, a fishing community affected by outside commercial interests, and a rubber plantation that is under study as part of the Office's project on large-scale agricultural plantations. The mission also visited the prison in Siem Reap. The report of the evaluation mission and its recommendations are internal to OHCHR and will be reviewed in early 2004 with a view to their implementation. The mission made a series of recommendations to restructure and improve the efficiency of the Office in relation to management, administration, staffing and related budget issues. The recommendations of an external United Nations audit of the Office that was undertaken in early December 2003, once they are available, will also be taken up as part of this process.

12. The mission reported that all those interviewed acknowledged the important role played by the OHCHR/Cambodia, and supported its continued presence in Cambodia, at least until the human rights context improves to a satisfactory extent. It concluded that the presence of the Office represents a positive commitment of the international community to Cambodia after decades of turmoil, that it acts as a "safety valve" or "watchdog" against human rights violations and as a check-and-balance against abuses of power, pending the development of effective and independent national human rights institutions for the promotion and protection of human rights. The mission found that the Office and its programmes are providing an enabling environment for the growth of civil society, especially non-governmental organizations that work in the field of human rights. The Office was found to "add value" in the field of protection and acts as a catalyst to nurture and support the human rights work of other actors, including public institutions and civil society, as well as acting as an intermediary to facilitate access by key actors—governmental and non-governmental—to external funding sources, and vice versa.

---

[1] The evaluation team consisted of Vitit Muntarbhorn (Professor of Law, team leader, Thailand), Peter Hellmers, (OHCHR/Geneva) and Raymond Fell (consultant, United Kingdom).

13. The mission's recommendations include the following:

(a) It is essential to support and sustain the Special Representative's mandate and the continued presence of the Office as the situation relating to human rights remains one of concern, bearing in mind Cambodia's recent past and the international responsibility towards the Cambodian people;

(b) The protection role of the Office adds value to the existing human rights context in Cambodia, and should be maximized through increasing staff capacity, selection of cases illustrating key trends, adequate follow-up, policy and technical assistance, and clear criteria for action. The Office should offer protection to those in need, especially where others are unable or unwilling to act;

(c) The Office should continue to provide legal and other technical assistance aimed at promoting structural change and cooperation to benefit the Cambodian people. The Office should highlight the effective implementation of laws and policies responsive to human rights, and help to build the capacity of mechanisms and personnel for human rights promotion and protection at national and local levels;

(d) The Office should provide expertise on the relationship between the national system and the international system on human rights, and help to inform the national community about the recommendations of the human rights treaty bodies and special procedures established by the Commission on Human Rights, putting them into accessible and understandable forms. It should monitor the Government of Cambodia's strategy and programme of action to reform the legal and judicial sector, which was adopted in June 2003, to assess implementation in conformity with Cambodia's international obligations;

(e) The Office should continue to support civil society, including non-governmental organizations, as a vigilant force for human rights, and build bridges between human rights and development non-governmental organizations, while extending access beyond non-governmental organizations to local communities and their leaders;

(f) The Office should support intergovernmental organizations and others on human rights-based programming. It should raise new areas of concern such as the negative impact of globalization, in concert with other United Nations agencies;

(g) The role of the Office should be consolidated as a catalyst rather than as a funder, with the capacity to cross-refer and cross-link with other agencies as appropriate. The Office should promote sustained and balanced support for local actors, and nurture self-reliance;

(h) The Office should emphasize and encourage effective implementation of human rights obligations by government authorities and other partners, with equitable and timely resource allocation from the State. It should identify good practices and utilize them for structural reforms and sustained capacity to overcome negative practices; and

(i) The current memorandum of understanding between the Office and the Government of Cambodia should be renewed in its present form.

14. OHCHR agrees that it is essential to support and sustain the mandate of the Special Representative of the Secretary-General and that the continued presence of the Office is necessary. It welcomes the assurances provided by Prime Minister Hun Sen during the Special Representative's tenth mission to both the Special Representative and the director of the Cambodia Office regarding the Office's continued operation.

C. *Protection of human rights: monitoring, investigation and reporting*

15. OHCHR/Cambodia continued to monitor the human rights situation throughout the country, to investigate reports involving serious violations of human rights and document patterns of such violations. It regularly brought its concerns to the attention of local and national government authorities, and proposed means of redress. The Office also remained in regular communication with the judiciary, non-governmental organizations and the international community on these issues.

16. During the reporting period, the Office gave particular attention to investigating human rights violations in the context of the National Assembly elections of July 2003. In particular, it investigated a number of murders of persons affiliated with political parties. It also monitored restrictions on freedoms of assembly and association in the post-election period, and other reports of serious human rights violations.

17. OHCHR/Cambodia continued to receive complaints from the public about human rights violations, and took up serious cases, including cases of violence and intimidation of political activists; land disputes and land grabbing; torture and cruel, inhuman or degrading treatment in places of detention; and serious breaches of criminal process guarantees. Staff also followed the progress of cases involving those charged with offences relating to the anti-Thai riots of 29 January 2003 who were eventually tried in September 2003. Forty-seven persons who were found guilty of offences directly relating to the riots, were given prison sentences equivalent to time already served, and released. Two students, convicted of incitement and handed longer sentences, were released three weeks later, after being granted royal pardons. Charges remain against two journalists accused of incitement who are on bail awaiting trial. The Office followed up on previous

work on street retribution (mob killings) and prison conditions, continued to investigate unresolved cases and assisted human rights non-governmental organizations in the effective commission of their work. It also assisted national human rights defenders facing threats to their safety.

D. *Election programme*

18. Through the reporting period, OHCHR/Cambodia continued its programme in relation to the National Assembly elections held in July 2003 in order to promote a political climate free from violence and intimidation, and an electoral process administered by neutral State institutions. Three mobile teams continued to investigate reports of election-related human rights violations throughout the country and monitored the general political situation. The Kompong Cham election office continued to closely monitor the situation in the province, investigating serious cases, and requesting intervention by local and provincial authorities. The election programme is due to be completed by the end of January 2004.

19. OHCHR/Cambodia staff met frequently with representatives and staff of the National Election Committee to raise general issues of concern and specific case-related matters, especially about the handling of complaints of intimidation and violence in the context of the election, and the application of sanctions. During the post-election period, the Office repeatedly raised its concerns with the Ministry of the Interior, police and municipal authorities about restrictions placed upon freedom of assembly, and the excessive force used to disperse unauthorized demonstrations.

20. OHCHR/Cambodia continued to monitor law enforcement efforts and court proceedings in connection with several murders and suspicious deaths with possible political motivation, in addition to other forms of violence and intimidation against political party activists. It continued to develop a database to record reported human rights violations relating to the election. Staff held meetings with representatives of all major political parties, and provided briefings for diplomats, the donor community and international organizations. The Office continued coordination efforts with local election and human rights non-governmental organizations, hosting regular meetings to discuss issues of common concern. This cooperation extended to the provinces, with staff supporting non-governmental organizations on monitoring and investigation.

E. *Study on impunity*

21. The Office started a project in November 2003 to review and follow up on human rights violations that were the subject of action by the United

Nations Transitional Authority in Cambodia in 1992 and 1993, as well as by the Office and the Special Representatives during the subsequent decade. On the basis of this review and an analysis of relevant political and legal developments, a report containing recommendations will be prepared. The Office will also develop a long-term strategy on how to effectively address impunity.

F. *The land project*

22. OHCHR/Cambodia continued its study of large-scale agricultural plantations—a term which includes both land concessions and rubber plantations operated by the State—to identify their effect on the human rights of people living within or close to their boundaries. The Office continued to research, report, analyse and monitor the situation of the human rights of local populations. It conducted fieldwork in selected areas during the reporting period, and investigated and documented the situation of human rights in four land concessions in Phnom Srouch district, Kompong Speu province (owned by several companies: Cambodia Haining, CJ Cambodia and Aduok), one land concession in Kompong Chhnang province (Pheapimex) and in the Tumring rubber plantation.

23. Fieldwork has now been conducted in nine land concessions and one rubber plantation. Detailed research has been undertaken in three of these locations, including semi-structured qualitative interviews with local populations, activists, authorities and concession company representatives. Staff also conducted open interviews with non-governmental organizations at national and provincial levels, and met regularly during the course of the study with those involved in land policy and administration in Cambodia, including relevant government officials at both national and provincial levels, civil society and international agencies.

24. The study has also sought to identify the extent to which land concessions have contributed to the development and economic and social well-being of the Cambodian people as a whole, specifically in terms of their contributions to overall State revenue and to the livelihood of affected local populations. The Office collected data about existing concessions, and assessed compliance by concessionaires with both the Land Law of 2001 and the terms of the concession contracts. The Office has also sought to contribute to the process of drafting sub-decrees that are essential to implement the Land Law, most specifically the sub-decrees on the procedures for granting land concessions for economic purposes, and on the reduction and specific exemptions of land concessions exceeding 10,000 hectares.

25. According to information provided by the Ministry of Agriculture in February 2003, the Council of Ministers has approved 42 land con-

cessions for agricultural purposes, covering over 800,000 hectares. In only 27 cases have the necessary concession agreements or contracts been executed with the Ministry. Since the Office began the study, 5 approvals for concessions were rescinded in August 2003 and 11 more cancellations have been foreshadowed by the Minister of Agriculture. However, no existing contracts have been terminated even when some companies are in clear breach of their contracts and Cambodian law. The Special Representative has recommended the cancellation of those contracts where the concessionaires are violating the law or are in serious breach of the terms of the contracts.

26. In undertaking this study, staff have had considerable difficulty in obtaining information relating to land concessions although this information concerns matters of significant public interest that should be in the public domain (such as the process for granting new land concessions, fees, contracts, shareholders, payment of deposit, fees and maps). Even where the Office was able to obtain access to the contracts, individual shareholders of relevant companies could not be identified. The difficulties in accessing this information have highlighted the urgency for more open administrative practices and policies to enable informed debate about land in Cambodia and better decision-making in the administration of land and the development of policy. There is also a need for a consultative process with local populations and a regulatory environment effective in monitoring the activities of the companies and ensuring compliance with the law and the terms of the contracts. The Special Representative has also recommended the adoption of freedom of information legislation that permits scrutiny of executive action and encourages greater accountability. Several non-governmental organizations are now working on this issue.

27. The Office also investigated and documented disputes over land and other natural resources over the reporting period. They often involved disputes between local populations or fishermen and those with political and economic influence, including military officers and business interests. Detailed study of these cases has helped to document and raise recurring problems both in the management of natural resources, and the mechanisms for dealing with land disputes and related violations of human rights. At present, neither the Cadastral Commission structure, established in July 2002, nor the courts function effectively to resolve disputes involving land or to provide remedies for related human rights violations.

G. *Human rights in development, including economic, social and cultural rights*

28. The Office continued to advocate for national policies based on international human rights obligations relevant to areas such as urban development, health, the environment, poverty reduction and management of natural resources, and for international human rights norms to be fully integrated into the National Poverty Reduction Strategy and the realization of the Millennium Development Goals. The Office worked with development organizations to integrate human rights, specifically focusing on human rights obligations with a view to strengthening accountability.

29. OHCHR/Cambodia continued to cooperate with and support the work of non-governmental and community organizations advocating for economic and social rights. It prepared a note on the right to adequate housing to inform affected groups and their representatives. It raised concerns with the Phnom Penh municipality relating to the relocation and forced evictions of squatters and the urban poor in Phnom Penh, and intervened on several occasions to try to stop forced evictions.

30. The Office also focused on the right to health as a central issue, which was taken up by the Special Representative during his tenth mission. There is a strong relationship between poverty and health in Cambodia. People living in poverty do not have equal access to health care, often becoming indebted to cover medical expenses, which in turn adversely affect their living conditions. The Office continued to provide financial and other support to the work of the Fisheries Action Coalition Team, a non-governmental organization that promotes legal knowledge, networking and advocacy among fishing communities around the Tonle Sap Lake.

31. Staff are revising and updating a basic training course on economic, social and cultural rights which focuses on the right to health, education and housing, and to a basic livelihood.

H. *Rule of law framework*

(a) *The judiciary and the administration of justice*

32. OHCHR/Cambodia continued to monitor reform of the justice sector to facilitate the incorporation of international human rights law into domestic law and practice, and to better link the reform agenda to other areas of government policy such as the National Poverty Reduction Strategy and private sector investment that are dependent upon competent, accountable and transparent legal institutions. It advocated for structural reform of key institutions, such as the Supreme Council of Magistracy. The Office maintained a presence in the municipal court of Phnom Penh and continued its links with the appeal court and Supreme Court. It continued

cooperation with the Battambang provincial court through its regional office, supplemented by regular visits by staff from the national office. In order to make more efficient use of resources, as well as to reinforce its office in the court of Phnom Penh (which has a caseload of 8,000 cases a year), the small office in the Sihanoukville provincial court was closed, with staff continuing to assist from Phnom Penh.

33. The Office continued to assist the courts to promote compliance with human rights standards and to address the many practices in the criminal justice system that do not appear to be sanctioned by law. Staff observed key trials of concern, including those relating to trafficking, torture, sexual violence against children, the anti-Thai riots of 29 January 2003, and the trial held in October into the murder of Om Radsady, a senior advisor to FUNCINPEC (National United Front for an Independent, Neutral, Peaceful and Cooperative Cambodia). In addition to cases at the Phnom Penh municipal court, the appeal court and the Supreme Court, the Office followed cases in the courts of Prey Veng, Kompong Cham, Kompong Speu, Sihanoukville and Battambang. The Office provided advice on due process rights and trial procedures, and addressed issues relating to legal representation and access to justice, seeking to facilitate contacts between accused persons and legal aid lawyers whenever serious cases were tried in courts without legal representation. The Office also monitored police-court relations.

34. A technical assessment mission by the United Nations Assistance to the Khmer Rouge Trials was undertaken in Phnom Penh in early December. The mission reached "substantial" agreement with the Government Task Force on several issues, including on staffing and the sequencing of work to prepare for the phased establishment of the Extraordinary Chambers, which will prosecute crimes committed during the period of Democratic Kampuchea under Cambodian law. The Office has continued to follow developments in Cambodia and has provided briefings about the human rights situation and the administration of justice. The Office sees its functions as being primarily those related to public education, with the possibility of also playing a role in monitoring the trials.

35. The Office met regularly with members of the judiciary, the legislature and Government officials to discuss juridical and broader policy issues relating to human rights in the administration of justice, including meetings with jurists, judges and prosecutors, the Council for Legal and Judicial Reform, the Supreme Council of Magistracy, officials from the Ministry of Justice and the Presidents of parliamentary committees. Topics of discussion included the independence of the judiciary; reform issues relating to judicial bodies and the legal profession; security concerns of judges and court personnel; the backlog of cases within the court system; sen-

tencing and the appeals policies of prosecutors. The Office also worked in close cooperation with non-governmental organizations working on legal and judicial reform issues.

36. Most recently, it has participated in consultations on the legal and judicial reform strategy document adopted by the Government on 20 June 2003. A series of workshops began in October 2003 to prioritize the Government's draft programme of action, which contains over 90 activities. The Office has welcomed the inclusion of a broader range of participants at this stage of the discussion, especially as a broad consultative process was not undertaken in preparing the strategy document. OHCHR/ Cambodia has consistently advocated that the reform process needs to be more inclusive to obtain the broader support of the Cambodian people.

37. The failure of the Supreme Council of Magistracy to carry out its responsibilities in scrutinizing and safeguarding the independence and professional conduct of judges and prosecutors remains one of the obstacles to the effective functioning of the judiciary in Cambodia. Restructuring of the Council remains a priority in the reform agenda, and yet is not adequately dealt with in draft amendment bills on the issue. The Office has engaged a legal expert to help prepare an analytical paper to examine the current status of the Council and recommend appropriate measures for its reform.

38. In April 2003, the Office began consultations with the Bar Association, concerned authorities of the Ministry of Justice and non-governmental organizations involved in the provision of legal aid, in order to examine the state of legal representation in Cambodia. The Office also started a modest study of legal representation in four provincial courts in Cambodia. The initial phase was conducted in three courts located in provinces where legal aid providers are present (Sihanoukville, Battambang, Kompong Chhnang) and in one province where they are not (Prey Veng). Staff examined court registers and determined the total number of cases heard during 2001 and 2002; recorded the number of cases in which there was legal representation during those years; and disaggregated these statistics by reference to whether they involved felonies, misdemeanours or civil cases, and further by reference to the type of case. In civil cases, note was made of whether one or both parties was legally represented. Staff also conducted semi-structured interviews of judges and prosecutors and those involved in the provision of legal aid. A preliminary discussion paper will be produced on the basis of the findings of the study, and distributed in early 2004. It aims to depict the current situation with respect to legal representation before the courts and access to legal assistance more generally in order to assessing Cambodia's needs in ensuring access to justice for the majority of its citizens who cannot afford to pay for legal repre-

sentation and advice. The Office hopes that this could offer a basis for developing a legal aid scheme to provide basic legal services for the poor and the possibility of a State-assisted legal aid fund, as has been established in other countries.

39. The Office also cooperated with the Royal School for Training Judges and Prosecutors, which began in November 2003, to ascertain how it can best assist the school in order to ensure that human rights are adequately included in the curriculum. The Office provided resource materials, arranged an address of the Special Representative to the student judges, and hopes to provide assistance to teach a specialized human rights component in the curriculum in early 2004.

(b) *Assistance in the legislative process: drafting and implementation of legislation to promote and protect human rights*

40. The Office continued to follow and advise on the drafting of legislation and regulations both to promote compliance with international human rights law and to improve the technical quality of draft laws, focusing on those laws that are directly relevant to its mandate and overall priorities. Laws that have been of particular interest include those relating to anti-corruption, the suppression of trafficking in human beings and sexual exploitation and sub-decrees relating to land and forestry. Staff continued to follow progress in the preparation of the Penal Code and the Code of Criminal Procedure (drafted with the assistance of experts from France) and the Civil Code and Code of Civil Procedure (drafted with the assistance of experts from Japan), all of which were recently submitted to the Council of Ministers. The Office has noted the importance of ensuring consistency between these foundation codes and the laws that are being passed in connection with accession to the World Trade Organization.

41. Legislative activity effectively stopped during the reporting period due to the failure to form a government in the wake of the elections. However, the Office has continued to promote a participatory law-making process, emphasizing a repeatedly raised but often overlooked concern regarding the need for consultation in the drafting process and for public scrutiny before the adoption of laws. It has also underlined the necessity of straightforward and accessible laws.

I. *Regional office in Battambang*

42. The regional office in Battambang covers the provinces of Battambang, Banteay Meanchey and Oddar Meanchey, as well as the municipality of Pailin, working under the supervision of the Phnom Penh office. During the reporting period, staff monitored and investigated complaints of viola-

tions of human rights related to the elections, making regular interventions with local and provincial authorities. This work was undertaken in close cooperation with non-governmental organizations, and through liaison with local and international election monitoring organizations. The office remained in regular contact with provincial authorities, such as the courts, police and military, throughout the reporting period.

43. The Office investigated sensitive cases involving alleged violations in isolated areas which local human rights groups have difficulties accessing, and in areas with systemic or widespread breaches of human rights. They also carried out routine monitoring in districts still dealing with the transition from military to civilian rule, linking this work with education and training efforts.

44. It also investigated and joined efforts to resolve disputes involving conflicts over natural resources, such as a long-standing land dispute in Koh Kralor district, and a conflict involving the Prek Chas fishing community, whose representatives face imprisonment and fines after confiscating illegal fishing equipment from a local merchant. The case is now before the court of appeal. During the reporting period, staff conducted several one-day training courses in economic, social and cultural rights for villagers and the local authorities, particularly in those districts affected by land disputes.

J. *Human rights reporting obligations and implementation of recommendations made by treaty monitoring bodies*

45. Cambodia is party to the six main international human rights instruments. OHCHR/Cambodia has been providing assistance in the preparation of treaty reports to the Government since 1994, and has assisted in the preparation of all initial reports. Since August 2001, the responsibility of drafting most reports has been entrusted to the Cambodian Human Rights Committee. Currently, Committee staff working on treaty reporting is divided into two subcommittees to prepare the initial report on compliance with the International Covenant on Economic, Social and Cultural Rights and the periodic report for the Committee on the Elimination of Racial Discrimination. The Cambodian National Council for Children has responsibility for preparing reports on the Convention on the Rights of the Child and for monitoring its implementation. The Ministry of Women's and Veterans' Affairs is responsible for reporting under the Convention on the Elimination of All Forms of Discrimination against Women (CEDAW). The initial report under CEDAW, which also encompasses the second and third reports, is now in its final stages and is expected to be transmitted to the Committee by the end of the year.

46. While not at the same level as in previous years, OHCHR/Cambodia will continue to help in the preparation of reports for the treaty bodies, through technical assistance, targeted training sessions, and relevant documentation and resource materials to help the Cambodian Human Rights Committee build a basic collection of resource materials on international human rights law and on domestic human rights issues. Working with Government institutions, international agencies and non-governmental organizations, the Office will now focus attention on promoting follow up to concluding observations made by the treaty bodies.

47. The Committee against Torture, at its thirtieth session in April/May 2003, considered Cambodia's initial report under the Convention against Torture and Other Cruel, Inhuman or Degrading Treatment or Punishment, which was due in November 1993. However, no delegation representing the Government from Phnom Penh was present to respond to the Committee's questions. The Committee issued provisional conclusions and recommendations, asking for a response from the Government by the end of August 2003. The Office translated these conclusions and recommendations into Khmer and brought them to the attention of relevant Government institutions, including the Cambodian Human Rights Committee, the Director of the Prison Department and the co-Ministers of the Interior. In the absence of a Government response, the Committee adopted them as final at its thirty-first session in November 2003.

K. *Educational, technical assistance and public information programmes*

48. OHCHR/Cambodia, jointly with others, works to create an enabling environment for human rights work, including through public outreach and facilitating discussion and dialogue. For example, during the tenth mission of the Special Representative, it organized round-table discussions, bringing together people from the Government, non-governmental organizations, and donor agencies to discuss justice sector reform, health and land issues.

49. OHCHR/Cambodia has continued to provide training, legal and other technical advice to Cambodian non-governmental and community-based organizations in all areas of its work.

50. Human rights publications, laws and information materials continued to be distributed to the general public, non-governmental organizations, students and government officials. The Office and the Special Representative's reports and statements as well as resolutions of the General Assembly and the Commission on Human Rights were translated into Khmer as a matter of regular practice. Revised and first-time translations into Khmer of those international human rights instruments particularly relevant to Cambodia will be published in early 2004.

51. OHCHR/Cambodia is currently developing a web page to make reports of the Special Representatives and the Office, and information on the history and mandate of the Office and Special Representative, available to a wider public. The resource room of the Office is now being reorganized, including classification of material and use of technology with television, videotape player, and limited Internet access.

52. The Office liased regularly with the media in Cambodia, with both the local English-language newspapers and the Khmer press and wire services.

L. *Cooperation and coordination with the United Nations system, donors and the diplomatic community*

53. OHCHR/Cambodia is a member of the United Nations Country Team (UNCT), and has provided to the members of UNCT, the World Bank and other relevant actors, information on the integration of international human rights norms and standards into poverty reduction strategies and the Millennium Development Goals in accordance with OHCHR draft guidelines on this topic.

54. The United Nations Country Team decided in September 2003 to take up human rights as an issue of shared concern, and the Office is participating in efforts to integrate human rights more fully into the work of UNCT and its member agencies. It is also contributing to the midterm review of the United Nations Development Assistance Framework and to advisory bodies on the Millennium Development Goals in order to promote the centrality of human rights and rights-based approach. One staff member is now working in dedicated fashion on these tasks.

55. The Office provided regular briefings for visiting and resident diplomats and international organizations and prepared regular reports for OHCHR Headquarters to meet the reporting requirements of the United Nations system. The Office also provided reports to the United Nations Resident Coordinator and donors where required.

III. *OHCHR/Cambodia Staff and the Financial situation of the United Nations Trust Fund for a Human Rights Education Programme in Cambodia*

56. The Office implemented its activities through its main office in Phnom Penh, a regional office in Battambang, an election office in Kompong Cham, and small offices in the municipal court of Phnom Penh, and the Sihanoukville provincial court which was closed in September. The management structure consists of the Director's Office, the Administration Unit,

the Protection and Policy Development Team, the Legal Assistance and Education, Training and Information Units. At the time of writing, the Office had 32 national staff and 8 international staff members.

57. The Director's Office is responsible for policy and management, including coordinating support to the Special Representative of the Secretary-General, participating in the United Nations system, working with other international agencies and non-governmental organizations, and external and donor relations.

58. The Administration Unit provides personnel, administrative and finance services to the office and coordinates transport and logistics. It is also responsible for information management.

59. The Protection and Policy Development Team is responsible for conducting the election programme, investigating complaints of human rights violations, preparing thematic reports, and working with other units on issues relating to the administration of justice and impunity.

60. The Legal Assistance Unit is responsible for assisting in the judicial reform process, and working with the courts to help address deficiencies in the administration of justice. The Unit works with the legal profession and comments on selected draft laws to ensure compliance with the international human rights treaties to which Cambodia is party.

61. The Education, Training and Information Unit is responsible for public outreach, and education, training and advocacy to promote the implementation of economic, social and cultural rights. It also works with the Government, the United Nations Country Team, and intergovernmental agencies on a human rights-based approach to development.

62. The United Nations regular budget covered the operational expenses of OHCHR/Cambodia, including the salaries of 7 professional international staff members and of 16 national staff members. Voluntary contributions to the United Nations Trust Fund for a Human Rights Education Programme in Cambodia cover all other expenditures (including the salaries of staff members not covered under the regular budget). The Trust Fund is administered by the United Nations Office at Geneva.

ANNEX V

ANNUAL REPORT OF THE OHCHR FIELD OFFICE IN COLOMBIA (2004)

Summary

This report on Colombia by the United Nations High Commissioner for Human Rights covers the year 2003, and responds to the request made by the Commission on Human Rights at its fifty-ninth session.

National context and dynamics of the internal armed conflict

The evolution of the internal armed conflict and the problems of indebtedness, the fiscal deficit, as well as legislative policy, marked new challenges for the country. The first months of the year transpired under a state of internal disorder, in the context of which public order measures and restrictions of fundamental rights and liberties were adopted, particularly in the "rehabilitation and consolidation zones". The Government increased operations aimed at maintaining or re-establishing public order, in the context of the policy of "democratic security". Combat between the Security Forces and the illegal armed groups, particularly the guerrillas, intensified, with the guerrillas retreating to traditional rural areas and resorting to acts of terrorism when faced with the increasing pressure exerted by the Security Forces. The illegal armed groups continued to finance their activities by means of the practice of kidnapping and the illicit traffic of drugs. During the year, while the President's popularity, as reflected in opinion polls, remained high, a higher degree of tension and polarization was observed in Colombian society. The Government promoted the adoption of a constitutional referendum, held on 25 October, to introduce changes of a political and economic nature in the Constitution. The preliminary results showed that practically none of the proposals has the minimum support needed from voters for their approval (25 per cent of eligible voters), although the final decision of authorities is still pending. The results of the departmental and municipal elections held on 26 October showed the political plurality of the country. In spite of the threats and attacks of the illegal armed groups it was possible to hold the referendum and the elections because of the measures adopted by the Government. After the

B.G. Ramcharan (Ed.), Human Rights Protection in the Field, 311–385.

elections, the President proceeded to substitute some of his most important ministers and to carry out changes in the upper echelons of the Security Forces. The Government and a significant part of the paramilitary groups increased the contacts and dialogues begun in 2002 and, after the declaration of a ceasefire they signed in July 2003 an agreement of gradual demobilization concluding at the end of 2005. As for the guerrilla groups, no advances in dialogues were registered. In the London declaration in July, 24 countries expressed their strong support for the Government, within the framework of certain qualifications. In particular, they urged the prompt implementation of the recommendations of the United Nations High Commissioner for Human Rights, and the adoption of measures against impunity and connivance with paramilitary groups.

State policy and follow-up of the international recommendations

Interlocution was developed between the office in Colombia of the High Commissioner and the Government, in particular with the Vice-President, and other State entities in order to promote the implementation of the recommendations. There were some advances, but the implementation of the majority of the recommendations was still pending at the moment the present report was completed. In general, it could be observed that the recommendations were not integrated in a consistent manner in the Government's policies. Actions taken in the context of "democratic security" influenced particularly the legislative agenda and the actions of the Security Forces and of the judicial organs and those of control. The office in Colombia took note of the so-called Antiterrorist Statute approved on 10 December 2003, a decision contrary to the express recommendations of the High Commissioner and other competent international organs. The Government was able to extend the presence of the Security Forces to almost all of the country's municipalities. However, some regions with a greater presence of the Security Forces continued to suffer from serious problems of governability and public order. The military reinforcement was not accompanied by the strengthening of civil institutions. There was a tendency to consider all violence as terrorist acts and in this way deny the existence of an internal armed conflict and the necessity of applying, in a consequent manner, international humanitarian law. Actions taken against paramilitarism and its links with public servants did not show sufficiently significant results.

Measures taken against impunity continued registering few concrete results. In its policy related to demobilization of members of illegal armed organizations, the Government adopted norms that grant juridical benefits, and proposed projects that raised questions as regards impunity and the rights to truth, justice and reparation. The Government's legislative proposals were characterized, in general, by making prison sentences harsher and by the creation of new crimes, as well as the weakening of constitutional and legal guarantees. Also observed were the increased difficulties in exercising independent and impartial control. As regards prevention and protection measures, positive actions were registered. However, difficulties persist as regards risk evaluation and the effectiveness of measures adopted. Positive actions were observed with regard to the destruction of anti-personnel mines. Public expenditure on education and health increased but the inequality gap did not decrease nor did the most disadvantaged sectors of society benefit proportionately. The illegal armed groups did not comply in the slightest with the High Commissioner's recommendations as regards armed conflict, the observance of international humanitarian law and respect for human rights.

International humanitarian law: Breaches by the armed actors

According to official figures, the number of homicides, massacres, attacks upon the civilian population, indiscriminate attacks, acts of hostage taking, terrorism and new forced displacements diminished. However, the levels of these infractions continued to be high. The civil population continued being the most affected in areas under the influence of the illegal armed groups. Infractions continued to be registered relating to the use of anti-personnel mines, particularly by FARC-EP and of ELN, and the recruitment of minors by all the illegal armed groups, The guerrillas, particularly FARC-EP, continued with their strategy of terrifying the civilian population, committing acts of terrorism and kidnappings. Not only did they not consent to unconditionally liberate their hostages, but rather, in some cases, FARC-EP and ELN killed them.

The main paramilitary groups did not honour, in most regions of the country, the commitment given to the Government to cease hostilities. Infractions, including massacres, homicides and displacements as well the recruitment of minors, continued to be registered. In the regions where the Armed Forces intensified their actions, infractions for disrespecting the principle of distinction, including cases of indiscriminate machine-gunning and homicides were denounced and attributed to members of the military. Actions adopted to cut supplies to the guerrillas affected, in some cases, the civilian population.

Human rights situation

The human rights situation in Colombia continued to be critical. During the year, the office in Colombia registered complaints of violations of the right to life, to physical integrity, to personal freedoms and security, to due process and judicial guarantees, to the independence and impartiality of the judicial system, to respect for privacy and intimacy, as well as the fundamental freedoms of circulation, residence, opinion and expression, and to the political rights. The office in Colombia continued receiving, in growing numbers, complaints of violations with direct responsibility of public servants, and in particular the Security Forces, on several occasions jointly with the Attorney-General's Office. Of concern was the increase in numbers of complaints regarding arbitrary or illegal detentions, forced disappearances, extrajudicial executions, violations of the right to due process and the right to intimacy.

There was an increase in the number of complaints of torture and mistreatment. Equally, various cases were denounced that involved State responsibility for omission or for connivance between public servants and paramilitary groups. The armed conflict and, in particular, the behaviour of the illegal armed actors impacted negatively on the human rights situation and aggravated the conditions and the resources that the State has to respond efficiently to existing problems. Economic, social and cultural rights continued being affected by the large gap in the distribution of the wealth, the extreme poverty, exclusion and social injustice.

Situation of particularly vulnerable groups

Although there was a decrease in killings of union leaders, the situation of human rights defenders and union leaders continued to be critical. Ethnic groups continued suffering discrimination and violations to economic, social and cultural rights. The internal armed conflict aggravated the situation of indigenous communities and Afro-Colombians, with an increase in selective violence by the illegal armed groups being observed. In spite of some legislative efforts and the signing of the National Agreement for Gender Equality, sexist forms of discrimination, exclusion and violence persisted against women, particularly in the context of the internal armed conflict. The human rights of a great number of children continued to be affected by economic and social inequity, extreme poverty, domestic and sexual violence, labour exploitation, as well as the internal armed conflict.

The situation of journalists continued to be precarious and demonstrated limitations with regard to the exercise of the right to freedom of opinion, expression and information, particularly because of the actions of the illegal armed groups. The growing trend of forced displacement was reversed in 2003, but continued to register high levels. Setbacks were registered in policies with regard to positive discrimination measures. The municipal and departmental functionaries (mayors, councillors, and local ombudsmen), members of the Patriotic Union (UP), judicial functionaries, and the religious practitioners were also affected by the internal armed conflict.

Recommendations

The High Commissioner presents a series of concrete, priority recommendations for the year 2004, convinced that their application would contribute notably to improving the situation in Colombia. The recommendations cover important matters relating to prevention and protection, the internal armed conflict, the rule of law and impunity, economic and social policies, the promotion of a culture of human rights and the advisory services and technical cooperation of his office in Colombia. The recipients of these recommendations are the State authorities, the illegal armed groups, representative sectors of the civil society, and the international community.

CONTENTS

	Paragraphs
Introduction	1–4
I. National Context and Dynamics of the Internal Armed Conflict	5–15
II. State Policies and Follow-up on International Recommendations	16–40
III. International Humanitarian Law: Breaches by Armed Actors	41–65
IV. Human Rights Situation	66–84
V. Situation of Particularly Vulnerable Groups	85–102
VI. Recommendations	103–131

Annexes

I. Status of implementation of the recommendations formulated by the United Nations High Commissioner for Human Rights in his 2003 report on the human rights situation in Colombia in 2002	1–45
II. Representative cases of human rights violations and breaches of international humanitarian law	1–36
III. Legislative policy	1–21
IV. Activities of the office in Colombia of the United Nations High Commissioner for Human Rights	1–39

Abbreviations

AUC	Autodefensas Unidas de Colombia
ELN	Ejército de Liberación Nacional de Colombia
FARC-EP	Fuerzas Armadas Revolucionarias de Colombia—Ejército del Pueblo
UP	Unión Patriótica

Introduction

1. The Commission on Human Rights has been following the human rights situation in Colombia, for several years, with concern. This concern has been reflected in successive statements of the Commission's Chairperson. In 1996, the Commission on Human Rights requested the Office of the High Commissioner for Human Rights to establish an office in Colombia, pursuant to the invitation of the Government of Colombia.

2. The office in Colombia of the United Nations High Commissioner for Human Rights (OACNUDH) was established on 26 November 1996 under an agreement between the Government of Colombia and the United Nations High Commissioner for Human Rights. Under the terms of the agreement, the office in Colombia of the High Commissioner is to observe the situation regarding human rights and international humanitarian law with a view to advising Colombian authorities on the formulation and implementation of policies, programmes and measures intended to promote and protect human rights, in the country's current context of violence and internal armed conflict. The High Commissioner should thus be able to submit analytical reports to the Commission on Human Rights. In September 2002, at the initiative of President Uribe, the agreement was extended for a four-year period until October 2006.

3. In its statement on the human rights situation in Colombia, the Chairperson of the Commission on Human Rights at its fifty-eighth session, in April 2003, reaffirmed that the office in Colombia "played a vital role in addressing the ongoing violations of human rights and international humanitarian law" and requested the High Commissioner to submit "a detailed report containing an analysis by his office of the human rights situation in Colombia".

4. The office in Colombia of the High Commissioner carried on with its duties of observation, advice, technical cooperation, as well as promotion and dissemination. More than 160 field missions were carried out and more than 900 complaints were admitted. The office in Colombia participated in numerous activities related to advising the Government, other

State entities and civil society. Technical cooperation had as main focus the recommendations of the High Commissioner and tried to promote the active participation of national institutions in order to strengthen the respect, protection and guarantees for human rights. The office in Colombia participated in several promotion activities for the public in general and communication media. It continued to produce a series of publications related to human rights, and distribution throughout the territory of Colombia reached 100,000 publications.[1] The office in Colombia also continued to develop the dialogue with diplomatic representations of the interested countries. This report covers the period between January and December 2003 and is based on the information gathered by the office in Colombia of the United Nations High Commissioner for Human Rights, either directly or through its contacts. The information collected through contacts, among which State and Government authorities are of particular importance, has been subsequently analysed by the office in Colombia. Four documents are annexed to this report: one relates to the follow-up on international recommendations; another covers violations of human rights and breaches of international humanitarian law; a third concerns legislative policy; and the final one relates to the observation, advisory, promotion and technical cooperation activities carried out by the office in Colombia of the High Commissioner.

I. *National Context and Dynamics of the Internal Armed Conflict*

5. During the year 2003, the evolution of the internal armed conflict and the serious issues of indebtedness, fiscal deficit, and legislative policy set new challenges for this country. While opinion polls showed that the President continued to enjoy a high degree of popularity, civil society showed a high level of polarization in various fields. During the year, there have been moments when tensions increased between senior Government and State officials and sectors of civil society organizations.

6. The aim of the Government has been to recover territorial control of the country and keep the roads free from illegal roadblocks and attacks with explosives, methods frequently used by the guerrillas. Therefore, military and police numbers have been considerably increased, including the so called "peasant soldiers" or "soldiers from my village", and operations intended to maintain or restore public order have multiplied as part of the "democratic security policy". By the end of 2003, the National Police

[1] For more information, see annex IV.

was present in nearly all of the country's municipalities. New military units and bases were also created in several strategic parts of the country.

7. During 2003, combats between security forces and illegal armed groups, particularly the guerrillas, intensified. Hostilities took place mainly in the Departments of Antioquia, Cundinamarca, Santander and Norte de Santander, the southern part of Bolívar, Guaviare and Caquetá. According to official figures from the Ministry of Defense, all of the illegal armed groups, especially the Revolutionary Armed Forces of Colombia—People's Army (FARC-EP), suffered a higher number of casualties and captures. Such confrontation had a significant impact on the civil population. Facing increased pressure by the security forces, the guerrilla groups retired into their more traditional and inaccessible areas. FARC-EP and the National Liberation Army (ELN) extended their strategic and military alliance in several parts of the national territory. Illegal armed groups continued to fund their activities through kidnapping, charging levying "taxes" on illegal drug trafficking, managing narcotics processing laboratories, guarding and maintaining secret airstrips for loading and unloading psychoactive substances or raw materials for their manufacture, and, in some cases, the direct export of drugs.

8. The Government continued developing policies designed to restructure the State, achieve "democratic security" and economic recovery. To this end, numerous bills were submitted to the Congress, some of them aimed at reforming the Constitution and others at introducing modifications to current legislation. Many of these bills posed new challenges to the strengthening of the rule of law, the civil oversight of the security forces, and for effective respect for human rights and international humanitarian law. Several of these governmental proposals contributed to the polarization of Colombian society regarding subjects such as the fight against terrorism and measures to overcome the internal armed conflict.

9. During the first months of this year, the country continued to live under the "state of internal commotion" (*state of emergency*), enforced under Decree 1837 of 11 August 2002. This was used as the basis for the adoption of several measures to control public order and create special geographical areas called "rehabilitation and consolidation zones" in the Departments of Arauca, Sucre and Bolívar. The application of these measures led to the constraint of fundamental rights and freedoms, mass arrests and raids. On 29 April the Constitutional Court put an end to the state of commotion by declaring its second extension incompatible with the Constitution.

10. Most political activities this year centred on the calling and holding of a referendum that took place on 25 October and involved submitting 15 proposals for constitutional reform to the voting public. These proposals

covered a wide variety of issues: from the loss of political rights for those convicted of crimes against State property to limiting the level of pensions and salaries paid with government funds, the elimination of some offices of the municipal comptroller, and the application of measures aimed at rationalizing public expenditure. The counting of votes became complicated and in the month of December the final result was not yet known. However, preliminary data indicated that practically none of the proposals achieved the number of required votes (25 per cent of total eligible voters).

11. On 26 October elections were held to choose governors, mayors, deputies, town councillors and aldermen. Thanks to special efforts made by the State, the majority of the citizenry was able to exercise their political rights without great difficulties. Despite this, complaints were made regarding the perpetration of electoral offences. The election results reflected the country's political pluralism, considering the victory of several independent or centre-left candidates. Several independent or centre-left candidates did better than candidates who supported the Government. A significant example was the victory of centre-left candidates for the positions of mayor in the capital district of Bogotá and governor in the Department of Valle. During the weeks that followed the two-day elections, the President of the Republic replaced the Interior and Justice Ministers, the Minister of Defense and the Minister of the Environment as part of his strategy to improve relations between the Government and Congress and between civilians and military forces. Against the background of internal issues and some corruption scandals, the President also made broad changes at the level of the highest-ranking officers within the security forces.

12. The international community continued to provide Colombia with support and cooperation in various fields. In this respect, the participation of 24 countries, with the presence of several multilateral organizations that included the United Nations, at the international meeting in London in July 2003 was significant. The participating countries took favourable note of the commitment undertaken by the Government of Colombia to implement the recommendations of the United Nations High Commissioner for Human Rights and urged the Government of Colombia to promptly implement such recommendations and adopt effective actions against impunity and the collusion of public servants with illegal armed groups, especially paramilitary groups. Significant progress concerning follow-up to the Government's commitments assumed in London was not registered when the present report was finished.

13. During the year, contacts and talks intensified between the Government and a significant number of the paramilitary groups. Following the decla-

ration of a ceasefire in December 2002 and the development of an exploratory phase aimed at bringing together the Government and the United Self-Defence Groups of Colombia (AUC), the Santa Fe de Ralito Agreement was signed on 15 July 2003. Under that agreement, the parties agreed to total demobilization of their paramilitary forces by 2005. Despite the ceasefire commitment, it must be noted that violent actions on the part of paramilitary group members continued to occur throughout the year against the civilian population. At the end of November, the demobilization process began with the celebration of an act in Medellín where a group of 870 paramilitaries surrendered their weapons and were concentrated at a holiday resort in La Ceja (Antioquia) where for three weeks they would prepare for reintegration into society. Several questions were raised during this process. Some of these have to do with the legal treatment the Government is going to give to the demobilized paramilitaries and how the right to truth, justice and reparation for the victims can be guaranteed.

14. With respect to the guerrilla groups, the Government declared itself willing to have a dialogue with them eventually, provided that they declare a ceasefire and free all hostages. The Executive Branch also warned that, under no circumstances would it create "demilitarized zones" for the rebel forces. To facilitate a negotiated solution of the conflict, the Government reaffirmed its confidence in the good offices of the United Nations Secretary-General, through his Special Adviser for Colombia.

15. FARC-EP and ELN, in a joint communiqué issued in August, refused any "process for political rapprochement and a national dialogue" with the Government. Nevertheless, FARC-EP continued its attempts to sign an agreement providing for the liberation of persons in their custody in exchange for imprisoned guerrillas. Last May, in a failed attempt by the Army to free a group of hostages, FARC-EP killed 10 people, among whom were the Governor of Antioquia and a former Minister of Defence and adviser to the Governor. This dimmed the possibility of making progress towards special agreements, an option that had been fostered by several sectors of the society throughout the year.

II. *State Policies and Follow-up on International Recommendations*

16. In order for State policies to properly and comprehensively include the High Commissioner's recommendations, the office in Colombia of the High Commissioner encouraged follow-up with the Government, led by the Vice-President, and worked with the authorities in analysing and evaluating progress made in compliance with the recommendations. In general terms, it can be said that the Government has considered the

recommendations and has opened channels for discussion and planning with respect to them among its institutions and with the office in Colombia. Nevertheless, the recommendations seem not to have received priority and remain unintegrated in the Government's public policies, and this may explain the fact that there is a contradiction between the actions recommended and some of the measures adopted by the Government. This might also suggest that the Government has not yet captured, in its full dimension, the usefulness of a tool that aims at positively contributing to and supporting the country's progress in improving the humanitarian and human rights situation in this country.[2]

17. During 2003, human rights and international humanitarian law policies were strongly influenced by the government policy called "democratic security". This particularly affected the legislative agenda and the actions of the security forces and of the judicial and oversight bodies. Equally, the evolution of the armed conflict and the conduct of the illegal armed groups had a negative effect on the enjoyment of fundamental rights and freedoms and on the validity of the rule of law.

18. The purpose stated in the "democratic security" policy is that of "intensifying and guaranteeing the rule of law throughout the entire country through the strengthening of democratic authority", and guaranteeing the security of all citizens alike. The policy also aspires to attain full recovery of State control over the national territory and to defeat terrorism. It also aims to involve civilian populations in maintaining security, particularly by supporting and collaborating with the authorities and the armed forces.[3] In the development of its policy, the Government was able to extend the presence of security forces to nearly all municipalities in the country. In order for the State to perform its duties in terms of security, prevention and protection, such presence is of significant importance. This process probably explains, in part, the positive overall decrease in the rate of violent acts and in several breaches of international humanitarian law on the part of the illegal armed groups. Additionally, it could be a positive element in the search for conditions that improve the ability to govern and make local democracy feasible, goals that are also included in the Government's policy.

19. Nevertheless, the legitimate goals of such a policy have not been achieved to the extent hoped for. The regions with greater presence of the security forces, such as the Department of Arauca and the municipalities

---

[2] See annex I.

[3] See document "Política de Defensa y Seguridad Democrática" (Defense and Democratic Security Policy) Ministry of Defense, Presidency of the Republic, 2003.

that formed the geographic areas known as rehabilitation and consolidation zones, continued to have serious problems in terms of their ability to be governed and with respect to public order, including an increase in crime in some municipalities. Likewise, apart from irregularities reported in the conduct of the security forces and weaknesses in terms of judicial control, the paramilitary presence continued, investment in social services was left unrealized, and there was a limited presence on the part of the State, apart from the security forces. At times, the Ombudsman's Office was the only civil institution to be found. This was pointed out by the relevant reports of the Ombudsman's Office and Procurator General's Office.[4]

20. The great majority of the adopted measures were aimed at strengthening the presence of the security forces across the national territory and granting additional resources to the State in terms of security and protection. The same determination has not been noted as regards strengthening the State's civil institutions. In some cases, the strengthening of security forces and the related policies have been applied to the detriment of civil institutions, constitutional guarantees for citizens and the powers of judicial and control bodies. According to the Government, the participation of the citizenry in security activities jointly carried out with military and police forces, which goes against the principle of distinction, played an essential role in the "democratic security" policy, by consolidating the network of informers and collaborators cooperating with the security forces as well as the recruitment of peasant soldiers.

21. There is no doubt that the enormous challenges the Government faces, in terms of security and protection of fundamental rights and freedoms, could be undertaken with greater effectiveness and legitimacy if the State's control institutions enjoyed the necessary range of action and resources. During this year, the reduced field of action that tends to exist for independent and impartial work on the part of officials of the Ministry of Justice and the Procurator General's Office has been a problem. On repeated occasions, those institutions that have shown greater independence and vigour in fulfilling their auditing and control duties have been threatened with limitations on their powers by means of legislative proposals presented by the Government. This situation has mainly affected the Constitutional Court and the Procurator General's Office.[5]

---

[4] See note A, annex II.

[5] The first case was part of the proposed reform of justice, a bill that eventually was not formally presented to the Congress and was left for the next legislature. In the second case, the Congress withdrew the bill, taking into account the short terms left in the current legislature. See annex III of this report.

22. Similarly, it is worth pointing out that the office in Colombia has not noticed specific actions by the Government and the Congress aimed at strengthening the Ombudsman's Office, in accordance with the recommendations of the High Commissioner. Nevertheless, positive mention has to be made of the creation of the Community Ombudsmen, a position that has been implemented with the support of the international community in several regions where there is a concentration of communities at risk. This partly complies with the recommendation of the High Commissioner to guarantee the presence of the Ombudsman's Office in regions with a high rate of indigenous, Afro-Colombian and displaced populations. The above-mentioned indicates that the application of the Government's policies did not achieve the strengthening of the rule of law.

23. The policy aimed at fighting the paramilitary phenomenon and the existing ties between public servants and those groups has not shown sufficiently significant results as to effectively match the statements made by the Government. The revival, towards the end of 2003, of the Center for Fighting the illegal self-defence groups and other unlawful armed groups, as well as the directives and circulars issued in September and October by the Ministry of Defense relating to "the unrestricted fight against the illegal self-defense groups" show the extent to which this continues to be a problem and explains why the Government indicates that one of its leading activities is "internal control and surveillance in order to prevent members of the military institutions from collaborating with such groups".[6]

24. The office in Colombia continued to receive complaints regarding the persistence or strengthening of the above-mentioned ties. The following has been reported: paramilitary operations with inexcusable knowledge of the security forces, undue contacts between civil authorities and paramilitary commanders, statements made by members of the military forces concerning the imminent arrival of paramilitary groups, inaction on the part of the security forces in spite of the existence of fixed paramilitary bases close to military installations, and even the alleged provision of information to paramilitary groups by members of the police regarding possible targets.[7] The office in Colombia was able to observe and continued to receive complaints concerning the positioning and consolidation of paramilitary groups in areas where the security forces had previously carried out counter-rebel operations, such as, for example, the area of Comuna 13 in Medellín or municipalities in eastern Antioquia.

25. From the results of field observations, it is possible to state that the measures adopted under the "democratic security" policy have been aimed,

[6] According to information provided by the Government in reply to the Office's request.
[7] See annex II, para. 3.

with greater emphasis, at fighting rebel groups rather than paramilitary groups. The increase in the number of operations and captures of members of paramilitary groups has not been large or meaningful enough in order to constitute blows to the paramilitary structure or to slow down its expansion and consolidation or prevent crimes against the population.26. The impunity with which paramilitary groups continue to act is a demonstration that more suitable and consistent conduct by the authorities in the face of this kind of violence is needed. Following the recommendation of the High Commissioner, the adoption of more effective measures by the Government and the Ministry of Defense is necessary in order to sanction actions and omissions on the part of public servants who support or tolerate paramilitary groups. The negotiations between the Government and AUC have not duly taken into account the possible legal consequences and have led to serious concerns over the impunity of those responsible for acts that amount to war crimes and crimes against humanity, and of public servants who may have been involved in them, as well as with respect to follow-up on the recommendation of the High Commissioner in terms of the right to truth, justice and reparation.[8]

27. Additionally, to date, a sufficiently effective commitment to the fight against impunity, in the institutional policy of the Attorney-General's Office, has not been perceived with respect to progress in investigations related to serious human rights violations or actions linked to paramilitary groups and involving public servants. What is striking is the absence of investigations into several complaints relating to situations such as these.[9] In November 2003, the Attorney-General, by way of a letter of understanding with the office in Colombia of the High Commissioner, committed himself to assigning a specialized group, within the human rights and international humanitarian law unit, for the investigation of such possible ties, in accordance with the recommendation of the High Commissioner. Compliance with this commitment is to be evaluated in next year's report.[10]

28. State policy in terms of the fight against impunity has continued to show few concrete results. The Government created the Fight against Impunity Unit inside the human rights and international humanitarian law Presidential Programme within the Office of the Vice-President of the Republic. Under a cooperation agreement with the Netherlands, the

[8] See annex III, paras. 9, 10 and 11.

[9] An example, the responsibilities of the institutions in the indiscriminate attack of Bojayá, in May 2002 (see Follow-up Report of the Office of the High Commissioner in Colombia, of June 2003); and in homicides and disappearances in the Comuna 13 of Medellín, as a consequence of Operation Orion, developed on 16 October 2002.

[10] See annexes I and IV.

Government committed itself to stimulate and follow up on the investigations into serious human rights violations and breaches of international humanitarian law, through the work of a special committee and the design and implementation of a public policy on fighting impunity. Despite the High Commissioner's recommendation on this matter, the office in Colombia observed that the special committee, an inter-institutional mechanism coordinated by the Vice-President and responsible for driving the investigations on human rights violations, has not achieved the expected results. The committee was able to agree upon the selection of cases requiring priority attention along with their respective work plan but, until now, it has not produced significant results regarding the fight against impunity and effective progress in the investigations.

29. Together with its military strategy and its strategy against violence and terrorism, the Government encouraged a demobilization policy for members of the illegal armed groups. In this context, on 22 January 2003, Decree 128 was adopted establishing a series of legal benefits, including the granting of pardons and administrative and welfare benefits, for the members of armed groups responsible for political or related crimes who decide to voluntarily demobilize. From 1 January to 19 November 2003, the Government recorded the demobilization of 2,136 members of illegal groups, 1,139 of whom belonged to FARC-EP, 350 to ELN and 647 to paramilitary groups; 329 of them are minors and 300 are women. The office in Colombia was informed of several difficulties during implementation of the reintegration process that caused some people to decide to again take up arms by joining groups that oppose the groups that they had originally belonged to, particularly cases of FARC-EP members deciding to join paramilitary groups.

30. In addition to the above decree, in August 2003 the Government presented a bill aimed at granting legal benefits to those members of illegal armed groups who were not eligible to benefit from the provisions of the above decree because of their involvement in serious crimes, not even excluding war crimes and crimes against humanity. This bill establishes the suspension of the custodial sentence and proposes a series of measures that the bill calls "alternative sentences". Setting aside the concern that provisions of this kind can generate in terms of impunity, several doubts arise in relation to the advisability and the modality of such a proposal, which refers not only to members of armed groups that have signed peace agreements but also includes among the beneficiaries members "who lay down their arms individually and voluntarily". The bill, to date, is not in accordance with international norms and principles, nor with the High Commissioner's recommendation to take into account the rights to

truth, justice and reparation when talking and negotiating with the illegal armed groups.

31. The State's policy in terms of international humanitarian law has been linked to the previously mentioned elements, related to negotiations and the struggle against violence and terrorism. Despite the Government's clearly expressed commitment in its Democratic Security and Defence Policy document—in which it declares that "there will be rigorous observance of human rights, and strict adherence to international humanitarian law"[11] often the Government's language and strategies in practice were inconsistent. The Government tended to not recognize the existence of an internal armed conflict and the specific legal issues linked to it, comprising everything in the fight against terrorism. The office in Colombia of the High Commissioner reiterated the importance of recognizing the humanitarian obligations and rules relating to the armed conflict and, particularly, the principles of distinction, limitation and proportionality, as pointed out by the High Commissioner in his recommendations.

32. In following up on the recommendation of the High Commissioner with respect to compliance with international obligations regarding anti-personnel mines, positive actions have been taken through governmental policies, particularly in the framework of the Anti-personnel Mines Observatory and specifically in the drafting of a detailed Comprehensive National Plan of Action against anti-personnel mines. Another positive area has been the strengthening of the Information System on Action against Anti-personnel Mines (MISMA). The office in Colombia has noted with interest that, on 26 June 2003, the Colombian State began the destruction of stored mines, in accordance with the Convention on the Prohibition of the Use, Stockpiling, Production and Transfer of Anti-Personnel Mines and on Their Destruction signed in Ottawa in 1997. Despite the progress of the Observatory, difficulties remain in placing signposts in minefields and in danger areas, in preventing and limiting risks to the population, especially for displaced and returned persons, as well as strengthening of mechanisms for assisting victims of anti-personnel mines.

33. Legislative policy has been a central tool of the Government's policy with the expectation that, through changes in the rules, the Government's policy can achieve greater impact and results.[12] One of the first laws approved was the National Development Plan, containing economic, social

[11] See previously mentioned document "Política de Defensa y Seguridad Democrática", p. 19, para. 24.

[12] See annex III.

and environmental provisions. It is worth stressing the adoption of several laws whereby international treaties were internally approved. It is worth stressing also that, with the exception of the Optional Protocol to the Convention on the Rights of the Child relative to the sale of children, child prostitution and child pornography, during the current administration no other instruments have been ratified that obligate the State internationally.

34. Several bills proposed to modify the Constitution; among them, three bills for legislative acts, one known as the "Anti-Terrorist Statute", another that modifies the competence of the Procurator General's Office in examining disciplinary offences by members of the Armed Forces, and a third aimed at making structural changes to the organization of the State. Bills have also been promoted to modify the Criminal Code and the Code of Criminal Procedure, the Penitentiary and Prison Code, the Organizational By-laws of the Attorney-General's Office, the Statutory Law for Administration of Justice and some norms regarding compulsory military service. Also proposed were the National Statute to face terrorism and the bill on national security and defence. The legislative proposals have generally been characterized by harsher sentences and the creation of new types of crimes, as well as by the weakening of constitutional and legal guarantees. At the same time, and paradoxically, bills showing great leniency were submitted in order to judicially respond to conduct that constitutes war crimes and crimes against humanity, such as the statutory bill regarding the reintegration of members of illegal armed groups.

35. It is worth mentioning the bill presented in April and approved in December 2003, known as the "Anti-Terrorist Statute", which proposes constitutional modifications. According to its articles, it provides the Armed Forces with judicial police powers, in direct contradiction to the recommendation expressed by the High Commissioner and by the Chairperson of the Commission on Human Rights in its fifty-ninth session in 2003. The changes also provide for administrative detentions and searches of homes, as well as interceptions of private communications, to be carried out without a previously issued warrant, and with excessively prolonged terms for submitting administrative detentions to judicial control in cases of terrorism, thus putting at risk the effective application of habeas corpus.

36. Beyond the incompatibility with international obligations, analysis of the legislative policy raises questions about the relevance and usefulness of the changes sought in the regulations. It would seem as though, in the Government's view, the achievement of the goals of its policies depended more on the laws than on the adoption and impact of concrete actions. Given the solidity of the Colombian juridical structure and tradition, it is worth asking whether full compliance with existing laws and the strength-

ening of public institutions may not be a more appropriate manner in which to attain the goals of the security policy.

37. In terms of prevention, the policy has been mainly focused on strengthening the Early Warning System (Sistema de Alerta Temprana, or SAT), particularly through creation of the Inter-Institutional Early Warning Committee (Comité Interinstitucional de Alerta Temprana, or CIAT), aimed at improving the State's coordination and response. This positive initiative, following the High Commissioner's recommendation, has demonstrated deficiencies, however, in terms of the effectiveness of risk assessment and response. On several occasions, the responses were unable to avoid the occurrence of violations or breaches, due to diverse factors detailed in annex II of this report.

38. As far as the policy regarding protection for certain vulnerable groups, such as human rights defenders, trade union representatives, journalists, Unión Patriótica (UP) and Communist Party members, and local officials, the Government began implementing several of the recommendations included in the external evaluation of the Ministry of the Interior, an evaluation implemented by the Government with the support of the International Labour Organization and the office in Colombia last year. Nevertheless, operational issues, particularly in terms of risk assessment, remained. The absence of more effective processes capable of acting in a preventive way over risk factors and the lack of a consistent policy on the part of the State and all of its public servants have so far not permitted the necessary degree of compliance with the High Commissioner's recommendations on this matter.

39. A main feature of the economic and social policies was the increase in public spending related to certain basic rights, although in detriment to quality with respect to several vulnerable sectors and without being proportionately reflected in coverage. Economic policy set its priority on reducing the fiscal deficit and increasing resources available for security. Social policy was affected by such priorities. The inequity gap was not reduced and the most disadvantaged sectors of the population were not benefited, thus leaving unresolved the recommendation of the High Commissioner on the subject.

40. It is worth emphasizing that the illegal armed groups have not observed in the slightest the recommendations made to them by the High Commissioner in terms of armed conflict and respect for international humanitarian law.

III. *International Humanitarian Law: Breaches by Armed Actors*

41. In the context of the Colombian armed conflict, breaches of international humanitarian law (IHL) are actions or omissions contrary to common article 3 to the Geneva Convention of 12 August 1949, its Additional Protocol II, international criminal law, and customary law. All parties involved in the hostilities, be it the State, the guerrilla or the paramilitary groups, must comply with the obligations imposed by international humanitarian law. Many of the breaches pointed out in this report, when carried out as part of a plan or a policy, or as part of a large-scale occurrence, constitute war crimes. Several of these breaches may also constitute crimes against humanity. These two types of crimes may be subject to trial by the International Criminal Court, if they occurred after 1 November 2002, date of the entry into force for Colombia.

42. According to figures provided by the Office of the Vice-President, during the first eight months of 2003 there has been a decrease, as compared to 2002, in the number of massacres, attacks on the civilian population, indiscriminate attacks, hostage-taking, forced displacements and acts of terrorism. Despite this decrease, it is worth stressing that such breaches continue to occur at very worrisome levels, as the 312 victims of the 54 massacres recorded by the Government show.[13] With respect to acts of terrorism, it is worth pointing out that they were the cause of a greater percentage of breaches of international humanitarian law since it was mainly the guerrilla groups who resorted to this kind of attacks rather than to other types of assaults.

43. In areas with a large presence of the illegal armed groups, victimization of the civilian population was even greater. Inhabitants have been subjected to growing pressure and subjugation through acts of terrorism, homicides and tortures, restrictions on freedom of movement and transport of basic necessities, destruction of personal effects and property and pillage.

44. The country's homicide rate, according to figures for 2003 up until October, showed a reduction at the national level in comparison with the previous year. However, the rate increased or remained at the same high levels of 2002 in cities such as Sincelejo (Sucre), Santa Marta (Magdalena), Bucaramanga (Santander) and Cœcuta (Norte de Santander). Massacres continued to occur mainly in the Departments of Antioquia, Chocó, Norte de Santander and Valle. It is striking that the figures of the Government assign 55 per cent of the massacres to unknown authors. The question

[13] See statistics from the "Observatorio de Derechos Humanos de la Vicepresidencia".

arises as to whether the majority of these acts are to be attributed to the paramilitary groups, as the Government pointed out last year.[14] The protection to be provided for civilians, as required under international humanitarian law, was equally disregarded due to terrorist actions, particularly by FARC-EP, and due to the strategy used by paramilitary groups who disappear their victims by killing them after having tortured them, mutilating their bodies and burying them in mass graves.

45. In some cases, the deaths of civilians were blamed on members of the security forces, in violation of the principles of distinction, limitation and proportionality. Likewise, cases of wounded civilians and the destruction of the personal property of civilians was the result of activities on the part of the security forces.[15]

46. Numerous cases of breaches of international humanitarian law were registered, resulting from indiscriminate attacks, death threats, hostage-taking and forced displacements. Guerrilla and paramilitary groups were responsible for these breaches. In some cases, the security forces were responsible for indiscriminate attacks, threats and forced displacements.[16]

47. The use of anti-personnel mines and other explosive devices by guerrilla groups, in violation of international humanitarian law, increased, causing the death of more than 90 civilians (up until October 2003) and nearly 200 members of the security forces. The reduction of attacks against electrical and communications infrastructure was accompanied by an increase in attacks against pipelines, carried out mainly by the guerrillas. Additionally, the illegal armed groups continued to practise recruitment of minors. Children, ethnic minorities and women continued to be the victims of the main breaches of international humanitarian law, including cases of sexual abuse and enslavement of women.[17]

48. Illegal armed groups, particularly FARC-EP, continued carrying out serious attacks or threats against public officials, such as mayors, town councillors and municipal representatives, or against candidates during the municipal and departmental elections of 26 October 2003.

Guerrilla groups

49. Guerrilla groups continued attacking civilian populations and to disregard their immunity. Even though a reduction in the number of raids

[14] See the report of the United Nations High Commissioner for Human Rights on the human rights situation in Colombia, E/CN.4/2003/13, p. 54, para. 27 and note O.

[15] See annex II, para. 20.

[16] See annex II, paras. 10, 13, 14, 15, 16, 17, 18, 19, 24 and 26.

[17] See annex II, paras. 27–30.

into urban areas of municipalities was observed, the Departments of Cauca and Nariño particularly suffered from these attacks. Guerrilla groups, and particularly FARC-EP, have continued with their strategy of terrorizing civilian populations, by recurrently perpetrating acts of terrorism. The terrorist attacks in Neiva (Huila), Cúcuta (Norte de Santander), Puerto Rico (Meta), Florencia (Caquetá) and Chita (Boyacá), where many civilians lost their lives or were wounded, have been attributed by the Attorney-General's Office to FARC-EP, with the exception of the second attack attributed to ELN (although ELN denied responsibility for it). FARC-EP were also considered responsible for the explosion of a car bomb in the building of El Nogal Club, in the city of Bogotá, on 7 February 2003, causing the death of 36 people and wounding over 100 people.[18]

50. Likewise, FARC-EP, and in some cases also ELN, have been responsible for frequent indiscriminate attacks with explosive devices, in total disrespect of civilians' lives and personal safety. Such practices have victimized hundreds of civilians, including children, young peopleand women, and have occurred with greater intensity in the Departments of Caquetá, Meta, Antioquia and Arauca. On several occasions, civilians utilized by FARC-EP to transport explosive devices lost their lives as a result of their detonation, as was the case on 17 April in Fortul (Arauca) where an 8-year-old boy was killed when the bicycle he was riding on exploded near a military control post.

51. Additionally, the inhabitants of rural areas, characterized by a strong presence on the part of the guerrilla groups, have been subject to increasing pressure by the rebels, frequently through restrictions on freedom of movement as well as on the transportation of basic necessities. In these same areas, FARC-EP and ELN have resorted to the practice of selective homicides against local officials, social leaders, teachers and candidates, as well as against people whom they accuse of belonging to the State's network of informers or of collaborating with paramilitary groups.

52. FARC-EP and ELN continued to use anti-personnel mines. The guerrilla groups also continued recruiting minors, in some cases forcibly. Several thousand minors are estimated to be in the ranks of the guerrilla groups.

53. Both guerrilla groups have repeatedly resorted to hostage-taking for reasons of financial extortion or political pressure and have not agreed to free hostages unconditionally; on the contrary, in some cases, FARC-EP have killed hostages in their power. Such was the case of the Governor

[18] However, one month later, through a public communiqué, FARC-EP denied being responsible for this act.

of Antioquia, his peace adviser and eight captive members of the military, of the Colombian Bickenbach couple, and of the Japanese citizen Chikao Muramatsu. ELN finally released the eight foreigners taken as hostages in the Sierra Nevada de Santa Marta.[19]

Paramilitary groups

54. The commitment to a ceasefire was the basic assumption for any process for dialogue between the Government and the largest paramilitary group, the Autodefensas Unidas de Colombia, or AUC. The lack of adherence to this commitment in the majority of regions must be emphasized. The large number of breaches of international humanitarian law attributable to paramilitary groups in 2003, regardless of the fact that these breaches are fewer than those recorded during the previous year, are in contradiction to the above commitment and to the existence of a unilateral truce declared by them at the end of 2002.

55. Several massacres were perpetrated by these groups, although in lesser number than in 2002, as occurred in Antioquia, Santander, Sucre and Tolima. It is also probable that the number of these massacres has been underestimated. The practice of selective homicides has continued, attributed to paramilitary groups who repeatedly have chosen to kill their victims after having detained them, tortured them and made them disappear in a strategy of terror directed against civilian populations. At the same time, such a strategy, which makes it difficult to identify those responsible, is noteworthy at a time when they have made a political commitment to demobilization and ceasefire. In the city of Barrancabermeja alone, between January and August 2003, the Ombudsman's Office received 45 complaints with respect to disappeared persons. The number of complaints submitted to the office in Colombia of the High Commissioner regarding discoveries of mass graves, mainly in Tolima and Antioquia, and of bodies with obvious signs of torture and mutilation increased during this year.[20]

56. The victims of paramilitary groups are usually people whom they accuse of having ties to rebel forces; social leaders and public officials who are opposed to the paramilitary groups' process of expansion and social, economic and political consolidation; rivals for control of illegal businesses (drug trafficking, theft of fuel, etc.); and victims of social cleansing.

57. During the year 2003, it was also striking to observe the internal disputes within the paramilitary groups that caused a large number of

[19] See annex II, para. 24.
[20] See annex II, para. 23.

deaths. The office in Colombia observed a significant increase in confrontations between paramilitary groups and especially between the Cacique Nutibara Block and the Metro Block, and between AUC and the Autodefensas Campesinas of Casanare.

58. The presence of minors in the paramilitary groups was evidenced by the surrender of 40 minors from the Central Bolivar Block and the surrender of minors by the Autodefensas Campesinas of Meta and Vichada, as well as more than 40 minors from the demobilized group of the Nutibara Block. Forced displacement of the population by paramilitary threats or activities has been a recurring strategy.

59. Based on the information received by the office in Colombia and its field observations, in several cases of breaches of international humanitarian law, the paramilitary groups received support, collusion or complicity on the part of public servants.[21]

Security forces

60. In regions where the Army carried out its renewed offensive, it was reported that, on some occasions, members of the security forces were responsible for breaches of international humanitarian law due to disregard for the principle of distinction.[22]

61. The office in Colombia of the High Commissioner received complaints of several cases of indiscriminate air bombardments or machine-gunning that caused damages to personal effects and properties, especially in Cauca, as well as civilian dead or wounded, such as in the area of Culebritas, in the municipality of El Carmen (Norte de Santander). On other occasions, military airplane or helicopter operations caused the displacement of the civilian population in rural areas, as in the municipality of San Francisco, in eastern Antioquia, as a result of "Operación Marcial", in March 2003. In the context of that same operation, the office in Colombia received complaints related to the killing of two civilians. Similarly, in the context of "Operation Emperador", in January 2003, in Santa Ana, in the jurisdiction of Granada, in eastern Antioquia, four civilians, including a minor, were reportedly executed. In both cases, the office in Colombia also received complaints of civilians being abused by members of the Army breaking into homes, destroying personal effects and property and engaging in pillage.[23]

62. The Army's strategy to try to cut the flow of supplies to the guerrillas has in some cases affected the civilian population, due to their being

[21] See annex II.
[22] See annex II, para. 20.
[23] See annex II, para. 34.

stigmatized and targets of abuse, pillage and threats on the part of the Army. The use of civilians as human shields during a counter-rebel operation has also been reported. This exposed civilians to serious risks and also caused the death of one person (during the "Independencia" operation of July 2003 in Arauca).

63. It is worth pointing out that cases were reported of restrictions by members of the security forces on the transportation of food products, gasoline and other basic necessities, particularly in the areas of Medio Atrato, Sierra Nevada of Santa Marta and eastern Antioquia. There were also cases reported of Army or Marine Corps troops occupying housing or such public places as schools and health-care centres, as occurred in the municipality of Colosó (Sucre), exposing the civilian population to risk and violating the principle of distinction.

64. Additionally, governors and authorities of the indigenous councils of Nariño reported that, in March 2003, military forces indiscriminately recruited young indigenous people, in violation of current regulations exempting ethnic minorities from compulsory military service. The office in Colombia also received complaints regarding the use of minors by members of the security forces, especially in intelligence operations.

65. Similarly, complaints of breaches of international humanitarian law were received where responsibility was attributed to members of the security forces due to omission, tolerance or complicity with paramilitary groups.[24]

IV. *Human Rights Situation*

66. Actions or omissions affecting rights established in international human rights and criminal law instruments or in general international law norms, constitute violations of those rights and norms when perpetrated by public servants or with the acquiescence of the authorities. Responsibility for these violations shall be for omission when the obligation to guarantee is not fulfilled, provided that this lack of fulfilment is not deliberate and there is no participation of State agents in the preparation, commission or concealment of the acts. Responsibility shall be for commission when State agents are either involved in the preparation or perpetration of the act, or in covering it up or protecting the culprits.

67. The human rights situation in Colombia continues to be critical. During the year, complaints of violations of the following rights were recorded: the right to life, to physical integrity, to personal freedom and

[24] See annex II. See also paras. 23 and 24 of this report.

safety, to due process and legal guarantees, to independence and impartiality in the administration of justice, to the respect for privacy and the home, as well as the rights to fundamental freedoms of movement, residence, opinion and expression, and political rights. Increasingly, the office in Colombia continued to receive complaints about human rights violations implying the direct responsibility on the part of public servants, and in particular members of the security forces, on several occasions jointly with members of the Attorney-General's Office. From the information provided by the Procurator General's Office, one may note an increase in disciplinary investigations undertaken in 2003, particularly as regards torture, forced disappearances, illegal detentions and irregular searches. Many of the violations, due to their serious, massive or systematic nature, constitute crimes against humanity and are susceptible to trial by the International Criminal Court.

68. Economic, social and cultural rights continued to be affected by the increase of poverty, exclusion, social injustice and the gap in terms of wealth distribution. This situation has worsened because of the armed conflict, particularly due to displacement, and has had an even greater effect on the rights of vulnerable groups. Similarly, the lack of official updated statistics, that would make it possible to appropriately evaluate the impact of policies on the above-mentioned groups, is a source of concern.

69. During the year 2003, the policy of restructuring of the State has affected institutions in charge of providing social assistance. Despite the fact that public spending has increased in relation to education and health, the poorest sectors continue to be highly neglected. An inequitable educational system continues to exist, without free basic primary education being guaranteed. A small decrease in unemployment has been observed but the rate continues to be high. Indirect taxes have been raised, affecting to a greater degree the most disadvantaged segment of the population. With respect to the right to housing, subsidies have been insufficient, taking into account the impoverishment of the population and the high interest rates.

70. The armed conflict and, particularly, the conduct of the illegal armed groups, has had a negative effect on the human rights situation and worsened the conditions and resources the State relies upon in order to effectively respond to the problems. In this respect, it is of particular importance that authorities identify priorities in order to guarantee an appropriate response and fulfilment of their obligations.

71. Complaints of summary, extrajudicial or arbitrary executions continued to be reported. An increasing trend was registered of complaints regarding serious violations such as forced disappearances, arbitrary arrests, arbitrary interference with private life and homes, torture and ill-treatment,

and disregard of judicial guarantees. Several such violations were perpetrated, by the security forces in the context of government security policies, and due to poor judicial control by officials of the Attorney-General's Office, and, on occasions, to poor control by officials of the State Procurator's institutions (*Ministerio Público*). In other cases, violations occurred due to powers, granted by certain regulations to the security forces, including military forces, to act without a warrant in the restriction of human rights and fundamental freedoms.[25]

72. Several extrajudicial executions directly attributed to security forces were reported.[26] Additionally, collective executions or massacres perpetrated by paramilitary groups were reported where responsibility was attributed to the State due to omission or collusion on the part of public servants, such as, in Tolima and Arauca, respectively. The responsibility of the State due to omission or collusion with paramilitary groups in summary executions in departments such as Antioquia, Arauca, Cauca, Cesar, and Cundinamarca was also reported.[27]

73. As compared to 2002, it is a source of concern to note the increase in complaints received by the office in Colombia in relation to forced disappearances, mainly perpetrated by paramilitary groups, in which responsibility is also attributed to the security forces. These complaints involve geographical areas where the security forces were widely present and in control and where tolerance and complicity of public servants with respect to paramilitary activities was reported. Additionally, the investigations aimed at finding the authors and determining their responsibility did not produce results. A number of forced disappearances directly attributed to the security forces were also reported.[28]

74. The office in Colombia equally recorded an increase in complaints of violations of the right to individual freedom due to arbitrary arrests perpetrated by State authorities. Several of these violations occurred under the security policy through the practice of mass arrests, detentions without a warrant by police and military forces, or with irregular warrants, as some people deprived of their liberty were not previously identified, or for being based on descriptions provided by hooded informers or intelligence reports.[29]

75. The office in Colombia has received numerous complaints regarding the conduct of officials from the Attorney-General's Office in several

[25] See annex III.
[26] See annex II, paras. 2 and 3.
[27] Ibid., para. 3.
[28] Ibid., para. 6.
[29] Ibid., para. 12.

of the above-mentioned cases. It was also reported that the Attorney-General's Office has subsequently endorsed initiatives on the part of the security forces in carrying out so-called "voluntary" searches and raids, arrests that did not satisfy the necessary requirements in order to be justified or legitimate, or the application of the notion of "permanent flagrancy", a concept incompatible with international rules. Additionally, the office in Colombia received complaints of cases where warrants for arrest were issued after the detainee had been singled out by former guerrillas reintegrated into civilian life. These irregular practices allegedly occurred inside military installations with the collaboration of the Attorney-General's Office.[30]

76. Compared to last year, an increase of complaints about violations of the right to personal integrity was reported, due to cruel, inhuman and degrading treatment and torture by members of the security forces.[31] Complaints of such violations also increased, including the disproportionate use of force, by security officials carried out against arrested individuals or penitentiary inmates. The latter cases were mainly registered in prison facilities built under the so-called new penitentiary culture,[32] prisons located in Acacias (Villavicencio), Cómbita (Boyacá), La Dorada (Caldas), Palo Gordo (Bucaramanga), Valledupar (Cesar) and, in particular, San Isidro (Popayán).[33] Additionally, the high level of overcrowding in the country's prisons is a source of concern.[34]

77. The administration of justice continued to experience problems related to access to justice, judicial independence and impartiality, judicial guarantees and presumption of innocence, as well as impunity. Issues of access to justice were observed not only due to the absence of prosecutors and judges in several municipalities of the country, but also as a result of the impact of the armed conflict.

78. Judicial independence and impartiality have been affected by several factors. In some cases, the legislative provisions have precluded respect for this principle, as in the case of the rules that, under the "state of internal commotion" (*state of emergency*), empowered security forces, including

---

[30] Ibid., para. 8.

[31] The Committee Against Torture reiterated "its concern for the great number of acts of torture and ill-treatments allegedly perpetrated in a generalized and usual way by the forces or corps of the State . . .". See document CAT/C/CR/31/1, para. 8, of 18 November 2003.

[32] The conditions and the internal regulations, under which these establishments function, may constitute cruel, inhuman or degrading treatments in giving excessive priority to the criteria of security and discipline.

[33] See annex II, para. 5.

[34] The Committee Against Torture has indicated that this situation could be equivalent to cruel, inhuman or degrading treatments (see documents CAT/CR/31/1, page 5, para. 10, point D.e).

military forces, to perform arrests, raids, searches and other operations with judicial police functions, but without a warrant having been previously issued by the competent authority. Similarly, prosecutors' independence has been cast in doubt by the presence of branches of the Attorney-General's Office inside military installations, as for example in Arauca. On other occasions, the decisions of prosecutors or the course of their investigations have led to their dismissal or to the reassigning of their investigations to other prosecutors, by decision of the Attorney-General, in contradiction to the principle of judicial independence and the autonomy of the prosecutors.[35]

79. Special mention has to be made of the efforts of the Procurator General's Office in following up and controlling the elaboration or application of certain provisions such as the evaluation of reports on the conduct of public servants in the so-called rehabilitation and consolidation zones, the follow-up on the situation in Bojayá (Chocó), or its formal opinion of the Government's proposed referendum.[36] On the other hand, the office in Colombia has been able to observe situations where the conduct of representatives of the State Procurator's institutions (*Ministerio Público*) has been inconsistent. In some cases, the State Procurator's institutions (*Ministerio Público*) has had a critical and rigorous attitude in the performance of its duties as an institution for both preventive and disciplinary control, as for example in Medell'n. In others, the Procurator General's Office has accompanied and endorsed, with the same tolerance and lack of rigour of the Attorney-General's Office, the actions of the security forces and prosecutors, as for example in Arauca.

80. An additional element for concern has been the reiterated practice on the part of State authorities to parade arrested or captured individuals before the media presenting them as members of guerrilla groups, thus disregarding the principles of presumption of innocence and respect of human dignity.

81. Another element that has affected judicial independence and impartiality is related to cases of violations of human rights or breaches of international humanitarian law that have been assigned to the military criminal justice system or continue under that jurisdiction.[37]

82. The general Colombian population, journalists and media representatives as well as the country's academics and intellectuals, continue to experience difficulties in fully exercising their right to freedom of opinion and expression. Due to implementation of the security policy and the

---

[35] See annex II, paras. 9 and 10.

[36] Ibid., para. 10.

[37] Ibid., para. 3.

impact of certain legislative measures, several complaints of violations of these fundamental freedoms were reported in some parts of the country, mainly in the Department of Arauca. The office in Colombia observed and received information of violations by the security forces that imposed arbitrary or illegal restrictions on the exercise of freedom of the press, as well as violations of their obligation to guarantee and protect.[38]

83. With respect to freedom of movement and residence, it is worth underlining the decrease in new forced internal displacements, as compared to last year, although worrisome levels are still being reported, particularly in Antioquia, Bolivar, Norte de Santander, Cesar and Cundinamarca. The Social Solidarity Network reported more than 130,000 newly displaced people, in the period up until September 2003. The State has been responsible for some of these incidents because of the absence or inefficiency of measures that could have prevented them or protected the victims.

84. Despite Government measures adopted to guarantee the safety of the population and the holding of municipal and departmental elections during the month of October, several candidates and electors could not exercise their political right to vote and be elected. In some cases, the inhabitants of rural areas could not register their personal identification documents in order to vote and, similarly, a significant number of candidates had to conduct their campaigns under conditions of inequality and insecurity.

V. *Situation of Particularly Vulnerable Groups*

Human rights defenders

85. The situation of human rights defenders, including trade unionists (particularly school and health personnel) continued to be critical. Although a decrease in homicides, attacks, forced disappearances and hostage-taking against them has been noted, these violent actions continued to affect them. These crimes were mainly attributed to paramilitary groups and, in some cases, to FARC-EP and, to a lesser degree, ELN.

86. The dynamics of the armed conflict evidenced a change in the modus operandi of the armed groups, particularly the paramilitaries, that makes use of more subtle strategies, which have less public impact than direct attacks on the defenders' right to life. A change in the risk factors for this

[38] See chapter III of this report.

group should also be mentioned. In fact, the policies of mass arrests and large-scale raids that included the offices of civil society organizations and trade unions, as well as the conduct of certain governmental authorities, caused the defenders to be more restrained in their work, to be more reserved when expressing opinions, and led them to limit their activities.

87. Under the leadership of the Office of the Vice-President, the Government made arrangements for exchanges with human rights and peace organizations, and trade unions. It is worth mentioning the adoption of Directive 09, issued by the Ministry of Defense, on July 2003, and which ratified Presidential Directive 07 of the previous administration, dated September 1999, whereby public servants are instructed to respect human rights defenders and the work of their organizations.

88. The positive impact of the start of this partnership and of the directives was, nevertheless, offset by certain public declarations made by governmental authorities. Top government officials[39] questioned the nature of the work of human rights organizations and accused them of being at the service of terrorism. This weakens the legitimacy and the possibilities that the above-mentioned directives be respected and can encourage actions against the freedom and privacy of people involved in the defence of human rights or in trade union movements.

89. Under the policy of democratic security, members of NGOs and social and trade union leaders were subject to arbitrary arrest and accused of rebellion. At the moment of their arrest, several of them were under the protection of precautionary measures requested by the Inter-American Commission on Human Rights (CIDH) and were benefiting from the protection programme of the Ministry of Justice and Interior.

Ethnic groups

90. The human rights situation for ethnic groups continued to be critical, especially for indigenous people and Afro-Colombian communities. In addition, these groups, including the *Raizales* (the Creole-English-speaking inhabitants of San Andrés, Providencia and Santa Catalina) and the Roma, continued to suffer from violations of their economic, social and cultural rights and to be affected by racial discrimination, poverty, exclusion and the repudiation of their specific rights. The above is reflected in the absence of social and economic data on the ethnic groups and the resulting absence of differentiating policies capable of addressing their specific needs.

[39] Among them, the President of the Republic, a few ministers and military commanders.

91. The armed conflict contributed to worsen the situation of indigenous and Afro-Colombian communities. An increase in selective violence against traditional authorities and leaders has been reported, with homicides, death threats and forced displacements, as well as greater confinement of the communities on the part of the illegal armed groups. This affected the communities' right to autonomy, thus weakening their internal organization and the level of representation of their authorities. More than 100 indigenous individuals and authorities were the victims of homicide, 50 of which were perpetrated against the political and spiritual authorities of the Kankuamo people (Sierra Nevada de Santa Marta) and mainly attributed to AUC. The lack of effective actions on the part of the security forces in order to protect these communities has occasionally been questioned, as well as their stigmatization.

92. Certain progress made by the State should be stressed in terms of protection and prevention, particularly in relation to indigenous people, as well as a stronger presence on the part of the Ombudsman's Office through community defenders in regions that have been characterized by a minimal State presence and a high concentration of indigenous and Afro-Colombian populations. Nevertheless, State responses aimed at satisfying education, health care, employment, housing and basic sanitation requirements continue to be insufficient. Despite the important decision of the Constitutional Court recognizing the right of the indigenous communities to prior consultation where fumigation of illegal crops is to take place in their reservations, this right continues to be violated by the State in cases of projects for exploiting resources.

Women

93. It is worth mentioning the signing of the national agreement on gender equality in October 2003 by all of the branches of the Government, and the adoption of the National Policy on Sexual and Reproductive Health. In spite of this, and of some legislative progress, the persistence of sexual discrimination, exclusion and violence continue to affect real equality between men and women. Greater advances are required in the execution and effectiveness of this policy for women. The commitment of the Government on this matter is weakened by the lack of institutional strengthening and the resulting absence of administrative, budgetary and technical autonomy.

94. The diverse forms of violence perpetrated against women, in the context of the armed conflict, continue to affect their rights. The office in Colombia received complaints of rapes by paramilitary groups and members of the security forces, as well as complaints of sexual enslavement on

the part of the guerrilla groups. The illegal armed groups continue exercising social pressure on women aimed at weakening their organizational process and their participation in public activities. In the face of this situation, effective responses provided by the State are insufficient in terms of the protection, prevention, investigation and punishment of these acts. Of special concern are the rape cases currently under the jurisdiction of the military criminal justice system.[40]

95. The rights of women participating in the hostilities, especially sexual and reproductive rights, are particularly affected by abuse of power inside the illegal armed groups. Similarly, FARC-EP continues compulsory use of contraceptives and forced abortion.

Children

96. Large numbers of children continued to be the victims of violations of the right to life and are also affected by abandonment, child labour, sexual exploitation and abuse, physical ill-treatment and familial violence.[41] In terms of economic, social and cultural rights, children and adolescents are the principal victims of neglect in this area. Similarly, the armed conflict has a strong negative impact on children, particularly because of hostage-taking,[42] recruitment, displacement, and the consequences of breaches of humanitarian law perpetrated against their communities and families.[43]

Journalists

97. The situation of journalists continued to be precarious, with limited space for free and independent exercise of their profession and the freedom of opinion, expression and information. During 2003, at least four homicides and executions of journalists were registered. Two of them were covered by the Protection Programme of the Ministry of Justice and the Interior and their risk level had been assessed as medium-low. Illegal armed groups continued to threaten and intimidate journalists as well as resorting to hostage-taking. Increased pressure by paramilitary groups on journalists covering their crimes, especially in Bogatá, coincided with the

---

[40] See annex II, para. 10.

[41] According to UNICEF, 35,000 children are sexually exploited and 653,000 are child workers, aged between 5 and 11 years old. It is estimated that around 2 million children are maltreated in their homes, 850,000 of them in a severe manner.

[42] According to *Fundación Pais Libre* (Free Country Foundation), 243 minors have been taken as hostages between January and September 2003.

[43] See annex II, paras. 27 and 28.

negotiation process between the Government and the paramilitary groups. Threats in the regions have also been are also attributed to the guerrilla groups. Other threats, of unknown origin, were made in order to prevent the reporting of cases of corruption involving public servants.

98. It was reported that, on some occasions, State authorities in the Departments of Arauca and César hindered the work of journalists by detaining them and confiscating their press material. The application of the democratic security policy in the Department of Arauca did not avoid the forced displacement of 15 journalists during the months of March and April because of threats by the illegal armed groups or the homicide of one threatened journalist who was a beneficiary of the Protection Programme of the Ministry of Justice and the Interior. It can be concluded then that the measures adopted in Arauca have not created favourable conditions for the full exercise of freedom of the press and the right of the population to be informed in a true and impartial way. For this reason many journalists have shown an increase in self-censorship, which they define as "self-regulation in order to survive".

Communities at risk

99. The growing tendency in forced displacement has been reversed in 2003, with a reported decrease in the number of new events. This change may be explained by factors such as the impact of the security policy and of returns arranged by the Government, the confinement of communities by the illegal armed groups, for example in Gabarra (Norte de Santander), the magnitude of displacement in previous years, which had left several rural areas practically abandoned, as in eastern Antioquia or in Putumayo, and also the impact of negotiations between the Government and AUC. The increased presence on the part of the security forces did not lead to avoidance of new forced displacements in some municipalities that were part of the rehabilitation and consolidation zones.

100. According to the Social Solidarity Network, between 1 January and 30 September, around 76 per cent of forced displacement occurred in 12 departments, the most affected being Antioquia, César, Bolivar, and Putumayo, with 4 per cent of the displaced population being minors, 50 per cent women (19 per cent heads of household), 4 per cent indigenous and 5 per cent Afro-Colombians. The Social Solidarity Network points to the overall insecurity, armed confrontations, selective threats, massacres and the occupation of municipalities by illegal armed groups as being the causes of displacement. According to the same source, the *autodefensas* were responsible for nearly 33 per cent of the displacements, the guerrilla groups for

24 per cent and the security forces for 0.8 per cent; 35 per cent of the displacements were caused by more than one armed group.[44]

101. The policy of attention to displaced populations suffered setbacks. The differentiated attention regarding health, housing, access to land and production projects, has been affected by the process of restructuring of public entities, the lack of definition of policies, the limited budgets and the weakening of positive discrimination measures. The Constitutional Court, in a ruling made on March 2003, protected the right of intra-urban displaced people to receive benefits and assistance provided for by national regulations. Despite achievements in emergency assistance, especially in the case of mass displacements, there is a high degree of neglect of the economic, social and cultural rights of the displaced population, particularly of women, children and ethnic groups. Additionally, there is a particular interest in Government policy in favour of the return of the displaced to their places of origin. Nevertheless, in the returns promoted by the network, the willingness of the displaced continues to be questionable due to the lack of social and economic options, of information, of a process implying participation and guarantees of security, due to the still existing time limit on the duration of aid, the continuation of the conflict and the few options for re-establishing and relocating.

Other vulnerable groups

102. Municipal and departmental officials (mayors, councillors and representatives), the members of the *Unión Patriótica* (UP), prosecutors, members of religious orders and homosexuals can be included among groups particularly affected by the armed conflict and by the human rights situation in this country. The Colombian Federation of Municipalities and the National Federation of Councils recorded 8 homicides of mayors and 56 of town or city councillors, until October 2003. Up until May of the same year, 107 mayors had to carry out their functions from outside of their municipalities, mostly in departmental capitals. Additionally, the vulnerability of UP members continued. According to *Reiniciar*, they suffered 16 homicides (among them two town or city councillors, one candidate for mayor and one for governor) and six forced disappearances (including one candidate for mayor). Similarly *ASONAL Judicial* (National Judicial Association) reported 17 homicides, 5 attacks and 56 death threats against judicial officials, until October. Homicides, threats and the taking of their mem-

[44] According to information provided by the Government in reply to the Office's request.

bers as hostages have also affected Catholic and Protestant religious communities. Finally, other groups, such as homosexuals, apart from being the victims of acts of violence inspired by intolerance, were not able to achieve legislative progress in the protection of their rights.

VI. *Recommendations*

103. On the basis of his detailed analysis, the High Commissioner puts forward a series of concrete priority recommendations for 2004. These recommendations, which are not exhaustive, are grouped under six headings: prevention and protection; internal armed conflict; the rule of law and impunity; economic and social policies; promotion of a human rights culture; and technical cooperation and advice on the part of his office in Colombia.

104. The recommendations are addressed to the national authorities in the three branches of government as well as to the supervisory bodies responsible for protecting and promoting human rights, to all of the parties to the internal armed conflict, and to civil society. The High Commissioner is firmly convinced that the situation regarding human rights and international humanitarian law would improve notably if the following recommendations were to be applied during the year 2004 by those to whom they are addressed.

(a) *Prevention and protection*

105. The High Commissioner encourages the Government to strengthen coordination between the Early Warning System (SAT), established in the Office of the Ombudsman, and the Inter-Institutional Early Warning Committee (CIAT), following up on the actions taken by authorities in areas identified by risk reports. The Committee ought also to include the Office of the Ombudsman, the Social Solidarity Network and the Ministry of Justice and the Interior's Programme for protection of human rights defenders.

106. The High Commissioner encourages the Government to ensure that the programmes for the protection of human rights defenders and other groups, for which the Ministry of the Interior's Human Rights Department is responsible, operate with the necessary coverage and effectiveness. The Ministry, together with other State institutions, ought to search for new mechanisms aimed at reducing risk factors and at acting preventively against them.

107. The High Commissioner encourages the Social Solidarity Network, together with other government and State institutions, to put into prac-

tice, as soon as possible, preventive and protective actions and programmes that have been agreed upon with the communities at risk. With respect to displacement, the United Nations Guiding Principles should be strictly applied.

108. The High Commissioner exhorts the Government and Congress to ensure inclusion in the national budget of funds required to provide the Procurator General's Office and the Office of the Ombudsman with the necessary means to establish themselves in localities in which they are currently absent, especially in areas with a high proportion of indigenous, Afro-Colombian and displaced persons. The High Commissioner also recommends that the Procurator General's Office and the Office of the Ombudsman comprehensively include Municipal Ombudsmen in their activities and programmes related to human rights protection and promotion.

109. The High Commissioner encourages the Procurator General to carry out, during the first semester of 2004, the pending review of military intelligence records concerning human rights defenders and organizations. This review ought to be carried out at least once a year.

110. The High Commissioner recommends the State Procurator's institutions (*Ministerio Público*) and senior public service officials to comply with their duty to take disciplinary action against any State employees who through their declarations, actions or omissions in any way discredit or jeopardize the work of human rights defenders.

111. The High Commissioner encourages the Minister of Defense to develop, on the basis of the results of an independent study, in a comprehensive, systematic and operational way, the training in human rights and international humanitarian law of all members of the security forces.

(b) *Internal armed conflict*

112. The High Commissioner urges FARC-EP, ELN, AUC and other guerrilla and paramilitary groups to respect the right to life of all civilians. The High Commissioner urges them in particular to refrain at all times from attacks on the civilian population, indiscriminate attacks, the unacceptable practice of kidnapping, recruitment of minors, and acts of terrorism.

113. The High Commissioner urges FARC-EP, ELN, AUC and all other illegal armed groups to immediately and unconditionally release everyone they have taken hostage and anyone who has laid down their arms or has ceased to take part in hostilities.

114. The High Commissioner urges FARC-EP, ELN, AUC and all other illegal armed groups to refrain from any action that may affect the civil-

ian population's enjoyment of human rights and diminish the ability of the Colombian State to fulfil its obligation to protect and safeguard those rights.

115. The High Commissioner urges the illegal armed groups, in particular FARC-EP and ELN, to comply with the obligations imposed on them by international rules that prohibit the employment, storage, production and transfer of anti-personnel mines.

116. The High Commissioner urges all those directly involved in the hostilities in the context of the internal armed conflict to observe, without restriction, the humanitarian principles of limitation, distinction, and proportionality and the general obligation to protect the civilian population, as well as to guarantee humanitarian access to vulnerable populations.

117. The High Commissioner recommends that the Government, the illegal armed groups and representative sectors of civil society spare no effort to establish contacts for dialogue and negotiation in order to resolve the internal armed conflict and achieve a lasting peace. The dialogues and negotiations should from the outset take human rights and international humanitarian law into account. The High Commissioner exhorts the Government and Congress to fully honour the fundamental principles of truth, justice and reparation for victims, in all dialogues and negotiations with illegal armed groups.

(c) *The rule of law and impunity*

118. The High Commissioner exhorts the Government and Congress to pay due attention to the obligations assumed by Colombia as a State party to international human rights, international humanitarian law and international labour law instruments. The High Commissioner recommends the Government to carry out the ratification of international treaties relating to such matters and to deposit the ratification instruments of treaties that have been internally approved. The High Commissioner urges that no rule incompatible with such instruments should be introduced or maintained in Colombian legislation. He further recommends that greater use be made of the advisory services of the office in Colombia of the High Commissioner.

119. The High Commissioner calls upon the Special Committee on the conduct of investigations into human rights violations and breaches of international humanitarian law to present concrete results concerning the selected cases and to present quarterly reports to the President of the Republic on the progress achieved in the investigation of these cases.

120. The High Commissioner exhorts the Attorney-General to guarantee, pursuant to the letter of understanding signed in November 2003 with his office in Colombia, compliance with the recommendations of 2002 during the first half of 2004. These recommendations relate to the programme

for the protection of witnesses and victims, the bill on a career structure for officials and employees of his office, the strengthening of the Unit of Human Rights and International Humanitarian Law, and the creation of a group specializing in the investigation of possible links between members of the security forces and paramilitary groups.

121. The High Commissioner exhorts the Attorney-General to safeguard and respect the independence of prosecutors in the performance of all of their duties and to guarantee that procedures involving detentions and searches are supported by sufficient evidence and carried out with respect for due process.

122. The High Commissioner calls on the Procurator General and the Ombudsman to promote and instil respect for procedural guarantees for those deprived of liberty whose legal situation has not yet been defined. The High Commissioner invites the Procurator General and the Ombudsman to present public reports on this matter. The High Commissioner exhorts the National Prison and Penitentiary Institute (INPEC) to guarantee and respect the rights of all inmates.

123. The High Commissioner recommends the Minister of Defense to ensure the effectiveness of all disciplinary investigations into serious human rights violations or war crimes attributed to members of the security forces, and to suspend them from duty as a preventive measure. The High Commissioner also exhorts that the military criminal jurisdiction be limited to crimes related to service.

124. The High Commissioner recommends the President of the Republic, in his capacity as Head of State and Commander-in-Chief of the security forces, to take all necessary steps to ensure that, independently of any dialogue conducted between the Government and the paramilitary groups, all links between public officials and members of such groups be severed. The High Commissioner also recommends the President to present a report to the State Prosecutor's institutions (*Ministerio Público*) every six months on the measures adopted and the results of their application.

(d) *Economic and social policies*

125. The High Commissioner exhorts the Government to develop a consistent policy, based on updated statistics, to reduce inequality, confront the extreme poverty that exists in the country and ensure that all necessary steps are taken to decrease illiteracy and unemployment rates and improve access to health care, education and housing. Primary education should be free and health services and housing subsidies ought to be guaranteed for the most disadvantaged sectors of the population.

(e) *Promotion of a human rights culture*

126. The High Commissioner recommends that the Government and the organizations of human rights defenders develop and institutionalize stable communication channels, both at the national as well as the regional levels, in order to achieve a greater degree of understanding and improve the promotion and protection of human rights throughout the country.

127. The High Commissioner recommends that the Government, through the Standing Intersectorial Commission on Human Rights and International Humanitarian Law, prepare a concerted plan of action on human rights and international humanitarian law, to be created in collaboration with broad sectors of society and which includes an integral gender approach. Within the first semester of 2004, a timetable ought to be agreed upon in order to enable that the action plan be concluded by the end of the year.

128. The High Commissioner recommends that the Minister of Education adopt, in 2004, a working plan that effectively makes comprehensive teaching of human rights part of the primary and secondary school education.

129. The High Commissioner encourages Congress, the High Council of the Judiciary, the Attorney-General, the Higher School of Public Administration and the associations of Governors and Mayors to make arrangements with the Procurator General's Office and the Office of the Ombudsman for continuous training in human rights and international humanitarian law. The High Commissioner also recommends that the Office of the Ombudsman and other institutions make use of the network of human rights educators trained by his office in Colombia.

(f) *Advisory services and technical assistance by the office*

130. The High Commissioner urges the State to implement in a coherent and efficient manner the international recommendations, including those made in this report, and exhorts the Vice-President of the Republic, the relevant Ministers, the High Commissioner for Peace and all other State institutions to adequately coordinate among themselves. The aforementioned institutions ought to prepare, within the first semester of 2004, a timetable for the implementation of these recommendations. In this respect, the High Commissioner invites them to make use of the advisory capacity of his office in Colombia.

131. The High Commissioner invites the Government, the Congress, the Attorney-General's Office, the Procurator General's Office, the Office of the Ombudsman and the organizations of civil society to enhance their interlocution with his office in Colombia, taking full advantage of its mandate regarding advisory services and technical cooperation. The High

Commissioner also invites the international community to provide financial and technical support to the different State institutions, to the organizations of civil society and to his office in Colombia in order to contribute towards the effective implementation of the recommendations.

Annex I

Status of implementation of the recommendations formulated by the United Nations High Commissioner for Human Rights in his 2003 report on the human rights situation in Colombia IN 2002

1. Since 1997, the United Nations High Commissioner for Human Rights has presented an annual analytical report on the human rights situation in Colombia to the Commission on Human Rights. This report, as provided for in the Agreement reached between the Government of Colombia and the United Nations in November of 1996—and currently renewed until 30 October 2006—includes the recommendations considered pertinent by the High Commissioner.

2. The 27 recommendations contained in the report for the year 2002 and submitted in April 2003 are addressed to the executive, legislative and judicial authorities of the Colombian State, to the organisms for control charged with protection and promotion of human rights and to the civil society, aimed at supporting the efforts made in the country directed at improving the overall situation of human rights and international humanitarian law. They are also addressed to the armed illegal groups.

3. In his report for the year 2002, the High Commissioner expressed "the firm conviction that the situation regarding human rights and international humanitarian law could be noticeably improved if the (É) recommendations were to be taken into account and applied in 2003" (E/CN.4/2003/13, para. 154).

4. The statement on Colombia formulated by the Chairperson of the Commission on Human Rights in April 2003 expresses the consensus reached between the international community and the Government of Colombia. The latter was urged to fully comply with the recommendations made in the High Commissioner's report (E/CN.4/2002/200, para. 45).

5. The commitment to implement the recommendations was later reiterated by the Republic of Colombia when, in July 2003, government representatives met in London with senior level representatives of the Governments of Argentina, Brazil, Canada, Chile, Japan, Mexico, Norway, Switzerland and the United States of America, the member States of the European Union, of the United Nations, of the Andean Development

Corporation, the Inter-American Development Bank, the International Monetary Fund and the World Bank. In the Declaration of London, the countries "noted with satisfaction the commitment on the part of the Government of Colombia to implement the recommendations of the United Nations High Commissioner for Human Rights and urged the Government of Colombia to implement these recommendations promptly as well as to adopt effective measures against impunity and complicity, especially with the paramilitary groups".

6. The efforts on the part of the State to initiate actions aimed at achieving effective implementation of the recommendations must be recognized, although they are just beginning. There are promising initiatives which, if strengthened, could have a positive impact on the fulfilment of Colombian commitments in this field.

7. The office in Colombia of the High Commissioner has achieved a fluid dialogue with the diverse entities of the Colombian State in the course of following up on the recommendations. However, the international commitment made by the Government to put these recommendations into effect was rejected by some of its highest officials, which limited satisfactory implementation of the majority of them on the part of institutions charged with their fulfilment. Other factors having an influence on unsatisfactory compliance with the recommendations, at the moment the report was completed, included the insufficient priority placed on human rights and international humanitarian law by senior government officials, the limited importance given to these topics in some public policies, failings in inter-institutional coordination, the presentation of projects for constitutional change and for new laws that are incompatible with international norms, the limited dialogue and failure to create established forums for discussion between the executive branch and non-governmental organizations and the infrequent use made of the office in Colombia's advisory services on the part of the State.

8. With regard to the recommendations made to the illegal armed groups, which include FARC-EP, ELN and AUC, they were not taken into account by these groups who throughout 2003 continued to contribute to the ongoing degradation of the internal armed conflict through acts of extreme violence and terrorism, characterized by an intense victimization of civilians.

9. In the following section, we will analyse actions by the State aimed at implementing the recommendations made to it. These recommendations are grouped under six headings: prevention and protection; internal armed conflict; democracy and impunity; economic and social policies; promotion of a human rights culture; and advisory services and technical cooperation on the part of the office in Colombia of the High Commissioner.

Prevention and protection

10. The eight recommendations grouped together under this heading were formulated in order to empower and strengthen the work of institutions charged with the prevention of human rights violations and breaches of international humanitarian law, protection for human rights defenders, witnesses and victims, preventive action with respect to risk factors for communities affected by the armed conflict and the application of disciplinary sanctions against agents of the State who, by action or omission, endanger the work of defending human rights.

11. In this respect, the Government's decision at the end of 2002 to establish the Inter-Institutional Early Warning Committee (or CIAT, from its initials in Spanish), inside the Ministry of Justice and Law, must be greeted with satisfaction. This committee is made up of public servants from that ministry as well as from the Ministry of Defense, the Security Forces and the Presidential Programme for Human Rights. This initiative from its very beginnings had to overcome great challenges, such as establishing its way of operating, the criteria for determining risk and the measures to be adopted for preventing an alert. It must be noted, however, that the establishment of the SAT represents a positive element to counter the difficult human rights and international humanitarian law situation.

12. It should be mentioned that analysis of the reports on risks and, as a result, timely actions identified by the CIAT, have for the most part adhered to a military approach. At the same time, measures that are the responsibility of the civil authorities have been delegated to the departmental level, without effective follow-up mechanisms being drawn up in order to ensure their implementation.

13. In the course of carrying out the committee's activities, certain failures also became evident, including the weak hierarchical representation of the participating officials, the utilization of the Ombudsman's Office reports on risks as the only source, excessive decentralization and the lack of adequate follow-up procedure on the alerts after they have been issued.

14. At the same time, it became evident that the warning system, initially created for the prevention of grave and massive human rights violations and breaches of international humanitarian law, lacked the necessary capacity and flexibility to coordinate with other governmental bodies the task of preventing certain types of conduct that constitute violations and that occurred throughout the year, such as selective homicides, forced disappearances and acts of terrorism.

15. In some cases in which the Ombudsman's Office did not issue reports on risk, the CIAT abstained from producing alerts. In other cases, in spite of the existence of reports on risk from the Ombudsman's Office, the

Committee did not act upon them. There were also situations in which, despite reports on risk provided by the Ombudsman's Office and the issuing of alerts on the part of the CIAT, the violation or infraction that the reports aimed to prevent unfortunately occurred nonetheless.

16. On the other hand, the Ministry of the Interior's Programme for Protection was able to initiate, although with delays, application of the recommendations for external evaluation made in 2001. This led to progress in providing pending plans for security. The office in Colombia was informed that a proposal exists on the part of the Office of the Vice-President to resolve the problem of the so-called "trusted bodyguards" but this has not yet been formalized.

17. It must also be noted that there has been no progress in the work of preventing the risk factors generated by public servants whose public declarations have sometimes contributed towards making evident the vulnerabilities of the system for prevention and protection, thus intensifying the danger to its beneficiaries while increasing the budgetary needs of the programmes that cover them.

18. With respect to the recommendation directed at the Attorney-General's Office regarding the programme for the protection of witnesses and victims, that institution has not implemented it. However, it must be noted that in November 2003, the office in Colombia of the High Commissioner and the Attorney-General's Office signed an agreement for cooperation that, if executed according to its timetable, will make it possible during the first half of 2004 to incorporate the recommendations formulated by the office in its 2001 study.

19. With respect to the identification of communities at risk due to the internal armed conflict and the implementation of programmes for preventive attention and protection for these communities, it must be stated that the hoped-for progress has not been observed. The working group made up of the Social Solidarity Network, representing the Government, the Ombudsman's Office, the NGO Consultoría para los Derechos Humanos y el Desplazamiento (CODHES) and agencies of the United Nations system, has met, although not as frequently as desired, and has made progress in formulating the theoretical framework as well as the instrument for carrying out this work. However, it has only carried out a mission to Catatumbo, in which the difficulties for defining the institutional offer of programmes aimed at communities at risk, and particularly those not included in the target population of the regulations on internal displacement, were evident.

20. At the same time, the Procurator General's Office, the Ombudsman's Office and the Government have not been able to determine the budgetary needs that would make it possible for them to establish a presence in those municipalities in which they do not yet have one. This limits the

operations of the institutions for control and defence of human rights precisely in the areas where they are most needed. Although the Ombudsman's Office was able to designate community ombudsmen in some of the country's most remote zones, this was achieved thanks to international contributions.

21. There has not been full compliance with the recommendation formulated and submitted to the State Procurator's offices and the higher members of the hierarchy so that they will apply disciplinary sanctions to public servants responsible by action or omission for endangering human rights defenders. The prohibition on making declarations that could affect the safety of these defenders, which was reinforced by Presidential Directive No. 07 of 1999 and Ministry of Defense Directive No. 09 of 2003, has been disobeyed by a number of public servants without any known disciplinary action being taken.

22. With respect to the recommendation made to the Procurator General that the accuracy and objectivity of information contained in the military intelligence files on human rights defenders be verified, we have yet to see a report on this topic.

23. With respect to the recommendation for incorporating systematic study of international human rights law and international humanitarian law into the training given to members of the Security Forces, and for signing an agreement with the Ministry of Defense and the Ombudsman's Office for continuous training, some working sessions have been held between the Ministry and the office in Colombia of the High Commissioner. However, at the time of finishing the report, there have not been concrete actions or results to report.

Internal armed conflict

24. Of the six recommendations grouped together under this topic, three were aimed at the illegal armed groups, such as FARC-EP, ELN and AUC along with the other guerrilla and paramilitary groups, one at the military and police forces and two at all of the parties involved in the internal armed conflict and at the civil society. They were formulated by the High Commissioner to encourage observance of international humanitarian law, respect for the civilian population and the search for ways to resolve the internal armed conflict by means of dialogue and negotiation, respecting certain important rights.

25. These recommendations were neither adopted nor respected by the outlawed armed groups, who continued to commit grave crimes against the civilian population.

26. Regarding the recommendations made to the Security Forces in terms of observance of the humanitarian principles of limitation, distinction, proportionality and general protection of the civilian population, the office in Colombia has corroborated that they are not always put into practice by the members of the government armed forces. This has given rise to a number of breaches of international humanitarian law. In addition, some of the actions undertaken by the Government in implementing its "democratic security" policy were contrary to the international principle of distinction.

27. In this sense, dispositions contrary to the principle of distinction established in international norms have been detected in the proposed legislation on the organization of national security and defence presented to Congress at the initiative of the Government.

28. With respect to the recommendation, addressed to all of the parties to the conflict, to comply with obligations arising from international norms regarding anti-personnel mines, it must be emphasized that the illegal armed groups, and especially FARC-EP, have continued illegal, massive and indiscriminate use of anti-personnel mines and other explosive devices. On the other hand, the Colombian State has made progress with respect to international norms, has commenced execution of a plan to destroy mines in storage, has strengthened the Anti-personnel Mines Observatory, has prepared a detailed National Plan of Action for Comprehensive Action against Anti-personnel Mines and has concluded agreements for technical assistance with international organisms. However, there is a need to strengthen mechanisms for protecting the civilian population and preventing accidents due to anti-personnel mines through locating and placing signposts and demarcations on the minefields as well as for guaranteeing better attention for the victims.

29. Regarding the recommendation to take human rights and international humanitarian law into account during the dialogues and negotiations for resolving the internal armed conflict, this has not been fully carried out. The Government has initiated dialogue and negotiations with the paramilitary groups aimed at their demobilization. However, to date, the process has given rise to serious questions with respect to guarantees for victims' rights to truth, justice and reparation in the course of these dialogues. Nor is there clarity with regard to the legal treatment to be given by the State to paramilitaries responsible for grave human rights violations, war crimes and crimes against humanity.

Rule of law and impunity

30. The seven recommendations grouped together under this heading were formulated by the High Commissioner to obtain compatibility between internal policies and norms and the international obligations of the State, strengthen the independence and impartiality of the Attorney-General's Office, increase the effectiveness of the fight against the paramilitary groups, begin to lower the rate of impunity and to cut every link between agents of the State and the illegal armed groups, particularly the self-defence forces and paramilitaries.

31. With respect to the recommendation against introducing regulations into domestic law that are incompatible with international precepts, it must be noted that the Government submitted legislation to Congress, aimed at constitutional amendment and change of current laws, whose content is not compatible with that stipulated in various international instruments that have been ratified (see annex III).

32. In relation to the three recommendations addressed to the Attorney-General's Office, that institution was unable to fulfil any of them. It should be noted that the Attorney-General's Office, along with the office in Colombia of the High Commissioner, signed a letter of understanding for implementation of the recommendations. Such cooperation could help to reaffirm the independence of the prosecutors, strengthen the Human Rights Unit, intensify the struggle against the paramilitary groups and investigate links between the military and police forces and the paramilitary groups in the first half of 2004. However, follow-up will have to be made on the Attorney-General's Office's fulfilment of the timetable and of the recommendations arising from the study.

33. Regarding the Special Committee to promote investigations of human rights violations and breaches of international humanitarian law, it must be noted that the work of revising these cases could only begin in the second half of the year. However, the results of the Committee's work are not known. It is to be hoped that the quarterly report that the Committee must make to the President will show progress in this area. If the Committee is able to produce concrete results in the investigations it is charged with carrying out, it could become a valuable instrument in the fight against impunity. To this end, greater action on the part of the institutions making up the committee is required, as well as concrete support by the highest levels of the Executive.

34. Regarding preventive disciplinary suspension of members of the Security Forces involved in grave human rights violations and war crimes, the office in Colombia is not aware of a single case in which such a suspension has been applied in disciplinary proceedings carried out by officials

of the Ministry of Defense. It may therefore be concluded that this legal power, established in the recommendation formulated with regard to this area, has until this moment not been used.

35. With respect to the measures taken in order to cut ties between public servants and paramilitary groups, the office in Colombia has not received notice of the President informing the Procurator General and the Ombudsman's Office on a quarterly basis regarding his actions in this field. Nor did the office in Colombia observe significant progress in investigating and punishing such ties. However, it appears that the recommendation for the dismissal of certain public servants has been taken into account.

Economic and social policies

36. With regard to the recommendation to reduce the inequality gap, decrease the rates of illiteracy and unemployment as well as regarding the right to health care, education and housing, the results are far from satisfactory.

37. The State doubled public expenditure on education during the period from 1997 to 2002. It has also expanded coverage of secondary education, with the exception of middle school. However, departments with fewer resources and less educational infrastructure were affected to a greater degree because they could not benefit from a preferential regimen. The application of legislative act 012 and Law 715 have decreased these municipalities' possibilities of receiving greater resources. At the same time, the dual educational system, public and private, that is in effect in Colombia and the lack of adequate resources for the public system have increased the gap between these two sectors, of which the private sector benefits to a greater extent.

38. In health care, the national expenditure by the State in the period between 1994 and 2002 also doubled. However, this has not been matched in public utilities, nor has it benefited the less favoured sectors and regions. In fact, the most progress in terms of coverage has been made in Bogotá and Medellín, and the least progress in the most backward and conflictive regions.

39. Unemployment, according to sources at the National Administrative Department for Statistics (DANE), has continued in the range of 13–14 per cent, which is not far from the average since 2001. In October 2003, the employed population numbered 18.2 million, while those economically active were 49 per cent of the total.

40. According to DANE, the proportion of the population that possesses their own homes is much less than it was 10 years ago. The financial sector crisis and the impoverishment of the population have proven an obsta-

cle for access to housing. It is significant that over the last few years, housing for the poorer segments of the population has fallen by 50 per cent.

Promotion of a human rights culture

41. The three recommendations grouped together under this topic were formulated by the High Commissioner to encourage the drawing up of an action plan for human rights, with an integrated gender approach, to achieve the incorporation of these rights into primary and secondary education and promote constant training of officials and employees of the judiciary branch in human rights and international humanitarian law.

42. With respect to the national action plan on human rights that was agreed to at the 1993 World Conference on Human Rights, the Government of Colombia was unable to draw it up in 2003 or to begin a sustainable process for negotiating with important sectors of civil society. The Government has indicated that it will have drawn this plan up by August 2004.

43. Regarding incorporation of human rights teaching in primary and secondary school programmes, the office in Colombia of the High Commissioner has taken note of the signing of an agreement between the Ombudsman's Office and the Ministry of Defense aimed at training teachers on this subject.

44. The office in Colombia is unaware of the establishment of agreements between the Ombudsman's Office and the judicial authorities to ensure constant training of the employees of this branch in human rights and international humanitarian law.

Technical cooperation and advice on the part of the office in Colombia of the High Commissioner

45. The two recommendations grouped together under this heading were formulated by the High Commissioner so that the Colombian authorities would follow-up on international recommendations and so that the different institutions of the Government and the State would intensify their dialogue with the office in Colombia and fully benefit from its mandate to provide technical assistance and advice.

46. In this sense, some authorities have not understood the value of the advice and technical cooperation of the office in Colombia in order to strengthen their efforts in areas relating to our mandate. It must be stated that, with some exceptions, the office in Colombia has not been consulted in the drawing up of proposed laws relating to human rights and international humanitarian law.

Annex II
Representative Cases of Human Rights Violations and Breaches of International Humanitarian Law

A. *Introduction*

1. The principal violations and breaches recorded by the office in Colombia of the High Commissioner during 2003 are incorporated here, including the modalities identified, those to whom they are attributed or who are considered to be responsible and the groups that were specifically affected. With respect to the investigations begun into a number of these occurrences or the progress made, the office in Colombia has not been able to obtain in a timely fashion the information requested from the Attorney-General's Office.

B. *Human rights*

Civil and political rights

(a) *The right to life*

2. This right was affected by extrajudicial executions, both individual and collective, and by death threats. Complaints have been made with respect to various extrajudicial executions directly attributed to the Security Forces. Examples include the executions of seven people, of whom two were minors, between February and September of from the indigenous communities of the Upper Atrato, in Lloró and Bagadó (Cihocó), which were attributed to members of the Army who, in almost all of these cases, presented the bodies as having been killed in combat. Another case refers to the execution of an individual in Arauquita (Arauca), in February, on the same day on which the victim had filed a complaint against members of the Army. The execution of a three-year-old girl in March in the community of San José de Apartadó that was attributed to members of the Army was also denounced.

3. Executions, both individual and collective, were committed by paramilitaries. Reliable information continued to be received that State responsibility was involved. Examples of responsibility due to omission include the massacre of 11 people in January in Tolima. Complaints were made with respect to collusion on the part of members of the National Police

due to links between them and paramilitary hired assassins in the massacre of five people in July in Saravena (Arauca), which occurred moments after the police had arrived. Some of the victims had been repeatedly detained by the police and stigmatized as collaborators of the guerrilla groups. Also, responsibility was attributed to the State due to omission or complicity on the part of members of the Security Forces, particularly in executions carried out this year in Viotá (Cundinamarca), in Tame and Saravena (Arauca), in Cajibío and Timbio (Cauca) and in the executions of Kankuamo indigenous people in Cesar. The homicides perpetrated by paramilitaries in the Comuna 13 of Medellín (Antioquia), involved responsibility on the part of the State due to omission and as a result of disregarding their duty to prevent violations and to protect the civilian population, considering the control and the strong military and police presence in the zone.

(b) *Right to personal integrity*

4. There was an increase recorded in the complaints of violations of this right due to acts of torture and cruel, inhuman or degrading treatment and the excessive use of force on the part of members of the Security Forces and government employees in the field of security, particularly in Bogotá and in the departments of Antioquia, Arauca and Tolima. The Ombudsman's Office recorded 374 complaints of violations of personal integrity. Complaints of torture on the part of members of the Army against various members of the Comunidad de Paz (Community of Peace) of San José de Apartadó (Antioquia) in March, and against a person in Viotá (Cundinamarca) in May are a source of concern. There were complaints in both cases that the aim had been to gather information and that the victims had to sign a document stating that they had been well treated.

5. Persons who were detained or imprisoned in the penitentiaries were also affected by these violations. It is pertinent here to mention the case of the torture and death of the inmate José Lara Lloreda in Peñas Blancas (Calarca, Quindío) jail and the torture of six prisoners along with the mistreatment of other prisoners and their families in the jail at San Isidro in Popayán, Cauca. Torture continues to be under-recorded, mainly because in various cases it is not denounced. In other cases, because it is associated with the death of the victim, torture is not recorded. In this sense, it must be pointed out that these acts along with rapes are rarely mentioned in forensic reports on deceased victims.

(c) *Right to individual freedom and personal safety*

6. The office in Colombia recorded an increase in complaints of forced disappearances and illegal or arbitrary detentions. Among the cases of forced disappearances attributed to the Security Forces, is the case of three young people in Granada (Antioquia) in January. There was also a complaint of joint action by members of the Security Forces and paramilitary groups in the events that led to the forced disappearance of two persons, in addition to the execution of others, in Cajamarca (Tolima) in November.

7. The office in Colombia of the High Commissioner recorded various complaints of forced disappearances perpetrated by the paramilitaries in zones controlled by the Security Forces and involving attribution of State responsibility due to omission, complicity or collusion on the part of public servants. These include the disappearance of a member of the Unión Patriótica in March in the Comuna 7 of Medellín (Antioquia) and that of six people in Corocito (Arauca) in February. The increase in forced disappearances carried out by paramilitaries in Barrancabermeja (Santander) and in the Comuna 13 of Medellín must be emphasized.

8. The office in Colombia received information on massive or individual arrests carried out by members of the Security Forces, particularly the Army, without prior court orders and not in situations of flagrante delicto. In other cases, the actions of the Attorney-General's Office were questioned because the arrest orders were drawn up after the arrests had been carried out or had been undertaken in an irregular manner because the persons had not been previously identified or the basis for their detention had been intelligence reports or mere identifications, which in some cases were made by hooded informants.[a] During the operation Estrella VI ("Star VI") in the Comuna 3 of Medellín (Antioquia) in January, 68 people were captured, of whom only 6 were the subject of arrest warrants. This operation was based on application of the concept of "flagrancy in the permanent crime of rebellion" a concept that is incompatible with international principles.[b] In the case of the 156 people detained during Operation "Ovejas" (Sucre) in August, complaints were made of the use of hooded informants and the drawing up of the warrants a posteriori. A prosecutor

[a] These same observations were made by the Prosecutor-General's Office in their special reports on the zones for rehabilitation and consolidation in Arauca and Sucre-Bolívar. See, for example, chapter II, point 7.2 (ii) of the latter report.

[b] According to this concept, because it is a permanent crime, a person accused of rebellion is found to be permanently in a situation of "flagrante delicto", without requiring application of such elements as immediacy, identification or individualization, or the possession of incriminating elements.

from the Attorney-General's Office subsequently ordered the release of these persons after being unable to find any elements to justify their arrest. Complaints were made to the effect that in the capture of more than 70 people in September on the part of the Security Forces and the Attorney-General's Office in Cartagena del Chairá (Caquetá), half of those detained did not have an outstanding arrest warrant and were accused based on information from intelligence and from the network of cooperating persons.

(d) *Right to due process*

9. There was an increase in denunciations of violations of due process resulting from disregard for independence and impartiality in the administration of justice, for procedural guarantees and for the principle of the presumption of innocence. A number of these actions occurred within the framework of the "democratic security" policy, in the context of arbitrary or illegal detentions, with the participation of the Attorney-General's Office and, on occasion, the Prosecutor General's Office.

10. There were complaints of violations of judicial independence and the autonomy of investigators who, due to their decisions or the course of their investigations, were removed from the case or from their posts. Such was the case of the prosecutor from the Attorney-General's Office charged with investigating the terrorist act in the Club El Nogal who was transferred to another office. In the above-mentioned case of Operation "Ovejas" (Sucre), the Attorney-General initially declared his intention to remove the prosecutor responsible for freeing the 128 people detained during this operation. He subsequently announced that he would be the subject of a disciplinary investigation, as he is one of the few prosecutors whose continuity in his post is protected by career status. In other cases, judicial independence was disregarded as a result of the persistence of investigations into human rights violations in the military justice system, such as the one undertaken by the 154th Military Criminal Investigating Magistrate's Office into the conduct of police agents in the Valle de Aburra (Antioquia) in the rape of a woman.

(e) *Right to freedom of movement and residence*

11. Forced displacements and illegitimate impediments to internal transit continue to be the gravest violations of this right. The office in Colombia was able to observe that, during the first months of this year, the civilian population of the Middle Atrato suffered from the imposition by the Military Forces of limitations and restrictions on freedom of movement as well as other impediments to the entry and exit of foodstuffs, pharmaceuticals, fuel

and construction materials. In April, members of the Army, the communities and the church reached an agreement to ease these restrictions.

(f) *Right to privacy and right to inviolability of the home*

12. Both during the time in which the state of exception was in force with the application of Decree 2002, as well as afterwards, these rights were affected by the carrying out of illegal and arbitrary raids and searches. These were undertaken without a court order or under the modality of "voluntary raids or searches", in which a court order is dispensed with, owing to the supposed authorization by the targets of these procedures. It is worth noting those carried out in the Comuna 13 of Medellín (Antioquia), in Saravena and Arauquita (Arauca), in the rural zones of Caquetá and Santander, and those undertaken in July by the Army in the Sabanetas reservation at El Tambo (Cauca). Complaints were also recorded with respect to violations of privacy in the carrying out of Army roadblocks (the taking of fingerprints and photographs), including cases of abuses committed against certain ethnic groups who were the victims of stigmatization, such as the indigenous populations of the Embera-Katíos (Córdoba) and of the Sierra Nevada de Santa Marta (Magdalena, La Guajira, Cesar).

C. *International humanitarian law*

(a) *Homicide and threats directed at protected persons*

13. The illegal armed groups continued to carry out homicides, both individual and collective, although lesser in number than in 2002. The massacre of seven people in Caldas (Antioquia), six of whom had their throats cut, and another that claimed the lives of five people in Suratá (Santander), both of which occurred in April, as well as that of five persons in a village near Sincelejo (Sucre) in August were attributed to the paramilitary groups. The January massacre of 17 people in three villages of San Carlos (eastern Antioquia) was attributed to FARC-EP.

14. In 2003, the paramilitaries and, increasingly, the guerrillas continued to make use of selective homicides and social cleansing as a military strategy. High rates of selective homicides were recorded in the Middle Magdalena, in the Montes de María (between Sucre and Bolívar), in Tolima, Antioquia, Meta, north Santander and Arauca. These were routine practices on the part of the paramilitaries in the Sierra Nevada de Santa Marta and specifically affected the Kankuamo indigenous people. In some cases, these communities were also the victims of homicides committed by FARC-

EP. The paramilitary groups also carried out a strategy of making their victims disappear and then killing them, as in Barrancabermeja (Santander). The murder of local officials in Arauca, Cauca, Caldas and Antioquia demonstrate the victimization of mayors, municipal representatives and town and city councillors as part of a strategy involving systematic attacks by FARC-EP and, to a lesser extent, the paramilitary groups, especially in Cundinamarca.

15. The office in Colombia of the High Commissioner also received complaints about homicides that were attributed to members of the Security Forces. For example, during *Operación Marcial* (eastern Antioquia) in March, the murder of two civilians, one of whom was a minor, was denounced, and in *Operación Emperador* in January in Granada (eastern Antioquia) a complaint was made with respect to the killing of four civilians, including a minor.

16. Death threats continued to be the most frequent means employed by the illegal armed groups to cause the displacement or subjugation of civilians, to take over their properties or to force them to make a financial contribution.

17. The office in Colombia also received various complaints of threats to the civilian population that were attributed to the Army, such as those related to the above-mentioned operations in eastern Antioquia, or to an operation carried out in Bolívar (Cauca) in February.

(b) *Attacks on the civilian population and indiscriminate attacks*

18. The humanitarian principles of distinction, limitation, proportionality and immunity of the civilian population continued to be violated by all of the parties to the conflict and particularly by the illegal armed groups. FARC-EP have resorted to the indiscriminate use of explosive devices, killing many civilians. The death of five civilians, including two minors, were recorded in Saravena (Arauca) in August as a result of the detonation of a car bomb directed at a military patrol. The same thing occurred in Granada (Antioquia), claiming the lives of three minors and one adult and leaving 14 civilians wounded. In other cases, FARC-EP used the civilian population as human shields or for transporting explosive devices. In Fortul (Arauca) in April, a minor died when the bicycle he was riding exploded near a military checkpoint. Complaints were made of guerrilla attacks on the civilian population, especially on the part of FARC-EP, such as in the municipal centres of Jambaló and Toribío (Cauca). A policeman was killed and three civilians were wounded in the locality of Ricaurte (Nariño).

19. The paramilitary groups also continued to carry out attacks and indiscriminate attacks on the civilian population, such as one that took the lives of four people in Tierralta (Córdoba), in May. An attack by AUC on the indigenous reservation at Aponte (Nariño) in May, in which there was a complaint of joint action with members of the Army, resulted in one person dead and various wounded.

20. The office in Colombia of the High Commissioner received reports of attacks on the civilian population and indiscriminate attacks attributed to members of the Military Forces. Reports were made of joint action between members of the Army and AUC in April during an operation in the Sierra Nevada de Santa Marta (La Guajira), with respect to which there were reports of the killing of a Wiwa indigenous person, whose body was found dismembered, as well as of threats, mistreatment, looting and the desecration of tombs. Other examples were connected to the above-mentioned *Operación Emperador* and *Operación Marcial.* The latter operation also caused a massive displacement. There were cases of indiscriminate aerial bombardment and machine-gunning that damaged civilian property in Cauca, in February and September, as well as civilian dead and wounded in El Carmen (north Santander), in February and in *Operación Independencia* (Arauca), in July.

(c) *Acts of terrorism*

21. These acts were part of the systematic strategy of the guerrillas, particularly FARC-EP. Various cases were attributed to the latter, such as the explosion of a car bomb in a shopping centre next to the Attorney-General's Office in Medellín (Antioquia) that took the lives of 5 persons, including a minor, while wounding 41, and the February car bomb at the Club Nogal in Bogotá that killed 36 and wounded more than 160, many of them minors. Other examples were the explosion of a house bomb in Neiva (Huila) in February during a raid by members of the Attorney-General's Office and the National Police that killed 15, including a number of minors, as well as wounding more than 50 others, and the explosion of a bomb in Puerto Rico (Meta) in August that claimed the lives of 5 people, including 2 minors and left 46 wounded. FARC-EP were also blamed for the detonation of a house bomb in Chita (Boyaca) in September that killed 8 and wounded 20 and for the attack in Florencia (Caquetá) in September that took the lives of 12 persons, among whom 2 were minors. An attack on a commercial centre in Cœcuta (north Santander) in March, which caused the deaths of 13 people and more than 60 wounded, was attributed to ELN.

22. The paramilitary groups also carried out actions and threats aimed at creating terror among the civilian population, such as in the case of an incursion into Ituango (Antioquia) in June that included acts of pillage and violence in a church.

(d) *Torture and other attacks on personal dignity*

23. Torture continues to be practised by the illegal armed groups. There were complaints of the torture and killing of two peasants by paramilitary forces in El Salado, El Tarra (north Santander) in February as well as the use of torture on the part of paramilitaries in the Comuna 13 in Medellín (Antioquia) and in Viotá (Cundinamarca). The cadavers found in various mass graves and individual graves and whose deaths are attributed to the paramilitary forces, showed signs of torture and mutilation, particularly in Tolima, Arauca and Antioquia. The torture and subsequent deaths of two people, including an unarmed soldier on leave in Turbo (Antioquia) in January are attributed to FARC-EP.

(e) *Hostage taking*

24. The guerrilla groups and, to a lesser extent, the paramilitary groups, have continued with the practice of taking hostages, although a decrease was recorded. It affected diverse sectors of the population along with departmental and municipal officials, including the Peace Adviser of Meta, who was taken hostage by FARC-EP in October. According to the office of the Vice-President, during the first nine months of the year, the responsibility of this group in the taking of 545 hostages was established, along with that of ELN with respect to 281 others and the paramilitary groups in 149 cases.

25. On occasion, FARC-EP killed their hostages, as in the case of the Governor of Antioquia, Guillermo Gaviria Correa, and his Peace Adviser, Gilberto Echeverri Mejía, along with eight captured members of the military forces, during a rescue operation mounted by the Military Forces in Urrao (Antioquia) in May. This was also the case in the deaths of Helmut and Doris Bickenback in June and that of a Japanese citizen, Chikao Muramatsu, in November.

(f) *Forced displacements*

26. The illegal armed groups have continued to cause forced displacements, both individual and collective. The paramilitary forces were respon-

sible for massive displacements in El Tarra (north Santander) and Viotá (Cundinamarca) in April. The massive displacement in Argelia (eastern Antioquia) in June was attributed to FARC-EP. There were complaints in some cases of displacements caused by members of the Security Forces, such as during *Operación Marcial* in San Francisco (eastern Antioquia) in March.

(g) *Children who are victims of the armed conflict*

27. Children continued to be the victims of hostage-taking, recruitment, the use of anti-personnel mines, forced displacement, indiscriminate attacks and acts of terrorism on the part of the illegal armed groups. The *Fundación País Libre* ("Free Country Foundation") recorded 243 children kidnapped as of September. The office in Colombia received information on various cases of recruitment of indigenous minors in Cauca by FARC-EP and in Cesar on the part of ELN. The paramilitary forces also recruited young people, in many cases in exchange for remuneration, or they made use of them for investigating or following certain persons in exchange for money or clothing, such as in Barrancabermeja (Santander).

28. The office in Colombia received reports of the use of minors by the Army as informants or within the framework of intelligence operations, such as in the case of minors belonging to the Esperanza de Dios ("God's Hope") humanitarian zone in the Lower Atrato (Chocó) in May.

(h) *Women victims of the armed conflict*

29. The office in Colombia received information about the diverse forms of violence, particularly sexual, with which the illegal armed groups afflict women in different areas of the country, such as Córdoba and Tolima, on the part of the paramilitary forces, as well as in Putumayo, where cases of sexual slavery by the guerrillas were denounced. The illegal armed groups, and especially the paramilitaries, continued threatening women and their organizations, as in the case of the leaders of the National Association of Indigenous and Peasant Women of Colombia (ANMUCIC, from its Spanish initials) and of the Popular Women's Organization (OFP). In this last case, it is pertinent to point out the murder of human rights defender Esperanza Amaris Miranda in Barrancabermeja (Santander) in October. Women are often the victims of violence on the part of the illegal armed groups when they have a family member in an opposition group, or are viewed as having contacts with members of an opposing group, or for a personal relationship with a member. The case of the killing in April of a schoolteacher in Cocorná (Antioquia) by ELN was observed with con-

cern. Complaints of the deaths of sexual professionals with sexually transmitted diseases at the hands of illegal groups in north Santander are a source of concern.

30. There were also complaints recorded of rapes on the part of members of the Security Forces in Antioquia, Chocó and Cauca. At the same time, judicial underreporting of sexual crimes persists, because the women tend not to denounce them out of fear, modesty or mistrust of the judicial system. The lack of entries in the forensic reports, as we have already stated, is an additional factor that contributes to impunity.

(i) *Attacks on the medical mission*

31. The members of the medical mission were affected by homicides, threats and harassments on the part of the illegal armed groups, especially FARC-EP, in the departments of Arauca and Cauca. The office in Colombia recorded the disappearance and subsequent homicide of a doctor in March and the planting of an explosive device in a hospital in September, as well as the killing of a hospital director in Santander de Quilichao (Cauca) during the same month. Cases of attacks on ambulances must also be mentioned, mainly on the part of FARC-EP, as in Cocorná (Antioquia) in October.

(j) *Attacks on civilian property*

32. The guerrilla groups continued their attacks on civilian property and on State infrastructure. According to the Office of the Vice-President, infrastructure attacks decreased by 35 per cent in the period up until September, destruction of bridges by 66 per cent and of electrical towers by 61 per cent. In contrast, attacks on oil pipelines increased by 61 per cent.

33. FARC-EP caused damage to civilian property in repeated attacks using explosive devices, such as the one at Coloso (Sucre) in April that left the local aqueduct in ruins. The illegal armed groups committed acts of pillage and destruction of civilian property, such as the pillage committed by paramilitaries in Abejorral (Antioquia) in October. In other cases, these groups forced civilians to sign over title to their farms, threatening to kill them if they refused.

34. There were also cases of pillage attributed to the Military Forces in operations in eastern Antioquia and the Guajira. There were also complaints made of damage to civilian property in indiscriminate operations carried out by the Air Force in Cauca in February 2003.

(k) *Use of anti-personnel mines*

35. Massive use of mines on the part of the illegal armed groups continued to be recorded. FARC, ELN and the paramilitary groups have been those principally responsible, in that order. According to the Observatory for Anti-personnel Mines, a large number of incidents continued to occur in 2003, with 253 new victims (69 dead) between January and August, of whom 87 were civilians.

36. The illegal armed groups have continued to use home-made mines that are difficult to detect, such as home-made plastic mines. It has been reported that FARC-EP indiscriminately planted mines and booby traps in Piamonte (Cauca), locating them in private residences, on outlying paths and heavily travelled roads. In May, mines wounded one person in this municipality and, hours later a young girl was killed and her child disfigured in the same place due to failure to take immediate measures for posting warnings or re-routing transit. In another episode perpetrated by FARC-EP, 11 members of the military were killed and 8 more wounded when they came across a minefield in Aracataca (Magdalena) in March.

Annex III
Legislative policy[a]

Introduction

1. Legislative policy has been closely linked to the goals and implementation of the so-called policy for democratic security. The Government emphasized that "strengthening democracy requires not only effective institutions . . . and a judicial system that provides support for the exercise of rights and liberties. It equally supposes that all of the State's actions will be subject to this organization. . . . This is the guarantee that the constitutional order and respect for human rights will prevail over the arbitrary actions and abuses of the illegal armed organizations".[b] Nonetheless, various regulations and projects turned out to be incompatible with interna-

[a] This annex complements the High Commissioner's report on the human rights situation in Colombia.

[b] See the document entitled "*Política de Defensa y Seguridad Democrática*" ("Democratic Defense and Security Policy"), Office of the President of the Republic, Ministry of Defense, 2003, p. 15, para. 12.

tional principles in terms of restrictions on basic rights and liberties, and imply changes to the Constitution.

2. On 5 February 2003, the Government approved Legislative Decree 245, by means of which it extended the state of internal commotion (state of emergency). On 29 April of this same year, the Constitutional Court issued ruling C-327/03, in which it declared that this decree was unconstitutional. Faced with this situation, the Government considered it necessary to seek constitutional modifications with the aim of implementing certain restrictive measures on rights and liberties that it deemed necessary in order to achieve the objectives of its security policy. Approval of the National Development Plan was another of the Government's legislative priorities in 2003.

3. Various legislative projects aimed at modifying the Constitution were presented. Proposed laws were submitted, one known as the "Antiterrorist Statute" and another that attempted to remove jurisdiction from the Procurator General's Office to specifically examine disciplinary violations committed by members of the Armed Forces.[c] Another such proposed law aimed at decreeing structural reforms in the organization of the State. Projects were also presented for modification of the penal code, the code of criminal procedure, the penitentiary and prison code, the Organic Statute of the Attorney-General's Office, the Statutory Law on the Administration of Justice as well as with respect to some regulations regarding compulsory military service. Additionally, other proposed legislation aimed at the inclusion of new regulations, such as the National Statute For Countering Terrorism, a proposed law dealing with national defence and security and the proposed Statutory Law on the Re-Incorporation of Members of Armed Groups. Law 418 was also regulated by means of Decree 128 of 2003.

4. In a parallel initiative, the Government promoted adoption of a referendum that proposed amendments to 15 articles of the Constitution in the economic and political fields. After the referendum, whose proposals were almost entirely rejected, the Government pushed forward a series of proposed laws in order to obtain legislative approval of the unapproved proposals.

5. A number of these legislative projects have been the object of analysis and observations on the part of the office in Colombia of the United Nations High Commissioner for Human Rights pursuant to its mandate to advise and ensure that projects that adopt or modify norms be respectful of international norms and obligations.

[c] Its sponsor withdrew this project due to the fact that it was unable to fulfil the terms contained in the Constitution for its approval during the current legislative session.

Progress and difficulties relating to the ratification of international treaties

6. In the legislative field, it is worth noting the adoption of laws by means of which different international treaties have been internally approved as a prior step towards their ratification. Among these, it is worth mentioning Law 800 of 13 March 2003, by means of which the Protocol to Prevent, Suppress and Punish Trafficking in Persons, Especially Women and Children was approved, supplementing the United Nations Convention against Transnational Organized Crime; Law 833 of 10 July 2003, by means of which the Optional Protocol to the Convention on the Rights of the Child on the involvement of children in armed conflict was approved; and Law 837 of 16 July 2003, by means of which the International Convention against the Taking of Hostages was approved. It is also important to point to the adoption of Law 823 of 10 July 2003 containing rules with respect to equal opportunities for men and women.

7. In spite of these important legislative initiatives, it must be mentioned that, with the exception of the Optional Protocol to the Convention on the Rights of the Child relative to the sale of children, child prostitution, and child pornography, they have not been accompanied by action on the part of the Government to deposit instruments of ratification and assume the corresponding international obligations, in accordance with the recommendations of the High Commissioner and other international bodies. Ratification is thus pending of ILO Convention No. 182 (1999) on the worst forms of child labour (Law 704 of 2001); the Inter-American Convention on the Forced Disappearance of Persons (Law 707 of 2001); and the Inter-American Convention on the Elimination of All Forms of Discrimination against Persons with Disabilities, (Law 762 of 2002). Also, the process of approval for the Optional Protocols to the Convention for the Elimination of All Forms of Discrimination against Women and the Convention against Torture and Other Cruel, Inhuman and Degrading Treatment or Punishment has yet to be initiated. Nor has the Government promoted actions aimed at recognition of the competence of the Committee against Torture and the Committee on Racial Discrimination to examine individual communications.

Analysis of certain projects and regulations

(a) *Regulation of Benefits for the Demobilized (Decree 128)*

8. Decree 128, of 22 January 2003, regulates Law 418 of 1997, extended and modified by Law 548 of 1999 and Law 782 of 2002, with respect to re-incorporation into civil society of demobilized members of outlaw groups (guerrilla groups and self-defence groups). In the matter of legal benefits for the demobilized, the decree refers to regulations established under Law 418 and its amendments for the granting of pardons, conditional stays of enforcement of penalties, discontinuance of proceedings and preclusion of investigation or inhibitory orders, limiting them to political and related crimes and excluding heinous crimes. Analysis of the text raises certain questions regarding the fight against impunity and the rights of victims to truth, justice and reparation, in that it makes no explicit reference to these international obligations of the State.

(b) *"Draft law for penal alternatives"*

9. On 21 August 2003, the Government presented the draft Statutory Law 85 of 2003 to the Senate, which proposes to award legal benefits to those members of the illegal armed groups who are unable to benefit from the regulations contained in Decree 128, due to their responsibility for grave crimes, which include conduct constituting war crimes and crimes against humanity. The project establishes the possibility of suspension of prison sentences and proposes a series of measures that it calls "alternative penalties".

10. The office in Colombia of the High Commissioner, by means of a communiqué issued on 8 September 2003 and during the public hearing carried out on 23 September 2003 in the First Committee of the Senate, provided observations regarding the incompatibility of its dispositions with international obligations. Among these, the project allows the State to suspend the execution of prison sentences of persons who have not even begun to serve the sentences imposed for the commission of heinous crimes; it allows the application of so-called alternative punishments instead of imprisonment to those responsible for international crimes that are so lenient and of such short duration that they violate the principles of just retribution and proportionality in penal sanctions. It does not clearly recognize the State's obligation with respect to reparation when they are not remedied by the party directly responsible for the crimes; it establishes reparation mechanisms that do not adequately compensate or indemnify the victims; at the same time it does not adopt measures to

impede the victimizers from benefiting from the suspension of the penalties before the victims have received effective reparation. The alternative punishments included in the project are neither quantitatively nor qualitatively comparable to being deprived of liberty, nor to the gravity of the crimes, reason for which they do not respect the principle of proportionality of punishments. All of these belong to the realm of what in comparative criminal law are referred to as accessory penalties, and which are imposed as a compliment to the main penalty and, therefore, do not replace it.

11. The office in Colombia also commented on the opportunity, convenience and modalities of the proposal. Among these, it raised various questions considering that the proposal refers not only to members of illegal armed groups that have signed peace agreements, in that it includes among the beneficiaries members "who individually and voluntarily give up their arms", a reason for which it is not circumscribed as a corollary to the peace negotiations. In this respect, the office in Colombia stated that the concession of certain benefits to isolated persons, without reference to negotiations and without establishing serious commitments with the illegal armed organizations with respect to future behaviour, does not necessarily strengthen efforts aimed at the search for a lasting peace and the achievement of national reconciliation. The office in Colombia also presented elements for reflection on this topic regarding the future.

(c) *"Antiterrorist Statute"*

12. The draft Legislative Act 223 of 2003 of the Lower Chamber and 015 of the Senate, known as the "Antiterrorist Statute", was presented by the Government on 24 April 2003 with the aim of modifying articles 15, 24, 28 and 250 of the Constitution in order to fight terrorism. In its articles, the proposal provides the Military Forces with judicial police powers, in contradiction to the expressed recommendation of the High Commissioner. It also orders restrictions on the right to privacy and the right to appeals and provides for administrative detentions and other procedures without a court order. The project was approved on 10 December. The office in Colombia of the High Commissioner sent two messages to the members of Congress and participated in a public hearing held in the House of Representatives on 23 September 2003. The office in Colombia has voiced several objections to the project, as follow below.

13. The international organs for the protection of human rights have stated that the exercise of the functions of judicial police by persons of a military character violates the principles of independence and impartiality in the administration of justice, as enunciated in international instruments

ratified by Colombia. The office in Colombia also observed that this proposal concedes faculties to the administrative authorities whereby, without a previous court order, they can carry out detentions as well as intercept or search correspondence and other private communications. In accordance with that stipulated in international norms and jurisprudence, jurisdiction in these matters must belong to the public servants of the judicial branch. The office in Colombia considered the establishment of excessively long time periods for submitting administrative detentions of persons deprived of their liberty to judicial control "in cases of terrorism" to be incompatible with international obligations. At the same time, there are observations with respect to the applicability of habeas corpus during this period. The office in Colombia emphasized that the right to submit this type of measure to the competent judicial authorities must be applicable at all times and without temporary restrictions.

(d) *National Statute for Countering Terrorism*

14. The Senate's draft Statutory Law 18 of 2003, by means of which an antiterrorist statute is created, provides for new crimes and increases the punishments for crimes perpetrated with terrorist objectives and in support of terrorism. At the same time, it modifies certain penal classifications, such as terrorism, or the management of terrorist resources. This project includes a number of crimes that are not necessarily related to terrorism and constitute breaches of international humanitarian law, thus identifying these breaches of international humanitarian law (IHL) with crimes related to terrorism. The office in Colombia declared that, given the particular circumstances and gravity of terrorist acts, it is of fundamental importance that the strategies and policies of the fight against terrorism be specifically oriented to this type of conduct and that it be differentiated from others that constitute violations of IHL. The project also contains dispositions that raise questions in the area of due process and judicial guarantees, particularly those related to the autonomy of the investigating prosecutor, the right of the accused to defend themselves, of discrimination against foreigners and of insufficient clarity in certain criminal classifications.

(e) *"Law of national security and defense"*

15. The Senate's draft Law 022 of 2003, which contains rules on the policy for national security and defence, includes certain dispositions that could endanger the principle of distinction. It is important to establish clear limits with respect to the solidarity and support provided by the civilian population in the task of national security and defence, so as not to involve

the civilian population in the armed conflict and so that the principle of distinction is not placed in question. This signifies a limit on the imposition of duties on private individuals in the field of public order. Clear separation between the actions, duties and responsibilities of authorities and those of the civilian population in relation to security and defence also permits and facilitates concrete application of the humanitarian principle of distinction.

(f) *"Reform of the justice system"*

16. On 29 October 2002, the Government submitted proposed Legislative Act 10 of 2002, which had the goal of modifying certain dispositions of the Constitution with respect to the administration of justice. The draft law proposed modification of the tutela (action in search of relief of a violation of a constitutional right), making it inapplicable for the protection of economic, social and cultural rights, including the rights of children and young people, the right to healthcare, the rights of the aged or the right to review of arbitrary judicial decisions that had been handed down without recognizing fundamental rights. It also proposed to limit the faculties of the Constitutional Court for guaranteeing the supremacy of the Constitution, restricting its competence and the effects of its decisions. Lastly, the draft proposed elimination of the Superior Council of the Judiciary and the creation of a new body that would be charged with administration of the judicial branch and would include members of the executive branch.

17. The draft law was later shelved because it was unable to fulfil the terms for its approval.[d] The Government declared its intention to submit the project to Congress when it had obtained the approval of the High Courts. The Constitutional Court publicly stated that the draft "eliminates the effectiveness of the tutela . . . it impedes the Constitutional Court from defending the supremacy of the Constitution and from protecting people from arbitrary acts and abuses of power, by drastically restricting its competences, all of which gravely affects the principle of the social and democratic rule of law. Additionally, there are proposed reforms in the project that go against the autonomy and independence of the judicial branch".[e] The new Minister of the Interior and Justice has stated that the Government will present this draft next year.

[d] The Colombian Constitution mandates that legislative projects aimed at modifying the Constitution must be approved in eight debates during two ordinary and consecutive sessions (from 20 July to 16 December and from 16 March to 20 June).

[e] Constitutional Court, press communiqué, 29 April 2003.

(g) *Penal and Criminal Procedural Codes*

18. On 20 July 2003, proposed Laws 01 of the Senate and the Lower Chamber, were presented to modify the penal and criminal procedure codes and introduce the accusatory system. Of concern is the fact that the democratic aspiration to implement an accusatory penal procedure, as a contribution towards more transparent and democratic administration of justice, appears frustrated by the presence in this comprehensive reform proposal of such elements as the evident imbalance between the accuser (the Attorney-General's Office) and the defence, the secret character of an important phase of the investigation and the widespread use of preventive detention.

19. The model suggested by the reforms is not in accord with a criminal justice policy capable of guaranteeing the civil liberties of the individual versus the arbitrary exercise of State power. Nor is it in concurrence with the principle of minimum intervention, the acknowledgement of absolute limits for the exercise of the power of the criminal justice system, control over the institutions in charge of exercising punitive actions, or with respect to dignified treatment for people deprived of their liberty. In general terms, one notes an incongruity between the elements that provide guarantees, and the guiding rules that recognize principles in accordance with the State's international obligations, on the one hand, and the changes contained in the articles, on the other. If they are not approved before 20 June 2004 due to a lack of consensus, the President of the Republic, endowed with extraordinary powers, can approve and enact these codes.

(h) *Penitentiary and Prison Code*

20. On 20 July 2003, the proposed Senate Law 03, which proposes modification of the Penitentiary and Prison Code, was submitted. This draft law is directly linked to the accusatory system with respect to criminal procedural reform in Colombia. The draft lacks documentary support in the form of an empirical study on the problems afflicting the prison and penitentiary system. Even when it gives formal recognition to the basic rights of persons deprived of their liberty, it repeatedly emphasizes "the limitations inherent to their special condition". On the other hand, the project delegates regulation of many aspects of the prisons' and penitentiaries' internal regulations to the administrative authority. In addition, the project announces restructuring and fundamental changes in the entity that coordinates the national prison and penitentiary system without there being any mention of the authority or entity responsible for this reform.

(i) *National Development Plan*

21. The National Development Plan (NDP) was adopted on 26 June 2003 by means of Law 812. NDP sets out State policy in the economic, social and environmental fields. In a general way, it could indicate that the Government has given priority to the areas of social investment, democratic security and economic revival. The largest item in social investment, comprising 61 per cent, is directed at the social sector. According to NDP, social investment is composed of monies assigned to healthcare, employment, education, culture, housing, basic medical treatment and royalties. At the same time, democratic security and economic reactivation constitute important concerns for the Government at the moment when expenditures are allocated. The budget for social investment represents slightly more than 11 per cent of the total budget.

22. It should be noted that the Government is not sufficiently investing in areas where there are human rights concerns in order to effectively improve their situation. This can probably be explained by the fact that the Government's policies during this year have not given this topic a sufficiently comprehensive and priority treatment, nor have they done so with respect to the High Commissioner's recommendations. At the same time, the lack of a national plan for action on human rights can be another factor that led to this weakness.

Annex IV
Activities of the Office in Colombia of the United Nations High Commissioner for Human Rights

1. The High Commissioner for Human Rights of the office in Colombia continued to carry out its mandate in the area of observation, advice, technical cooperation, promotion and dissemination.

Observation

2. The office in Colombia of the High Commissioner fulfils its task with respect to observation based on thematic and geographical priorities that enable analytical and systematic follow-up on the situation of human rights and international humanitarian law in Colombia.

3. During 2003, 168 field missions were carried out and 1,144 complaints were received, of which 936 were admitted.

4. Field missions and the permanent presence in the branch offices in Cali and Medellín, enable the office in Colombia to follow up on the

regional and local situation as well as to provide advice to the authorities and institutions of civil society in the field of human rights and international humanitarian law while accompanying local processes undertaken in the areas included in the mandate. In order to facilitate this work, the office in Colombia of the High Commissioner will open a new branch office in Bucaramanga in January 2004.

5. Additionally, although it is difficult to measure their impact, field missions fulfil the purpose of promoting preventive and protective measures for the communities. These visits, carried out mostly with the Colombian authorities, are made to zones in which the presence of the State has been traditionally weak or non-existent.

Advisory services

6. The office in Colombia of the High Commissioner participated in numerous activities related to advising State entities and civil society. In addition to providing documents relating to the compatibility of proposed legislation with international norms, it provided the authorities with advice in the definition of policies and programmes and stimulated follow-up on recommendations in committees and other inter-institutional bodies. Periodic dialogue was established with the authorities, in particular with the Office of the Vice-President, with various ministers, members of Congress and judicial and control bodies. The office in Colombia provided quality and impartial advice to State institutions and civil society organizations. It promoted international human rights and international humanitarian law instruments through forums, workshops and seminars.

7. The office in Colombia aided in substantive and logistical preparation for the carrying out of missions in October 2003 to Colombia by the Special Rapporteurs on the right to education and on contemporary forms of racism, racial discrimination, xenophobia and related forms of intolerance. It issued two publications that afforded a better understanding of their mandates and the fields in which they work.

Technical assistance and cooperation

8. In order to fulfil its mandate to advise governmental and non-governmental institutions, the office in Colombia began with the supposition that initiatives for technical cooperation must promote the active participation of these institutions in tasks that imply respect, protection and guarantees for human rights. International recommendations formulated on this subject, and especially those of the United Nations High Commissioner for

Human Rights, constituted the basis for the office in Colombia's development of diverse projects for institutional strengthening and training.

9. In November, the office in Colombia of the High Commissioner signed a letter of understanding with the Office of the Attorney-General aimed at carrying out a project for institutional strengthening, in which the recommendations formulated and addressed to that institution by the High Commissioner were gathered together.

(a) *National Plan of Action on Human Rights*

10. The office in Colombia of the High Commissioner received a first draft proposal for a concerted National Plan of Action on Human Rights from the Presidential Programme for the Promotion, Respect and Guarantee of Human Rights and the Application of International Humanitarian Law. The office in Colombia has shared its observations with the Office of the Vice-President with respect to this document and has offered its technical cooperation and advice.

(b) *Institutional strengthening*

11. The studies carried out by the office in Colombia in a number of important State institutions, and the recommendations contained in them, have been the subject of accompaniment and follow-up aimed at contributing to their implementation.

1. *Ombudsman's Office*

12. *National Office of the Ombudsman (DNDP)*: Based on its study of the civil criminal programme of the Public Ombudsman, four areas of work were developed during the first half of 2003: (a) technical advice in drawing up a study of the functioning of the public defender; (b) establishment of a permanent national observatory on deprivation of liberty in the national sphere; (c) adoption of a system for management and control to enable the measurement of quality, promptness and effectiveness of the service, and (d) technical assistance in the fields of internal regulation and legislative proposals.

13. The office in Colombia has provided advice to the National Office of the Ombudsman regarding legal concepts related to the right to legal defence. In the context of penal reform, it contributed analytical documents comparing the different experiences in Latin America as regards the figure of the public defender. With respect to the proposed legislation on

the National System for Public Defenders, the office in Colombia analysed the proposal of the Ombudsman's Office and made contributions and observations in this respect.

14. *National Directorate for Receiving and Processing Complaints*: The office in Colombia completed its *Manual de Conductas Violatorias de Derechos Humanos* (Manual on Conduct in Violation of Human Rights). This document incorporates national and international jurisprudence and legislation in this field, with the aim of improving the classification that the Ombudsman's Office makes with respect to conduct reported to it that constitutes human rights violations and infractions of international humanitarian law.

2. *Office of the Procurator General*

15. The Procurator General issued the document "*Función preventiva de la Procuraduría en materia de derechos humanos*" ("Preventive function of the Office of the Procurator General in the field of human rights"), drawn up within the framework of the agreement for technical cooperation signed with the office in Colombia. This document has been widely disseminated within the Office of the Procurator as the basis for the work of the institution's employees in the area of prevention.

16. As a follow-up to the study made of the role of the Procurator's Office in disciplinary actions, the office in Colombia drew up the *Guía práctica de pruebas para las investigaciones disciplinarias por violaciones de derechos humanos e infracciones al derecho internacional humanitario* ("Practical guide to evidence in disciplinary investigations for human rights violations and breaches of international humanitarian law"). This document is aimed at public servants charged with investigating human rights violations and establishes guidelines and parameters for action that permit prompt, exhaustive and impartial action.

3. *Inter-institutional project on the situation of persons deprived of their liberty*

17. This project is aimed at strengthening the Office of the Procurator, the Ombudsman's Office, the Ministry of Justice and the National Institute of Penitentiaries and Prisons, with the goal of endowing their work with greater impact in improving the living conditions of persons deprived of their liberty. The project was initiated in July 2003 with co-financing from the European Union.

18. With respect to the Office of the Procurator, the office in Colombia of the High Commissioner has provided advice to the Delegate for Prevention

in the Field of Human Rights and Ethnic Affairs in drawing up thematic documents that serve as inputs for the adoption of instructions for internal coordination as well as in the development of a policy for protection and prevention in the field of imprisonment.

19. The Ministry of Justice and the National Institute for Penitentiaries and Prisons (INPEC for its Spanish initials) have facilitated the work of the office in Colombia with all of their offices with the aim of identifying the areas that are to receive assistance and advice as part of the project. Visits to 16 prisons at all levels have been carried out in order to provide suitable advice with respect to their needs. Additionally, a study was completed of the National Penitentiary School and the training of penitentiary personnel in general, a document that will be jointly analysed with INPEC authorities.

20. The Ombudsman's Office has accompanied various visits that were undertaken and has begun a process of active intervention with the Delegate for Criminal Policy and the Regional Offices of the Ombudsman in order to formulate an institutional strategy that will permit the strengthening of this control organ in the field of penitentiaries and prisons.

(c) *Training in human rights and international humanitarian law*

21. Training in the field of human rights and international humanitarian law for governmental institutions and civil society organizations, as well as for the agencies of the United Nations system, continues to be a very important activity for the office in Colombia. The development of techniques for teaching these subjects has made it possible to update this teaching and involve the recipients more closely with human rights in an open and active manner. With respect to the publications that support this training, updates were made of compilations of international human rights law, international humanitarian law and international criminal law.

22. *Training for public servants*: The office in Colombia, within the framework of agreements signed with diverse State institutions, has carried out courses and workshops for training in human rights and international humanitarian law with: (a) 7 congressmen, 30 advisers and collaborators from this branch; (b) 357 public servants from the entities charged with supervising the legality of actions on the part of the Government (Office of the Procurator, Ombudsman's Office and the municipal ombudsmen); (c) 34 military penal judges; (d) 80 directors and aspiring directors of prisons and penitentiaries, and 60 guards and custodial and supervisory staff from the INPEC; (e) 141 magistrates, judges and prosecutors from the College of Judges and Prosecutors of Antioquia; and (f) 52 members of the network of trainers of the justice sector.

23. *Training for municipal ombudsmen*: During the period 2002–2003, 90 per cent of the country's municipal ombudsmen have been the beneficiaries of the training programme in human rights, which contributed towards strengthening the important work carried out by these functionaries. The populations of 980 of the country's 1,098 municipalities have benefited from the presence of a local public servant who is more able to provide them with representation and defence in the field of human rights. This year, 16 training workshops, 4 in evaluation and validation and a national forum on municipal ombudsmen were carried out.

24. The programme benefits from the inter-institutional effort represented by the agreement signed between the Office of the Procurator, the Ombudsman's Office and the Office in Colombia of the High Commissioner, with co-financing on the part of the European Union.

25. The project intends to invigorate the functions fulfilled by the municipal ombudsmen in defence of human rights. A sense of belonging with the State Procurator's offices has been encouraged among municipal ombudsmen and joint actions between the Office of the Procurator and the Ombudsman's Office aimed at strengthening this institution regionally and locally, have been promoted.

26. The production of teaching tools has facilitated the Municipal Ombudsmen's work of dissemination, prevention and protection of human rights. The Institute for Studies of the State Procurator's offices will be entrusted with all of these tools and will undertake the future formation of municipal ombudsmen.

27. *International symposium on human rights and international humanitarian law*: The College of Judges and Prosecutors of Antioquia, with the support of the office in Colombia and the Embassy of Sweden, carried out a symposium in Medellín that was attended by 150 participants and included presentations by distinguished national and international speakers.

28. *Programme of scholarships for human rights defenders*: The office in Colombia of the High Commissioner, the Universidad Alcalá de Henares of Spain and the American University of the United States awarded five scholarships for human rights studies to human rights defenders and public servants.

29. *Civil society and the Church*: A basic course on human rights and national protection mechanisms was given in Rivera (Huila) to 30 priests, religious workers and lay people from the diocese of San Vicente del Caguan and the diocese of Florencia. At the same time, the office in Colombia and the Centre for Research, Training and Information for the Amazon Service has agreed to execute the project "Training for pastoral agents of the diocese of Florencia and the Apostolic Vicariate of San Vicente del Caguan-Puerto Leguizamo from the perspective of rights".

30. The office in Colombia and the organization *Planeta Paz* ("Peace Planet") drew up a communication manual that will be published in early 2004. Also, a document was written on the right to information for low-income sectors of society, a document that was used in the preliminary work of the World Conference on the right to communication held in late 2003.

31. *Global Programme "Assisting Communities Together (ACT)"*: Seven projects for training and promotion in human rights were executed in the departments of Nariño, Arauca, Boyacá, Chocó, Antioquia, Caldas and Bolívar.

32. *United Nations system*: In fulfilment of the Plan for Action contained in the Secretary-General of the United Nations' reform programme, the office in Colombia has initiated a close working relationship with the Resident Coordinator and the representatives of the system's agencies in order to gradually incorporate human rights as a central focus of its programmes, plans and activities. Four courses for training and up-dating in human rights, humanitarian law and international criminal law were provided to 79 United Nations system employees.

Information, promotion and dissemination

33. With the goal of reaching the most remote and isolated populations, an agreement was signed with the Radio Nederland Training Center. The office in Colombia received 2,000 CDs containing children's stories about human rights, which are disseminated by 300 community radio stations throughout the country through the radio programme *Naciones Unidas Manos Amigas* (United Nations, Friendly Hands).

34. Among the publications created by the office in Colombia, it is worth mentioning the 5,000 copies of *Compilación de Derecho Penal Internacional* (Compilation of International Criminal Law); 3,000 copies of the *Informe annual* (Annual Report); 20,000 newspaper supplements of the *Recomendaciones para Colombia 2003* (Recommendations for Colombia 2003); 20,000 copies of the pocket edition of the Universal Declaration of Human Rights; 40,000 copies of the Universal Declaration (children's version); and 10,000 copies of the calendar *Colombia: Imágenes y realidades 2004* (Colombia: Images and Realities 2004) were printed for nationwide distribution. The total number of copies of publications of the office in Colombia distributed throughout the territory of Colombia reached 100,000.

35. The office in Colombia participated in numerous activities (seminars, forums, workshops and conferences) and was present at the Bogotá Book Fair where all of its publications were for sale. Within the framework of its work with the media, the office in Colombia organized nine

workshops with regional journalists and three thematic discussions with journalists from Bogotá. Training was provided to 170 journalists.

36. Advice was provided to different civil society organizations with respect to managing communications, including the Fundación Dos Mundos (the "Two Worlds Foundation") on creating human rights murals in the department of Cauca. The office in Colombia disseminated information with various public libraries in Bogotá and organized a painting contest on human rights with children from six different schools.

37. The office in Colombia issued 37 press releases and organized eight press conferences. There appeared 1,100 press articles, 700 radio reports and 290 television reports concerning the office.

38. A National Photography Contest on human rights was undertaken jointly with the Fundación Dos Mundos, in which professional and amateur photographers, graphic reporters and students participated. An exposition of 100 photographs on human rights, out of the 1,130 submitted to the contest, was presented in the National Museum of Bogotá.

39. The office in Colombia commissioned an opinion poll with respect to its image and impact. The results showed that all of the sectors interviewed considered the presence of the office and the work it is carrying out to be of great importance for the country.

ANNEX VI

ANNUAL REPORT ON HUMAN RIGHTS FIELD OPERATIONS IN SIERRA LEONE (2004)

Summary

The last months have seen further progress in the implementation of the peace process, stabilization of the human rights situation and consolidation of State authority in Sierra Leone. The administration of justice has benefited from increased staffing of courts with magistrates and Justices of the Peace, as well as from the rehabilitation of court buildings, especially in the provinces. Similarly, police and prison administration have seen their capacity increase, both in terms of recruitment of officers and strengthening of physical infrastructure.

The transition to peace has been aided by the work of the Truth and Reconciliation Commission (TRC) and the Special Court. While the TRC is already preparing its final report, which is scheduled for submission to the President during the first quarter of 2004, the Special Court conducted pre-trial hearings for nine individuals and is poised to start hearings in early 2004.

Nonetheless, the root causes of the conflict persist, creating a perception that too many impediments remain for the attainment of economic and social rights in Sierra Leone.

With the expected conclusion of the United Nations Mission in Sierra Leone (UNAMSIL) in December 2004, support by the Office of the United Nations High Commissioner for Human Rights (OHCHR) to the Mission, and to Sierra Leone, will be guided by the need to transfer responsibility for human rights monitoring and training, capacity-building and advocacy to local partners, including the yet to be established National Human Rights Commission. Another main objective during 2004 will be to ensure appropriate follow-up to the TRC by supporting the Government in the implementation of its recommendations. It is imperative that the post-UNAMSIL residual United Nations presence in Sierra Leone should include a substantial human rights component with the capacity and personnel to monitor and report on the human rights situation and to help build national capacity through training and human rights advocacy.

Bertrand G. Ramcharan (Ed.), Human Rights Protection in the Field, 387–405.

CONTENTS

	Paragraphs
Introduction	1–4
I. The Human Rights Situation in Sierra Leone	2–32
A. Reports of the Secretary-General and the High Commissioner for Human Rights	2–4
B. The right to life and security of the person	5–11
C. Amputees	12
D. Children's rights	13–22
E. Gender-based violence and women's rights	23–28
F. Refugees, internees and internally displaced persons	29–31
G. Economic, social and cultural rights	32
II. Human Rights Activities of the United Nations in Sierra Leone	33–48
A. UNAMSIL and the Human Rights Section	33–34
B. Activities in the districts	35
C. Monitoring of the courts, police stations and prisons	36–41
D. Training	42
E. Capacity-building, technical cooperation and advocacy	43–45
F. A national human rights commission and the Office of the Ombudsman	46–48
III. Transitional Justice	49–62
A. Truth and Reconciliation Commission	49–59
B. Special Court	60–62
IV. Conclusions and Recommendations	63–64

Introduction

1. The Commission on Human Rights, in its resolution 2003/80, requested the High Commissioner to report to the General Assembly at its fifty-eighth session and to the Commission at its sixtieth session on the human rights situation in Sierra Leone, including with reference to reports from the Human Rights Section of the United Nations Mission in Sierra Leone (UNAMSIL).

I. *The Human Rights Situation in Sierra Leone*

A. *Reports of the Secretary-General and the High Commissioner for Human Rights*

2. Since the High Commissioner submitted his reports to the General Assembly at its fifty-eighth session (A/58/379) and to the Commission on Human Rights at its fifty-ninth session (E/CN.4/2003/35), the Secretary-General has submitted two reports to the Security Council: the nineteenth (S/2003/863 and Add.1) and the twentieth (S/2003/1201).

3. As reported in the twentieth report, by 15 December 2003, the troop strength of UNAMSIL stood at 11,528, with a further reduction of 1,000 troops planned by June 2004 and another 5,500 by November 2004. The remaining 5,000 troops would be repatriated by the end of December 2004. This planning is in accordance with a security assessment that presupposes a continuing favourable security environment for Sierra Leone. The overall security situation in the subregion benefited considerably from the initial establishment of the United Nations Mission in Liberia (UNMIL) on 19 September 2003, and the continuing deployment of UNMIL troops is expected to have a further stabilizing effect on the subregion.

4. In connection with the downsizing of UNAMSIL, both the Sierra Leone Police and the Republic of Sierra Leone Armed Forces have been strengthened to facilitate the transfer of responsibility for public security to the State.

B. *The right to life and security of the person*

5. The consolidation of the human rights situation in the area of civil and political rights has continued to be a source of encouragement. It will be recalled that at its fifty-ninth session the Commission on Human Rights transferred the consideration of the situation in Sierra Leone to item 19 ("Advisory services and technical cooperation") from item 9 ("Question of

the violation of human rights and fundamental freedoms in any part of the world").

6. As suggested by this reclassification of the human rights situation, Sierra Leone is not at present affected by serious violations of the right to life and security comparable to the situation in the past few years. However, there remain some problems, such as the 14 death sentences which were passed in 2003 and the continuing illegal detention of some 90 members of the Revolutionary United Front (RUF) and the West Side Boys, who were arrested in May 2000. Their trials have not yet begun, which constitutes a disconcerting violation of international standards.

7. Remarkable progress in the implementation of the peace process has been accompanied by parallel accomplishments in the area of transitional justice. The issuance of indictments by the Special Court and the completion by the Truth and Reconciliation Commission (TRC) of its hearings and statement-taking processes have contributed to a climate of increasing respect for human rights, including the rights to life and security of the person.

8. Attacks against civilians by any of the former parties to the conflict have ceased to be an issue altogether. Since the deployment of UNMIL in Liberia there have been no incursions by Liberian fighting forces into Sierra Leonean territory. As a result, there have been no allegations of grave breaches of international humanitarian law by Liberian actors on Sierra Leonean territory.

9. At the Mape Internment Camp set up to confine Liberian combatants, which at present holds 340 ex-combatants, internment conditions have improved with regard to hygiene standards and respect for children's rights. Access to health care remains an issue that has not yet been resolved satisfactorily.

10. The Prison Administration has similarly made strides in improving its performance in accordance with international norms, including in a number of crisis situations such as the attempted escape from the Port Loko jail in November 2003. Where conditions are unsatisfactory, this is normally the result of a lack of resources and not a lack of commitment to or an understanding of international standards.

11. Over the reporting period the Human Rights Section of UNAMSIL has continued to work on its databases of war-related violations. Its databases include violations categorized by violation type, location and date. Principal violation types are massacres, killings, torture including rape and mutilation, abductions and forced labour. In this context, the Human Rights Section carried out preliminary investigations of newly discovered mass graves in Bo and Pujehun districts in July 2003. These included graves at Sahn and Bendu Mahlen, which may hold more than 300 bod-

ies. It is noteworthy that with the continuing normalization of public life throughout the country there has been a further increase in support from concerned Sierra Leoneans in efforts by the human rights community to document previously unreported sites.

C. *Amputees*

12. In following up on its amputee report based on interviews with 239 amputees and war wounded, which was completed in March 2003, the Human Rights and Civil Affairs Sections of UNAMSIL jointly developed activities to address the economic and social rights of amputees. Cognizant of demands by amputee associations in Freetown and Kenema addressed to the Government of Sierra Leone and the Truth and Reconciliation Commission, which include the provision of free education for the children of amputees and free medical care and pensions for the amputees themselves, the concerned UNAMSIL sections began implementing an amputee subsistence farming and income generation project under the technical guidance of the Food and Agriculture Organization of the United Nations (FAO) in January 2004. The project, which is funded by UNAMSIL's Trust Fund, is designed as a stopgap measure until such time as the Government will be able to address the amputees' concerns through the implementation of related recommendations in the final report of the TRC. The conceptualization of the project was instrumental in persuading amputees to cooperate with the TRC in its statement-taking and hearings processes, which the amputees had initially intended to boycott in view of their unfulfilled economic and social rights. In this context, it should be recalled that in resolution 2003/80, the Commission urged the Government of Sierra Leone to give priority attention, in cooperation with the international community, to the special needs of mutilated victims (para. 4 (e)).

D. *Children's rights*

13. The UNAMSIL Human Rights Section, in line with the Mission's transition from peacekeeping to peace-building, has adopted a more holistic approach to understanding the plight of children in Sierra Leone. While efforts at rehabilitating and reintegrating child ex-combatants into the fabric of the society deserve sustained support while other salient harmful societal practices affecting children, such as child detention, child labour and child abuse, compete for immediate attention. The paucity of health and educational facilities, particularly in the provinces, has compounded the dilemma of children in poorer communities.

14. Owing to concerted efforts by the Government of Sierra Leone, the United Kingdom Department for International Development (DFID), the United Nations Development Programme (UNDP) and UNAMSIL, rehabilitation of police stations has commenced in earnest throughout Sierra Leone. Concurrently, the Human Rights Section has mounted a series of sustained human rights training sessions for police officers designed specifically to highlight the unique status of children as a vulnerable group. These efforts have noticeably improved the way juveniles in conflict with the law are perceived and treated. Efforts are under way in all police stations to separate children from adults in police cells.

15. As the number of sitting magistrates remains inadequate, prolonged detention is still common. As cited above, in some parts of the country, magistrates cover more than two districts and service as many as five courts. The redeployment of the Justices of the Peace has partially alleviated the burden, but there is still a dire need for more magistrates to be appointed. The Human Rights Section frequently advises the police not to resort to pre-trial detention except as a last resort and recommends instead that children be granted bail. The Section also encourages police personnel, welfare officers and specialized agencies to interact regularly, in the spirit of community policing, with local communities and families with a view to promoting the interests of children. Recently, the Director of Prisons instructed all prison officers in the districts to refrain from interning children, citing as a reason the inadequacy of available detention facilities.

16. Owing to the high illiteracy rate in Sierra Leone, coupled with lack of access to health care, many children born to poor rural parents are not registered at birth. This creates problems when they come in conflict with the law as there are no statutory documents to establish their age. In the absence of a birth certificate, children usually lose the legal protection normally accorded them by reason of their status. It is common to find children who look like adults locked up with recidivists and other adult criminal suspects.

17. The dearth of approved schools and remand homes constitutes a major impediment in responding to the needs of children in conflict with the law. There is only one approved school and one remand home in Sierra Leone and both are located in Freetown. Even they do not meet the required international standards and are in need of urgent improvement. Because of a lack of remand homes and approved schools, children continue to be detained in police stations and prisons. This is a major cause of concern and undermines the establishment of a credible juvenile justice system. As part of efforts to build and strengthen the capacity of the Government, UNAMSIL and UNDP have offered to help open two remand homes, in Kenema and Bo.

18. Access to education is a prerequisite for the implementation of the rights of the child. The northern and eastern provinces of Sierra Leone are severely disadvantaged in that only a small percentage of children have access to education. Additionally, there is noticeable favouritism of boys in those areas where children do have access to primary and secondary education. In 2002/03, 90,578 children enrolled in primary schools in Port Loko District. Of this number, 53,377 were boys while only 37,201 were girls. In response to this situation, the Government of Sierra Leone has initiated a policy aimed at creating equal opportunities through seeking to ensure free education and school materials for girls attending secondary schools in the north and east.

19. The Human Rights Section, in concert with the National Commission for Social Action (NaCSA), Plan International, the World Food Programme, the International Red Cross, and War Child, recently pioneered a Girl Child and Education Project aimed at improving access to education for girls in the northern province. The project aims to retain at least 700 girls in primary and secondary schools in Sanda Magbolontor, Maforki and Koya chiefdoms by April 2004. Within the same period, the programme proposes to facilitate the absorption of 300 more girls in the same chiefdoms. At present, the majority of girls who do not have access to education are engaged in street peddling, while boys of the same age spend their childhood labouring in diamond mines.

20. The use of child labour in the diamond mines is a matter of serious concern, especially in Kono district and Tongo fields village. The 10-year civil war impoverished the population such that families are compelled to send their children to work in the diamond mines in order to eke out a living. This reality is an important factor in any consideration of long-term investment in child education in Kono and Tongo fields. Children between the ages of 6 and 18, mostly boys, are engaged in mining activities in conditions akin to slavery. Recently, licence holders have been instructed to provide the names and ages of labourers on their payrolls, making sure no labourer is below 18 years of age. Unfortunately, this measure is difficult to enforce owing to the problem of lack of birth certificates referred to earlier. The UNAMSIL Child Protection Office and the Human Rights Section continue to campaign for formal or vocational education for these children.

21. Child abuse remains one of the most widespread violations of human rights in Sierra Leone. Such abuse may be physical or psychological. Many children are regularly subjected to domestic violence, sexual exploitation and/or gross neglect. In most of the country, especially in the north, girls are forced into early marriages. The practice of female genital mutilation (FGM) is also widespread.

22. Children constitute the majority of the population of Sierra Leone and are also the most exposed to health hazards; they also have little or no access to proper health care. Hospitals and medical clinics throughout the country are ill-equipped and lacking in qualified medical personnel, a situation which encourages illegal medical practitioners, popularly known as "pepper doctors", particularly in remote towns and villages. Although pepper doctors frequently prescribe harmful medicines for children, they continue to be recognized by many as the primary health-care providers for most poor families who cannot reach or afford conventional medical treatment for their children. The Government's efforts to crack down on these illegal and untrained practitioners and the use of illegal pharmaceutical products have so far come to naught. In addition, HIV/AIDS education remains inaccessible to many families and their children.

E. *Gender-based violence and women's rights*

23. Closely analogous to the status of children is the position of women in Sierra Leonean society. Domestic violence remains a major problem and affected women often lack access to information on any possible assistance or advice. The Human Rights Section has increased its public awareness programmes on the issue of domestic violence and continues to develop its working relations with the Family Support Unit of the Sierra Leone Police Force in Freetown and in the districts. The Section offers specialized training to police personnel on how to handle cases of domestic violence. Victims of domestic violence are often reluctant to file complaints against perpetrators in an open court for fear of stigmatization and other forms of psychological pressure, and prosecutors are therefore often unable to press charges. The latest surveys, however, reveal a sharp increase in the number of cases reported by women, in contrast to previous years.

24. One of the major obstacles in addressing the problem of sexual violence against girls and women is the slow pace of the administration of justice. The situation of women is further exacerbated by poverty, which forces many to succumb to sexual exploitation. The Human Rights Section is currently investigating allegations of trafficking in girls and young women. While cases of sexual violence against women often go unreported, few of the reported cases are processed because of the inability of the victims to pay the required fees for medical and other reports necessary for the police to pursue further the allegations.

25. As mentioned above, female genital mutilation is still being widely practised in Sierra Leone. So far, the Government has shown little interest in putting an end to this harmful practice. Secret societies in rural areas still encourage FGM, touting the practice as a cultural legacy worth

preserving. They fail to recognize the true nature of female circumcision as genital mutilation with far-reaching harmful effects on the health of women. The cultural aura that surrounds FGM, along with the absence of laws expressly prohibiting the practice, have stalled efforts at sensitizing the population against it. Following her visit to Sierra Leone, the Special Rapporteur on violence against women urged the Government to pass legislation banning FGM and to conduct immediate sensitization and public awareness campaigns against such harmful practices (E/CN.4/2003/75/Add.1, paras. 507–521).

26. On 8 September 2000, Sierra Leone signed the Optional Protocol to the Convention on the Elimination of All Forms of Discrimination against Women, which it ratified on 11 November 1988. However it has yet to submit a report to the Committee on the Elimination of Discrimination against Women (CEDAW) outlining the legislative, judicial and administrative measures it has adopted to implement the Convention. To assist the Government in meeting its treaty body obligations, OHCHR technical cooperation programmes for Sierra Leone in 2004 envisage training for government officials and representatives of civil society in reporting to human rights treaty bodies.

27. UNAMSIL has continued to pay priority attention to mainstreaming women's rights in all its activities. The Mission closely monitors and reports on all gender-based violence, whether physical, psychological, and abuses of women's social and economic rights, for example through wilful denial of the right to inherit. Depriving women of their inheritance rights perpetuates a culture of dependency and encourages patriarchy and male domination. Victims of such discrimination normally experience various forms of psychological humiliation and loss of self-worth. While the common law system provides little satisfaction for women, women's rights suffer even more at the level of customary law where cultural practices favour communal over individual rights.

28. The International Human Rights Law Group recently organized a series of seminars in Freetown, Kenema, Koidu, Port Loko and Bo to sensitize communities on the concept of equality between men and women. As a result of this exercise, civil society groups and the UNAMSIL Human Rights Section have commenced consultations aimed at recommending a government-sponsored bill that would guarantee women their full inheritance rights.

F. *Refugees, internees and internally displaced persons*

29. Since the repatriation operations for Sierra Leonean refugees run jointly by the Office of the United Nations High Commissioner for Refugees

(UNHCR) and the International Organization for Migration (IOM) began in September 2000, a total of 245,732 Sierra Leoneans have returned to Sierra Leone and resettled in the 12 districts and the Western Area. Of these returnees, 153,252 were assisted in their repatriation by UNHCR/IOM. In 2003, a total of 33,170 Sierra Leoneans returned, the majority of whom were assisted by UNHCR/IOM.

30. Because of elections in Guinea in December 2003, repatriations from Guinea were suspended until early 2004. With the evolving situation in Liberia since the departure of President Taylor and the establishment of UNMIL, reports are being received of the clandestine return of Sierra Leoneans affiliated with former President Taylor's forces. There is concern that if the borders are not closely monitored this influx of ex-combatants may create problems in the near future, in particular after UNAMSIL ends.

31. Approximately 63,908 Liberian refugees reside in camps in the eastern and southern provinces. The Human Rights Section has continued to monitor the human rights situation in the refugee camps, including Mape camp near Lungi (northern province). In the eastern and southern provinces, the Section conducted training on the rights of refugees, women and children and on the Sierra Leonean Constitution for refugees' executive committees, camp managers, UNHCR implementing partners, the Sierra Leone Police, and NaCSA, as well as for the refugees themselves.

G. *Economic, social and cultural rights*

32. While Sierra Leone has made much progress in terms of civil and political rights, the record remains bleak in the area of economic, social and cultural rights. This imbalance needs to be addressed as a matter of urgency if the progress made in the implementation of the peace process is to be consolidated. The poverty reduction strategy paper (PRSP), which was recently prepared by the Ministry of Development and Economic Planning, underlined this point by drawing attention to low per capita income and great inequalities in income distribution, coupled with other unfavourable indicators. The PRSP states that these were some of the root causes of the conflict in Sierra Leone. Against the backdrop of governmental commitments and commitments by the international community to the realization of the rights to food, health and education, it is important to realize that 25 per cent of children under the age of 5 remain malnourished; maternal mortality is still at 1,800 per 100,000 live births; illiteracy rates stand at nearly 80 per cent, with female illiteracy at 89 per cent; and 81.6 per cent of Sierra Leoneans live below the poverty line of US$ 1 per day.

II. *Human rights activities of the United Nations in Sierra Leone*

A. *UNAMSIL and the Human Rights Section*

33. With the guidance and the substantive support of OHCHR, the UNAMSIL Human Rights Section continued to implement its mandate through monitoring and reporting on the situation in police stations and prisons, the functioning of the judicial system and the state of national human rights institutions; documenting war-related violations; and organizing training and capacity-building activities for members of the judiciary, law enforcement officials, local human rights non-governmental organizations (NGOs) and civil society organizations.

34. The Section also strengthened its cooperation with the Civil Affairs and Demobilization, Disarmament and Reintegration (DDR) Sections within UNAMSIL. It has been taking an active part in the design and approval process of Quick Impact Projects, which serve to foster community development and fill gaps in international project support. The Section has assisted DDR in identifying and funding suitable microprojects to the benefit of young Sierra Leoneans under the transition to peace-building theme. Microprojects funded from the DDR-managed Trust Fund have included a number of human rights training projects in the provinces. Human rights officers have also participated in the sensitization campaign on HIV/AIDS, both in Freetown and in the provinces. The Human Rights Section was also active in the United Nations Development Assistance Framework for 2004–2007 and has continued to provide substantial inputs on human rights and the rule of law to the National Recovery Strategy for Sierra Leone through the Office of the Deputy Special Representative of the Secretary-General for Governance and Stabilization.

B. *Activities in the districts*

35. The UNAMSIL Human Rights Section has undertaken human rights monitoring, advocacy, training and capacity-building activities with an increasing focus on the country's provinces. The Section, already present in Kenema, Koidu, Port Loko and Magburaka/Makeni, was able to extend its regional coverage by opening new offices in Moyamba, Kailahun, Bo/Pujehun and Koinadugu, bringing to eight the number of UNAMSIL human rights offices at the district level. This adjustment in the deployment of human rights officers and related resources corresponds to an ongoing human rights needs assessment which has revealed strong demand for the development of human rights infrastructure in the districts. The redeployments within the Human Rights Section are designed to reinforce

local capacity where it is most needed with the impending withdrawal of UNAMSIL.

C. *Monitoring of the courts, police stations and prisons*

36. During the reporting period, the UNAMSIL Human Rights Section stepped up its prison monitoring activities, extending them to all provincial penitentiary facilities. Eight human rights officers, assisted by a number of national staff, have been deployed in 8 districts where they monitor and report on the developments in conditions of detention throughout the 12 districts of Sierra Leone.

37. Reports from the field offices, particularly in the first half of the year, contain recurrent themes with regard to detention facilities, prisons and police outposts throughout Sierra Leone. These include: overcrowding, prolonged detention without trial, escapes, deplorable detention conditions and understaffing. Lactating mothers are often detained with their babies under living conditions that may threaten the health of both mother and baby. A constant feature in all detention centres is the persistent practice of locking up juveniles with convicted adult criminals or adults accused of serious criminal offences.

38. UNAMSIL, UNDP, DFID and other agencies are working assiduously to help the Government of Sierra Leone introduce the necessary changes in the penitentiary system. Most prison and detention facilities have either been reconstructed or are scheduled for reconstruction. These measures, along with close monitoring and reporting by human rights officers, have forced some, if limited, structural improvement in prisons and detention centres throughout the country.

39. Despite a persistent shortage of judges and magistrates, judicial authority is steadily being reinstated in the districts. Following an absence of nearly a decade, a High Court now sits regularly in the southern and eastern provinces of the country. Four itinerant magistrates, each covering at least three districts and assisted by newly sworn-in Justices of the Peace, have been assigned. While these measures have significantly alleviated the acute backlog in the number of cases pending before the courts, prolonged pre-trial detention remains a major cause of concern. The UNAMSIL Human Rights Section has informed the Chief Justice of frequent and arguably unwarranted adjournments, in one case 53.

40. While the revival of the High Court in the provinces is a welcome development aimed at consolidating the return to the rule of law, worryingly, UNAMSIL has reported a marked increase in the issuance of death sentences. Reports from Bo and Kenema speak of a High Court Judge sentencing 14 persons to death for their alleged complicity in a murder

case. Most of the accused were either represented by poorly remunerated or disinterested counsel or not represented by qualified counsel at all. This was the first time in four years that a death sentence had been handed down by a High Court. While the national courts retain and apply capital punishment, the Special Court for Sierra Leone, established to judge those who bear the greatest responsibility for crimes committed during the 10-year civil war, is prevented from doing so.

41. The drawn-out saga of the RUF and West Side Boys members detained since May 2000 has continued. The status of the two cases has remained unchanged since they were charged in court in March 2002. Since then, the accused have been brought to court only to be remanded without trial or hearing. Owing to a lack of funds, none of the accused has retained the services of a qualified attorney and there is no indication the impasse will soon be overcome. Since their detention, the detainees have been denied all legal rights normally available to persons under detention, such as the right to family visits and the right to consult with attorneys of their choice. The Government has recently taken an encouraging step by allowing the accused supervised family visits. This is the first time since their arrest and detention in 2000 that they have had contact with the outside world. This positive development aside, prolonged detention before and during trial remains a constant feature of the justice system in Sierra Leone.

D. *Training*

42. The Human Rights Section has further stepped up its training activities, cognizant of the need to leave behind well-trained State actors as well as a well-trained human rights NGO community upon the departure of UNAMSIL from Sierra Leone. During the third quarter of 2003 the Human Rights Section trained 227 members of UNAMSIL national contingents, 314 members of the Sierra Leone Police and 260 members of NGOs/civil society on human rights standards, principles and norms as provided in international, regional and national human rights instruments. All training sessions have also included gender and the rights of women and children. Numbers for the fourth quarter of 2003 were considerably higher given the programmes leading up to and following Human Rights Day, when thousands of Sierra Leoneans participated in human rights symposiums and other sensitization and training activities. UNAMSIL has also developed important training materials on human rights for the Sierra Leone Police and Sierra Leone Armed Forces. The set of manuals developed for senior military command and staff officers include: a human rights training manual for senior military officers, a compendium of relevant

human rights instruments, a compilation of relevant humanitarian law instruments, a compendium of command and staff exercises for senior military officers and a code of conduct for military personnel and units deployed for law enforcement duties.

E. *Capacity-building, technical cooperation and advocacy*

43. The Human Rights Section played an active role in monitoring the implementation of several programmes of advocacy and technical assistance designed by OHCHR, including a pro bono legal service. The Lawyers Center for Legal Assistance, which provides legal assistance to indigent persons, has been working closely with the Human Rights Section in identifying cases deserving legal assistance.

44. Assistance to six grass-roots organizations has been made available through the Assisting Communities Together (ACT) Programme, designed by OHCHR to address the main emerging human rights issues in the post-conflict phase. ACT projects have covered several areas including domestic violence, the death penalty and FGM. ACT projects have provided NGOs, which are often used to operating in isolation or competition, with opportunities for collaboration.

45. OHCHR, in conjunction with the UNAMSIL Human Rights Section, designed technical assistance activities to be carried out in 2004, including a series of seminars on human rights treaty reporting. The programme is specifically tailored for officials from the Ministries of Foreign Affairs and Justice, as well as civil society groups. The OHCHR programme for 2004 also foresees the establishment of human rights resource and documentation centres with Internet workstations in Kailahun, Koidu, Kenema, Makeni, Magburaka, Bo, Pujehun and Port Loko. These centres will act as a reference library for law officers and human rights activists and support training activities for law enforcement officers and civil society groups. The implementation of these activities, to be funded from extrabudgetary contributions, will depend on donor support to the OHCHR Annual Appeal and activities included in the 2004 Consolidated Inter-Agency Appeal.

F. *A national human rights commission and the Office of the Ombudsman*

46. OHCHR, in collaboration with UNAMSIL, is providing technical support to the Government as it prepares to establish a national human rights commission. The commission, unlike the Truth and Reconciliation Commission, will become a permanent institution with the mandate of monitoring the implementation of the international human rights obligations of the Government. The Human Rights Section, with the support of

OHCHR and in consultation with local stakeholders, earlier submitted to the Government of Sierra Leone for its consideration and adoption draft legislation which covers the terms of reference of the commission and its standard operating procedures. In an encouraging development, in December 2003 the Cabinet endorsed the establishment of a national human rights commission. It is expected that the draft legislation will soon be submitted to the Parliament.

47. The main challenge remains the extent to which the commission will maintain its independence from government control and political manoeuvring. The full participation of civil society at all levels of the commission is imperative in order to safeguard its independence and to encourage transparency and objectivity. A working group has been established comprising representatives of the non-governmental human rights community and other stakeholders to advocate for and lead the way towards the establishment of an effective and independent national human rights commission. It is expected that additional assistance in terms of training and resources may be made available to the commission upon its establishment.

48. While the Act establishing the Office of the Ombudsman was passed in 1997, the Office only became operational in 2000 when the President of Sierra Leone appointed the Ombudsman. Recent cases handled by the Ombudsman's Office include unlawful dismissals, age discrimination and denial of property rights. According to the Ombudsman's records for 2003, the Office had a caseload of 800 complaints, only 250 cases of which were within its mandate. Sixty-three of these cases were resolved successfully. In view of the considerable public interest in its services, the Office of the Ombudsman plans to set up four offices in the provinces. In this context, the Ombudsman has expressed an interest in collaborating with the eight human rights reference centres to be established in the districts. In addition to its work with government agencies on behalf of complainants, the Ombudsman's activities for 2004 will include sensitization programmes at universities, schools, mosques and community centres.

III. *Transitional Justice*

A. *Truth and Reconciliation Commission*

49. Since my last report to the Commission on Human Rights (E/CN.4/2003/35) and to the General Assembly (A/59/379), the TRC has continued to make progress in the implementation of its mandate. On 6 August 2003, the Commission marked the conclusion of its public hear-

ings phase by holding a national reconciliation ceremony in Freetown. This commenced with a procession, in which political associations and representatives of the Government, NGOs, the army, the police, local and international organizations and faith group organizations marched from Victoria Park to the National Stadium. At the stadium a number of speeches were made, including apologies by the army, the police and the Revolutionary United Front Party. After the celebration the procession moved to the Congo Cross Bridge—the symbolic site at which the forces of the Economic Community of West African States Monitoring Group had halted the rebel RUF march on Freetown in January 1999. The bridge was renamed and dedicated as the Peace Bridge.

50. With the conclusion of its public hearings, the TRC embarked on the final reporting stages of its work. Owing to the amount of outstanding work still to be done on its report, the mandate of the Commission, scheduled to terminate in October, was extended until 31 December 2003. On that day, the TRC administratively ended its mandate, but a small report-writing group, under the supervision of the commissioners, will continue to finalize the report as well as oversee its editing and printing before its presentation to the President, scheduled for April 2004.

51. During the last quarter of 2003, the TRC, in collaboration with the Inter-Religious Council, carried out several reconciliation activities, including district reconciliation workshops in the districts and in Freetown. These activities, funded by UNDP, were aimed at reinforcing reconciliation at the community level and led to the establishment of district support committees, under the leadership of the Council. These committees are designed to continue local reconciliation activities during 2004. The follow-up project to the TRC, which OHCHR will implement in 2004, foresees assistance to these committees, among other activities.

52. To assist the TRC in developing its recommendations on reparation, the International Center for Transitional Justice (ICTJ) facilitated consultations among civil society groups to develop general recommendations for the consideration of the TRC. These recommendations were presented to the TRC in late October after which the ICTJ seconded a consultant to assist the Commission in developing its recommendations on reparation.

53. In September 2003, the TRC issued a call for contributions for a "National Vision" for Sierra Leone. Sierra Leoneans were requested to set out their hopes for a post-conflict Sierra Leone and to describe a new Sierra Leone of peace, unity and pride. In two months, the TRC received over 250 contributions, representing the efforts of over 300 individuals, including adults, children, war victims, prisoners and ex-combatants. The contributions included written and recorded essays, slogans, plays and poems, paintings, etchings and drawings, sculptures and wood carvings.

On 10 December 2003, Human Rights Day, the National Vision Exhibition was launched at the National Stadium in Freetown. Over 400 individuals, many of them contributors, attended the event, during which prizes were awarded to selected contributors. The exhibition was subsequently moved to the National Museum on 15 December and has attracted numerous visitors, including President Kabbah. Arrangements are being made to conduct similar exhibitions in the districts.

54. In collaboration with the TRC, the New York-based NGO WITNESS has produced a 50-minute video documentary on the findings of the Truth and Reconciliation Commission. Once the TRC report is made public, the UNAMSIL Human Rights Section and others are planning to show the documentary in the districts, as part of a broader TRC dissemination strategy.

55. During the reporting period, the TRC made unsuccessful efforts to secure the public appearance before it of Chief Sam Hinga Norman, former Minister of Internal Affairs and leader of the Civil Defence Forces (CDF) militia, and Augustine Gbao, a former RUF commander. In September, the Registrar of the Special Court issued a Practice Direction, which placed stringent conditions on access to detainees by the TRC. An application by the TRC for the public appearance before it of the detainees was rejected by the Special Court which, in a ruling on 30 October, held that Chief Hinga Norman should not appear before the TRC as this would be irreconcilable with his right to a fair trial. An appeal by the TRC against this finding was turned down by the President of the Special Court on 28 November 2003. The Court, however, ruled that the TRC could receive written testimonies from the indicted. This action, in the view of the TRC, dealt a serious blow to its work and constituted a serious injustice to the detainees and people of Sierra Leone. It denied the TRC an opportunity to hear from a major figure in the conflict, not least since all the other main actors, including the President, and even detainees in the local Pademba Road prison, had given testimonies. The decision closed the door to participation in the TRC for all those detained, at the request of the Prosecutor of the Special Court.

56. The differences between the TRC and the Special Court on this matter generated media and public attention, with most of the public supporting the former, arguing that the comprehensiveness of the historical record to be produced by the TRC would benefit from public testimonies by those under the custody of the Special Court.

57. By virtue of their contemporaneous existence, the TRC and the Special Court offered a unique framework for moving from conflict to peace. The inability of the TRC and the Special Court to resolve their differences concerning the appearance of those indicted by the Special

Court arguably is a missed opportunity for the effective parallel operation of truth and justice mechanisms.

58. With the impending conclusion of the TRC and the need to ensure proper management of resources and securing of the fixed assets of the Commission, OHCHR intensified its monitoring of the implementation of its project to support the TRC. During the last quarter of 2003, four monitoring missions were deployed to the Commission to, among other activities, report on the implementation of OHCHR technical assistance and use of resources. An interim financial and systems audit of the TRC was conducted by an external auditor who has been engaged to verify the fixed assets of the Commission in preparation for the final auditing, as provided in the TRC Act (2000).

59. As part of its established practice of keeping donors informed of progress in the operations of the TRC, OHCHR organized several briefings during 2003 to apprise donors of progress in the operations of the TRC as its mandate draws to a close.

B. *Special Court*

60. On 10 March 2003 the Sierra Leone Special Court issued its first set of indictments against seven persons accused of war crimes, crimes against humanity and other violations of international humanitarian law. The Court's action targeted members of the RUF, the Armed Forces Revolutionary Council (AFRC) and the CDF who are perceived as bearing the greatest responsibility for crimes committed during the war. Among the persons first indicted were two former RUF leaders, Foday Saybana Sankoh and Issa Sessay, as well as Alex Tamba Brima (AFRC), Morris Kallon (RUF) and Sam Hinga Norman (CDF). Johnny Paul Koroma and Sam "Maskita" Bockarie were also indicted in absentia. Augustine Gbao, Brima "Bazzy" Kamara, Moinina Fofana, Allieu Kondewa, Charles Taylor and Santigie Kano were indicted thereafter.

61. At a preliminary hearing subsequently held at the remote Bonthe Island, all the indicted pleaded not guilty. Foday Sankoh, then bedridden and terminally ill, could not enter any plea; he died on 30 July 2003 in Choithram Hospital in Freetown. Three months after his indictment, in May 2003, Sam Bockarie reportedly died of multiple gunshot wounds in Liberia. On 5 December 2003, the Prosecutor of the Special Court withdrew his indictments against the two men.

62. All the indicted persons are under the custody of the Special Court except for Johnny Paul Koroma, whose whereabouts are unknown, and Charles Taylor, ex-President of Liberia, in exile in Nigeria. The Appellate Chambers of the Special Court has heard and approved the Prosecution's

application requesting that the nine accused persons be tried jointly under two indictments: RUF/AFRC, on the one hand, and CDF, on the other. The Special Court has cleared all the jurisdictional issues raised by the defence team and is poised to start trials in the first quarter of 2004.

IV. *Conclusions and Recommendations*

63. Considerable progress has been made in the field of human rights in Sierra Leone since my last report to the Commission on Human Rights. Sustained progress in the transition from relief to recovery and from peace-keeping to peace-building has led to the gradual withdrawal of UNAMSIL, which is scheduled to be completed by December 2004. It is imperative that the planned completion of UNAMSIL, which has been the catalyst for positive change in Sierra Leone, including in the establishment of a nascent national human rights protection infrastructure, not leave a void that national institutions will be unable to fill.

64. To further consolidate progress in the area of human rights and avoid any reversals, it is imperative that the post-UNAMSIL residual United Nations presence in Sierra Leone retain a substantial human rights component with the capacity and personnel to deploy nationwide in order to monitor human rights and provide technical cooperation and advisory services.

ANNEX VII

CONSOLIDATING THE PROFESSION: THE HUMAN RIGHTS FIELD OFFICER

Report on Phase One: Initial Research and Expert Consultation

Michael O'Flaherty

1. *Introduction: The Challenge of Professionalisation*

In recognition of the multiple forms of interaction between human rights and armed conflict, the United Nations as well as different regional organisations have in recent years increasingly inserted human rights programmes within the civilian components of their peace-related field missions. Dozens of human rights mandated missions, staffed with many hundreds of personnel, have been deployed to locations affected by armed conflict. They have evolved into multifaceted operations that must keep pace with changing perceptions of the nature of conflict and of the relevance of international human rights law for its resolution.

One of the most critical challenges arising from the increased deployment of human rights field officers is that of the professionalisation of this sector: overarching principles, methods and goals need to be elaborated, a core 'doctrine' of human rights fieldwork articulated. There are vast gaps in this respect—work areas where little or no guidance is available and the practitioner is obliged to proceed in a trial-and-error process of experimentation. Similarly, there is a lack of comprehensive codes of practice and of performance indicators whereby fieldwork can be properly evaluated.

Given the youth of the sector, these deficiencies are perhaps not too surprising—good practice can only emerge from a phase of case-specific experimentation. Yet such a phase may prove to be wasteful if it is not matched by an ongoing and system-wide assessment of practice in the field.

It is thus now time to identify and describe the profession of the human rights field officer, clarify the role of other actors in the context of mainstreamed approaches to human rights work and propose models for the different forms of partnerships. This process of establishing a core doctrine must be accompanied by comprehensive training programmes of a type conducive to the maintenance of professional consistency and coherence; such training efforts may greatly benefit from the single organising framework that the process of professionalisation will provide.

Bertrand G. Ramcharan (Ed.), Human Rights Protection in the Field, 407–417.

In order to address the complex challenge of consolidating the profession of the human rights field officer, Michael O'Flaherty, Co-Director of the University of Nottingham Human Rights Law Centre (HRLC), in association with the United Nations Office of the High Commissioner for Human Rights (OHCHR) and the European Inter-University Centre for Human Rights and Democratisation (EIUC), has initiated the research and capacity-building project "Consolidating the Profession: the Human Rights Field Officer". The goals of this project are to: (1) assess the evolving function of the civilian human rights field officers of international organisations who are deployed to locations affected by armed conflict, (2) undertake a stocktaking of those training and professional development supports which are in place or are required, (3) establish a network of institutions to provide training and related research support to human rights field operations, and (4) generate the basis for adoption of a set of guiding principles for the profession. The project is directed by Michael O'Flaherty.

During 2004, phase one of the project was undertaken, consisting of a number of research initiatives and an expert consultation that took place on 20 and 21 November 2004 in Geneva. The consultation led to the adoption of a set of recommendations which were presented to the UN High Commissioner for Human Rights and discussed with the Heads of UN Human Rights Field Presences at their annual meeting. Phase one was funded by the Government of Ireland (Development Cooperation Ireland).

2. *Initial Research: Identifying Gaps and Strengths*

In order to facilitate a stocktaking of the views on the professional role of human rights field officers, as well as to identify weaknesses and strengths in terms of existing professional development and training support, HRLC carried out two closely related surveys: one on the professional role of human rights field officers and one on materials and resources addressing the training needs of such officers.

2.1. *Survey on the Profession*

For the survey on the professional role of human rights field officers a questionnaire with thirty-two questions was designed, asking respondents to provide information on five subject areas: the respondents themselves, the profession of the human rights field officer, training, training materials and other resources, and a register of qualified human rights field officers. The questionnaire was sent to some eighty current and former human rights field officers of international and regional organisations, headquarters staff supporting human rights field operations, and specialists in academic and training institutions. The target group included the heads of all OHCHR human rights field presences as well as other persons with relevant expertise, including experts in OSCE and other non-UN missions. Forty-five persons completed the questionnaire.

Most of the respondents are currently working in a function directly related to a human rights or peace mission of an international or regional organisation, be it as a human rights officer/adviser in the field, as the head of such a mission, or as a desk officer in the headquarters. Respondents carrying out functions *not directly* related to a field mission include people working in academia, in training institutions or for NGOs who provide training support to human rights officers and/or carry out research in relevant fields. A large number of those respondents who are not currently carrying out work directly related to a field mission have *previous* experience of human rights field work: of the forty-five respondents, thirty-nine have worked in the field at some stage. In total, the answers to the survey reflect the experience of more than two hundred years of human rights field work, acquired in all regions of the world.

The answers to the questions on the role of human rights field officers demonstrate that there is no uniform perception of the profession: most respondents stressed that—depending on the specific mission mandate and the concrete situation in the field—it may be appropriate for a human rights officer to get involved in a broad range of very diverse activities. None the less, a number of common priorities and trends are clearly discernible from the answers. Almost all respondents mentioned the following components as being central to a human rights field officer's role: monitoring the human rights situation, reporting human rights abuses, protecting and promoting human rights. As far as partnerships that human rights officers might maintain in the field are concerned, those with three entities at the host state level, namely national human rights institutions, national civil society and the national government, were rated as particularly crucial.

The survey further showed that what could be called 'applied knowledge of international human rights standards' is seen as by far the most important technical skill required to fulfil a human rights field officer's role, followed by local knowledge/knowledge of the local language. Cultural/political/gender sensitivity and teamwork were described as the two most essential personal competencies.

In terms of existing methodological guidance and support, functions which were described as not well supported include advocacy/intervention and analysis/research. Partnerships rated as well supported include those with national human rights institutions, national governments and UN country teams, whereas those with national civil society and non-state actors in control of territory were seen as not well supported.

The survey also identified several common problems as far as the training of human rights field officers is concerned. First, there appears to be a general lack of training opportunities preparing people for their work relating to human rights field operations. The majority of the respondents with field experience stated that they did not receive any specific training whatsoever before they were deployed to their field missions. Second, a large number of the respondents who did receive some form of training before deployment expressed varying degrees of dissatisfaction with the training offered, often describing it as too general or too theoretical. Third, although the training and professional support offered during the respective field operations themselves was in general assessed somewhat more positively, several respondents stated that they did not receive any training at all during their field missions.

The most fundamental challenge in terms of training was identified as finding the right balance between keeping field workers up-to-date with theoretical developments in the human rights area and instructing them on how to translate their theoretical knowledge into practice. As far as training methods are concerned, short training courses and workshops of up to one week were ranked as particularly useful, followed by mentoring and organised mutual training. In terms of suitable training venues, the respondents expressed a slight preference for regional over local and international venues.

Finally, the survey tried to gauge support for the establishment of a register of qualified international human rights field officers for professional recognition purposes. About half of the respondents were supportive or rather supportive of the suggestion, although some of them were sceptical about details concerning the implementation of such a register. By contrast, ten respondents were not convinced by the idea.

2.2. *Survey of Training Resources*

The survey of materials and resources addressing the training and professional development of human rights field officers was mainly carried out in the form of a desktop review process of training materials which are available on the Internet. In the course of this process, the websites of about one hundred international and regional organisations, NGOs, platforms for human rights-related resources and educational institutions were searched for relevant training materials. Over 250 sources covering the whole range of subject matters relevant to the training of human rights field officers were identified. The outcome of this review is a directory of

English language web-based training materials which both illustrates the quality of existing resources and itself serves as a helpful research tool. It allows the user to access a myriad of training materials and guidebooks by one mouse click. In addition to the review process, the results of the corresponding survey by questionnaire mentioned above were relied upon to assess the usefulness of existing training materials.

The directory reveals that the wealth of available information dealing with the substance of almost all the subject matters relevant to the work of human rights field officers is striking. At the same time, the number of resources which are tailored to the specific needs of these officers in terms of subject coverage is rather small and mainly limited to a few publications by the OHCHR. Similarly, there are hardly any materials which address the practical aspects of a human rights field officer's work, such as how to deal with stress or how to work with national governments, civil society, non-state actors, the media etc. Accordingly, many respondents to the survey by questionnaire expressed a desire for materials which are more suitable for use in the field.

The survey concludes that the most comprehensive existing training resource addressing the needs of human rights field officers is the OHCHR *Training Manual on Human Rights Monitoring*. The Monitoring Manual was also the training resource mentioned most often by the respondents as being particularly helpful. This high rating seems to reflect a need for a training tool which, in a comprehensive and integrated manner, addresses both the substantive issues which human rights field officers have to deal with and the more practical and personal aspects of their work. However, the Manual also has a number of shortcomings. First, it is not comprehensive in terms of what human rights field officers do, as it does not cover several important functions apart from monitoring. Second, it concentrates almost exclusively on civil and political rights, devoting only very limited space to the increasingly important subject of economic, social and cultural rights. Finally, it has not been updated since 2001. A supplementation and updating of the Manual in these three respects would undoubtedly help to accommodate the need of human rights field officers for both practical guidance and topical information on relevant subject matters.

3. *Expert Consultation: Finding a Way Forward*

To launch the process of authoritatively and comprehensively mapping out the professional role of human rights field officers and of identifying training requirements, the HRLC, in close cooperation with OHCHR and

EIUC, convened an expert consultation in Geneva. The meeting, which took place on 20 and 21 November 2004, assembled a group of internationally recognised specialists in the area; their discussions were informed by the surveys described in the previous section. After two days of intensive discussions in the plenary and in smaller working groups, the participants adopted a set of recommendations which were then presented to the High Commissioner and discussed with the Heads of UN Human Rights Field Presences.

3.1. *Invitees*

Great importance was attached to inviting persons to attend the expert consultation who come from very diverse professional and cultural backgrounds. Therefore, there were among the invitees a number of civil society experts from countries in which there is, or has been, an international human rights operation, such as Sierra Leone, Afghanistan, Liberia and East Timor. International and regional organisations were represented by human rights officers/advisers working in field missions in all regions of the world, current and past heads of such missions, desk officers and senior staff in the headquarters supporting these missions, as well as training specialists. Institutional affiliations of invitees included OHCHR, other UN bodies, such as OCHA, DPKO, UNDP and UNICEF, and regional organisations such as OSCE, OAU and OAS. Other invitees included experts from academic institutions, training centres and international NGOs (including Human Rights Watch, the Centre for Humanitarian Dialogue, the International Service for Human Rights and the International Center for Transitional Justice).

3.2. *The Meeting*

After an introduction to the goals and methods of the expert consultation and a plenary discussion in which the participants explained what they expected from the consultation process, the remainder of the agenda was devoted to four main subject areas: (1) The professional identity of the human rights field officer, (2) the regulation of the profession, (3) the training of the profession, and (4) the formulation of recommendations "to and through" the High Commissioner regarding the further professionalisation of the sector. Each of these sessions consisted of introductory comments by specialists in the respective fields, discussion of the relevant issues in three alternating working groups, and presentation and discussion of the findings of the working groups in the plenary. The recommendations were finalised in plenary session.

3.2.1. *The Professional Identity*

Representatives of the UN and an international NGO opened the session on the professional identity of human rights field officers by addressing questions as to whether it is possible (and desirable) to identify core functions of a human rights officer, what partnerships an officer should maintain in the field, and what methodological guidance and support exists. In the discussions in the working groups, the participants attempted to identify the most important goals of human rights field work, the main obstacles to achieving these goals, and different options to overcome them. The working groups generally agreed that the key functions of a human rights officer include the protection of the rights of individuals through monitoring and reporting, the promotion of human rights and, in the longer term, the building up of national human rights communities. The participants identified several major challenges which human rights operations have to face in the course of this process: the diversity of the political contexts in which international standards have to be translated into practice; the different problems presented by pre-conflict, conflict, and post-conflict situations; the common lack of understanding how to translate certain policies (such as the rights-based approach) into practice; shortcomings in terms of strategic thinking and problem-solving skills within human rights missions; inter-agency competition; and different skill levels of persons working in the respective missions. Furthermore, several participants stressed that human rights operations can create false expectations that can eventually weaken civil society and warned that human rights officers should not take over the role of national institutions. As far as a basic profile is concerned that human rights officers would have to fulfil to be able to address these challenges, there was agreement that they need to base their work upon consolidated standards, mechanisms and methods. Yet at the same time it was stressed that human rights field professionals must be flexible enough to adapt to the particular context of their work and to make use of partnerships as appropriate, including of partnerships with other in-mission actors. Finally, the importance of a number of other personal competencies and skills, including cultural, gender and political sensitivity, inclusiveness and communication skills were highlighted.

3.2.2. *Regulation of the Profession*

In the second session of the first day, the need to regulate the profession and different ways of doing so were dealt with. A representative of the UN and a specialist from an academic institution introduced the subject by addressing issues concerning the central ethical problem areas related to human rights field missions, the underlying values guiding the profession, the desirability of establishing a code of conduct for human rights field professionals and the definition of sites of accountability. Accordingly, discussions in the working groups focused on principles and standards underlying the work of human rights field officers, in particular the question as to what degree human rights norms themselves can serve as a value system guiding professional activity, indicators regarding professional performance, different systems of accountability and the development of a system of professional accreditation. As far as a code of conduct for human rights officers is concerned, a UN participant pointed out that the OHCHR had in fact developed a basic code in earlier years (albeit the code seems to have been overlooked in practice). That code of conduct was identified and brought to the attention of the participants on the following day of the consultation meeting; it informed further discussions on the subject. In terms of the desirability of regulating the profession, one of the working groups pointed to the following fundamental advantages: enhanced recognition and protection of the profession, clarification of entrance requirements to the profession, unified assessment of qualifications, facilitation of professional support and creation of a forum for the sharing of experiences. Yet, according to this working group, these benefits contrast with a number of downsides: systems of regulation tended to emphasise the values of the regulators; there was a danger that the required qualifications could be reduced to a set of very formal criteria which are not necessarily relevant for the work in the field; and the enforcement and implementation of any system of regulation was problematic (who regulates and evaluates according to what criteria?). Moreover, there was the fundamental challenge that a human rights field officer's work depends to a large extent on the specific mandate and the particular political context of a mission. Therefore, whereas the participants generally welcomed the idea of reviewing and improving existing rosters of human rights field officers, most of them described a formal accreditation system as premature. By contrast, there was wide support for an informal 'association' of human rights field professionals. As far as fundamental standards that should guide the work of human rights field officers are concerned, the participants highlighted the following principles: impartiality and independence, universality and indivisibility, non-discrimination, non-substitution for national actors, partnership between various actors, and operation within the framework of international human rights and humanitarian law. Finally, the participants agreed that frameworks of both institutional and personal accountability, internally and externally, should be strengthened. At the same time, it was stressed that parameters for individual accountability should be matched by institutional support to human rights field officers.

3.2.3. *Training of the Profession*

The first session of the second day of the expert consultation was opened by introductory comments from a UN representative and a specialist from a training institution who both stressed the need for training initiatives targeted at human rights field officers and addressing different professional stages. Discussion in the working groups centred on the content of existing and required training initiatives for human rights professionals, the methodologies to be used for such training modules and the range of relevant training materials. The participants highlighted the importance of designing training initiatives that aim at different levels of specialisation: general human rights education at the pre-recruitment level (in universities and other educational institutions), training on core knowledge areas (e.g. knowledge of treaty system, Action 2, role of the ICRC, monitoring skills etc.) at the pre-deployment level, and in-mission training that takes account of the specific mandate and the local situation. It was pointed out that any training modules and materials should be tested before dissemination and systematically evaluated and followed up by the headquarters for effectiveness. In addition, end-of-mission debriefings could be used as a way of identifying training needs. Specific suggestions for improving training approaches included the development of internship programmes in the field, designing training modules that include real life/case studies and the development of management training modules. Furthermore, training initiatives should address skills of political analysis and inter-cultural communication. Finally, the use of the expertise which exists both within the missions and in outside institutions should be coordinated more effectively, avoiding duplications. As far as training materials are concerned, one working group pointed out that the directory produced for the present project could serve as a good starting point but should be made more accessible (by being put on a website), expanded by including materials produced in other languages than English, and further developed and further categorised. Moreover, it was suggested that a corresponding directory listing training institutions and modules should be developed. Finally, the participants identified a lack of training materials addressing important practical skills such as stress management, communication skills, intervening in violent situations, human rights advocacy and negotiating in human rights contexts.

3.3. *Recommendations*

In the final session of the expert consultation, each of the three working groups formulated five to six specific recommendations "to and through" the High Commissioner and presented them to the plenary. After discussion of the recommendations in the plenary, the participants, in an anonymous voting process, identified the recommendations which they regarded as most important. After a drafting group had refined the wording of these recommendations, they were finalised and adopted by the plenary.

The recommendations centre on the following broad areas: development of a basic profile for human rights field officers, review of recruitment and deployment policies, development of a code of conduct, strengthening of accountability frameworks, creation of a range of training curricula, and identification and effective use of training materials and resources.

The final recommendations adopted by the expert consultation ask the High Commissioner to:

1. Review and improve existing rosters of Human Rights Field Officers (HRFOs) and recruitment procedures in co-operation with relevant regional organisations with a view to enhancing capacity, diversity and professionalism.
2. Review and develop basic profiles for all civilian staff of intergovernmental organisations who have a human rights function. This process should include review of essential skills, core competencies and standards of professional integrity.
3. Develop operational guiding principles for HRFOs, with a view to enhancing individual and organisational effectiveness, reputation and integrity, and taking into account international law, the OHCHR code of conduct and other established human rights methodologies.
4. Strengthen institutional and personal accountability frameworks through the development of indicators, clarification of the responsibility and capacity of management, support to personnel and systematic, independent evaluation and auditing.

In recognition that training should be a prerequisite for recruitment and deployment of HRFOs, and in acknowledgement of the need for training partnerships, the expert consultation recommended that the High Commissioner for Human Rights, in partnership with other entities:

5. Develop and sustain a robust inventory of training courses and training materials in as many languages as possible, offered by a broad array of institutions from different regions around the world which would be available to all staff via electronic means. This list should be categorised in a variety of ways including (but not limited to): Geography, Institutions, Language, Content, Methodologies.
6. Create curricula for systematic training of potential and new staff at different levels of specialisation, including pre-recruitment (basic) and pre-deployment training.

7. Support the development of mission specific training, organised by the Head of Mission, in situ, using existing expertise within field missions.
8. Develop curricula for systematic training of existing staff at different levels of responsibilities. Training should make use of the expertise of staff serving in missions and emphasise the exchange of experience on human rights field work. This training should include various methodologies such as, skill building, Mentoring and coaching.
9. To ensure that these recommendations will be acted upon, the partners in the project "Consolidation of the Profession—the Human Rights Field Officer", i.e. the High Commissioner, the University of Nottingham and the European Inter-university Centre for Human Rights and Democratisation are encouraged to move to the next phase. There is a sense of urgency that the range of necessary outputs be delivered within a reasonable timeframe.

On 22 November 2004, these recommendations were presented to the High Commissioner and constructively discussed with the Heads of UN Human Rights Field Presences at their annual meeting.

4. *Next Steps*

Participants in the expert consultation, together with the primary institutions involved in the project, identified two different sets of activities to move the project to the next phase. On the basis of the recommendations adopted at the consultation, there is a need for continued research and documentation activities, including the review of best practices, concerning a wide range of areas. On the other hand, core training modules need to be created and tested, a network of training institutions established, a comprehensive inventory of training materials developed and existing rosters of human rights field officers reviewed. It was agreed that these two tracks should be implemented simultaneously and in close coordination.

Following the consultation, HRLC drafted a concept paper identifying a set of next steps. The concept paper is the basis for current initiatives to move the project to its next phase during 2005.

INDEX

Abkhazia 130, 153–154
Access, Problems of 63–65, 338, 392, 394
Action and activities 80, 221
Additional Protocols to the Geneva Conventions 4, 8, 89, 90 n. 12, 91, 105, 330
Advisory Opinion of ICJ 3, 91 n. 19, 97, 103, 105–106
Afghanistan 41, 45, 47, 72, 80, 99, 106 n. 82, 123, 130, 155, 220–221, 267–268, 412
African Union 48, 48 n. 44, 71, 94, 96, 240
Agenda for protection 4, 8, 8 n. 15, 27, 72–73, 75–76, 78, 80, 82–83
Aide Memoire 4, 60, 66, 83, 120 n. 6, 254–256
AIDS 31, 61, 72, 221, 238, 241, 264, 268, 284, 394, 397
Amnesty International 13, 19, 19 n. 15, 24, 24 n. 18, 41 n. 3, 42 n. 8, 53, 95, 103 n. 73, 115
Angola 51 n. 53, 73, 108 n. 87, 124, 130, 143, 156–158, 198, 237, 267
Application of the law 95 n. 44, 102, 113, 324, 358, 380
Arab League 96
Arms control 102, 105
Aspen Institute 49 n. 49

Better use of implementation mechanisms 102
Bosnia 41, 47, 48 nn. 42–43, 49, 49 n. 48, 72, 109, 130, 136–137, 143, 146, 158–159, 217, 268
Bowden, Mark 59
Brahimi report 9, 125, 269
Burundi 48 n. 42, 72, 72 n. 4, 79, 123, 130, 143, 161–164, 217, 220–221, 237, 268

Cambodia 289–290, 293–304, 306–309
CEDAW 206, 208, 218, 306, 395
Celebration 87, 110, 321, 402
Centre for Human Rights and Democracy in Central Africa 236–237
Central Africa 165–166, 220, 236–237, 241–242
Central Asia 169–170, 208
Civil and political rights 3, 31, 35, 37–38, 102, 103 n. 72, 110, 185, 360, 389, 396, 411
Challenges 1, 4, 14, 14 n. 5, 15, 15 n. 9, 17–20, 22, 24, 28, 28 n. 28, 32–33, 46 n. 30, 49 n. 46, 52, 55, 57, 59, 71, 75–76, 78, 82, 87, 98 n. 54, 131–132, 135, 137, 201, 211–216, 220, 231, 235, 238, 241, 244, 295, 311, 318–319, 323, 353, 401, 407–408, 410, 413–414
Changing environment 59
Children in armed conflicts 5, 372
Civilians in armed conflicts 4, 42 n. 9, 60–61, 68, 80, 82, 105 n. 79, 119, 122, 247, 253–256, 268
Codification 87–88
Conscience 116–117, 285
Cold War 49, 60, 67, 69, 127, 131
Colombia 48 n. 42, 73–74, 95 n. 44, 100 n. 64, 106 n. 80, 108 n. 88, 130, 140–144, 148–149, 171–172, 231, 233–234, 311–312, 314–315, 317–322, 324–325, 325 n. 9, 326–327, 329–330, 331 n. 14, 333–340, 342, 346, 348, 350–352, 354–360, 362–363, 365–366, 368–369, 370 n. a, 371, 373–375, 377–385
Commissions of Inquiry 41 n. 5, 73, 77
Commission on Human Rights 7, 13–14, 17–21, 23–24, 26, 26 n. 25, 28–31, 31 n. 32, 33, 46, 94, 98, 131, 141, 143, 145, 160–161, 163–164, 171, 186, 192, 199–202, 205, 225, 228, 231, 275, 289, 293–295, 297, 307, 311, 317, 328, 341, 350–351, 389, 401, 405
Compensation 29, 102, 106–107, 107 n. 84, 280, 287
Conceptual issues 121
Conceptual pillars 218
Congo 47, 48 n. 42, 59, 106 n. 80, 108 n. 87, 116 n. 115, 130, 140, 143, 172–173, 215, 220, 237, 242–243, 267–268, 402
Coordination 6–7, 66–67, 83–84, 99 n. 55, 124, 131, 138, 142–143, 160, 165, 174, 176–177, 179–180, 183, 188, 191, 195, 213, 231–232, 261, 264–265, 275, 299, 308, 329, 346, 352, 382, 417
Consultations on protection 81

Council of Europe 90, 96, 201–202, 204
Convention on the rights of the child 306, 328, 372
Convention Plus 18
Crises in protection 13, 59
Crisis response 47, 146, 228
Custom 115, 117
Cultural objects 102, 105

Darfur 14, 41, 41 n. 5, 48 n. 44, 52, 59, 73–74, 84, 115 n. 111, 124, 130, 140, 206–207, 248
Delegation 20, 22–23, 125, 186, 208, 236, 307
Depositary 90 n. 13, 97–98
DDDR 72, 72 n. 4, 83, 219–221, 397
Democracy 15, 18, 31, 35, 38, 50 n. 49, 106 n. 80, 134 n. 8, 157, 165–166, 169–170, 181–182, 184, 198, 209, 236–238, 241–242, 244, 294, 322, 352, 370
Democratic legitimacy 32, 34–35, 39
DPA 119, 127, 129, 159, 166–167, 181–182, 207
DPKO 10, 48 n. 40, 72 n. 5, 77, 82–83, 119, 123, 125, 130, 153, 155, 166–167, 175, 184, 196, 209, 213, 222–223, 269–275, 412
Dunant, Henry 88 n. 3

East Timor 47, 54, 109, 116, 129–130, 209, 267–268, 412
ECCAS 165, 236–240, 242, 244
ECHA 7, 120–121
Economic security challenge 216
Economic, social, and cultural rights 10, 24, 31, 46, 136, 141, 149, 185, 187, 214, 271, 294, 302, 306, 309, 314, 336, 341, 343, 345, 376, 396, 411
El Salvador 49, 109, 116, 128–129
Eritrea/Ethopia 175–176, 268
Environment 2, 10, 15–16, 59, 81, 102, 104–105, 117, 122, 146, 164, 181–183, 193–194, 197, 211, 213–217, 219, 221–223, 228, 259, 261, 296, 301–302, 307, 320, 389
Emerging risks 15
Empowerment 30, 214, 216, 222–223
Ensure 2, 4, 6, 9, 34, 37, 46, 68, 78, 85, 89, 89 n. 11, 90 n. 15, 91, 91 n. 19, 96, 96 n. 48, 97–98, 105, 111, 137, 143–144, 159–161, 170, 176, 180, 184, 202–203, 210–212, 214, 219, 222–223, 231–234, 253, 259, 264, 269, 274, 279, 283, 285, 287, 293, 295, 305, 309, 346–347, 349, 353, 359, 371, 387, 393, 404, 417
Equality and non-discrimination 34, 37, 39
European Union 24, 24 n. 19, 95, 95 n. 40, 130, 201, 351, 381, 383

Fact-finding 29, 73, 77, 93, 100, 100 n. 64
Failure to intervene 45–47
Failure to protect 56, 66
Failure to support 45, 48
Field 11, 17, 32, 46, 48, 48 n. 45, 49–50, 50 n. 49, 51, 51 n. 53, 55, 55 n. 67, 56, 68, 73, 88 n. 4, 95 n. 42, 113, 119, 123–124, 128–134, 136, 136 n. 9, 137, 140–141, 145, 149, 151, 153, 155–156, 158, 161–164, 166, 168–172, 176–184, 186, 191–192, 194, 196–199, 201–202, 205–207, 209, 216, 227–241, 243–244, 247–248, 274–275, 296, 318, 320, 323–324, 334, 352, 358, 361, 371–372, 376, 378–383, 393, 405, 407–417
Field Missions 50–51, 129, 148–149, 172, 204, 317, 378–379, 407, 409–410, 412–413, 417
Field protection 1, 11, 29, 248
Field Offices 1, 29, 49, 129, 141–143, 146, 148, 150–151, 159, 165, 171, 247–248, 274, 398
Field operations 1, 9, 48, 48 n. 43, 50 n. 49, 54, 128–130, 134–135, 166, 408–410
Flouting of international norms 16

Gender 2, 5, 8, 19, 26, 30, 72, 76, 82, 122, 159–160, 180, 197, 202, 211–215, 217–223, 233, 261, 264, 2881, 314, 342, 350, 359, 394–395, 399, 409, 413
Gender Laws 8, 19, 160, 350, 359
Gender Mainstreaming 160, 219–220, 223
General Assembly 5, 7, 13, 23, 27 n. 26, 31–32, 53, 94, 109 n. 98, 129, 164–165, 223, 236–238, 269, 293, 295, 307, 389, 401
Geneva Conventions 4, 8, 69, 84, 87–88, 88 nn. 4–5, 89, 89 nn. 8–9, 11, 90 nn. 12–13, 15, 91, 91 n. 19, 92, 92 nn. 24–31, 96–97, 97 n. 52, 98–100, 101 n. 65, 103, 105, 107, 110–113, 113 n. 107, 114–115, 136, 253, 330
Genocide 5, 11, 41, 46, 46 n. 30, 53, 88, 94, 96, 102–104, 104 n. 76, 106 n. 83, 108, 115, 129, 135, 150, 253, 263–264, 278, 280
Girls 5, 8, 30, 78, 197, 211–217, 221–222, 261, 285, 393–394
Golberg, Elissa 71, 250

Guatemala 109, 129, 178–180
Graca Machel 43, 217
Guiding Principles 9, 144, 203, 232, 277, 347, 408, 416
Guinea-Bissau 181
Guyana 183

Haiti 1, 49, 123, 129–130, 132, 133 n. 5, 134 n. 8, 183, 215, 220–221
High Commissioner for Human Rights 273, 289, 293, 295, 311–312, 317–318, 320, 331 n. 14, 346–348, 350–352, 357, 359, 370–371, 378–380, 383, 387, 389, 408, 412, 416–417
High Commissioner for Refugees 8, 17, 27, 27 n. 26, 131, 213, 395
High Contracting Parties 90 nn. 13, 15, 91 n. 19, 96–97, 97 n. 52, 111
High-level panel 14, 14 n. 5, 20, 22–23, 46 n. 30
HIV/AIDS 31, 61, 72, 221, 238, 241, 264, 268, 394, 397
Holocaust 43, 43 n. 17, 103–104, 140
Humanitarian actors 27, 66, 71, 122–123, 130, 216
Humanitarian law 1–4, 9–11, 17, 19, 25–26, 29, 34, 37–38, 46 n. 30, 60, 67, 74, 78, 80, 87, 87 n. 1, 88–89, 89 n. 11, 90, 90 n. 14, 91 nn. 17, 21, 92, 94–95, 95 nn. 43–44, 96, 96 n. 48, 97, 97 n. 50, 98, 100 n. 63, 101, 101 nn. 66–67, 102, 102 n. 72, 103–105, 105 n. 79, 106–107, 109 nn. 94, 98, 111, 111 n. 104, 112–114, 114 n. 109, 117, 121–122, 127–128, 131, 142, 144, 149, 158, 171–172, 185, 194, 197–198, 233, 247, 253, 258, 264, 274, 277–279, 312–313, 317–319, 322, 325–327, 330–331, 333–335, 339, 343, 346–353, 355–357, 359–360, 364, 375, 378–384, 390, 400, 404, 414
Human rights 1, 3–5, 9–11, 13–15, 15 n. 9, 16–17, 17 n. 11, 18–35, 37–39, 43–52, 52 n. 55, 53–57, 67–69, 71–74, 77–78, 80, 84, 87, 94–95, 96 n. 49, 98, 102, 102 n. 72, 103 n. 74, 108–109, 109 n. 98, 114, 114 n. 109, 115, 117, 119, 121–125, 127–130, 130 n. 1, 131–132, 132 n. 3, 133–151, 153–172, 175–210, 225–228, 231–233, 235–244, 247–248, 253, 258, 260, 262, 264, 269, 271–275, 277–279, 286, 289–291, 293–303, 305–309, 313–315, 317–319, 322, 325–327, 329, 331 n. 14, 335–337, 339–341, 345–353, 355–357, 359, 363, 368, 370, 374, 378–379, 381–385, 387, 389–393, 395–401, 405, 407–417
Human Rights Committee 35 nn. 35–36, 36–38, 41 n. 2, 83, 94, 194, 197–198, 294, 306–307
Human rights movement 13–14, 19–20, 24–25, 28–29, 31, 33, 235–236, 243–244
Human rights components 1, 10, 48, 119, 122–125, 129, 137, 153, 156, 166–167, 175–176, 185, 248, 269, 271–275, 305, 387, 405
Human rights defenders 13, 18–19, 24, 143–144, 148, 172, 180, 202, 232, 233, 299, 314, 329, 340–341, 346–347, 350, 353, 355, 368, 383
Human Rights Watch 14, 14 n. 4, 19, 41 n. 3, 44 n. 20, 53, 95, 95 n. 45, 108 n. 88, 115, 412
Humanity 5, 11, 15, 26, 94, 97 n. 50, 108, 111–114, 150, 212, 217–218, 253, 263–264, 278, 285, 325–326, 328, 330, 336, 356, 373, 404

Independent Commission on Intervention and State Sovereignty 36, 53, 53 n. 60
Impact of war on civilians 43, 56
Implementation 5, 8–10, 17, 19–21, 23, 26–27, 29, 31, 46 n. 33, 49, 60, 68, 71–73, 76–77, 87, 89, 91 n. 17, 91 n. 21, 92–93, 95, 102, 106, 109 n. 98, 112, 114, 120, 142, 154–155, 159, 166–167, 172, 175–177, 179, 182–186, 192, 195–197, 200–201, 206, 208–209, 217, 219–220, 222–223, 234–237, 261–262, 267, 269–271, 290, 293, 296–297, 305–306, 309, 312, 317, 326, 339, 350–354, 357, 370, 380, 387, 390–391, 393, 396, 400–401, 404, 410, 414
Impunity 5, 11, 54, 65, 73, 94, 122, 141, 150–151, 159, 186, 201, 204, 215, 221, 233, 253, 263, 294–295, 299–300, 309, 312–313, 315, 320, 325–326, 338, 346, 348, 352, 357, 369, 373
Institutional Issues 122
Internally displaced persons 4, 8–10, 18, 26, 81, 124, 131 n. 2, 154, 161, 184, 205, 247, 253, 271, 277–278, 280–287, 395
International Committee of the Red Cross 1, 17, 91 n. 17, 91 n. 18, 92, 98, 100, 103, 105 n. 79, 112, 116, 136, 247
International Council on Human Rights Policy 14, 15 n. 8, 18, 18 n. 13, 25, 25 n. 21
International Court of Justice 3, 46, 89 n. 8, 91, 91 n. 19, 97, 102, 102 n. 72, 105, 105 n. 77, 106, 111, 111 n. 104

International Covenants on Human Rights 67
International criminal court 8, 30, 73, 87–88, 88 n. 7, 93 n. 37, 94, 94 n. 38, 185, 212, 217–218, 247, 330, 336
International norms 16, 136, 193, 326, 352, 356, 371, 375, 379, 390
Kofi Annan 14, 32, 53, 55
Kosovo 48 n. 43, 129–130, 137–139, 199–204, 225–226, 228–229, 268

Lamptey, Comfort 211, 250
Land 44, 88, 106, 107 n. 84, 137, 141, 143, 145–149, 290, 292, 294, 298, 300–301, 305–307, 345
Legal mechanisms 89, 108
Legality 3, 34, 37, 39, 97 n. 50, 103 n. 72, 105 n. 77, 382
Liberia 42, 42 n. 8, 72, 72 n. 4, 80, 82, 108 n. 86, 123–124, 130, 130 n. 1, 184–185, 217, 219, 221, 266–267, 389–390, 396, 404, 412

Macedonia, FYR 92 n. 22, 137, 176, 225
Mandate 10, 22, 27, 27 n. 26, 28, 68, 75, 79–80, 82–84, 119, 121, 123–125, 128–129, 148–149, 153–154, 156–157, 159–160, 162, 164–165, 167, 169, 171, 175, 177–178, 181–182, 184, 186, 189, 191–192, 195–196, 198–201, 204, 206–207, 209–210, 226–227, 229, 237, 255, 266–267, 269, 271, 273, 277, 289, 294, 297–298, 305, 308, 350, 359, 371, 378–379, 397, 400–402, 404, 409, 414–415
Mexico 48, 186–187, 191, 351
MICIVIH 129, 132–134
Minorities 10, 31, 95 n. 40, 124, 138–139, 160–161, 203, 271, 280, 331, 335
Mitigatory protection 143, 146
Monitoring 5–7, 9–10, 21, 26–27, 48 n. 45, 49, 49 n. 46, 50 n. 49, 56, 61, 66, 74, 76–77, 102 105, 115, 122, 124, 128, 131, 133 n. 5, 141–142, 146–149, 154, 156, 158, 163–164, 167, 176–179, 182–185, 187, 189, 194, 196–197, 200, 202, 204, 210, 217, 219, 223, 225, 234, 259–261, 263–264, 271, 290, 292–293, 298–299, 301, 303, 306, 387–388, 397–398, 400, 402, 404, 409, 411, 413, 415
Morjane, Kamel 79, 250
MOU 10, 123, 125, 167, 270

National Human Rights Institutions 33, 33 n. 34, 148, 158, 165, 189, 199, 204–205, 240, 289, 296, 397, 409
Nepal 47, 82, 140, 147, 191
New Approaches 110, 115, 131, 248
New Actors 115
NGOs 1, 19, 23, 27, 48, 51–54, 56, 67, 73–77, 84, 88, 95, 98, 115, 124, 128–129, 154–155, 162–163, 165–166, 168, 172, 178–180, 186, 188, 190, 193–194, 198, 201–202, 204, 206, 208, 210, 213, 241, 243, 341, 397, 399–400, 402, 409–410, 412

OAS 90, 129–130, 133, 133 n. 5, 412
OCHA 68, 75 n. 8, 77, 116 n. 115, 119–120, 120 n. 5, 121, 123–124, 131, 131 n. 2, 203, 206, 213, 248, 412
Occupied Palestinian Territories 74, 98, 192
O'Flaherty, Michael 41, 250
OHCHR 10, 47 n. 35, 48 n. 41, 52 n. 55, 68, 109 n. 98, 119–121, 123–125, 129, 139–143, 145–147, 147 n. 1, 148, 150, 153–156, 158–167, 169–172, 175–187, 191–208, 210, 223, 225–229, 231–233, 239–240, 243–244, 250, 269–275, 289–290, 292–296, 296 n. 1, 298–300, 302, 304, 306–309, 311, 387, 395, 397, 400–404, 408–409, 411–412, 414, 416
O'Neill, William 127, 141, 250
OSCE 48, 48 n. 43, 90, 96, 130, 136, 136 n. 9, 137–139, 153, 160, 178, 201–204, 409, 412
Operationalising protection 71

Peacemaking 6, 119, 121, 212–213, 222, 236
Peacekeeping 1, 6, 9–10, 47–48, 48 n. 40, 49 n. 49, 56, 60–64, 66, 72, 75, 81–83, 101, 101 nn. 66–67, 120, 122–125, 129–130, 137, 139, 153, 212–213, 217, 219, 221–223, 247–248, 250, 254–256, 259, 264, 268–275, 391, 405
Peacebuilding 30, 61–62, 66, 153, 214–215, 240
Pitfalls 73
Preventive protection 143
Prevention of genocide 53
Present issues 61
Princeton principles 11
Principles 3–4, 9–11, 17, 26, 32, 34–39, 45 n. 24, 50, 55, 60, 80–81, 84, 89 n. 11, 90 nn. 14–15, 94, 97 n. 50, 107 n. 84, 111, 111 n. 104, 113, 113 n. 107, 117, 119, 121, 125, 144, 158, 160, 168, 179, 189, 198, 201, 203, 232–233, 253, 274, 277–280, 285–287, 326–327, 331, 339, 347–348, 356, 362,

365, 371, 373–374, 377, 399, 407–408, 414, 416
Profession of field officer 151, 407–408, 417
Progress 2, 6–7, 15, 71–74, 76, 85, 136, 147, 161, 201, 203, 218–220, 223, 233, 241, 243, 282, 298, 305, 320–322, 325–327, 342, 346, 348, 354, 356–358, 360, 372, 387, 390, 396, 401, 404–405
Promotion 10, 16, 25, 31, 33, 39, 73, 94, 121, 125, 144, 153–155, 157, 159, 162–163, 167–168, 173–174, 179–180, 183–184, 191, 195, 198, 200, 202–203, 205, 233, 237–238, 242–243, 269, 271, 275, 289, 292–293, 295–297, 315, 317–318, 346–347, 350–352, 359, 378, 380, 384, 413
Proposals for Better Respect of International Humanitarian Law 96
Prosecution 36, 65–66, 90, 96, 106, 107 n. 85, 108 n. 90, 150, 263
Prospects 33, 61, 64, 76, 162
Protecting Power 91–92, 92 n. 22, 100
Protection in Action 132, 138
Protection, meaning of, 1
Protection strategies 13, 29, 73, 138, 214, 216
Protection methods 141
Protection of civilians 4, 42 n. 9, 53, 59–61, 65, 68–69, 71, 71 n. 2, 72–79, 82–83, 119–123, 147, 211–214, 253–256, 265, 268
Protection of refugees 8, 26, 79, 82–83, 247
Protection of displaced persons 83
Protocol to the Geneva Conventions 4, 8, 69, 88 n. 5, 89, 90 n. 12, 91, 96, 105, 112 n. 106, 136
Public conscience 116–117

Ramcharan, Bertrand 14 n. 7, 28 n. 28, 29 n. 30, 32 n. 33, 33 n. 34, 72 n. 2, 95 n. 42, 141, 238, 250
Range of activities 141
Ratification 87, 89, 93, 97, 174, 185, 195, 199, 206, 348, 372
Reach individuals 116
Reaffirm rules 110
Reality of War 41
Reconciliation 9, 29, 36, 54, 54 n. 63, 87, 89, 108, 109 n. 95, 110 n. 99, 114, 120, 137, 142, 158, 181, 184, 198, 207, 253, 263, 374, 402
Refugees 1, 4, 8, 17–18, 24, 26–27, 27 n. 26, 45 n. 24, 60, 62, 78–85, 108 n. 87, 110, 131, 142, 154, 159, 161, 184, 202–203, 205, 213, 225–227, 250, 253, 257, 388, 395–396
Refugee convention 8, 83
Regional institutions 30, 71
Regional representatives 146, 195
Reinforce 96, 103, 129, 158, 163, 182, 214, 242, 274, 303, 397
Remedy 34, 38, 280
Reparation 2, 87, 89, 102, 106–107, 107 n. 84, 122, 287, 313, 321, 325, 327, 348, 356, 373–374, 402
Reporting 5–7, 20, 49, 52, 61, 66, 73, 83, 102, 122, 124–125, 131, 141–142, 147–149, 164, 177–179, 182, 185, 196–197, 199–200, 202, 204–206, 208–209, 228, 259–264, 272–273, 289–290, 292, 294, 298–301, 305–306, 308, 344, 390, 395, 397–398, 400, 402–203, 409, 413
Respect and ensure 9, 37, 89, 91, 279
Responsibility to protect 1, 36, 46 n. 30, 53 n. 60
Risks 15–16, 16 n. 10, 64, 133, 216, 235, 327, 335, 353
Risks facing women and girls 211
Road Map 60–61, 66
Robinson, Mary 15 n. 8, 46 n. 34, 241
Roles 27, 29, 56, 68, 76–78, 120, 125
Rule of Law 10, 15, 30–31, 35, 59, 65–67, 73, 83, 106 n. 80, 120, 141, 154, 156–157, 159–161, 166, 168–170, 181–183, 192, 197–198, 201, 205, 207, 235, 242, 253, 259, 292, 295, 302, 315, 319, 322, 324, 346, 348, 357, 376, 397–398
Rwanda 41, 46, 46 n. 27, 53, 59–60, 72, 79, 82, 93, 93 n. 36, 103–104, 104 n. 76, 109, 129–130, 135, 217, 237, 245, 268

Sanctions 3, 6, 36, 65, 72–73, 77, 96, 101, 101 n. 71, 102 n. 71, 114, 120, 215, 261, 265–266, 299, 353, 355, 373
Secretary-General, UN 5–7, 9, 14, 20, 27, 32, 42 n. 9, 43 n. 12, 52–53, 53 n. 59, n. 61, 55, 60, 77, 81, 95 n. 42, 119, 122, 131, 134 n. 8, 141–143, 153, 164, 169, 175, 183, 196, 218–219, 236, 273, 321, 384
Security 4, 6–7, 9, 14–15, 17–19, 26–27, 36–37, 53 n. 62, 60–61, 65, 67, 71–74, 76, 78–83, 87, 96 n. 49, 98 n. 54, 101, 101 n. 65, 108 nn. 87–88, 110, 114, 114 n. 109, 116 n. 113, 119–120, 122, 128, 130, 132, 137–138, 144, 155, 162, 164–165, 167–168, 175, 180, 184, 193, 200, 206, 209, 212–216, 218–220, 222–223, 226, 229, 233, 237, 253, 255, 257–259, 263–264, 267–269, 279–281, 303, 311–312, 314, 318–320, 322, 322

n. 3, 323–324, 327–329, 331, 334–338, 338 n. 32, 339–342, 344–345, 347, 349, 353–357, 360–363, 365, 368–370, 370 n. b, 371, 375–376, 378, 388–390
Security Council 4, 6–8, 20–21, 26, 28, 30, 41 n. 5, 42 n. 9, 43 n. 12, n. 16, 47, 47 n. 39, 53, 53 n. 61, 60–61, 66, 71, 71 n. 2, 72, 72 n. 3, 73–74, 76–78, 81–83, 93, 93 n. 36, 96, 99, 109 n. 98, 119–120, 120 n. 5, 121–123, 129, 141, 143, 153, 155, 157, 161, 166, 175, 181, 183–184, 196–197, 209, 212–213, 217–219, 221–223, 247, 253–256, 265, 267–269, 271
Serbia and Montenegro 48 n. 42, 199–202, 204
Sexual violence 5, 43, 43 n. 15, 61, 73, 221, 303, 314, 394
Shiawal-Kidanekal, Teffera 235, 250
Sierra Leone 41–43, 43 nn. 12–13, n. 15, 44, 44 n. 20, 45, 54, 54 n. 63, 72 n. 4, 82, 103, 103 n. 73, 108 n. 87, 109, 123–124, 130, 141–142, 148, 196–198, 217, 221, 266–268, 387–390, 391–399, 401–405, 412
Southern Africa 80, 198–199
Special procedures 18, 21–23, 27, 29, 147, 297
Strategies of protection 25, 39
Sub-Commission 22, 94
Sri Lanka 47–48, 116 n. 117, 140, 207
Stanley Foundation 249
Sudan 13 n. 2, 14, 41, 41 n. 3, 47–48, 52, 74, 80, 115 n. 111, 116 n. 115, 124, 130, 205–206, 221
Switzerland as depositary 90 n. 13, 97–98

Tajikistan 130, 169, 207–208
Targeting of humanitarian staff 64–65
Timor Leste 45, 141–142, 150, 209–210, 221
Transitional justice 53–54, 54 n. 63, n. 65, 54 nn. 65–66, 67, 122, 156, 221, 388, 390, 401–402, 412
Tribunals 5, 93, 93 n. 36, 107 n. 84, 263
Truth and Reconciliation 54, 54 n. 63, 108, 108 n. 92, 109, 109 n. 98, 142, 185, 196–197, 210, 263, 387–388, 390–391, 400–401, 403

UN High Commissioner for Human Rights 1, 8, 13 n. 1, 17, 28 n. 28, 41 n. 3, 248, 408
UN High Commissioner for Refugees 17, 27
UNICEF 44 n. 19, 51, 52 n. 55, 68, 116 n. 115, 120 n. 5, 132, 138, 139, 160, 180, 223, 343 n. 41, 412
United Nations 1, 4–9, 13–14, 14 n. 5, 19, 19 n. 14, 20–22, 24, 26–27, 31–34, 41 n. 2, 43 n. 16, 46, 49 n. 49, 53, 60, 71, 81, 87–88, 90, 92, 94, 95 n. 42, 97, 100, 101 n. 66, 104, 119, 128, 131, 140–142, 144, 146, 150, 153, 155–157, 164–167, 170–171, 175, 181–184, 195–196, 198–199, 209–210, 213, 218–219, 222–223, 232, 236–239, 241, 248, 250, 253, 255, 259, 262, 265, 268–271, 273–274, 289–293, 295–297, 303, 308–309, 311–312, 316–318, 320–321, 331 n. 14, 347, 351–352, 354, 371–372, 378–379, 382, 384, 387–389, 391–392, 395, 397, 405, 407–408
Universality of human rights 34, 235
Universal jurisdiction 11

Veuthey, Michel 87, 90 n. 14, 99 n. 57, 100 nn. 62–63, 101 n. 65, 116 n. 114, 250
Victims of war 41, 45, 55, 91 n. 20, 108
Vienna Convention 113
Violations 2–3, 5–7, 9, 11, 13–14, 16, 19, 25–26, 29–30, 38, 46 n. 30, 49, 65–67, 74, 78, 83, 87, 89, 92, 95 n. 43, 96, 96 n. 49, 98, 102, 105, 105 n. 79, 106–108, 110 n. 99, 114–119, 121, 128, 131–136, 139–140, 142–143, 147–150, 154, 156, 158, 162–163, 168, 173, 176, 179, 183, 185, 197, 200, 204, 209, 225–227, 231–233, 235, 253, 260, 263–264, 277, 289, 295–296, 298–299, 301, 306, 309, 314, 316–318, 325–326, 329, 335–341, 343, 348–349, 353, 356–357, 360–361, 363–364, 371, 375, 381, 390, 393, 397, 404
Violence against children 62, 303
Violence against IDPs 62
Violence against refugees 62

Yugoslavia 46, 46 n. 28, n. 32, 93, 93 n. 36, 99, 127, 130, 146, 159, 199–200, 217, 225–227, 268

Women 1, 5, 7–8, 10, 19, 24, 26, 26 n. 25, 30–31, 31 n. 32, 33–34, 42–44, 44 n. 21, 53, 61, 63, 67, 72–73, 76, 78, 120, 135, 137–139, 142–143, 146, 160, 162, 178–180, 182, 184, 194, 197, 211–223, 238, 241–242, 247, 253, 260–262, 267–268, 271, 280, 283–285, 294, 306, 314, 326, 331–332, 342–345, 368–369, 372, 388, 394–396, 399
Women in peacekeeping environments 217

1. Bertrand G. Ramcharan: *Humanitarian Good Offices in International Law.* The Good Offices of the United Nations Secretary General in the Field of Human Rights. 1983 ISBN 90-247-2805-3
2. Bertrand G. Ramcharan: *International Law and Fact-Finding in the Field of Human Rights.* 1983 ISBN 90-247-3042-2
3. Bertrand G. Ramcharan: *The Right to Life in International Law.* 1985 ISBN 90-247-3074-0
4. Katarina Tomaševski and Philip Alston: *Right to Food.* 1984 ISBN 90-247-3087-2
5. Arie Bloed, Pieter van Dijk: *Essays on Human Rights in the Helsinki Process.* 1985 ISBN 90-247-3211-5
6. K. Tornudd: *Finland and the International Norms of Human Rights.* 1986 ISBN 90-247-3257-3
7. Berth Verstappen and Hans Thoolen: *Human Rights Missions. A Study of the Fact-Finding Practice of Non-Governmental Organizations.* 1986 ISBN 90-247-3364-2
8. Hurst Hannum: *The Right to Leave and Return in International Law and Practice.* 1987 ISBN 90-247-3445-2
9. H. Danelius and Herman Burgers: *The United Nations Convention Against Torture. A Handbook on the Convention Against Torture and Other Cruel, Inhuman or Degrading Treatment or Punishment.* 1988 ISBN 90-247-3609-9
10. David A. Martin: *The New Asylum Seekers: Refugee Law in the 1980's.* The Ninth Sokol Colloquium on International Law. 1988 ISBN 90-247-3730-3
11. Cecilia Medina: *The Battle of Human Rights. Gross, Systematic Violations and the Inter-American System.* 1988 ISBN 90-247-3687-0
12. Claus Gulmann, Lars Adam Rehof: *Human Rights in Domestic Law and Development.* Assistance Policies of the Nordic Countries. 1989 ISBN 90-247-3743-5
13. Bertrand G. Ramcharan: *The Concept and Present Status of the International Protection of Human Rights. Forty Years After the Universal Declaration.* 1989 ISBN 90-247-3759-1
14. Angela D. Byre: *International Human Rights Law in the Commonwealth Caribbean.* 1991 ISBN 90-247-3785-0
15. Natan Lerner: *Group Rights and Discrimination in International Law.* 1990 ISBN 0-79230-853-0
16. Shimon Shetreet: *Free Speech and National Security.* 1991 ISBN 0-79231-030-6

17. Geoff Gilbert: *Aspects of Extradition Law.* 1991 ISBN 0-79231-162-0

18. Philip E. Veerman: *The Rights of the Child and the Changing Image of Childhood.* 1992 ISBN 0-79231-250-3

19. Mireille Delmas-Marty: *The European Convention for the Protection of Human Rights.* International Protection versus National Restrictions. 1992 ISBN 0-79231-283-X

20. Arie Bloed and Pieter van Dijk: *The Human Dimension of the Helsinki Process.* The Vienna Follow-up Meeting and its Aftermath. 1991 ISBN 0-79231-337-2

21. Lyal S. Sunga: *Individual Responsibility in International Law for Serious Human Rights Violations.* 1992 ISBN 0-79231-453-0

22. Dinah Shelton and Stanislaw J. Frankowski: *Preventive Detention.* A Comparative and International Law Perspective. 1992 ISBN 0-79231-465-4

23. Michael Freeman and Philip E. Veerman: *Ideologies of Children's Rights.* 1992 ISBN 0-79231-800-5

24. Stephanos Stavros: *The Guarantees for Accused Persons Under Article 6 of the European Convention on Human Rights.* An Analysis of the Application of the Convention and a Comparison with Other Instruments. 1993 ISBN 0-79231-897-8

25. Allan Rosas, Diane Goodman and Jan Helgesen: *Strength of Diversity.* Human Rights and Pluralist Democracy. 1992 ISBN 0-79231-987-7

26. Andrew Clapham and Kees Waaldijk: *Homosexuality: A European Community Issue.* Essays on Lesbian and Gay Rights in European Law and Policy. 1993 ISBN 0-79232-038-7

28. Howard Charles Yourow: *The Margin of Appreciation Doctrine in the Dynamics of European Human Rights Jurisprudence.* 1995 ISBN 0-79233-338-1

29. Lars Adam Rehof: *Guide to the Travaux Préparatoires of the United Nations Convention on the Elimination of all Forms of Discrimination against Women.* 1993. ISBN 0-79232-222-3

30. Allan Rosas, Arie Bloed, Liselotte Leicht and Manfred Nowak: *Monitoring Human Rights in Europe.* Comparing International Procedures and Mechanisms. 1993 ISBN 0-79232-383-1

31. Andrew Harding and John Hatchard: *Preventive Detention and Security Law: A Comparative Survey.* 1993 ISBN 0-79232-432-3

32. Yves Beigbeder: *International Monitoring of Plebiscites, Referenda and National Elections.* Self-Determination and Transition to Democracy. 1994 ISBN 0-79232-563-X

33. Thomas David Jones: *Human Rights: Group Defamation, Freedom of Expression and the Law of Nations.* 1997 ISBN 90-411-0265-5

34. David M. Beatty: *Human Rights and Judicial Review: A Comparative Perspective.* 1994 ISBN 0-79232-968-6

35. Geraldine Van Bueren: *The International Law on the Rights of the Child.* 1995 ISBN 0-79232-687-3

36. Tom Zwart: *The Admissibility of Human Rights Petitions.* The Case Law of the European Commission of Human Rights and the Human Rights Committee. 1994 ISBN 0-79233-146-X

37. Helene Lambert: *Seeking Asylum.* Comparative Law and Practice in Selected European Countries. 1995 0-79233-152-4

38. E. Lijnzaad: *Reservations to UN-Human Rights Treaties.* Ratify and Ruin? 1994 ISBN 0-7923-3256-3

39. L.G. Loucaides: *Essays on the Developing Law of Human Rights.* 1995 ISBN 0-7923-3276-8

40. T. Degener and Y. Koster-Dreese (eds.): *Human Rights and Disabled Persons.* Essays and Relevant Human Rights Instruments. 1995 ISBN 0-7923-3298-9

41. J.-M. Henckaerts: *Mass Expulsion in Modern International Union and Human Rights.* 1995 ISBN 90-411-0072-5

42. N.A. Neuwahl and A. Rosas (eds.): *The European Union and Human Rights.* 1995 ISBN 90-411-0124-1

43. H. Hey: *Gross Human Rights Violations: A Search for Causes.* A Study of Guatemala and Costa Rica. 1995 ISBN 90-411-0146-2

44. B.G. Tahzib: *Freedom of Religion or Belief.* Ensuring Effective International Legal Protection. 1996 ISBN 90-411-0159-4

45. F. de Varennes: *Language, Minorities and Human Rights.* 1996 ISBN 90-411-0206-X

46. J. Raikka (ed.): *Do We Need Minority Rights?* Conceptual Issues. 1996 ISBN 90-411-0309-0

47. J. Brohmer: *State Immunity and the Violation of Human Rights.* 1997 ISBN 90-411-0322-8

48. C.A. Gearty (ed.): *European Civil Liberties and the European Convention on Human Rights.* A Comparative Study. 1997 ISBN 90-411-0253-1

49. B. Conforti and F. Francioni (eds.): *Enforcing International Human Rights in Domestic Courts.* 1997 ISBN 90-411-0393-7

50. A. Spiliopoulou Akermark: *Justi.cations of Minority Protection in International Law*. 1997
ISBN 90-411-0424-0

51. A. Boulesbaa: *The U.N. Convention on Torture and the Prospects for Enforcement*. 1997
ISBN 90-411-0457-7

52. S. Bowen (ed.): *Human Rights, Self-Determination and Political Change in the Occupied Palestinian Territories*. 1997 ISBN 90-411-0502-6

53. M. O'Flaherty and G. Gisvold (eds.): *Post-War Protection of Human Rights in Bosnia and Herzegovina*. 1998 ISBN 90-411-1020-8

54. A.-L. Svensson-McCarthy: *The International Law of Human Rights and States of Exception*. With Special Reference to the Travaux Préparatoires and the Case-Law of the International Monitoring Organs. 1998 ISBN 90-411-1021-6

55. G. Gilbert: *Transnational Fugitive Offenders in International Law*. Extradition and Other Mechanisms. 1998 ISBN 90-411-1040-2

56. M. Jones and L.A. Basser Marks (eds.): *Disability, Divers-ability and Legal Change*. 1998
ISBN 90-411-1086-0

57. T. Barkhuysen, M.L. van Emmerik and RH.P.H.M.C. van Kempen (eds.): *The Execution of Strasbourg and Geneva Human Rights Decisions in the National Legal Order*. 1999
ISBN 90-411-1152-2

58. S. Coliver, P. Hoffman, J. Fitzpatrick and S. Bowen (eds.): *Secrecy and Liberty: National Security, Freedom of Expression and Access to Information*. 1999 ISBN 90-411-1191-3

59. W.S. Heinz and H. Fruhling: *Determinants of Gross Human Rights Violations by State and State-Sponsored Actors in Brazil, Uruguay, Chile, and Argentina*. 1960-1990. 1999
ISBN 90-411-1202-2

60. M. Kirilova Eriksson: *Reproductive Freedom*. In the Context of International Human Rights and Humanitarian Law. 1999 ISBN 90-411-1249-9

61. M.B. Eryilmaz: *Arrest and Detention Powers in English and Turkish Law and Practice in the Light of the European Convention on Human Rights*. 1999 ISBN 90-411-1269-3

62. K. Henrard: *Devising and Adequate System of Minority Protection*. Individual Human Rights, Minority Rights and the Right to Self-Determination. 2000 ISBN 90-411-1359-2

63. K. Tomasevski: *Responding to Human Rights Violations*. 1946-1999. 2000
ISBN 90-411-1368-1

64. L.-V.N. Tran: *Human Rights and Federalism*. A Comparative Study on Freedom, Democracy and Cultural Diversity. 2000 ISBN 90-411-1492-0

65. C. Tiburcio: *The Human Rights of Aliens under International and Comparative Law*. 2001 ISBN 90-411-1550-1

66. E. Brems: Human Rights: *Universality and Diversity*. 2001 ISBN 90-411-1618-4

67. C. Bourloyannis-Vrailas and L.-A. Sicilianos: *The Prevention of Human Rights Violations*. 2001 ISBN 90-411-1672-9

68. G. Ulrich and K. Hastrup: *Discrimination and Toleration*. New Perspectives. 2001 ISBN 90-411-1711-3

69. V.O. Orlu Nmehielle: *African Human Rights System*. Its Laws, Practice and Institutions. 2001 ISBN 90-411-1731-8

70. B.G. Ramcharan: *Human Rights and Human Security*. 2002 ISBN 90-411-818-7

71. B.G. Ramcharan: *The United Nations High Commissioner for Human Rights*. The Challenges of International Protection. 2002 ISBN 90-411-1832-2

72. C. Breen: *The Standard of the Best Interests of the Child*. A Western Tradition in International and Comparative Law. 2002 ISBN 90-411-1851-9

73. M. Katayanagi: *Human Rights Functions of United Nations Peacekeeping Operations*. 2002 ISBN 90-411-1910-8

74. O.M. Arnadottir: *Equality and Non-Discrimination under the European Convention on Human Rights*. 2002 ISBN 90-411-1912-4

75. B.G. Ramcharan: *The Security Council and the Protection of Human Rights*. 2002 ISBN 90-411-1878-0

76. E. Fierro: *The EU's Approach to Human Rights Conditionality in Practice*. 2002 ISBN 90-411-1936-1

77. Natan Lerner: *Group Rights and Discrimination in International Law*. Second Edition. 2002 ISBN 90-411-1982-5

78. S. Leckie (ed.): *National Perspectives on Housing Rights*. 2003 ISBN 90-411-2013-0

79. L.C. Reif: *The Ombudsman, Good Governance and the International Human Rights System*. 2004 ISBN 90-04-13903-6

80. Mary Dowell-Jones: *Contextualising the International Covenant on Economic, Social and Cultural Rights: Assessing the Economic Deficit*. 2004 ISBN 90-04-13908-7

81. Li-ann Thio: *Managing Babel: The International Legal Protection of Minorities in the Twentieth Century* ISBN 90-04-14198-7

INTERNATIONAL STUDIES IN HUMAN RIGHTS

82. K.D. Beiter: *The Protection of the Right to Education by International Law*. 2006 ISBN 90 04 14704 7

83. J.H. Gerards: *Judicial Review in Equal Treatment Cases*. 2005 ISBN 90 04 14379 3

84. V.A.Leary and D. Warner: *Social Issues, Globalization and International Institutions. Labour Rights and the EU, ILO, OECD and WTO*. 2005 ISBN 90 04 14579 6

85. J.K.M. Gevers, E.H. Hondius and J.H. Hubben (eds.): *Health Law, Human Rights and the Biomedicine Convention*. Essays in Honour of Henriette Roscam Abbing. 2005 ISBN 90 04 14822 1

86. C. Breen: *Age Discrimination and Children's Rights*. Ensuring Equality and Acknowledging Difference. 2006 ISBN 90 04 14827 2

87. B.G. Ramcharan (ed.): *Human Rights Protection in the Field*. 2006 ISBN 90 04 14847 7

This series is designed to shed light on current legal and political aspects of process and organization in the field of human rights

MARTINUS NIJHOFF PUBLISHERS – LEIDEN • BOSTON